TAO TE CHING

道德經

TAO TE CHING

The Definitive Edition

Lao Tzu

Translation and Commentary
by
Jonathan Star

JEREMY P. TARCHER/PENGUIN
a member of Penguin Group (USA) Inc.
New York

I would like to thank all those people who have supported this offering. Special thanks to Christel Sciarone, Sindu Porter, E. B. Weiss, Mitch Horowitz, and Stuart Calderwood.

Most Tarcher/Putnam books are available at special quantity discounts for bulk purchase for sales promotions, premiums, fund-raising, and educational needs. Special books or book excerpts also can be created to fit specific needs. For details, write Penguin Group (USA) Inc. Special Markets, 375 Hudson Street, New York, NY 10014.

Jeremy P. Tarcher/Putnam
a member of
Penguin Group (USA) Inc.
375 Hudson Street
New York, NY 10014
www.penguin.com

To submit translations, to provide feedback on the material
contained in this book, or to contact Jonathan Star, e-mail:
unity@ffc.net or unity10@aol.com

First trade paperback edition 2003
Copyright © 2001 by Jonathan Star

The Library of Congress cataloged the hardcover edition as follows:

Laozi.
  [Dao de jing. English]
  Tao te ching : the definitive edition / Lao Tzu;
    translation and commentary by Jonathan Star.
    p. cm.
  Includes bibliographical references.
  ISBN 1-58542-099-9
   I. Star, Jonathan.   II. Title.
BL1900.L26   E5   2001   00-054379
299'.51482—dc21
ISBN 1-58542-269-X (paperback edition)

Printed in the United States of America

10 9 8 7 6 5 4 3 2 1

BOOK DESIGN BY LEE FUKUI

To the one
who shares her purity,
reveals her wonder,
and touches the moon in her dreams.

CONTENTS

TAO TE CHING

INTRODUCTION

The *Tao Te Ching* is an ancient Chinese text consisting of spiritual teachings, folk wisdom, political instruction, cosmology, observations of nature, anti-Confucian doctrine, and mystical insights. Just as the Chinese language has experienced numerous transformations, the Tao Te Ching has changed and evolved over time. The present form of the Tao Te Ching is an amalgam of the combined wisdom and insights of many Chinese sages, which took form between the seventh and second centuries B.C.

Legend, however, gives us a more animated account of the Tao Te Ching's origin. It says that during the time of Confucius (around 500 B.C.) Lao-tsu practiced *Tao* and *Te* (the Supreme Way and its Expression) and focused his teachings on humility and being nameless. He was keeper of the royal archives in the state of Chou. After he foresaw that the state would fall into decay, he packed his belongings and decided to leave through the Western gateway. The gatekeeper, Yin-hsi, seeing that this great sage was about to leave the world said, "Master, you are about to renounce this world, please compose a book for me." Thereupon the "Old Master" came down from his oxcart, took out his pen and ink, and began to compose a book of two parts, discussing Tao and Te. Several hours later, Lao-tsu handed the finished text of slightly more than five thousand characters to the gatekeeper and then departed toward the West.

This popular story, however implausible, holds a symbolic charm that is consistent with the spirit of the Tao Te Ching: The verses were given to a gatekeeper—which represents their power to open the gate of understanding; it also symbolizes a turning point in one's life. The entire book was given at a simple request—which shows the generosity of the sage, and how he poured forth his knowledge at the first opening of a seeker. Lao-tsu wrote the book in a single sitting—which is an example of the sage's one-pointedness and perseverance. The sage came down from his oxcart (a scene often depicted in Chinese art), demonstrating his humility. He also "left toward the West," which symbolizes that the teachings of the Tao Te Ching are universal and meant for all people—a reality that we now see manifest.

Tao is the Supreme Reality, the all-pervasive substratum; it is the whole universe and the way the universe operates. Te is the shape and power of Tao; it is the way Tao manifests, it is Tao particularized to a form or a virtue. Tao is the transcendent reality; Te is the immanent reality. *Ching* means a book or a classic work. Hence, the Tao Te Ching literally means, "The Classic Book of the Supreme Reality (Tao) and its Perfect Manifestation (Te)," "The Book of the Way and Its Power," "The Classic of Tao and Its Virtue."

道

When I first read the Tao Te Ching, I was moved by the power of its words and the mystical spirit it imparted. I sensed the great and lofty vision of the ancient Chinese sages. But as I continued to read various English translations, I strained more and more to hold that sense of wonder, and the magic began to fade. Words and ideas that were baffling because they seemed beyond understanding were, in the end, baffling because they did not make sense. I felt more and more removed from the original text—I was not reading the Tao Te Ching, but someone's interpretation of it. So, in an attempt to penetrate the scripture's inner meaning, I read dozens of commentaries, studied the Chinese text in detail, and compared different texts and interpretations. This, finally, gave me the clarity I was looking for. But even with a complete understanding of the text, some sections still did not make sense—and I realized that they were not supposed to. The terse and mystical language of many of the verses serves as a marker, a hint suggesting a much larger meaning—and this meaning cannot be understood through the words of the text alone, but through one's own contemplation, spiritual practice, and by opening one's heart to the "doorway of all mysteries."

There is a Sanskrit treatise on hatha yoga called the *hatha yoga pradipika*, which supplies the basics of each hatha yoga posture—just enough to tell you about the posture but not enough for you to actually assume it. At the end of each description, the text says, "go and learn the rest from a qualified teacher." The posture can be "told about" in a book, but the only way to learn the correct posture is through one who knows it. The same is true of the Tao Te Ching: It was never meant to fully explain the mysteries of the universe, only to allude to them. The lessons and truths to which it points must be discovered within. That is the only way for the text to bring you past the words to the wonder of your own being.

道

The nature of ancient Chinese is one reason why this scripture, for thousands of years, has "baffled all inquiry." Ancient Chinese is a conceptual language; it is unlike English and other Western languages, which are perceptual. Western languages are rooted in grammar that frames events in real time, identifies subject and object, clarifies relationships, and establishes temporal sequences. Ancient Chinese is based on pictorial representations, without grammar. Characters symbolize concepts that can be interpreted as singular or plural; as a noun, a verb, or an adjective; as happening in the past, present, or future. Therefore, when translating from Chinese to English, the Chinese characters must be framed within a perceptual context to be understood.

For instance, most of the Chinese text of the Tao Te Ching does not identify the subject or the object. It is left up to the translator to identify who is doing the talking, from what perspective, and to whom the message is directed—and then find the English equivalents to support his interpretation. Various interpretations of the same verse can have the sage giving a message to the people, the Tao giving a message to the world, and even the people giving a message to the sage! In addition, there are no clear distinctions that group characters into lines or sentences; as a result, translators can begin and end sentences in different places.

To illustrate the flexibility of the Chinese, and the many possible translations it can yield, we can look at a few characters from verse 27, which reads, *shi wei hsi ming:*

shi: this

wei: is called

hsi: follow / one who follows / practice / unite / merge // conceal / cover / secret // penetrate / force / steal / "secure by devious means" // double / twofold // >*hsi* generally means to enter or secure by deceptive or secretive means, thus connoting an invasion, attack at night, penetration; something that is done in secret, concealed, etc.

ming: light / enlightenment / to enlighten / one who is enlightened / mystical vision / shine / luminous / illumined / brilliant // insight / discernment / awareness / understanding / wisdom // shines forth / conspicuous // > *ming* is comprised of the characters "sun" + "moon."

By using a combination of possible meanings, a translator can come up with dozens of plausible translations. For example, by using just the first definition of each character ("follow" and "light"), we could render the line thus:
"This is called . . .

> "following the light," "following one's own light," "one who follows the light," "followers of light," "following the path of light" (Ming), or "following the guidance of the inner light." (Wu)

Using the other definitions we could say,
"This is called . . .

> "the practice of mystical vision," "concealing your brilliance," "penetrating the luminous," "the shining practice," "blending the light," "the secret of enlightenment," or "penetrating into the mystical vision."

By adding interpretive modifiers, we could say,
"This is called . . .

> "shining the light on all that is hidden," "the practice of enlightened beings," or "the practice that leads to brilliant insight."

Some noted translators have rendered the line as follows:
"This is called . . .

"following one's discernment" (Lau); "stealing the Light" (Yutang); "inherited enlightenment" (Lin); "following the light [of Nature]" (Chan); or "double enlightenment" (Ta-Kao).

In addition to the fact that a wide range of English words can be considered as rough equivalents to each Chinese character, other issues have contributed to the diversity among translations. These are as follows:

Textual Issues

The original text was passed from hand to hand and was rewritten by numerous scribes. This has resulted in displaced lines, changed characters (due to clerical errors), "corrections," merged and repeated sections, added lines and characters, and altered or changed meanings. In addition, the Tao Te Ching passed through different political reigns, with each ruler modifying the text to fit his own view or political orientation. This arduous passage of the original text has resulted in many different "originals." Translators will often modify their translations by using a standard text and then "borrowing" characters from additional texts when it supports their understanding. This leads to increasingly different interpretations and translations, although the essence of them all remains the same.

Just before A.D. 249, Wang Pi wrote a commentary on the Tao Te Ching, which included a copy of a text. We can assume that the text used by Wang Pi in his commentary was, at that time, among the oldest and most established versions of the Tao Te Ching. So, while some texts may predate Wang Pi, it does not mean that those texts are older than the one he used—a text which may have been several centuries old at the time. The text used by Wang Pi is the standard version now used by most scholars. The Verbatim Translation found in this edition is based on that text. Other texts which are referenced in the Verbatim Translation include *Ho Shang Kung* (based on a commentary attributed to the Taoist master Ho Shang Kung, dated from the second century A.D.); *Fu I* (dated from the second century B.C.); the two texts recently found at *Ma Wang Tui* (the oldest known texts, dated from 206 B.C.); *Tang Dynasty Inscription* (a text carved into stone during the Tang Dynasty, beginning in the seventh century); and the *Tunhuang* texts (dated from the eighth century).

A) Different Chinese Texts

B) Verse Structure   The Tao Te Ching can be seen as a pastiche of many separate sayings (the contemporary scholar, D. C. Lau, has identified 196 in all) grouped together in 81 verses. Many times "sayings" within each verse are wholly unrelated to each other, and one is hard-pressed to find a reason why these lines have been grouped together. For example, let's look again at verse 27. Here we see five distinct ideas, none of which relates to the others:

   a) good walking leaves no tracks

   b) therefore, the sage is always good at saving men

   c) this is called "following the light"

   d) therefore, the good man is the teacher of the bad man

   e) this is the essential mystery of Tao

In order to preserve the integrity, unity, and wholeness of each verse (and, indeed, give reason as to why these distinct lines were grouped together in the first place), the translator often "slants," "tweaks," "stretches," or "bridges together" the meanings of the disparate sayings within a verse in a way that gives them some commonality. Keeping the same tense or perspective throughout the verse, adding connective lines, or imposing highly interpretive translations will, in some measure, bring about this cohesiveness. These methods used by translators and interpreters to improve the overall power of the verse, or to create an inner wholeness and unity, have led to more cohesive translations but also to a widening difference among them.

C) Poetic License   Many versions and "translations" of the Tao Te Ching are prepared by people who have no knowledge of Chinese. These renderings are made by mixing together several existing translations, by using literal texts (such as the one prepared by Paul Carus in 1898), or by "getting a feel for the true meaning" and then writing a new verse based on that feel. Many of these versions stay close to the original and have a poetic power in their own right. Other versions, admittedly, take more liberty and make no attempt to offer a translation. Sometimes an entire verse is discarded and the interpreter-poet rewrites his own poem based on the "spirit" of the original. Although these poetic versions can be helpful, and perhaps have literary merit of their own, they represent "poetic departures"— they are poems based on the Tao, not translations.

道

Some scholars (especially Martin Palmer, who worked on a translation of the Tao Te Ching in 1993) suggest that, initially, the Tao Te Ching may have been an oracle—much like the *I Ching*—consisting of many short, mystical "seed verses" or *sutras*. Each seed verse contained the essence, or seed, of some teaching or mystical view. The meanings of these seed verses were mysterious and impenetrable by design, like Zen koans—they were not meant to be grasped by the rational mind alone; their inner meanings were meant to be discovered through one's own insight and spiritual penetration. These seed verses contained two to four lines, which ended with rhyming characters for easy memorization. Many of these seed verses can still be found throughout the Tao Te Ching.

What we now have is a mixture of seed-like verses, which are short, cohesive, and mystical in nature—combined with commentaries, which are more instructive, understandable, and logical in nature. What may have begun as a structured, cohesive text is now more piecemeal and inconsistent.

There is little value in trying to "recapture" the original sutra format of the Tao Te Ching. As an exercise in understanding the text, however, the reader can go through each verse with the intent of identifying seed verses and commentary. In many poems the reader will see a clear change of wording and viewpoint. Seed verses will usually contain a few rhyming lines, which are mystical, complete, and whole in themselves. Commentaries will be clearer and more understandable, and they will often elaborate on another teaching. Commentaries often begin with "therefore" or "hence," which loosely connects them to the previous lines. They also include practical teachings, descriptions of the life of the sage (which show the highest application of the seed verse), and references to the seed verse, and they often use repetitions and logical progressions ("man follows the way of earth; earth follows the way of heaven; heaven follows . . .").

In verses 13 and 26 we see a consistent structure: a seed verse at the beginning and a possible commentary that follows. In verses 3, 17, and 31 we see a possible commentary but no seed verse. In verses 31, 32, and 66 we see commentaries on the commentaries! In verse 1, we see what may be several seed verses.

The division of the Tao Te Ching into 81 verses may have first occurred in an original oracle, or it may have been imposed at a later date for numerological empowerment. Anyone familiar with the significance of numbers will understand the power and mystical importance of 81 ($3 \times 3 \times 3 \times 3$, or 9×9). Nine, in ancient Chinese numerology, represented the divisions of earth, and came to mean completion, fulfillment, totality, and perfection. Nine is considered a magical and "spiritual" number. (The I Ching is based on the structure of 64 (8×8); 8 representing the structure of things and the nature of the physical world.)

Although the origins of the Tao Te Ching are lost, a possible evolution could have been as follows:

a) A collection of seed verses (short, mystical sayings) was grouped together; this collection represented a complete system or view of reality—similar to the complete system that is represented by the I Ching. The collection may have contained 81 (9×9) verses or some other "perfect" number, such as 36 (6×6), 49 (7×7), or 64 (8×8). The verses rhymed for easy memorization, and this collection might have begun as part of an oral tradition.

b) In order for people to understand and apply the teachings found in the sutras, commentaries and explanations were added. These commentaries were longer, more logical, and less cryptic than the original sutras and were separated from the original text in both use of language and content.

c) As the text evolved, additional commentaries were added. It is possible that more seed verses were added as well. It is also possible that the text was edited, and seed verses and commentaries were removed.

d) Ancient Chinese books were written on narrow slips of bamboo or wood, and each slip often contained only one line of characters. These slips were held together by a thong, which passed through a notch cut in the edge of each slip. It is likely that thongs holding together the bamboo slips may have broken, and that during attempted restorations lines were moved, sections lost, and seed verses and commentaries mixed together. In addition, scribes, copying the text, may have unwittingly combined sections. These changes may have happened several times. Lines may also have been added; it is surprising that in such a short scripture we often find the same line repeated in two or three different verses.

e) Additional commentaries, which applied to human affairs and politics (and which reflected the outlook of the present regime), were added and got mixed in with the original text and commentaries. What then remained were the original sutras, commentaries on those sutras, and commentaries on the commentaries. At this point, the cohesive structure of the original oracle was lost.

f) In order to clarify the scripture, and for numerological empowerment, the text was divided into 81 sections. This artificial division may have taken place during the Han Dynasty (206 B.C.–A.D. 221). A possible reshuffling of lines, and additional editing, may also have occurred at this time. (This division into 81 sections does not occur in all texts, and many Chinese texts make no verse distinction. The oldest known text, called "The Bamboo-Slip Lao-tzu," which dates back to approximately 300 B.C., is not divided into 81 verses.)

g) Over the years, small changes and clarifications were made by scholars and interpreters. Errors made by scribes also slipped into the text.

h) Using the oldest and most established text of his time, Wang Pi made a commentary on the Tao Te Ching just before A.D. 249. The text upon which Wang Pi based his commentary is the standard version used today.

道

The Definitive Tao Te Ching

In an attempt to give the reader a complete access to the text of the Tao Te Ching, we have included the following sections in this edition: (a) one possible translation, (b) a verbatim translation with notes, (c) a commentary on verse 1, (d) a concordance and a list of characters according to their radicals.

A) A Translation of the Text

My goal in this translation was to capture the heart and spirit of the Tao Te Ching, preserve its poetic power, and make clear its teachings, while at the same time being true to the original text. In most places I have stayed close to original Chinese—going so far as to translate some of the characters etymologically. In other places I have strayed from the original in order to make clear certain ideas, or emphasize teachings. Sometimes I have added a connective line to link disparate ideas, bring integrity to the verse, or reveal a hidden teaching. (This is most evident in verse 6, which significantly departs from the original.) This translation is certainly not definitive but is one possible version. It is a blending of the original text, the insights of many past translators, and years of contemplation of the spiritual truths and vision put forth in the Tao Te Ching.

To share some of the resonance with original texts, which often do not contain punctuation or line distinctions, very little punctuation is used in this translation. To honor the Chinese sense of space, or nothingness—which is a central concept in Chinese art and Taoist philosophy—the poems are laid out from the bottom to the top. In this layout, the weight of the printed words is placed below (like the earth) while the empty space remaining on the page is found above (like the sky). For poetic reasons, I have used "he," "his," and "him," which represent both males and females.

B) Verbatim Translation and Notes

The Verbatim Translation in this edition is designed to give the reader the fullest sense of the text, and a complete range of possible interpretations. Because many characters can be represented by a dozen or more English equivalents, no single translation is really possible. What are possible, however, are interpretations based on one's own understanding of the text. Hence, the inclusion of a Verbatim Translation is the definitive way to give the reader a framework and a context in which to interpret and compare the many different translations of the Tao Te Ching, and even to make his own version. A definitive translation is one by which all other translations are compared, and we have included a Verbatim Translation for this purpose.

In the end, a definitive translation is one that defines your own experience, that speaks to you in your own voice, that is so close to the mark that it becomes your own.

This Verbatim Translation was prepared by Jonathan Star and C. J. Ming.

The mystical teachings put forth in verse 1 can be viewed as a complete spiritual practice in themselves, and this is why we have chosen to include an extensive commentary on this verse. If a seeker could penetrate the mysteries of this verse alone, the "gates to all the mysteries" would open before him. Verse 1 also sets the framework in which to understand and interpret many of the verses and teachings that follow.

C) Commentary on Verse 1

This section is a reference guide that supplies (a) a definition of each character, (b) spelling of each character using the Wade-Giles and Pinyin systems, and (c) a concordance, which allows the reader to locate the exact verse and line position of every character found in the text.

D) Concordance, Definitions, and Wade-Pinyin Conversion

This list defines the 214 radicals. Radicals are the basic symbols upon which Chinese characters are grouped.

E) List of Radicals

TAO TE CHING

Translation

A way that can be walked
    is not The Way
A name that can be named
    is not The Name

Tao is both Named and Nameless
As Nameless, it is the origin of all things
As Named, it is the mother of all things

A mind free of thought,
    merged within itself,
    beholds the essence of Tao
A mind filled with thought,
    identified with its own perceptions,
    beholds the mere forms of this world

Tao and this world seem different
    but in truth they are one and the same
The only difference is in what we call them

How deep and mysterious is this unity
    How profound, how great!
It is the truth beyond the truth,
    the hidden within the hidden
It is the path to all wonder,
    the gate to the essence of everything!

Everyone recognizes beauty
    only because of ugliness
Everyone recognizes virtue
    only because of sin

Life and death are born together
Difficult and easy
Long and short
High and low—
    all these exist together
Sound and silence blend as one
Before and after arrive as one

名

The Sage acts without action
    and teaches without talking
All things flourish around him
    and he does not refuse any one of them
He gives but not to receive
He works but not for reward
He completes but not for results
He does nothing for himself in this passing world
    so nothing he does ever passes

VERSE 3

materialism and pursuit of wealth are viewed as distractions.

living in harmony with the Tao and embracing simplicity and moderation can lead to more fulfilling and balanced life.

Putting a value on status
    will cause people to compete
Hoarding treasure
    will turn them into thieves
Showing off possessions
    will disturb their daily lives

Thus the Sage rules
    by stilling minds and opening hearts
    by filling bellies and strengthening bones
He shows people how to be simple
    and live without desires
To be content
    and not look for other ways
With the people so pure
Who could trick them?
What clever ideas could lead them astray?

When action is pure and selfless
    everything settles into its own perfect place

tao = "The Way"
— ancient chinese interpretation
of the spiritual force in all life.

Tao is empty
      yet it fills every vessel with endless supply
Tao is hidden
      yet it shines in every corner of the universe

With it, the sharp edges become smooth
      the twisted knots loosen
      the sun is softened by a cloud
      the dust settles into place

So deep, so pure, so still
      It has been this way forever
You may ask, "Whose child is it?"—
      but I cannot say
This child was here before the Great Ancestor

Heaven and Earth have no preference

A man may choose one over another
    but to Heaven and Earth all are the same
The high, the low, the great, the small—
    all are given light
    all get a place to rest

The Sage is like Heaven and Earth
To him none are especially dear
    nor is there anyone he disfavors
He gives and gives without condition
    offering his treasure to everyone

徼

The universe is like a bellows
    It stays empty yet is never exhausted
    It gives out yet always brings forth more

Man is not like this
When he blows out air like a bellows
    he becomes exhausted
Man was not made to blow out air
He was made to sit quietly and find the truth within

— Someone who is wise or wisdom itself. Someone who understands and embraces the Tao.

metaphor for a humble, receptive, and gentle way of living that is in harmony with the tao.

Endlessly creating
Endlessly pulsating
The Spirit of the Valley never dies   — *female*
She is called the Hidden Creator   = *gives life*

valley
born in the void between the valley from nothing!
something from nothing.

Although She becomes the whole universe
    Her immaculate purity is never lost
Although She assumes countless forms
    Her true identity remains intact
Whatever we see or don't see
Whatever exists or doesn't exist
Is nothing but the creation of this Supreme Power

Tao is limitless, unborn, eternal—
    It can only be reached through the Hidden Creator
She is the very face of the Absolute
The gate to the source of all things eternal

Listen to Her voice
    Hear it echo through creation
Without fail, She reveals her presence
Without fail, She brings us to our own perfection

Heaven is ancient
Earth is long-lasting
Why is this so?—
    Because they have no claims to life
By having no claims to life
    they cannot be claimed by death

The Sage puts his own views behind
    so ends up ahead
He stays a witness to life
    so he endures
What could he grab for
    that he does not already have?
What could he do for himself
    that the universe itself has not already done?

"uncarved block"
— encourages people to return to
a state of simplicity, receptivity,
and naturalness.

"water"
— emulate the qualities
of water, such as
flexibility, humility, and
adaptability, people
can live more balanced,
peaceful, and aligned
life in accordance
with the idea of
tao.

The best way to live
　　is to be like water
For water benefits all things
　　and goes against none of them
It provides for all people
　　and even cleanses those places
　　a man is loath to go
In this way it is just like Tao

Live in accordance with the nature of things:
Build your house on solid ground
Keep your mind still
When giving, be kind
When speaking, be truthful
When ruling, be just
When working, be one-pointed
When acting, remember—timing is everything

One who lives in accordance with nature
　　does not go against the way of things
He moves in harmony with the present moment
　　always knowing the truth of just what to do

Grabbing and stuffing—
    there is no end to it

Sharpen a blade too much
    and its edge will soon be lost
Fill a house with gold and jade
    and no one can protect it
Puff yourself with honor and pride
    and no one can save you from a fall

Complete the task at hand
Be selfless in your actions
    This is the way of Heaven
    This is the way to Heaven

Hold fast to the Power of the One
It will unify the body
    and merge it with the spirit
It will cleanse the vision
    and reveal the world as flawless
It will focus the life-force
    and make one supple as a newborn

As you love the people and rule the state
    can you be free of self-interest?
As the gates of Heaven open and close
    can you remain steadfast as a mother bird
    who sits with her nest?
As your wisdom reaches the four corners of the world
    can you keep the innocence of a beginner?

常

Know this Primal Power
    that guides without forcing
    that serves without seeking
    that brings forth and sustains life
        yet does not own or possess it

One who holds this Power
    brings Tao to this very Earth
He can triumph over a raging fire
    or the freeze of winter weather
Yet when he comes to rule the world
    it's with the gentleness of a feather

Handwritten annotation (top): do that which consists in taking no action and order will prevail. Don't force action

Wu is nothingness, emptiness, non-existence

Thirty spokes of a wheel all join at a common hub
    yet only the hole at the center
    allows the wheel to spin
Clay is molded to form a cup
    yet only the space within
    allows the cup to hold water

Handwritten annotation: related to life

Handwritten annotation: something from nothing.

Walls are joined to make a room
    yet only by cutting out a door and a window
    can one enter the room and live there

Thus, when a thing has existence alone
    it is mere dead-weight
Only when it has *wu*, does it have life

The five colors blind the eye
The five tones deafen the ear
The five flavors dull the palate
Racing, hunting, and galloping about
    only disturb the mind
Wasting energy to obtain rare objects
    only impedes one's growth

So the Sage is led by his inner truth
    and not his outer eye   *wisdom*
He holds to what is deep
    and not what lies on the surface

"Be wary of both honor and disgrace"
"Endless affliction is bound to the body"

What does it mean,
        "Be wary of both honor and disgrace"?
Honor is founded on disgrace
        and disgrace is rooted in honor
Both should be avoided
Both bind a man to this world
That's why it says,
        "Be wary of both honor and disgrace"

What does it mean,
        "Endless affliction is bound to the body"?
Man's true self is eternal,
        yet he thinks, "I am this body, I will soon die"
This false sense of self
        is the cause of all his sorrow
When a person does not identify himself with the body
        tell me, what troubles could touch him?

One who sees himself as everything
        is fit to be guardian of the world
One who loves himself as everyone
        is fit to be teacher of the world

Eyes look but cannot see it
Ears listen but cannot hear it
Hands grasp but cannot touch it
Beyond the senses lies the great Unity—
        invisible, inaudible, intangible

What rises up appears bright
What settles down appears dark
Yet there is neither darkness nor light
        just an unbroken dance of shadows
From nothingness to fullness
        and back again to nothingness
This formless form
This imageless image
        cannot be grasped by mind or might
Try to face it
        In what place will you stand?
Try to follow it
        To what place will you go?

Know That which is beyond all beginnings
        and you will know everything here and now
Know everything in this moment
        and you will know the Eternal Tao

live in the moment?

The masters of this ancient path
     are mysterious and profound
Their inner state baffles all inquiry
Their depths go beyond all knowing
Thus, despite every effort,
     we can only tell of their outer signs—
Deliberate, as if treading over the stones of a winter brook
Watchful, as if meeting danger on all sides
Reverent, as if receiving an honored guest
Selfless, like a melting block of ice
Pure, like an uncarved block of wood
Accepting, like an open valley

調 5

Through the course of Nature
     muddy water becomes clear
Through the unfolding of life
     man reaches perfection
Through sustained activity
     that supreme rest is naturally found

Those who have Tao want nothing else   *wisdom*
Though seemingly empty
     they are ever full
Though seemingly old
     they are beyond the reach of birth and death

Become totally empty
Quiet the restlessness of the mind
Only then will you witness everything
    unfolding from emptiness
See all things flourish and dance
    in endless variation
And once again merge back into perfect emptiness—
    Their true repose
    Their true nature
Emerging, flourishing, dissolving back again
    This is the eternal process of return

To know this process brings enlightenment
To miss this process brings disaster

Be still
Stillness reveals the secrets of eternity
Eternity embraces the all-possible
The all-possible leads to a vision of oneness
A vision of oneness brings about universal love
Universal love supports the great truth of Nature
The great truth of Nature is Tao

Whoever knows this truth lives forever
The body may perish, deeds may be forgotten
But he who has Tao has all eternity

To know Tao alone,
  without trace of your own existence,
    is the highest
Next comes loving and praising it
Then fearing it
Then despising it

萬 6

If one doesn't trust himself
  how can he trust anyone else?

物 7

The great ruler speaks little
  and his words are priceless
He works without self-interest
  and leaves no trace
When all is finished, the people say,
  "It happened by itself"

When the greatness of Tao is present
    action arises from one's own heart
When the greatness of Tao is absent
    action comes from the rules
    of "kindness" and "justice"
If you need rules to be kind and just,
    if you *act* virtuous,
    this is a sure sign that virtue is absent
Thus we see the great hypocrisy

Only when the family loses its harmony
    do we hear of "dutiful sons"
Only when the state is in chaos
    do we hear of "loyal ministers"

Abandon holiness
Discard cleverness
  and the people will benefit a hundredfold
Abandon the rules of "kindness"
Discard "righteous" actions
  and the people will return
  to their own natural affections
Abandon book learning
Discard the rules of behavior
  and the people will have no worries
Abandon plots and schemes
Discard profit-seeking
  and the people will not become thieves

These lessons are mere elaborations
The essence of my teachings is this:
  See with original purity
  Embrace with original simplicity
  Reduce what you have
  Decrease what you want

The difference between a formal "yes"
     and a casual "yeah"—how slight!
The difference between knowing the Truth
     and not knowing it—how great!

Must I fear what others fear?
Should I fear desolation
     when there is abundance?
Should I fear darkness
     when that light is shining everywhere?
Nonsense!
The people of this world are steeped in their merrymaking
     as if gorging at a great feast
     or watching the sights of springtime
Yet here I sit, without a sign,
     staring blank-eyed like a child

I am but a guest in this world
While others rush about to get things done
     I accept what is offered
Oh, my mind is like that of a fool
     aloof to the clamor of life around me
Everyone seems so bright and alive
     with the sharp distinctions of day
I appear dark and dull
     with the blending of differences by night

I am drifting like an ocean, floating like the high winds
Everyone is so rooted in this world
     yet I have no place to rest my head
Indeed I am different. . . .
     I have no treasure but the Eternal Mother
     I have no food but what comes from her breast

[handwritten notes in margin: "women provide life." and "life"]

33

Perfect action,
True virtue,
Supreme power,
This is how Tao is revealed
　　　through those who follow it completely

無

Though formless and intangible
　　　It gives rise to form
Though vague and elusive
　　　It gives rise to shapes
Though dark and obscure
　　　It is the spirit, the essence,
　　　the life-breath of all things
"But is it real?" you ask—
　　　I say its evidence is all of creation!

名

From the first moment to the present
　　　The Name has been sounding
It is the gate
　　　through which the universe enters
The witness
　　　by which the universe sees

How have I come to know all this?
That very Name has told me,
That Name which is sounding right here,
　　　right now

"Surrender brings perfection"
The crooked become straight
The empty become full
The worn become new
    Have little and gain much
    Have much and be confused

So the Sage embraces the One
    and becomes a model for the world
Without showing himself, he shines forth
Without promoting himself, he is distinguished
Without claiming reward, he gains endless merit
Without seeking glory, his glory endures

The Sage knows how to follow
    so he comes to command
He does not compete
    so no one under Heaven can compete with him

The ancient saying,
    "Surrender brings perfection,"
    is not just empty words
Truly, surrender brings perfection
    and perfection brings the whole universe

Speak little
Hold to your own nature
A strong wind does not blow all morning
A cloudburst does not last all day
The wind and rain are from Heaven and Earth
        and even these do not last long
How much less so the efforts of man?

One who lives in accordance with the Truth
        becomes the embodiment of Tao
His actions become those of Nature
        his ways those of Heaven
It is through such a one
        that Heaven rejoices
        that Earth rejoices
        that all of life rejoices

On his tiptoes a man is not steady
Taking long strides he cannot keep pace

don't
be selfish

To the self-serving, nothing shines forth
To the self-promoting, nothing is distinguished
To the self-appointing, nothing bears fruit
To the self-righteous, nothing endures

From the viewpoint of Tao, this self-indulgence
    is like rotting food and painful growths on the body—
Things that all creatures despise
So why hold onto them?
When walking the path of Tao
        this is the very stuff
        that must be uprooted, thrown out, and left behind

Something formless, complete in itself
There before Heaven and Earth
Tranquil, vast, standing alone, unchanging
It provides for all things yet cannot be exhausted
It is the mother of the universe
I do not know its name
  so I call it "Tao"
Forced to name it further
I call it
  "The greatness of all things"
  "The end of all endings"
I call it
  "That which is beyond the beyond"
  "That to which all things return"

道

From Tao comes all greatness—
  It makes Heaven great
  It makes Earth great
  It makes man great

Mankind depends on the laws of Earth
Earth depends on the laws of Heaven
Heaven depends on the laws of Tao
But Tao depends on itself alone
  Supremely free, self-so, it rests in its own nature

The inner is foundation of the outer
The still is master of the restless

The Sage travels all day
     yet never leaves his inner treasure
Though the views are captivating and beg attention
     he remains calm and uninvolved
Tell me, does the lord of a great empire
     go out begging for rice?

One who seeks his treasure in the outer world
     is cut off from his own roots
Without roots, he becomes restless
Being restless, his mind is weak
And with a mind such as this
     he loses all command below Heaven

A knower of the Truth
    travels without leaving a trace
    speaks without causing harm
    gives without keeping an account
The door he shuts, though having no lock,
    cannot be opened
The knot he ties, though using no cord,
    cannot be undone

The Sage is always on the side of virtue
    so everyone around him prospers
He is always on the side of truth
    so everything around him is fulfilled

The path of the Sage is called
    "The Path of Illumination"
He who gives himself to this path
    is like a block of wood
    that gives itself to the chisel—
Cut by cut it is honed to perfection

Only a student who gives himself
    can receive the master's gift
If you think otherwise,
    despite your knowledge, you have blundered

Giving and receiving are one
This is called,
    "The great wonder"
    "The essential mystery"
    "The very heart of all that is true"

Hold your male side with your female side
Hold your bright side with your dull side
Hold your high side with your low side
Then you will be able to hold the whole world

When the opposing forces unite within
        there comes a power abundant in its giving
        and unerring in its effect
Flowing through everything
        It returns one to the First Breath
Guiding everything
        It returns one to No Limits
Embracing everything
        It returns one to the Uncarved Block

When the Block is divided
        it becomes something useful
        and leaders rule with a few pieces of it
But the Sage holds the Block complete
Holding all things within himself
        he preserves the Great Unity
        which cannot be ruled or divided

Those who look down upon this world
     will surely take hold and try to change things
But this is a plan
     I've always seen fail
The world is Tao's own vessel
It is perfection manifest
It cannot be changed
It cannot be improved
For those who go on tampering, it's ruined
For those who try to grasp, it's gone

Allow your life to unfold naturally
Know that it too is a vessel of perfection
Just as you breathe in and breathe out
     Sometimes you're ahead and other times behind
     Sometimes you're strong and other times weak
     Sometimes you're with people and other times alone

To the Sage
     all of life is a movement toward perfection
So what need has he
     for the excessive, the extravagant, or the extreme?

Those who rule in accordance with Tao
     do not use force against the world
For that which is forced is likely to return—
Where armies settle
     Nature offers nothing but briars and thorns
After a great battle has been fought
     the land is cursed, the crops fail,
     the Earth lies stripped of its motherhood

A knower of the Truth does what is called for
     then stops
He uses his strength but does not force things
In the same way
     complete your task
     seek no reward
     make no claims
Without faltering
     fully choose to do what you must do
This is to live without forcing
     to overcome without conquering

Things that gain a place by force
     will flourish for a time
     but then fade away
They are not in keeping with Tao
Whatever is not in keeping with Tao
     will come to an early end

Even the finest warrior is defeated
    when he goes against natural law
By his own hand he is doomed
    and all creatures are likely to despise him

One who knows Tao
    never turns from life's calling
When at home he honors the side of rest
When at war he honors the side of action
Peace and tranquility are what he holds most dear
    so he does not obtain weapons
But when their use is unavoidable
    he employs them with fortitude and zeal

Do not flaunt your excellence
Do not rejoice over victory
With the loss of others
    weep with sorrow and grief
After winning a battle
    do not celebrate,
    observe the rites of a funeral

One who is bound to action, proud of victory,
    and delights in the misfortune of others
will never gain a thing
    from this world below Heaven

Tao is eternal, one without a second
Simple indeed
    yet so subtle that no one can master it
If princes and kings could just hold it
All things would flock to their kingdom
Heaven and Earth would rejoice
    with the dripping of sweet dew
Everyone would live in harmony,
    not by official decree,
    but by their own inner goodness

This world is nothing but the glory of Tao
    expressed through different names and forms
One who sees the things of this world
    as being real and self-existent
    has lost sight of the truth
To him, every word becomes a trap
    every thing becomes a prison

One who knows the truth
    that underlies all things
    lives in this world without danger
To him, every word reflects the universe
    every moment brings enlightenment

Rivers and streams are born of the ocean
All creation is born of Tao
Just as all water flows back to become the ocean
All creation flows back to become Tao

One who knows others is intelligent
One who knows himself is enlightened

One who conquers others is strong
One who conquers himself is all-powerful

One who approaches life with force
        surely gets something
One who remains content where he is
        surely gets everything

One who gives himself to his position
        surely lives long
One who gives himself to Tao
        surely lives forever

The great Tao flows everywhere
It fills everything to the left
        and to the right
All things owe their existence to it
        and it cannot deny any one of them

Tao is eternal
It does not favor one over the other
It brings all things to completion
        without their even knowing it

Tao nourishes and protects all creatures
        yet does not claim lordship over them
So we class it with the most humble
Tao is the home to which all things return
        yet it wants nothing in return
So we call it "The Greatest"

The Sage is the same way—
        He does not claim greatness over anything
        He's not even aware of his own greatness
Tell me, what could be greater than this?

Hold fast to the Great Form within
    and let the world pass as it may
Then the changes of life will not bring pain
    but contentment, joy, and well-being

Music and sweets are passing pleasures
    yet they cause people to stop
How bland and insipid are the things of this world
    when one compares them with Tao!
One tastes, but the sweetness turns bitter
One sees, but the colors grow faint
One hears, but the sound fades into silence

One may look for fulfillment in this world
    but his longings will never be exhausted
The only thing he ever finds
    is that he himself is exhausted

Contraction pulls at that
    which extends too far
Weakness pulls at that
    which strengthens too much
Ruin pulls at that
    which rises too high
Loss pulls at life
    when you fill it with too much stuff

The lesson here is called
"The wisdom of obscurity"—
    The gentle outlast the strong
    The obscure outlast the obvious
Hence, a fish that ventures from deep water
    is soon snagged by a net
A country that reveals its strength
    is soon conquered by an enemy

Tao does not act
     yet it is the root of all action
Tao does not move
     yet it is the source of all creation

If princes and kings could hold it
     everyone under them would naturally turn within
Should a doubt or old desire rise up
     The Nameless Simplicity would push it down
The Nameless Simplicity frees the heart of desire
     and reveals its inner silence

When there is silence
     one finds peace
When there is silence
     one finds the anchor of the universe within himself

To give without seeking reward
To help without thinking it is virtuous—
    therein lies great virtue
To keep account of your actions
To help with the hope of gaining merit—
    therein lies no virtue

The highest virtue is to act without a sense of self
The highest kindness is to give without condition
The highest justice is to see without preference

When Tao is lost one must learn the rules of virtue
When virtue is lost, the rules of kindness
When kindness is lost, the rules of justice
When justice is lost, the rules of conduct
And when the high-blown rules of conduct are not followed
    people are seized by the arm and it is forced on them
The rules of conduct
    are just an outer show of devotion and loyalty—
    quite confusing to the heart
And when men rely on these rules for guidance—
    Oh, what ignorance abounds!

The great master follows his own nature
    and not the trappings of life
It is said,
    "He stays with the fruit and not the fluff"
    "He stays with the firm and not the flimsy"
    "He stays with the true and not the false"

From ancient times till now
    the One has been the source of all attainments
By realizing the One
    Heaven becomes clear, Earth becomes still
    spirits gain power and hearts fill up with joy
By realizing the One
    kings and lords become instruments of peace
    and all creatures live joyfully upon this earth
Without the One
    Heaven has no clarity and would crack
    Earth has no peace and would crumble
    spirits have no power and would lose their charm
Without the One
    hearts would dry up, empires would fall,
    all things would go lifelessly upon this earth

地

Long ago kings and lords called themselves
    "orphaned," "lonely," and "unworthy"
What honor can there be without humility?
    What heights can be reached without being low?

The pieces of a chariot are useless
    unless they work in accordance with the whole
A man's life brings nothing
    unless he lives in accordance with the whole universe
Playing one's part
    in accordance with the universe
    is true humility

So whether you're a gem in the royal court
    or a stone on the common path
If you accept your part with humility
    the glory of the universe will be yours

The movement of Tao is to return
The way of Tao is to yield

Heaven, Earth, and all things
        are born of the existent world
The existent world is born of the nothingness of Tao

When the best seeker hears of Tao
      he strives with great effort to know it
When an average seeker hears of Tao
      he thinks of it now and again
When the poorest seeker hears of Tao
      he laughs out loud

Tao is always becoming
      what we have need for it to become
If it could not do this
      it would not be Tao

There is an old saying,
      The clear way seems clouded
      The straight way seems crooked
      The sure way seems unsteady

The greatest power seems weak
The purest white seems tainted
The abundant seems empty
The stable seems shaky
The certain seems false
The Great Square has no corners
The Great Vessel is never filled

A beginner may be clumsy
      but after practice—what talent!
A large drum may sit silently
      but when banged—what noise!
Tao lies hidden
      yet it alone is the glorious light of this world

Tao gives life to the one
The one gives life to the two
The two give life to the three
The three give life to ten thousand things

All beings support *yin* and embrace *yang*
    and the interplay of these two forces
    fills the universe
Yet only at the still-point,
    between the breathing in and the breathing out,
    can one capture these two in perfect harmony

People suffer at the thought of being
    without parents, without food, or without worth
Yet this is the very way that
    kings and lords once described themselves

Who knows what fate may bring—
    one day your loss may be your fortune
    one day your fortune may be your loss

The age-old lesson that others teach, I also teach—
    "As you plant, so you reap"
    "As you live, so you die"
Know this to be the foundation of my teachings

The most yielding thing in the world
    will overcome the most rigid
The most empty thing in the world
    will overcome the most full
From this comes a lesson—
    Stillness benefits more than action
    Silence benefits more than words

Rare indeed are those who are still
Rare indeed are those who are silent
And so I say,
    Rare indeed are those
    who obtain the bounty of this world

One's own reputation—why the fuss?
One's own wealth—why the concern?
I say, what you gain
        is more trouble than what you lose

Love is the fruit of sacrifice
Wealth is the fruit of generosity

Be content,
        rest in your own fullness—
You will not suffer from loss
You'll avoid the snare of this world
You'll have long life and endless blessings

The Great Perfection seems imperfect
    yet this world it creates is never impaired
The Great Fullness seems empty
    yet this world it creates is never lacking

Great truth seems false
Great skill seems clumsy
Great eloquence seems like babble

Keep moving and you'll miss the cold
Keep silent and you'll beat the heat

Be tranquil like the rain of spring
Be pure like the sheen of silk
Then the Great Perfection will be perfect
    and the Great Fullness will be full

When Tao is present in the empire
    men follow their own nature
    and riding horses work the fields
When Tao is absent from the empire
    men go astray
    and war horses breed on sacred ground

There is no greater loss than losing Tao
    No greater curse than desire
    No greater tragedy than discontentment
    No greater fault than selfishness

Contentment alone is enough
Indeed, the bliss of eternity
    can be found in your contentment

Without going outside
    one can know the whole world
Without looking out the window
    one can see the ways of Heaven
The farther one goes
    the less one knows

Thus the Sage does not go, yet he knows
    He does not look, yet he sees
    He does not do, yet all is done

To become learned, gain daily
To obtain Tao, reduce daily
Reduce and reduce again
    until all action is reduced to non-action
Then no one is left
Nothing is done
    yet nothing is left undone

One who gives freely and without attachment
    gets a full life in return
One who gives with the secret hope of getting
    is merely engaged in business
Truly, they neither give nor receive
    any of the treasure from this world below Heaven

The Sage has no fixed heart of his own
Those who look at him
    see their own hearts

Those who are good he treats with goodness
Those who are bad he also treat with goodness
    because the nature of his being is good
Those who are truthful he treats with truth
Those who are not truthful he also treats with truth
    because the nature of his being is truthful

The Sage lives in harmony with all below Heaven
He sees everything as his own self
He loves everyone as his own child
All people are drawn to him
    every eye and ear is turned toward him

Again and again
Men come in with birth
        and go out with death
One in three are followers of life
One in three are followers of death
And those just passing from life to death
        also number one in three
But they all die in the end
Why is this so?
Because they clutch to life
        and cling to this passing world

I hear that one who lives by his own truth
        is not like this
He walks without making footprints in this world
Going about, he does not fear the rhinoceros or tiger
Entering a battlefield, he does not fear sharp weapons
For in him the rhino can find no place to pitch its horn
The tiger no place to fix its claw
The soldier no place to thrust his blade
Why is this so?
Because he dwells in that place
        where death cannot enter

Tao gives all things life
      Te gives them fulfillment
Nature is what shapes them
Living is what brings them to completion
Every creature honors Tao and worships Te
      not by force
      but through its own living and breathing

Though Tao gives life to all things
      Te is what cultivates them
Te is that magic power that
      raises and rears them
      completes and prepares them
      comforts and protects them

To create without owning
To give without expecting
To fill without claiming
      This is the profound action of Tao
      The highest expression of Te

That which creates the universe
      is the Mother of the world
By knowing the Mother
      one knows her children
By knowing her children
      one comes to know her
Such is their unity
      that one does not exist without the other

Fully embrace your life
      and you will share in the glory of creation
The Mother herself will be your guardian
And all her creation will be your guide

Stay with the Mother, shut the mouth, close the gates
      and you are never in trouble
Abandon the Mother, open the mouth, be busy with others
      and you are beyond all hope of rescue

Seeing your own smallness is called insight
Honoring your own tenderness is called strength

The sun in all its glory
      reveals but a passing world
Only the inner light illumines eternity
Only that light can guide us back home

Have faith
Follow your own shining
Be aware of your own awareness
On the darkest nights you will not stumble
On the brightest days you will not blink
This is called
      "The Practice of Eternal Light"

If I had the least bit of wisdom
    I could follow the path of Tao quite well
My only fear would be trying to go my own way
The Great Path is simple and direct
    yet people love to take the side-routes

See how magnificent the courts have become
The women dress in colorful gowns
The men carry well-crafted swords
Food and drink overflow
Wealth and finery abound
Yet in the shadow of all this splendor
    the fields grow barren
    the granaries are all but empty

I say this pomp at the expense of others
    is like the boasting of thieves after a looting
Surely it is contrary to Tao
Surely it cuts against the grain of the whole empire

Truth, once established, can never be uprooted
Goodness, once imbibed, can never be stripped away
    A sacrifice to a higher cause is never lost
    An offering to an ancestor never goes to waste

When a person embodies Tao
    his heart becomes true
When a family embodies Tao
    it thrives
When a village embodies Tao
    it is protected
When a country embodies Tao
    it prospers
When the world embodies Tao
    it reveals its perfection

Tao is everywhere
    it has become everything
To truly see it, see it as it is
In a person, see it *as* a person
In a family, see it *as* a family
In a country, see it *as* a country
In the world, see it *as* the world

How have I come to know all this?
Tao has shown me—
    Tao as all this!

One who embraces Tao
    will become pure and innocent
    like a newborn babe
Deadly insects will not sting him
Wild beasts will not attack him
Birds of prey will not strike him
He is oblivious to the union of male and female
    yet his vitality is full
    his inner spirit is complete
He can cry all day without straining
    so perfect is his harmony
    so magically does he blend with this world

Know this harmony—it brings the Eternal
Know the Eternal—it brings enlightenment

A full life—this is your blessing
A gentle heart—this is your strength

Things in harmony with Tao remain
Things that are forced, grow for a while
    but then wither away
This is not Tao
Whatever is not Tao
    comes to an early end

One who speaks does not know
One who knows does not speak

Shut the mouth
Close the gates
Blunt the sharpness
Loosen the knots
Temper the glare
Become one with the dust of the world
This is called
    "The Secret Embrace"

One who knows this secret
        is not moved by attachment or aversion,
        swayed by profit or loss,
        nor touched by honor or disgrace
He is far beyond the cares of men
        yet comes to hold the dearest place in their hearts

To rule the state, have a known plan
To win a battle, have an unknown plan
To gain the universe, have no plan at all

Let the universe itself
  reveal to you its splendor
How do I know this should be so?
  Because of this—
The more restrictions, the more poverty
The more weapons, the more fear in the land
The more cleverness, the more strange events
The more laws, the more lawbreakers

Thus the Sages say,
  Act with a pure heart and the people will be transformed
  Love your own life and the people will be uplifted
  Give without conditions and the people will prosper
  Want nothing and the people will find everything

When the ruler knows his own heart
     the people are simple and pure
When he meddles with their lives
     they become restless and disturbed

有

Bad fortune, yes—
     it rests upon good fortune
Good fortune, yes—
     it hides within bad fortune
Oh the things that Heaven sends—
     Who can know their final aim?
     Who can tell of their endless ways?
Today the righteous turn to trickery
Tomorrow the good turn to darkness
Oh what delusion abounds
     and every day it grows worse!

But the Sage is here upon the Earth
     to gently guide us back
He cuts but does not harm
He straightens but does not disrupt
He illumines but does not dazzle

Rule the people and serve Heaven
      yet hold nothing more dear than the Mother's harvest
Let every thought and every breath
      be the fruit of your offering—
Do it now
Let her power run thick in your blood
      There will be no obstacle you cannot overcome
      No limit you cannot surpass
      No empire you cannot rule

Ah, but in all your glory
      never lose sight of the Mother
Without her
      your empire will crumble
      your power will waste away
For the Mother brings the harvest
      She alone causes all things to endure

We call this
      "Deep roots and a solid trunk"
      "The way of long life and lasting insight"

Govern a nation as you would fry a small fish

山

When Tao is present in the empire
        dark spirits lose their power
It's not that they have no power
        it's that their power can't harm anyone
When Tao is present
        the people enjoy the blessings of Heaven
They find unity
They find peace

What's this about spirits doing harm?
The Sage is approaching
        and they are rushing in to sweep his path!

A great state is like a river basin
     that receives everything flowing into it
It is the place where all things come to rest
     where all the world is welcomed

The low is greater than the high
The still is greater than the restless
     The low country wins over its neighbor
     The still female wins over the male

The Sage wants to uplift the people
The people want to follow the Sage
     only by being low does this come to be
The Sage bows to the people
The people bow to the Sage
And when they lift up their heads
     only greatness remains

Tao is the treasure-house
  the true nature
  the secret source of everything
It is the great wealth of those who are awake
  the great protector of those still sleeping

If a person seems wicked
  do not cast him away—
Awaken him with your words
Elevate him with your deeds
Requite his injury with your kindness
Do not cast him away
  cast away his wickedness

欲

When the emperor is crowned
  or the three ministers installed
  they receive a gift of jade and horses
But how can this compare
  to sitting still and gaining the treasure of Tao
This is why the ancient masters
  honored the inward path of Tao
Did they not say
  "Seek and you will find"?
  "Err and you will be forgiven"?
Within, within
This is where the world's treasure has always been

Act without acting
Give without giving
Taste without tasting

Tao alone becomes all things great and all things small
It is the One in many
It is the many in One

Let Tao become all your actions
          then your wants will become your treasure
          your injury will become your blessing

後

Take on difficulties while they are still easy
Do great things while they are still small
Step by step the world's burden is lifted
Piece by piece the world's treasure is amassed

So the Sage stays with his daily task
          and accomplishes the greatest thing
Beware of those who promise a quick and easy way
          for much ease brings many difficulties

Follow your path to the end
Accept difficulty as an opportunity
This is the sure way to end up
          with no difficulties at all

A still mind can easily hold the truth
The difficulties yet to come can easily be avoided

The feeble are easily broken
The small are easily scattered
Begin your task before it becomes a burden
Put things in order before they get out of hand
Remember,
A tree that fills a man's embrace grows from a seedling
A tower nine stories high starts with one brick
A journey of a thousand miles begins with a single step

出

Act and it's ruined
Grab and it's gone
People on the verge of success often lose patience
        and fail in their undertakings
Be steady from the beginning to the end
        and you won't bring on failure

同

The Sage desires that which has no desires
        and teaches that which cannot be taught
He does not value the objects held by a few
        but only that which is held by everyone
He guides men back to their own treasure
        and helps all things come to know
        the truth they have forgotten
All this he does without a stir

The ancient ones were simple-hearted
    and blended with the common people
They did not shine forth
They did not rule with cleverness
    So the nation was blessed

Now the rulers are filled with clever ideas
    and the lives of people are filled with hardship
    So the nation is cursed

道

He who knows the play of Tao and Te
    knows the nature of the universe
Tao brings forth Te from its own being
Te expands in all directions
    filling every corner of the world
    becoming the splendor of all creation
Yet at every moment Te seeks Tao
This is the movement that guides the universe
This is the impulse
    that leads all things back home

Why do the hundred rivers
    turn and rush toward the sea?
Because it naturally stays below them

He who wishes to rule over the people
    must speak as if below them
He who wishes to lead the people
    must walk as if behind them
So the Sage rules over the people
    but he does not weigh them down
He leads the people
    but he does not block their way

The Sage stays low
    so the world never tires of exalting him
He remains a servant
    so the world never tires of making him its king

All the world talks about my Tao
          with such familiarity—
What folly!
Tao is not something found at the marketplace
          or passed on from father to son
It is not something gained by knowing
          or lost by forgetting
If Tao were like this
It would have been lost and forgotten long ago

玄

I have three treasures that I cherish and hold dear
          the first is love
          the second is moderation
          the third is humility
With love one is fearless
With moderation one is abundant
With humility one can fill the highest position
Now if one is fearless but has no love
          abundant but has no moderation
          rises up but has no humility
Surely he is doomed

Love vanquishes all attackers
It is impregnable in defense
When Heaven wants to protect someone
          does it send an army?
No, it protects him with love

The best warrior
      leads without haste
      fights without anger
      overcomes without confrontation
He puts himself below
      and brings out the highest in his men

This is the virtue of not confronting
      of working with the abilities you have
      of complying with the laws of Heaven

This is the ancient path that leads to perfection

The great warriors have a saying,
"I dare not act as host
    but would rather be a guest
I dare not advance an inch
    but would rather retreat a foot"

So advance but do not use your feet
Seize but do not use your arms
Cut but do not use your sword
Fight but do not use your own power

There is no greater misfortune than feeling
    "I have an enemy"
For when "I" and "enemy" exist together
    there is no room left for my treasure

Thus, when two opponents meet
    the one without an enemy
    will surely triumph

My teachings are very easy to understand
     and very easy to practice
Yet so few in this world understand
     and so few are able to practice

My words arise from that ancient source
My actions are those of the universe itself
If people do not know these
     how can they know me?

Those who follow my ways are rare
     and so I treasure them
Even if they wear the clothes of a beggar
     they carry a priceless gem within

Knowing what cannot be known—
    what a lofty aim!
Not knowing what needs to be known—
    what a terrible result!

Only when your sickness becomes sick
    will your sickness disappear

The Sage's illness has become ill
    his renunciation has been renounced
Now he is free
And every place in this world
    is the perfect place to be

When the people do not fear worldly power
    a greater power will arrive

Don't limit the view of yourself
Don't despise the conditions of your birth
Don't resist the natural course of your life
    In this way you will never weary of this world

The Sage knows himself, but not as himself
    he loves himself, but not as himself
    he honors himself, but not as himself
Thus, he discards the view of his own self
    and chooses the view of the universe

Bold action against others leads to death
Bold action in harmony with Tao leads to life

非

Good fortune, bad fortune
One seems to bring benefit
     the other to cause harm
But Heavens rejects them both
Both, in the end, tether men to this world

Who can know the reasons of Heaven?
     Who can know its endless ways?
Not even the Sage has an answer to this one

門

Heaven's way does not strive
     yet it always overcomes
It does not speak, yet it responds
It is not summoned, yet it appears
It does not hurry, yet it completes everything on time

The net of Heaven spans the universe
     yet not the slightest thing ever slips by

If people do not fear death
    why threaten them with it?
But suppose they did fear death
    and this was the fate handed to lawbreakers
Who would dare to do the killing?

There is always a Lord of Death
He who takes the place of the Lord of Death
    is like one who cuts with the blade
    of a master carpenter
Whoever cuts with the blade of a master carpenter
    is sure to cut his own hands

Why are the people starving?—
    Because their grain is being eaten up by taxes
    That's why they're starving

Why are the people rebellious?—
    Because those above them meddle in their lives
    That's why they're rebellious

Why do the people regard death so lightly?—
    Because they are so involved with their own living
    That's why they regard death so lightly

In the end,
The treasure of life is missed by those who hold on
    and gained by those who let go

When life begins
    we are tender and weak
When life ends
    we are stiff and rigid
All things, including the grass and trees,
    are soft and pliable in life
    dry and brittle in death

So the soft and supple
    are the companions of life
While the stiff and unyielding
    are the companions of death

An army that cannot yield
    will be defeated
A tree that cannot bend
    will crack in the wind
Thus by Nature's own decree
    the hard and strong are defeated
    while the soft and gentle are triumphant

Heaven operates like the bending of a bow—
    the high it pulls down
    the low it brings up
It takes from that which has too much
And gives to that which has too little
The way of man is otherwise—
    he takes from that which is depleted
    and gives to that which has too much

Who can offer an abundance to the world?—
One who has Tao
Such a one can give like the heavens

The Sage gives
    without relying on his own effort
He completes
    without waiting for reward
He illumines
    without stepping from the shadow

Nothing in this world
　　　is as soft and yielding as water
Yet for attacking the hard and strong
　　　none can triumph so easily
It is weak, yet none can equal it
It is soft, yet none can damage it
It is yielding, yet none can wear it away

Everyone knows that the soft overcomes the hard
　　　and the yielding triumphs over the rigid
Why then so little faith?
Why can no one practice it?

So the Sages say,
　　　fulfill even the lowest position
　　　love even the weakest creature
Then you will be called
　　　"Lord of every offering"
　　　"King of all below Heaven"

After settling a great dispute
    some resentment is sure to remain
Being content with what you have
    is always best in the end

The Sage always assumes the debt
    as if holding the left side of a contract
He gives and gives, and wants nothing in return

One with true virtue
    always seeks a way to give
One who lacks true virtue
    always seeks a way to get
To the giver comes the fullness of life
    to the taker just an empty hand

Though the Tao of Heaven has no favorites
    it always sides with one who has a pure heart

Let every state be simple
    like a small village with few people
There may be tools to speed things up
    ten or a hundred times
    yet no one will care to use them
There may be boats and carriages
    yet they will remain without riders
There may be armor and weaponry
    yet they will sit collecting dust

The people must take death seriously
    and not waste their lives in distant lands
Let them return
    to the knotting of cord
Let them enjoy their food
    and care for their clothing
Let them be content in their homes
    and joyful in the way they live

Neighboring villages are within sight of each other
Roosters and dogs can be heard in the distance
Should a man grow old and die
    without ever leaving his village
    let him feel as though there was nothing he missed

Words born of the mind are not true
True words are not born of the mind

Those who have virtue do not look for faults
Those who look for faults have no virtue

Those who come to know It
    do not rely on learning
Those who rely on learning
    do not come to know It

玄

The Sage sees the world
    as an expansion of his own self
So what need has he to accumulate things?
By giving to others
    he gains more and more
By serving others
    he receives everything

無

Heaven gives,
    and all things turn out for the best
The Sage lives,
    and all things go as Tao goes
    all things move as the wind blows

TAO TE CHING

Verbatim Translation, Commentary, and Notes

VERBATIM TRANSLATION

In this Verbatim Translation of the Tao Te Ching, each line contains five entries. They are, from left to right:

1. The verse and line position where the character is found in the text.

2 The Chinese character.

3. The number of the character's radical. A radical is a symbol within a Chinese character that is used to group together or classify various characters. Radical numbers, as used in this edition, also serve to distinguish between two characters that have a common spelling in English: for example, the word *ai* (lament) has the radical number 30, whereas another word, also *ai* (cherish), has the radical number 61. In cases where two Chinese characters have the same English spelling and the same radical, a letter is added to each radical: for example, *chi* (oneself) is 40a, and *chi* (near) is 40b.

4. An English transliteration of the character using the Wade-Giles system.

5. A list of English equivalents (definitions, interpretive meanings, and commonly used terms) that correspond to the character.

The following notations are used throughout the Verbatim Translation:

/ divides similar definitions of the same character

// divides dissimilar definitions of the same character

}} provides a meaning of the previous two Chinese characters
e.g.: *wu ming* = no + name   }} nameless

}}} provides a meaning for the previous three Chinese characters
(}}}} for the previous four Chinese characters, etc.)

(_____) indicates that the character may be left untranslated, such as in the case of a modifier or where two Chinese characters can be translated by one English word

( ) indicates an implied or contextual meaning or an entry that may be left untranslated

~ used for a word or phrase that is not a definition, but a suggested, implied, or interpretive meaning; or a meaning generated by context
e.g.: *ta*, great/ ~complete/ ~totally

" " used for a word or phrase that is unique or particular to a translator

[ ] enclose words or letters that are possible additions or alternatives

> denotes a suggested meaning or gives background information
e.g.: *k'ung*: vast / highest / grand / > surname of Confucius: *K'ung Fu Tzu*

• period or line ending

○ comma or line pause

>>Etm: gives the etymology of the character

Alt: supplies an alternative to the entry found in the standard Wang Pi text.

>Alt: supplies an alternative character to the one found in Wang Pi

+Alt: add supplies a character found in some texts, but not Wang Pi (++ For two characters, etc.)

X Alt: omit indicates that this character, found in Wang Pi, is omitted in some texts (XX for two characters, etc.)

^^Alt: move supplies an alternative placement for a character

Alternative texts used are: HSK (the text used for Ho Shang Kung's commentary); MWT (the two texts found at Ma Wang Tui: MWT is used when the entry is found in both texts, MWTA is used when the entry is specific to text A, and MWTB is used when the entry is specific to text B); Fu I; Tang Inscription; Tunhuang; and Okada.

NOTE: Double usage of the same Chinese character is often used to emphasize that character. For instance, the line *su jen chao chao* (common people are bright bright), suggests that common people are "very bright" or "doubly bright." Double characters can also be translated using two different meanings of the same word. For instance, *hsüan*, meaning "mysterious," "secret," "profound," "deep," or "dark," when doubled (*hsüan hsüan*) can be translated as "very dark," "secret secret," "mysterious and profound," "a profound mystery," etc.

Any work that deals with transposing an ancient Eastern language into a contemporary Western language is bound to have gaps and measures of discrepancy. Even a literal translation should not be taken literally. Many characters, such as *chi* ('s, its), *che* (the one, they, his), *tzu* (its), *i* (only), *hu* (!, very), are grammatical in nature. Sometimes they are used to change the orientation of the previous line or character, add emphasis to a sentence to create a feeling, or complete a rhyme, and they need not be regularly translated. Very often the English words will provide the context that suggests the meaning of these characters.

Names that appear in parentheses are those of English translators; their editions appear in the Sources section. Various Chinese commentators are also cited in the text, including Wang Pi (which refers to the commentator and not the standard text upon which his comments were based), HSK (Ho Shang Kung), MHL (Ma Hsu Lin), Kao Heng, Su-Che, Ssu-ma Kuang, and Erh Ya.

Verbatim Translation

				VERSE 1
01-01	道	162	**tao**	Tao / the Tao / way / path / paths / "That" / "The Absolute" / "Nature"
01-02	可	30	**k'o**	can / able to / can be / "becomes"
01-03	道 ｡	162	**tao**	Tao / path / way / walked / trodden // be told / talked about / spoken of
01-04	非	175	**fei**	not / cannot / surely not / opposes / "other than" / "not identical with" (Duy)　[the]
01-05	常	50	**ch'ang**	eternal / everlasting / constant / unchanging / always / fixed // the Absolute / the Eternal
01-06	道 ●	162	**tao**	Tao / way / path
01-07	名	30a	**ming**	Name / names / the Name
01-08	可	30	**k'o**	can / can be / able / "becomes"
01-09	名 ｡	30a	**ming**	name[d] / name / given a name / spoken of / ~divided　[is]
01-10	非	175	**fei**	not / surely not / opposite to　[the]
01-11	常	50	**ch'ang**	eternal / everlasting / fixed / constant // the Absolute / the Eternal
01-12	名 ●	30a	**ming**	Name / names / the Name / "labels" (Cleary)
01-13	無 ｡	86	**wu**	without / no / nothing / free of / void / empty // non-being / non-existence
01-14	名	30a	**ming**	name / is named / "manifests as" }} Nameless / unnameable / "non-being is the name of"　[is]
01-15	天	37	**t'ien**	Heaven　[and]
01-16	地	32	**ti**	earth　}} >Alt: replace *t'ien ti* (Heaven and earth) with *wan wu* (all things)—MWT
01-17	之	4	**chih**	's / of / its
01-18	始 ●	38	**shih**	origin / beginning / starting place / "Antecedent" // "maiden" (Pine) / "virgin" / ~that which gives birth /　>v. 6:15–18
01-19	有 ｡	74	**yu**	with / having / possessing // being / existence
01-20	名	30a	**ming**	name[s] / the Name / the Word /　}} "being is the name of"
01-21	萬	140	**wan**	ten thousand / myriad / all
01-22	物	93	**wu**	things / creatures / beings
01-23	之	4	**chih**	's / its / of
01-24	母 ●	80	**mu**	mother / the Mother
01-25	故	66	**ku**	Therefore / thus / hence / for / indeed / now / (reason)　[let there]
01-26	常	50	**ch'ang**	always / ever / constant[ly] / permanent[ly] / unchanging // the Eternal / the Absolute // ~a permanent state / ~established in / ~identified with
01-27	無 ｡	86	**wu**	without / free of / not having / rid // non-being / non-existence
01-28	欲	76	**yü**	deep-seated desire / mental patterns / desire[s] / longing / ~ attachment / ~identification / "thought-constructs" / "paradigm"　}} thought-free state
01-29	以	9a	**yi**	then / what follows / "so we may" / "in order to"
01-30	觀	147	**kuan**	perceive / see / truly see / recognize / observe / witness / behold // display / reveal / manifest / make evident
01-31	其	12	**ch'i**	its / his / 's / ~Tao's / ~the world's / ~the mind's
01-32	妙 ●	38	**miao**	essence / mystery / subtlety / secret[s] / true nature / wonderfulness / excellence/ spirituality / marvels // the Essence / the nature of the Absolute / one's true nature
01-33	常	50	**ch'ang**	always / ever / constant[ly] / permanent / unchanging // the Eternal / the Absolute
01-34	有 ｡	74	**yu**	hav[ing] / possess / (identifying yourself with) / "regard life with" (Yutang) / "manifest" / "allow yourself to have" // being

01-35	欲	76	**yü**	desires / thought-constructs / mental patterns / ~attachment / "fixed way of thinking" }} seeing the world through the lens of your mind / normal consciousness
01-36	以	9a	**yi**	then [one]
01-37	觀	147	**kuan**	perceive[s] / see[s] / truly see / recognize / witness // display / reveal / make evident
01-38	其	12	**ch'i**	its / his / ~Tao's / ~the world's / ~the mind's
01-39	徼	60	**chiao**	outer forms / manifestations / outcome / outer shell / end / limit / external / world appearance / "outer fringe" / "outer aspects" (Wu) / "the apparent" (Cleary) / bounds / borders / ~body
01-40	此	77	**tz'u**	These / this
01-41	兩	11	**liang**	two / both / pair[s] / duality / sameness // ~immanent and transcendent aspects of the Absolute / ~Tao-world / ~essence-manifestation // ~being-nonbeing
01-42	者	125	**chê**	those / (they are) / > makes the preceding character or clause into a noun
01-43	同	30	**t'ung**	alike / the same / one / together / unified / unity / merged / "issue from the same" // the One
01-44	出	17	**ch'u**	origin / source / birth // manifest / issue forth / arise / emerge
01-45	而	126	**erh**	but / yet / though
01-46	異	102	**yi**	differ / different[ly] / diverge [in]
01-47	名	30a	**ming**	name[d] / what they are called / how they are called forth / how they manifest ~[This]
01-48	同	30	**t'ung**	unity / oneness / likeness / sameness / together / both / "being the same" / "what they have in common" (Duy) // the One / ~the Absolute [is / are]
01-49	謂	149	**wei**	call[ed] / they are called / "appear as"
01-50	之	4	**chih**	its / (the) / (___)
01-51	玄	96	**hsüan**	mystery / secret / profound / hidden / dark[ness] / deep / obscure / mysterious / abyss // incomprehensible >Alt: *yüan* (origin, first cause, original or primal principle)
01-52	玄	96	**hsüan**	mystery / secret / profound / hidden / dark / deep / obscure >Alt: *yüan* (origin, first cause, primal)
01-53	之	4	**chih**	it is // (passes) / (becomes)
01-54	又	29	**yu**	again / also / ~to a higher degree / ~more }} upon / within
01-55	玄	96	**hsüan**	mystery / mysterious / profound / secret / obscure / dark / deep >Alt: *yüan* (origin, primal)
01-56	衆	143	**chung**	all / everything / "manifold" / "Collective" (Wing)
01-57	妙	38	**miao**	essence / mystery / subtlety / wonder / excellence // ~one's true nature
01-58	之	4	**chih**	's / of / its
01-59	門	169	**mên**	gate / gateway / door / opening / entrance // house / abode

NOTE: For a detailed explanation of all terms and concepts see Commentary on verse 1, page 271.

VERSE 2

02-01	天	37	**t'ien**	Heaven
02-02	下	1	**hsia**	below }} the world / the universe / all / everyone
02-03	皆	106	**chieh**	everyone / all }}} all below Heaven / everyone in the world / universal
02-04	知	111	**chih**	perceive[s] / knows / recognizes / affirms / becomes conscious of / (calls something)
02-05	美	123	**mei**	beautiful / beauty / delight / "desirable" / "agreeable" / (attractive)
02-06	之	4	**chih**	's / of / in its X Alt: omit—MWT
02-07	為	87	**wei**	being / making / acting / (manifestation as) X Alt: omit—MWT }} as
02-08	美	123	**mei**	beautiful / beauty // delight[ful] / (attractive) X Alt: omit—MWT

02-09	斯	69	ssu	because of / causes / thus / yet / "comes into being" / "arises" X Alt: omit—MWT
02-10	惡	61	wu	ugliness / ugly // hatred / evil / (aversion) / (repulsion)
02-11	已	49	yi	only / alone / ! / (____) / ~comes into being
02-12	皆	106	chieh	everyone / all
02-13	知	111	chih	perceive[s] / knows / recognizes
02-14	善	30	shan	virtue / good[ness] / the good *dharma*
02-15	之	4	chih	's / of / in its
02-16	為	87	wei	being / making / acting / be / (manifestation as) }} as
02-17	善	30	shan	virtue / good[ness] / the good
02-18	斯	69	ssu	because of / causes / thus / this / "comes into being"
02-19	不	1	pu	non- / no / lack of
02-20	善	30	shan	virtue / goodness }} bad / evil / wickedness
02-21	已	49	yi	alone / only / ! / (____) / ~comes into being
02-22	故	66	ku	for / thus / therefore / in this way / similarly
02-23	有	74	yu	existence / being / something / manifest / "is" / have / having [and]
02-24	無	86	wu	non-existence / non-being / nothing / emptiness / hidden / absent / "is-not" / not having
02-25	相	109	hsiang	each other / mutually / together / reciprocally / interdepend[ent] / co- / "mutually posited" (Chung)
02-26	生	100	shêng	produce[d] / born / grow[th] / live / give rise / birth / beget / exist[ence] / emerge / originate [1]
02-27	難	172	nan	difficult / hard [and]
02-28	易	72	yi	easy
02-29	相	109	hsiang	each other / mutually / co-
02-30	成	62	ch'êng	complete[d] [ion] / finish / complement[ary] / perfect / accomplish / produce
02-31	長	168	ch'ang	long [and]
02-32	短	111	tuan	short
02-33	相	109	hsiang	each other / mutually
02-34	較	159	chiao	compare / contrast / relate / confront / exhibit / test / appear / create / formulate / "offset" (Lau) >Alt: *hsing* (form, shape)
02-35	高	189	kao	High / the high / superior [and]
02-36	下	1	hsia	low / the low / inferior
02-37	相	109	hsiang	each other / mutually
02-38	傾	9	ch'ing	support / lean on / incline toward / rely on / determine / depend / distinguish / "position" / overturn
02-39	音	180	yin	tone / musical note / sound / pitch / treble [and]
02-40	聲	128b	shêng	voice / melody / mood / silence / "instruments" / base }} > Terms are vague; both refer to music. >Alt: *ying* (fill)—MWT
02-41	相	109	hsiang	each other / mutually
02-42	和	30b	ho	harmonize / harmony / conform / unity
02-43	前	18	ch'ien	front / before / "future" [and]
02-44	後	60	hou	back / after / behind / "past"
02-45	相	109	hsiang	each other / mutually

02-46	隨 .	170	sui	follow / comply / succession / accompany / company / ~may refer to the unbroken cycle of a circle
02-47	是	72a	shih	(this)
02-48	以	9a	yi	(for) }} therefore / thus / hence / accordingly / that is why
02-49	聖	128a	shêng	holy / saintly / high character
02-50	人	9a	jên	person / man / human }} the sage / saint / holy man [2]
02-51	處	141	ch'u	dwells / holds to / keeps to / lives by / abides by / stay / stop // manages / administers /embraces
02-52	無	86	wu	non- / empty / without
02-53	為	87	wei	action / doing / activity / effort / "interference" [3]
02-54	之	4	chih	in his / which are his
02-55	事 .	6	shih	activities / affairs / dealings / work / business / deeds / daily life
02-56	行	144	hsing	practices / teaches / acts / does / effects / spreads / carries out / disseminates
02-57	不	1	pu	non- / no / not / without
02-58	言	149	yen	talking / words / speech / spoken }} silence
02-59	之	4	chih	in his / which are his / (___)
02-60	教 .	66	chiao	teaching[s] / lesson / doctrine / instruct[ion] / philosophy }}}} doctrine without words
02-61	萬	140	wan	ten thousand / myriad / (all)
02-62	物	93	wu	things }} everything
02-63	作	9a	tso	arise / make / work / "he attends to"
02-64	焉	86a	yen	there / in it }} come to him / "take their rise"
02-65	而	126	erh	and / yet / but [he]
02-66	不	1	pu	does not / without / "claims no"
02-67	辭 .	160	tz'u	refuse / disown / reject / turn away / decline / overlook / hinder / "interrupt" [them] [4]
02-68	生	100	shêng	produces / rears / brings up / born / does / "create" / "give them life" / "assists in their development"
02-69	而	126	erh	and / yet / but
02-70	不	1	pu	does not / (no one)
02-71	有 .	74	yu	hold / have / own / possess / take possession [of them] / "presume" / "claim" [he]
02-72	為	87	wei	acts / works / does / "does his work"
02-73	而	126	erh	and / yet
02-74	不	1	pu	does not
02-75	恃 .	61	shih	claim / rely upon / hold on / assert / presume / appropriate / expect / depend upon / take credit / "rely upon his own ability" / "attach to the fruits of his actions"
02-76	功	19	kung	merit / achieve[ment] / reward / credit
02-77	成	62	ch'êng	complete[s][d] / finish / accomplish / achieve / succeed }} accomplishes [its][his] task
02-78	而	126	erh	and / yet
02-79	弗	57	fu	does not
02-80	居 .	44	chü	stop / stay / reside / dwell on it // "claim" / "take credit for it" }} is forgotten
02-81	夫	37	fu	because / since / truly
02-82	唯	30b	wei	exactly / only / alone / > this character shows a relationship and often remains untranslated }} for the very reason / precisely because / forasmuch [he]

02-83	弗	57	fu	does not / >Alt: *pu* (not)
02-84	居	141	ch'u	dwell / remain / occupy / reside // "take credit" / "regard as his own" / ~identify with limitations // ~how a person holds himself, his stance, his mental "posture"
02-85	是	72a	shih	(this)
02-86	以	9a	yi	(for) }} therefore / thus [he][it][his / its accomplishments, merit, credit]
02-87	不	1	pu	does not / not / "suffers no"
02-88	去	28	ch'ü	depart / desert / go away / die / loss }} stays with him / lasts forever / he loses nothing [5]

[1] *Hsiang shêng*: "give birth to each other" (Ta-Kao); "have a common birth" (Parker); "are interdependent in growth" (Yutang); "grow out of one another" (Waley); "are mutually arising" (Cheng)

[2] *Shêng jên:* a term for an enlightened or self-realized being. Variously translated as: sage, holy man, perfect sage, enlightened being, realized being, perfect being, etc. *Sheng jen* refers to one who embodies the virtues of the Tao and has realized his unity with the Absolute. (See NOTES)

[3] *Wu-wei* is a central concept to Taoism and translates as "non-action," "without action," "empty action," "no action," "without doing." It is action without the sense of doer-ship; it is egoless action; it is "taking no unnatural action"; action without ego or "force"; action in accord with the universe; action without attachment to its fruits. "Non-action" does not mean to avoid the call of your daily life, or be lazy, but rather to engage in all enterprises fully, knowing that the Supreme Power is the source of all action. In *wu-wei* a person sees himself as the universe, and, thus, he does nothing—all his actions are the actions of the universe itself. (See NOTES)

[4] a) >Alt: *ssu* (master, dominate, rule over, control, authority, "initiate") b) >Alt: *wei-shih* (make first, be in front, start, take the lead) —Fu I

[5] *Fu wei pu chu ssu i fu ch'ü*:
A. (The results of one's actions do not depart.)
"It is precisely because he does not claim credit that his accomplishment remains with him." (Chan); "Because he does not claim merit, his merit does not go away." (Chen); "Only when work is forgotten does it last forever." (Feng)
B. (The Sage does not die or depart.)
"The Master indeed rests not on rewards. That is why he passes not away." (Mears); "The very reason he does not die (and is reborn) is because he does not dwell in (identify with) his limited sense of self (i.e., his body, mind, or actions)." (Janwu)

VERSE 3

03-01	不	1	pu	Do not / not / not to / no / by not
03-02	尚	42	shang	exalt[ing] / honor / esteem / praise / elevate / "show partiality" [to the / those who are] >Alt: *shang* (above, superior, place above)
03-03	賢	154	hsien	worthy[ness] / good / virtuous / talented / ability / able ones / "the wise" / "the gIfted" / "men of worth" / "high character" / "persons of superior morality" [1]
03-04	使	9b	shih	so that / causes / thus
03-05	民	83	min	people
03-06	不	1	pu	do not / not to / (cease from) / (keep from) / (prevent them from)
03-07	爭	87	chêng	contest[ing] / compete / contend / contention / strife / quarrel / rivalry / fighting / be jealous / >lit: "pull in different directions" / "scheme and contend" (Yutang)
03-08	不	1	pu	do not / not / not to / no
03-09	貴	154	kuei	prize[ing] / value / honor / esteem / hold dear / treasure / "collect"
03-10	難	172	nan	difficult
03-11	得	60a	tê	to obtain / to get / procure }} rare
03-12	之	4	chih	(____) / its
03-13	貨	154	huo	goods / merchandise / objects / > v. 64 }}}} treasures

03-14	使	9b	**shih**	so that / causes
03-15	民	83	**min**	people
03-16	不	1	**pu**	will not / not to / free from / (prevent)
03-17	為	87	**wei**	commit[ting] / make / act / become
03-18	盜	108	**tao**	robbery / theft / steal[ing] // thieves / robbers }} become thieves / "illegal gain" (Chung)
03-19	不	1	**pu**	do not / not / no
03-20	見	147	**chien**	display[ing] / show / show off // see / look at / "focus on" [what] }} "shut out from sight"
03-21	可	30	**k'o**	can / is able to [bring about]
03-22	欲	76	**yü**	desire[able] / wants / thoughts / covet }} objects of desire / "attractions" / that which is desirable
03-23	使	9b	**shih**	so that / causes
03-24	民	83	**min**	people ['s]
03-25	心	61	**hsin**	heart / mind [to be]
03-26	不	1	**pu**	not / un- / "keep from" / (prevent)
03-27	亂	5	**luan**	trouble[d] / disturb[ed] / anxious / confuse / unsettle / distract / out of place }} remain placid / calm
03-28	是	72a	**shih**	(this)
03-29	以	9a	**yi**	(for) }} therefore [the]
03-30	聖	128a	**shêng**	holy
03-31	人	9a	**jên**	man / person }} the sage
03-32	之	4	**chih**	's
03-33	治	85	**chih**	rule / government / governing / way of ruling / "led by others" }}}} sage's way of ruling / sage's way of life (~how he governs himself) [is to]
03-34	虛	141	**hsü**	empty / empties / make empty / vacuous / "opening" / "relaxing" (Chung) / "unpreoccupied" (Parker) / ~pacify / calm / purify / peace / "put at ease"
03-35	其	12	**ch'i**	their / (the people's) / his
03-36	心	61	**hsin**	heart[s] / mind[s] / heart [of desire] / mind [of envy] / ~negative emotions, what upsets them }}} > open-minded / humble / mind free of too many ideas [and][but]
03-37	實	40b	**shih**	fill[s] / "reinforcing" / (make solid)
03-38	其	12	**ch'i**	their / (the people's) / his
03-39	腹	130	**fu**	bellies / stomachs / middle / "centers" / "seat of the mind" / (inward reality / resolve / soul) / ~as an adjective, "dear, "intimate"—"what is dear to them" (Carus)
03-40	弱	57	**jo**	weaken / make gentle / discourage / make pliant / relaxing
03-41	其	12	**ch'i**	their [personal]
03-42	志	61	**chih**	ambition[s] / will[fullness] / wish / desire [to get ahead] / ~self-willed / ~headstrong
03-43	強	57	**ch'iang**	strengthen / sturdy / make strong
03-44	其	12	**ch'i**	their
03-45	骨	188	**ku**	bones / frame / "backbone" / "character" / ~sturdiness, what supports them
03-46	常	50	**ch'ang**	always / [he] always / continually
03-47	使	9b	**shih**	because / since / causes / (keeps) / (keeping)
03-48	民	83	**min**	the people [are / to be]

03-49	無	86	**wu**	without / free of / (innocent of)
03-50	知	72	**chih**	knowledge / cunning / craftiness / knowing / erudition / "strategy" }} innocent / simple / simpleminded / "in no-knowledge" (Chen)
03-51	無	86	**wu**	without / free from
03-52	欲.	76	**yü**	desire / "excessive needs" / wanting / "demanding" / seeking [gain] }} content / passionless
03-53	使	9b	**shih**	causes / ensures / it makes / he causes / making
03-54	夫	37	**fu**	truly
03-55	知	72	**chih**	cunning / crafty / clever / sly / knowing / "sophisticated" / "world-wise" / "having knowledge"
03-56	者	125	**chê**	(the ones)
03-57	不	1	**pu**	not
03-58	敢	66	**kan**	to dare / presume / venture }} be afraid to / will not be able to / "given no scope for tempting" (Ould)
03-59	為	87	**wei**	interfere / act / plan / (trick them) / (take advantage of them)
03-60	也.	5	**yeh**	! / indeed [If one / he]
03-61	為	87	**wei**	acts / does / practices
03-62	無	86	**wu**	without / non-
03-63	為.	87	**wei**	action / acting / making / doing / "being the one acting" (Ming) / "contrivance" (Chen) }}} "if nothing is done" (Feng) / "be still while you work" (Blakney) [2]
03-64	則	18	**tsê**	then
03-65	無	86	**wu**	nothing / un- / without [is]
03-66	不	1	**pu**	not }} all
03-67	治.	85	**chih**	in place / in order / order[ed] / well-regulated / governed / controlled / (in harmony with nature) }}} all will "live in peace" (Yutang) / "no one is uncultivated" (Chung)

[1] *Pu shang hsien*: "when worth is not honored" (Medhurst)

[2] *Wu-wei* ("non-action")   (See v. 2, n. 3)

VERSE 4

04-01	道	162	**tao**	Tao [is][is like]
04-02	沖	85	**ch'ung**	empty / vacuous / void / hollow [bowl] / (an empty vessel) / "a whirling emptiness" (Chen) >Alt: *chung* (empty), which implies "center" or "within"—HSK [1]
04-03	而	126	**erh**	yet / and [when]
04-04	用	101	**yung**	used / in use / applied / put in operation / one who uses [2]
04-05	之	4	**chih**	its / it / it is [capacity][potential]
04-06	或	62	**huo**	perhaps / somehow / maybe [3]
04-07	不	1	**pu**	not / don't [become]
04-08	盈.	108	**ying**	exhausted / depleted / drained / empty // filled / full / at its limit / (a full vessel) }}}} it is not filled / there is nothing it does not fill / it is never drained / inexhaustible
04-09	淵	85	**yüan**	deep / fathomless / profound / bottomless / an abyss / in its depths >Alt: *hsiao* (deep, still)—MWT
04-10	兮	12	**hsi**	! / oh / indeed / so / (very) [it]
04-11	似	9	**ssu**	resembles / is like / seems to be / is likely / as if [the]
04-12	萬	140	**wan**	ten thousand / (all) / "myriad"

04-13	物	93	**wu**	things / creatures / forms }} all things / "all of us"
04-14	之	4	**chih**	's / of / (their) / (our)
04-15	宗	40	**tsung**	ancestor / [fore]father / origin / source / progenitor / "fountainhead" / ~"guiding rule, comprehensive principle, pattern" (Duy)
04-16	挫	64	**ts'o**	blunt[s][ing] / make dull / "round off" / dull[ing] / "file down" / "removes"
04-17	其	12	**ch'i**	its / it / (the) / (our)
04-18	銳	167	**jui**	sharp[ness] / point / sharp edges // acuteness / keenness }}} it blunts the sharpness / "in it all sharpness is blunted" (Waley)
04-19	解	148	**chieh**	loosen / unravel / undo / untie // explain / resolve / subdue
04-20	其	12	**ch'i**	its / (the)
04-21	紛	120	**fên**	knots / fetters / tangles / entangled // confusion / perplexity / turmoil / complexity / complications
04-22	和	30b	**ho**	harmonize / blend[ing] / soften / temper / diffuse
04-23	其	12	**ch'i**	its / (the) / (our)
04-24	光	10	**kuang**	light / bright[ness] / glare / brilliance / "discord" (Au-Young)
04-25	同	30	**t'ung**	becomes one / identify / unite / mix / merge with / share / "assimilate" [with]
04-26	其	12	**ch'i**	its / (the)
04-27	塵	32	**ch'ên**	dust / dust of the world / world / (common man) / "ways of the world" / ~"noise and fuss of daily life" // "clear" [4]
04-28	湛	85	**chan**	deep / dark / deep pool / tranquil / serene / still / "profoundly still" / "hidden in the deeps" (Wu) / ~quality of deep water—dark, tranquil, serene / "soak in"
04-29	兮	12	**hsi**	! / (very) / so
04-30	似	9	**ssu**	it seems / resembles / appears to
04-31	或	62	**huo**	likely / sometimes/ perhaps / apparently / (barely) / (hardly) / >v. 56, v. 12 >Alt: *ch'ang* (forever, eternal)—Tang Inscription >Alt: *jo* (like, seems, resembles) [5]
04-32	存	39	**ts'un**	continue / enduring / remain / exist / present }} continue forever }}} "it seems in its likeness to remain" (Carus)
04-33	吾	30	**wu**	I
04-34	不	1	**pu**	do not
04-35	知	111	**chih**	know
04-36	誰	149	**shui**	who
04-37	之	4	**chih**	its
04-38	子	39	**tzu**	child / son / offspring / "generated" (Duy)
04-39	象	152	**hsiang**	image[s] / reflection // seems / appears
04-40	帝	50	**ti**	Lord of Heaven / supreme ruler / the Creator / Ancestor / God / "creation" / "the gods" [6]
04-41	之	4	**chih**	's / its
04-42	先	10	**hsien**	preceded / existed before / forefather / antecedent / preface }}}} it came "before the creation of images" / "This image in front of the Source" (Wing)

[1] *Tao ch'ung* (tao empty): "Tao is like a hollow vessel." (Yutang); "Tao is infinite." (Au); "Tao is within." (Erkes); "The Tao is as emptiness, so are its operations. It resembles non-fullness." (Medhurst)

[2] "Used" = (a) pouring out from its emptiness / creating all things, (b) pouring into its emptiness / accepting the return of all things

[3] >Alt: *chiu* (a long time, enduring)—Tang Inscription >Alt: *yu* (again) > Alt: *ch'ang* (always)—HSK

[4] **T'ung ch'i ch'ên**: "It becomes one with the dusty world." (Chan); "It identifies with the ways of the world." (Wing); "It is lowly as the dust." (Mears); "Its turmoil is submerged." (Yutang); "It unites the world into one whole." (Wu); "It becomes one with everything that it has created." (Tze); "It brings unity to all beings." (Au); "Let your wheels move along old ruts." (Lau)

[5] **Ssu huo**: "resembles a certain existence" (Wing); "bears the apearance of permanence" (Medhurst)

[6] **Ti**: the Lord of Heaven or the Creator, such as the Hindu deity Brahma, who is responsible for the creation of the physical world. *Ti* does not refer to the all-pervasive God or Lord of Western theology.

NOTE: The three characters used to describe Tao in this verse all contain the character for water: **ch'ung** ("water" + "middle"): "Empty . . . used yet never exhausted"; **yüan** ("water" + "abyss"); "Deep . . . the ancestor of all things"; **chan** ("water" + "very / much"): "Dark . . . it remains forever."

VERSE 5

05-01	天	37	t'ien	Heaven [and]	
05-02	地	32	ti	earth	
05-03	不	1	pu	not / [are] not / do not [have] / are without / non-	
05-04	仁。	9b	jên	partial[ity] / sentimental[ity] / human sentiments / biased / "favorites" / humane / kindness / "preference to relatives" }} indifferent / dispassionate / "equal-vision"	[1][2]
05-05	以	9a	yi	thus / (regard) / (treat) / (see)	
05-06	萬	140	wan	ten thousand / myriad / (all)	
05-07	物	93	wu	things / beings / creatures }} "the creation"	
05-08	為	87	wei	(like) / acting / acting [toward them like] / (as if they were)	
05-09	芻	140	ch'u	straw / grass	
05-10	狗.	94	kou	dogs }}} ~indifferently, with dispassion, without sentimentality	[3]
05-11	聖	128a	shêng	holy	
05-12	人	9a	jên	person / man }} the sage	
05-13	不	1	pu	is not / does not [have]	
05-14	仁。	9b	jên	partial[ity] / biased / human sentiments—based on aversion and attraction	[4]
05-15	以	9a	yi	thus / (regards) [the]	
05-16	百	106b	pai	hundred	
05-17	姓	38	hsing	families / surnames }} everyone / the masses	
05-18	為	87	wei	acting / making / acting [toward them like] / (as if they were)	
05-19	芻	140	ch'u	straw / grass	
05-20	狗.	94	kou	dogs	
05-21	天	37	t'ien	Heaven [and]	
05-22	地	32	ti	earth	
05-23	之	4	chih	's / its	
05-24	間。	169	chien	space / crevice / (the space between them)	
05-25	其	12	ch'i	it	
05-26	猶	94	yu	is like	
05-27	橐	75	t'o	sack / bag / cover of a bellows	
05-28	籥	118	yo	pipe / bar of a bellows / flute—"which produces music due to its hollowness" (Chen) / "a tube through which potters blow air into a fire" }} a bellows	

05-29	乎	4	hu	! / indeed [It is]
05-30	虛	141	hsü	empty / emptied / vacant / hollow / vacuous
05-31	而	126	erh	and / yet
05-32	不	1	pu	does not [get] / is never / without
05-33	屈	44	ch'ü	get exhausted / fall in / collapse / is lacking / fails to supply [It] }}} "Though unsupported, it does not warp." (Medhurst)
05-34	動	19	tung	moves / moving / active / "the more it works" / "shakes" / "each movement" (Pine)
05-35	而	126	erh	and / yet / (_____)
05-36	愈	61a	yü	more and more / further
05-37	出	17	ch'u	produces / gives out / brings forth / comes out / pours out / begets / expels
05-38	多	36	to	many / too many / too much / more / numerous
05-39	言	149	yen	words / speech / talk / "dispensations" / ~"ordinances of the ruler" (Ku) / "the course of things or their history" }} the talkative [5]
05-40	數	66	shu	brings about / leads to / soon reaches / "will of course" (Chan) / "necessarily brings about" / numerous / much / "reckoning" / "wit" / "accelerate" / ~quick, soon, speed [6]
05-41	窮	116	ch'iung	exhaustion / the end / the limit / dead end / destruction / "silence" (Lau) }} "wastes it" (Pine) / "exhausts itself" (Wing)
05-42	不	1	pu	not / un- / nothing
05-43	如	38	ju	likely }} it is better to / rather / nothing is better
05-44	守	40	shou	hold / hold fast to / keep to / stay with / remain / abide in / maintain / preserve
05-45	中	2	chung	the center / centered / middle / core / the mean / middle path / moderation / what is within / inside / "your thoughts" (Blakney) / middle way [7][8]

[1] *Jên* refers to humanness, human-kindness, or benevolence, but in this context it refers to the partiality of humans and a condition based on personal bias, preference, and conditions. *Pu jen* (without humanness) represents dispassion, showing no favorites, treating all as equal. Translations such as "amoral," "ruthless" (Lau), "inhuman," and "not humane" (Duy) carry moral connotations that are not suggested here. "Unkind" (Yutang) and "heartless" (Pine) also miss. "Benevolent" (Chung) and "not sentimental" (Wu) are closer to the mark.

[2] *T'ien ti pu jên*: "Heaven and earth do not act from motives of benevolence." (Alexander); "Heaven and earth have no special love." (Chalmers); "Heaven and earth entertain no benevolence, making the innumerable objects serve their respective purposes, just as we utilize the straw hounds in exorcising at sacrifices." (Parker)

[3] *Ch'u kou* (straw dogs): "Before the straw dog has been offered in sacrifice," replied Shih Chin, "it is kept in a box, wrapped up in an embroidered cloth, and the augur fasts before using it. But when it has once been offered up, passersby trample over its body, and fuel-gatherers pick it up for burning." —Chuang-tsu (Giles, p. 145)

[4] "I am the same to all beings. I favor none and I hate none. But those who worship me with devotion, they live in me and I live in them." *Bhagavad Gita* (9:29). (See NOTES)

[5] >Alt: *wen* (hear, learning)—MWT

[6] *Shu* literally means "number" and suggests a repetition, continuity, course, or history of things; it can also mean truth, principle, or one's lot in life (Chan). Wang Pi interprets *shu* as the tendency or inertia of existence. Lit: "number, counting."

[7] *Chung*, center, one's center. *Chung* also implies "one's own nature," "the inner path," or "the path of truth." "Inner essence" (Medhurst); "that which dwells within the heart" (Ould)   >Alt: *ch'ung* (void, empty)—HSK

[8] *Pu ju shou chung*: "More words count less. / Hold fast to the center. " (Feng); "By many words wit is exhausted. / Rather, therefore, hold to the core." (Yutang); "By many words one's reckoning is exhausted. / It is better to abide by the center." (Chen); "Many words add up to much exhaustion: / Not as good as holding to your own nature." (Janwu); "All your talk leads to exhaustion. Better hold to the silence of your own center." (Ming); "No amount of words can fathom it. / Better look for it within you." (Wu);

"... There is nothing like keeping the inner man." (Chalmers); "... Nothing is better than to remain in the state before things are stirred." (Chung)

VERSE 6

06-01	谷	150	ku	Valley / vacuous / fountain / ~"to nourish"—HSK
06-02	神	113	shên	Spirit / Soul / "God" }} spirit that fills the world / "spiritual reality of the void" / ~Tao [1]
06-03	不	1	pu	does not / is not / never
06-04	死 。	78	ssu	die[s] / cease / dead / "expire" }} is immortal / deathless
06-05	是	72a	shih	(she) / it / this / ~the spirit
06-06	謂	149	wei	is called / call / known as / "styled"
06-07	玄	96	hsüan	mysterious / profound / secret / subtle / deep / hidden / dark / abyss >Alt: *yüan* (origin, primal principle)
06-08	牝 。	93	p'in	female / woman / mother / mare / womb / >lit: "mare" / ~female qualites / (creative power) }} mysterious female / abstruse womb / dark mare
06-09	玄	96	hsüan	mysterious / profound / secret / dark >Alt: *yüan* (origin, first cause, primal principle)
06-10	牝	93	p'in	female / woman / mother [2]
06-11	之	4	chih	's / its / of
06-12	門 。	169	mên	gate / door / entrance / opening / passage / mouth // house / abode
06-13	是	72a	shih	this / (she) / it
06-14	謂	149	wei	call / is called // tells of / reports / (reveals)
06-15	天	37	t'ien	heaven [and]
06-16	地	32	ti	earth ['s] }} creation
06-17	根 。	75	kên	root / origin / cause / source / foundation / fundamental beginning / "base from which it springs"
06-18	綿	120	mien	continual[ly] / continuous / enduring / perpetual / ceaseless / linger // silky / gossamer / (very) / > lit: "drawn out or prolonged like a thread of silk"
06-19	綿	120	mien	continual[ly] / continuous / enduring / without end / interminable / linger // silky / gossamer }} goes on forever / "lingering like gossamer" (Wu) / "dimly visible"
06-20	若	140	jo	seems [to] / like / the same / seeming / appears / barely / "has a hint" / "on the brink of" >Alt: *chiu* (long-lasting, forever, always)
06-21	存 。	39	ts'un	continue / exist[ence] / endure / remain }} seems to exist / "its invisible existence" (Ku) // remain forever / "as though ever abiding" (Medhurst) [3]
06-22	用	101	yung	use / [in] using / function / giving out / draw[ing] upon
06-23	之	4	chih	it / her [there is] [there will be] }} it can be used / its usefulness
06-24	不	1	pu	no / don't / without / never / [comes with] no
06-25	勤 。	19	ch'in	effort / exertion / labor / toil / "try to force" // exhaust[ion][ed] / wear[s][ing] out / weariness / come to an end / failure / fails / "run dry" / "drain it" [4][5]

[1] **Shên** is from "two hands extending a rope" + "influx from Heaven" / > sign by which the will of Heaven is known by mankind

[2] **Hsüan p'in**: "Mystic / Mysterious Female" (Yutang) (Blakney) (Lin) (Lau) (Chan) (Waley) (Wei) (Cheng), "Mysterious Feminine" (Wu), "mysterious feminine element" (Au-Young), "Mysterious Femininity" (LaFargue), "profound female" (Chan), "dark female" (Duy), "Subtle Female" (Wing), "Mysterious Mother" (Ould), "Mother of the Abyss" (Medhurst), "Mother-substance of the Deep" (Mears), "primal mother" (Feng), "Mother of Heaven" (Tze), "abstruse womb" (Ku), "mystery of passivity" (Chung), "Dark Mare" (Chen)

[3] **Mien mien jo ts'un**: "Ceaselessly it seems to endure." (Chalmers); "It is there within us all the while." (Waley); "Lingering like gossamer, it has only a hint of existence." (Wu); "It lingers in wisps." (Cheng); "It is like a veil barely seen." (Feng)

[4] **Pu chin**: comes naturally, inexhaustible, "without external coercion"

[5] **Yung chi pu ch'in**: "It is employed without effort." (Chalmers); "Use it without haste." (Cheng); "Use it; it will never fail." (Feng); "It is eternal becoming, effortless creation." (Runes); "Its functions are inexhaustible." (Ku); "Use it and you will never wear it out." (Chan); "Draw upon it as you will, it never runs dry." (Waley); "Its usefulness comes with no effort." (Wing); "Use her without labor." (Blakney); "Call on her—she will always be there to give." (Ming)

NOTE: This verse is similar in many respects to verse 4: Emptiness: v. 6:1–8 vs v. 4:1–2; Root of Heaven and Earth: v. 6:9–17 vs v. 1:13–18; Seems to continue forever: v. 6:18–21 vs v. 4:28–32; Used but never exhausted: v. 6:22–25 vs v. 4:3–7; (See NOTES for a more detailed description of this creative energy.)

VERSE 7

07-01	天	37	t'ien	Heaven [is]
07-02	長	168	ch'ang	everlasting / constant / eternal / enduring / constant / perpetual / long
07-03	地	32	ti	earth [is]
07-04	久.	3	chiu	lasting / ancient / enduring / long-lasting / permanent }} the universe is everlasting
07-05	天	37	t'ien	Heaven [and]
07-06	地	32	ti	earth }} nature
07-07	所	63	so	reason / that which
07-08	以	9a	yi	for / because }} the reason why
07-09	能	130	nêng	can [be] / able / have the power to
07-10	長	168	ch'ang	everlasting / eternal / enduring / last forever / "ever-renewing"
07-11	且	1	ch'ieh	and
07-12	久	4	chiu	enduring / lasting }}}}}} "what is the secret of their durability?" (Wu)
07-13	者.	125	chê	it / that
07-14	以	9a	yi	because / (accordingly)
07-15	其	12	ch'i	they [do]
07-16	不	1	pu	not [for]
07-17	自	132	tzu	themselves / self / [give] themselves
07-18	生.	100	shêng	live / life / exist / produce / arise / come forth / [aim] at life / }} do not live for themselves / "are unborn"
07-19	故	66	ku	that is the reason / thus / therefore / hence
07-20	能	130	nêng	[they] can / are able to
07-21	長	168	ch'ang	everlasting / forever / long-lived / constant[ly]
07-22	生.	100	shêng	live / exist / arise / produce
07-23	是	72a	shih	(this)
07-24	以	9a	yi	(for) }} therefore / thus
07-25	聖	128a	shêng	holy / saintly
07-26	人	9a	jên	person / man }} the sage [puts][places][positions]
07-27	後	60	hou	behind / last / in the background / second
07-28	其	12	ch'i	his / her / him
07-29	身	158	shên	self / person / (body) }}} puts himself behind / "pulls himself back"

07-30	而	126	erh	and / yet [his / her]
07-31	身	158	shên	person / self [is]
07-32	先 。	10	hsien	in front / first / in the foreground }} "finds himself in front"
07-33	外	36	wai	rejects / denies / excludes / puts away / outside / detached / indifferent / "not concerned with" / "treats as incidental / extraneous" / "regards as external" (Chan)
07-34	其	12	ch'i	his / her / him
07-35	身	158	shên	self / person }}} "reckons himself out" (Wu) / "unmindful of himself" (Ould) / }} "lets himself go" (Pine) [1]
07-36	而	126	erh	and [his / her]
07-37	身	158	shên	self / person / himself
07-38	存 。	39	ts'un	is preserved / continues / always remains / survives / is safe [is this]
07-39	非	175	fei	not / is this not
07-40	以	9a	yi	because
07-41	其	12	ch'i	he
07-42	無	86	wu	is without / lacks / has no
07-43	私	115	ssu	self / self-interest / personal concern / "thought of self" / ~limited identification with self }} forgets himself / is selfless
07-44	邪 。	163	hsieh	?
07-45	故	66	ku	therefore / thus / this is the reason why / is it not because [he][she]
07-46	能	130	nêng	can / is able to / has the power to
07-47	成	62	ch'êng	accomplish / complete / succeed / fulfill / perfect / realize / attain / secure
07-48	其	12	ch'i	his / her
07-49	私 。	115	ssu	self / own person / own / interests / "private ends" / ~attainment of higher self [?]

[1] **Wai ch'i shên**: "Rejects himself" means that the sage rejects the limited identification with his body and the small sense of self, and identifies himself with the universe. This is the state of unity, whereby the sage sees his own Self in everyone and everyone as his own Self.

VERSE 8

08-01	上	1	shang	Superior / supreme / highest / the best / "highest style of"
08-02	善	30	shan	goodness / excellence / virtue / skill / dharma / value // good person / skillful person }} the best of men / the highest goodness / a person of superior goodness [1]
08-03	若	140	jo	is like / follows / resembles
08-04	水	85	shui	water
08-05	水 。	85	shui	water [brings][is]
08-06	善	30	shan	good / excellent / excels / "greatly" [at][to] }} water is good at // the goodness of water
08-07	利	18	li	benefit[ting][s] / profit / gains [to the]
08-08	萬	140	wan	the ten thousand / (every) / (all)
08-09	物	93	wu	thing[s]
08-10	而	126	erh	yet
08-11	不	1	pu	does not
08-12	爭 。	87	chêng	contend[ing] / strive / go against / struggle / assert / compete / quarrel / "scramble" >Alt: replace pu chang (not contend) with ching (tranquil)—MWTA [with them]

08-13	處	141	ch'u	[it] dwells / stays / stops / rests / settles / "content to be where" (Waley) / "flows in" [where]
08-14	眾	143	chung	all / many
08-15	人	9a	jên	people / men
08-16	之	4	chih	their / its
08-17	所	63	so	place / (lowest place) [is]
08-18	惡﹒	61	wu	loath[ed] / hate / despise / shun / reject / disdain
08-19	故	66	ku	therefore / this is why [it / water][it comes]
08-20	幾	52	chi	very close / near / approaches / "approximates" / "is similar" / ~close in qualities or nature
08-21	於	70	yü	in / at / on / to / with / compared with
08-22	道﹒	162	tao	Tao / > because (a) it dwells in low places, (b) it dwells with all people, even those despised
08-23	居	44	chü	a place to live / home / dwelling / house / lodging // (to inhabit / occupy / be in)
08-24	善	30	shan	good / excellent / excel / best / value / virtue / skill / love / satisfied with / prefer / choose // a good man
08-25	地	32	ti	the earth / site / place / level ground / location / "dwelling in lowly places" (Ku)
08-26	心	61	hsin	heart / heart-mind / (matters of the heart) / (qualities of the mind)
08-27	善	30	shan	good / best / excellent / values / be good at
08-28	淵﹒	85	yüan	deep / depth / profound / fathomless / "seeking depth" / ~quality of deep water—still, serene / ~deep within / ~warmth, sentiment (Carus) / (welcoming) / > v. 4:09 [2]
08-29	與	134	yü	relationships / dealing with others / human relations / ally / associates / sharing / helping / generosity
08-30	善	30	shan	good / best / excellent / adept at [being]
08-31	仁﹒	9b	jên	humane / humanity / kindness / human-kindness / benevolent / kind people >Alt: *jen* (others, man)—Fu I >Alt: *t'ien* (Heaven)—MWT
08-32	言	149	yen	words / speech / speaking
08-33	善	30	shan	good / best / value / skill
08-34	信﹒	9	hsin	sincere[ity] / truth[ful][ness] / faith[ful] / trustworthy
08-35	正	77	chêng	governing / government / ruling / managing / leadership / administration >Alt: *cheng* (correct, upright)
08-36	善	30	shan	good / best / love / skill / "one should be adept at"
08-37	治﹒	85	chih	just[ice] / peace / fair / harmonious / righteous // govern / rule / order / proper order
08-38	事	6	shih	work / service / duty / serving others / deeds / doing business / daily life / projects / the affairs of life
08-39	善	30	shan	good / best / right
08-40	能﹒	130	nêng	able / competent / ability / efficient / effective[ness]
08-41	動	19	tung	action[s] / activity / movement / "making a move" / "in its own course" / effort / "practice"
08-42	善	30	shan	good / best / right / value
08-43	時﹒	72b	shih	[proper] timing / timeliness / the right moment / opportunity / "seizing the moment" / "in rhythm" / ~time / ~all the time [3]
08-44	夫ˊ	37	fu	above all / forasmuch / because // "a man of goodness" / ~one who is above
08-45	唯	30b	wei	(____) / just as / only / but / so }} for the very reason / since / whereas
08-46	不	1	pu	not

08-47	爭。	87	chêng	contend / compete / go against / strive [with others][with nature][natural law]	
08-48	故	66	ku	therefore [one is]	
08-49	無	86	wu	without / no / free from / -less / [commits] no / not / frees [himself from] / remains without	
08-50	尤.	43	yu	fault / calamity / wrong / error / blame / malign[ed] / reproach / "resentment" (Wing) / "extreme" (Cleary) }}}}} "no fight; no blame" (Feng)	[4]

[1] **Shan** resembles the Sanskrit word *dharma*—that which is in accord with the truth and the natural laws of the universe. By following the inherent laws of nature, one's actions are naturally skillful, empowered, and virtuous.

[2] **Chü shan ti hsin shan yüan**: "The value in dwelling is location, the value in a mind is depth." (Wing); "The good of the house is from the land / Or the good of the mind is its depth." (Blakney); "The quality of an abode is in its location / The quality of the heart is in its depths." (Mair); "(The best man) in his dwelling loves the earth / In his heart, he loves what is profound." (Chan)

[3] **Translation of lines 1–43:** "Everything has its own virtue, its own truth—that which gives it value. Of places to live, it is location, of the mind, it is stillness, of giving, it is kindness, of speaking, it is truthfulness, of ruling, it is justice, of working, it is ability, of action, it is timing."
"What gives a dwelling value is location, what gives a mind value is stillness, what gives giving value is love, what gives speaking value is sincerity, what gives ruling value is justice, what gives working value is ability, what gives activity value is the present moment."

[4] (See NOTES for an additional translation)

NOTE: > Alt: move last 7 lines [v. 8:44–50] between 8:22 and 8:23—Lau

VERSE 9

09-01	持	64	ch'ih	Holding / grasping / to hold / (stretch a bow)	
09-02	而	126	erh	and / yet / to / at	
09-03	盈	108	ying	filling to excess / overflowing / fullness / "fill to the brim" / very full / beyond / too much	
09-04	之。	4	chih	it / (a cup / a vessel) / (a bow)	
09-05	不	1	pu	not	
09-06	如	38	ju	likely / as good as / the same as	
09-07	其	12	ch'i	is / to be }}} it is better to / it is not as good as	
09-08	已.	49	yi	stop[ping] / finish [in time / before the limit] / leave it alone / desist	[1]
09-09	揣	64	ch'uai	sharpen / temper / sharpness / whet[ting] / knock / pound / handle >Alt: *ch'ueh* (scheme, calculate) >Alt: *cho* (beam, joist)	
09-10	而	126	erh	and / yet / (to a)	
09-11	銳	75	cho	beat / hammer / pound / "keep on beating" // sharpen[ing] / filing / point[ed] / acute / "be sharp" / shrewd	
09-12	之。	4	chih	it / (blade, edge, sword, one's keenness, sharpness) }}}} hammering a blade to a sharp edge	
09-13	不	1	pu	not	
09-14	可	30	k'o	able to / can	
09-15	長	168	ch'ang	last long / long time / endure	
09-16	保.	9	pao	keep / preserve / last / maintain / keep safe / guarantee [its sharpness]	[2]
09-17	金	167	chin	gold / bronze [and]	
09-18	玉	95	yü	jade / jewels	
09-19	滿	85	man	fill up a / full	
09-20	堂	32	t'ang	hall / court / residence	
09-21	莫	140	mo	no one / none of	

09-22	之	4	chih	it
09-23	能	130	nêng	can / able to
09-24	守	40	shou	guard[ed] / protect / keep [it]
09-25	富	40	fu	wealth[y] / rich[es] / opulence [and]
09-26	貴	154	kuei	honor[ed][s] / exalt[ed] / prize / high rank / position / "power" }}} "claim wealth and titles" / "success"
09-27	而	126	erh	and / but / yet / leads to
09-28	驕	187	chiao	proud / pride / haughty / arrogant / vanity / overbearing / "set store by" (Wu) / "define yourself by" [then]
09-29	自	132	tzu	oneself / themselves / (____)
09-30	遺	162	yi	what follows is / bring about / causes / invites / "sow the seeds of" / "reap the fruit of" / "in its strain" / "necessarily bequeaths" (Medhurst) / "is overlooking" (Wing)
09-31	其	12	ch'i	his / their / his own / one's
09-32	咎	30	chiu	downfall / calamity / misfortune / blame / run / disaster / evil / "invite blame" }}} "their legacy indicts them" (Cleary) / "bequeath their own doom" (Blakney)
09-33	功	19	kung	work / service / task / accomplishment / merit [3]
09-34	遂	162	sui	complet[ed] / establish / succeed / accomplish / done / made / "come to you"
09-35	身	158	shên	person / self
09-36	退	162	t'ui	retreat / draw back / withdraw / retire / "get out of the way" (Chalmers) [this is] }}} withdraw when your work is done }}}} "merit established, a name made" (Medhurst)
09-37	天	37	t'ien	Heaven / nature
09-38	之	4	chih	's / of
09-39	道	162	tao	Tao / way }}} Heaven's Tao / "the Tao in Nature" (Wing)

[1] *Ch'ih erh ying chih pu ju ch'i yl*: "Grasping and filling is not as good as desisting." (Ku); "To take all you want / Is never as good / As to stop when you should." (Blakney)
(Cup imagery): "To hold and fill a cup to overflowing / Is not as good as to stop in time." (Chan); "It is better to leave it alone, than forcibly to attempt to make it full." (Tze)
(Bow imagery): "Instead of keeping a bow taut while holding it straight, / Better to relax." (Mair)

[2] *Ch'uai erh cho chih pu k'o ch'ang pao*: "Temper a (sword-edge) to its very sharpest, / And the edge will not last long." (Yutang); "Pounding and whetting it cannot be long maintained." (Ku); "Scheme and be sharp / And you'll not keep it long." (Blakney)

[3] +Alt: insert *ch'ing* (finish, accomplish, complete, done) and *ming* (name, fame, reputation, "duty proper to one's name") between 9:33 and 9:34—HSK

VERSE 10

10-01	載	159	tsai	Carry[ing] / hold / keep / transport / begin / bear / in keeping / "husbanding" / regulate / arrange / organize / govern / manage // sustain / cultivate / nourish // "while" / "now"/ "new" / ! (ending particle) ^^Alt: move to the end of verse 9
10-02	營	86	ying	spiritual soul / spirit
10-03	魄	194	p'o	physical soul / bodily soul / "animal nature" / "vitality" // instincts / senses / "dark of the moon" [1]
10-04	抱	64	pao	embrace [in your arms] / enfold / carry / conceal / hold within
10-05	一	1	yi	unity / unify / the One / together }} ~see everything as a manifestation of the One
10-06	能	130	nêng	can / able to / has the power to / is it possible [one][one be][you be] [keep them]

10-07	無	86	wu	without / not / free of / avoid / un- / never / prevent them from
10-08	離	172	li	separat[ion] / disintegration / divided / parting // depart / leave / wander / "forsake the Tao" (Lau) / "seeing differences" }}} "and not let go" / "maintain harmony" [2]
10-09	乎.	4	hu	? / !
10-10	專	41	chuan	concentrate[ing] / gather / attend / regulate / focus / control / attention / care for / "preserve"
10-11	氣	84	ch'i	*chi* / breath / vital force / power / (Sanskrit: *prana*) / "fully" / "your influence" (Wing)
10-12	致	133b	chih	cause / induce / reach / bring about / achieve / render / become / attain // extreme / highest degree
10-13	柔。	75	jou	soft[ness] / tender / gentle / pliant / supple / weak / passive / yield / "harmony" (Chung)
10-14	能	130	nêng	can one [be][reach the state of] +Alt: add *ju* (like, resemble)——Fu I
10-15	嬰	39	ying	newborn / infant
10-16	兒	10	erh	child / baby }} infant / "innocent babe"
10-17	乎.	4	hu	? / ! / (oh)
10-18	滌	85	ti	wash[ing] / cleanse
10-19	除	170	ch'u	purify / clean / polish / wipe / "sponge away the dust" (Ould) }} cleaning
10-20	玄	96	hsüan	profound / deep / hidden / (inner) / mysterious / abstruse / dark / secret / mystic >Alt: *yuan* (primal)
10-21	覽。	147	lan	vision / behold[ing] / perception / insight // mirror / reflection >Alt: *chien* (bronze mirror)——MWT }} ~"heart" / "mirror of the dark" (Chen) [3]
10-22	能	130	nêng	can [it][one be][you] [strive after][become]
10-23	無	86	wu	without / free of / -less / "leave no" / (purified of)
10-24	疵	104	tz'u	fault[s] / flaw / stain / malady / blemish / dross / dust / imperfections / error / blur
10-25	乎.	4	hu	? / !
10-26	愛	61	ai	caring for / lov[ing] / acting kindly / "perfecting" / (the exhibition of humanity)
10-27	民	83	min	the people / the common people / all men [and]
10-28	治	85	chih	rul[ing] / governing / ordering / leading / "pacifying"
10-29	國。	31	kuo	the country / state / kingdom / empire
10-30	能	130	nêng	can / is it possible [one be][you be][you take][one practice]
10-31	無	86	wu	without / non- / no / "dispense with"
10-32	知	111	chih	knowing / intellect / cleverness / cunning >Alt: *wei* (action, make, do) }} unknown / remain unknown [4]
10-33	乎.	4	hu	? / !
10-34	天	37	t'ien	Heaven / (nature) / what is natural / ['s]
10-35	門	169	mên	gate / door / gateway
10-36	開	169	k'ai	open[s][ing] / begins to open [and]
10-37	闔。	169	ho	closes / closing / shut[s] / (complete) }}}} ~"way of nature" / ~movements of life, destiny, fate / >"creation of the world" (Chen) / ~breathing in and out [5]
10-38	能	130	nêng	can one
10-39	為	87	wei	be / become / act / do / keep / play the role of / >*wei* appears in MWT and Fu I >Alt: *wu* (not, without)——Wang Pi Commentary
10-40	雌	172	tz'u	female bird / woman / mother bird / female // ~passive / "[tranquility of] the female" (Ku) }} not weaken (Wing)

10-41	乎	4	hu	? / !	[6] [6a]
10-42	明	72	ming	understanding / awareness / bright / illumined / enlightened / "mind"	
10-43	白	106a	pai	pure / clear / discern[ing]　}} clear-minded / pure awareness / seeing clearly	
10-44	四	31	ssu	the four [directions] / the four [quarters] / "all directions" / (everywhere / all places)	
10-45	達	162	ta	penetrate / reach / comprehend / see through / shine forth	
10-46	能	130	nêng	can one　[be / remain]	
10-47	無	86	wu	without / free of / renounce	
10-48	為	111	wei	action / doing / make　>Alt: *chih* (knowing)　}} innocent / unknown / unknowing	
10-49	乎	4	hu	? / !　[Tao / the sage]	
10-50	生	100	shêng	produce[s] / gives life / gives birth / rears / engenders / quickens	
10-51	之	4	chih	them / things / (the people)	
10-52	畜	17	ch'u	feed / rear / nurture / nourish / cultivate / develop	
10-53	之	4	chih	them / things	
10-54	生	100	shêng	produce[s] / gives life / rears / engenders / develops	
10-55	而	126	erh	yet / but / and	
10-56	不	1	pu	does not / do not	
10-57	有	74	yu	own / claim / possess[ing] / take possession　}} "without self-consciousness" (Medhurst)	
10-58	為	87	wei	acts / does / work	
10-59	而	126	erh	yet / but / and	
10-60	不	1	pu	does not / do not / without	
10-61	恃	61	shih	claim [results] / rely upon / take credit for / hold on to / presume / "expectation" / "seek the fruits of" / "set any store by it" (Wu) / "rely upon his own ability" (Chen)　[The sage][Tao]	
10-62	長	168	ch'ang	lead[s] / grow / develop / excel / progress / advance / "enlarge" / a leader / a chief / "the steward"	
10-63	而	126	erh	yet / but / and	
10-64	不	1	pu	does not	
10-65	宰	40	tsai	dominat[ing] / lord over / master / control / rule / govern // "butcher" / "cut off" / >lit: "the slaughter of animals" / > can imply a ruthless method of ruling	
10-66	是	72a	shih	this / these	
10-67	謂	149	wei	is called / describes	
10-68	玄	96	hsüan	dark / deep / profound / mysterious / secret　>Alt: *yüan* (primal, origin, first cause)	
10-69	德	60b	tê	Te / virtue / power / (embodiment of Tao)	[7]

[1] Chinese held the view that there were two souls: **hun**, the bright, spiritual, yang soul, which is associated with the upper body; and **p'o**, the dark, physical, earthly, yin soul, which is associated with the lower body. (In this passage only p'o is mentioned, but this can imply both the physical (p'o) and spiritual (hun) souls.) P'o is variously translated as: "physical soul," "bodily soul," "animal nature," and "dark of the soul." Implied meanings are "vitality," "sexual fluid" (which must be protected), "senses," "instincts," and "crescent moon" (Pine). P'o can also refer to the darkness of the moon.

[2] **Tsai ying p'o pao yi nêng wu li**: "Can you keep the spirit and embrace the One without departing from them?" (Chan); "Carrying vitality and consciousness, embracing them as one, can you keep them from parting?" (Cleary); "In keeping the spirit and the vital soul together, are you able to maintain their perfect harmony?" (Wu); "In managing your instincts and embracing Oneness, can you be undivided?" (Wing); "By causing the reason-mind-soul and the human-mind-soul to be united (at the Middle), it is possible to prevent their dissolution." (Tze); "Can you hold fast your crescent soul and not let it wander?" (Pine)

[3] **Hsüan lan**: "Mystic vision" (Yutang) (Blakney) (Lin), "Mysterious Vision" (Cheng), "inner vision" (Wu), "Primal vision" (Feng), "profound insight" (Chan), "the abstruse reflections [of his mind]" (Ku), "vision of the Mystery" (Waley), "hidden perception" (Chan), "the channels of deep perception" (Mears), "secret seeing" (Wilhelm), "mind of phantasms" (Medhurst), "the dark look" (Erkes), "mirror of the dark" (Chen), "Mysterious mirror (i.e., the mind)" (Lau), "secret mirror" (Duy), "dark mirror" (Chung); "insight" (Wing), "eye of the heart" (Chalmers), "Mystical Mirror"—the imaging line that divides the conscious from the so-called unconscious (Ould)

[4] **Wu chih**: Refers to the state of a beginner: innocence, openness, and humility. It is a state in which one is not burdened, limited, or closed off (to his true nature) by his own knowledge. Zen calls this state "beginner's mind." It is a state of unlimited possibilities and infinite potential.

[5] **T'ien mên k'ai ho**: "The opening and closing of Heaven's gate" represents a pair of opposites, possibly gain and loss, ups and downs of life, good fate and bad fate, or attraction and aversion—all in the realm of the senses.

[6] **Nêng wei tz'u hu**: "Playing the role, or acting the part of the female" refers to a state of holding to one's one nature (represented by the bird's nest), or the steadfast devotion to one's duty (as a mother bird who never abandons the hatchlings in her nest). Feminine can also be interpreted as being patient, passive, humble, and content where you are—all Taoist virtues. This line can also be interpreted as: Can you accept what life offers you? Can you stay centered? Can you remain steadfast in your duty? Can you stay calm within yourself? Can you remain content in your place?

[6a] "Like the Ocean when it is calm and placid, the wise man is tranquil, poised, deep in knowledge. The brimful ocean does not overflow nor do the rivers dry up; similarly the wise man, his heart united with God, remains calm and unchanged amidst the opposites of life."—Shrimad Bhagavatam

[7] **Hsüan tê**: "Profound Teh" (Cheng), "Mysterious Te" (LaFargue), "profound Teh, which is Tao in manifestation," (Au), "profoundest virtue of TAO" (Wei-Tao), "mystic attainment" (Chung), "Deepest Truth" (Janwu), "secret Life" (Wilhelm), "mysterious integrity" (Mair), "Mystic Virtue" (Yutang) (Wei), "profound and secret virtue" (Chan), "profound virtue" (Lin), "dark virtue" (Chen), "hidden Virtue" (Wu), "Primal Virtue" (Feng), "Mysterious Power" (Waley), "Subtle Powers" (Wing), "the abyss of energy" (Medhurst)

NOTE: Much of this verse relates to the mystical practice of integrating opposites into unity by holding the boundless point where the pairs of opposites meet. Lines 1–3 relate to the breath and the still-point between the breathing in and breathing out. Lines 4–6 relate to the soul and the integration of physical and spiritual souls. Lines 7–10 relate to the mind and integration of the heart and mind and/or the conscious and unconscious mind.

NOTE: Line 10:66–10:69 is also found at the end of verse 51. Some commentators have omitted this line here, believing it was erroneously inserted.

VERSE 11

11-01	三	1	**san**	Three [times]
11-02	十	24	**shih**	ten }} thirty
11-03	輻	159b	**fu**	spokes [are]
11-04	共	12b	**kung**	unite[d] / share / have in common / all / joined / converge [upon]
11-05	一	1	**yi**	one / a single
11-06	轂.	159	**ku**	hub / knave [to make a wheel]
11-07	當	102	**tang**	because of / but / by way of / upon / through / owing to / from
11-08	其	12	**ch'i**	its / their
11-09	無。	86	**wu**	empti[ness] / non-being / non-existence / nothingness / "empty space" / vacancy / "what is not there" / "where it is not" / (hole) / "loss of individuality" (Yutang)
11-10	有	74	**yu**	is / there is / exists / (depends on / lies / arises) [the]
11-11	車	159a	**ch'ê**	wheel / carriage wheel / carriage / cart / wheel
11-12	之	4	**chih**	's / it's

11-13	用	101	yung	use[ful][ness] / utility / function / purpose / "work" / "power of being to act, work, and serve" / "coming to be" (Chen)
11-14	埏	32	yen	mold / shape / turn on wheel / knead / "throw" / mix >Alt: *jan* (bake, fire)—MWT
11-15	埴	32	ch'ih	clay / earth
11-16	以	9a	yi	thereby / thus / in order to
11-17	為	87	wei	make / form / fashion [into a]
11-18	器	30	ch'i	vessel / (bowl) / utensil
11-19	當	102	tang	because of / but / by way of / upon / through / owing to / from
11-20	其	12	ch'i	its
11-21	無	86	wu	emptiness / non-being / non-existence / nothingness / empty space
11-22	有	74	yu	is / exists / (depends) [the]
11-23	器	30	ch'i	vessel
11-24	之	4	chih	's / (of)
11-25	用	101	yung	use[ful][ness] / utility / function / purpose
11-26	鑿	167	tso	cutting out
11-27	戶	63	hu	doors [and]
11-28	牖	91	yu	windows
11-29	以	9a	yi	thereby / thus
11-30	為	87	wei	to make / build
11-31	室	40a	shih	a room / house
11-32	當	102	tang	because of / but / by way of / upon / through
11-33	其	12	ch'i	its
11-34	無	86	wu	emptiness / non-being / non-existence / nothingness / empty space
11-35	有	74	yu	is / exists / depends / lies [the]
11-36	室	40a	shih	room / house
11-37	之	4	chih	's / of
11-38	用	101	yung	use[ful][ness] / utility / function / purpose
11-39	故	66	ku	therefore / thus / hence
11-40	有	74	yu	existence / being / "something" / the tangible / "what is" / "what is there"
11-41	之	4	chih	's / of [a thing] }} "being of a thing"
11-42	以	9a	yi	thus / thereby / (turn into)
11-43	為	87	wei	make[s] / act / take / lead to / become / turn into / "constitutes" / "corresponds to" / (there lies)
11-44	利	18	li	benefit / advantage / gain / profit[able] [1]
11-45	無	86	wu	non-existence / emptiness / non-being / nothing / intangible / "what is not there" / absent
11-46	之	4	chih	its
11-47	以	9a	yi	thus / thereby
11-48	為	87	wei	makes / acts / leads to / becomes / (turn into) / "recognize"
11-49	用	101	yung	use / useful[ness] / utilize / function / "work" / "served" (Yutang) [2]

[1] *Li* is derived from "to cut" + "wheat or corn" and suggests the profit, benefit, or gain that comes from the harvest season. It can also mean "sharp," "acute," "that which cuts."

[2] **Yu chih yi wei li—wu chih yi wei yung**: "Turn being into advantage, and turn non-being into utility." (Chan); "Existence renders actual but non-existence renders useful." (Carus); "Benefit comes from what is there; usefulness from what is not there." (Feng); "What we gain is Something, yet it is by virtue of Nothing that this can be put to use." (Lau); "By the existence of things we profit. And by the non-existence of things we are served." (Yutang); "Take advantage of what is there, by making use of what is not." (Wing); "Existence may be said to correspond to gain, but non-existence to use." (Chalmers)

VERSE 12

12-01	五	7	wu	Five / the five / ~numerous / ~many / ~too many / ~all / ~the complete range of	
12-02	色	139	sê	colors / (sights) }} seeing too many sights	[1]
12-03	令	9	ling	make / cause / bring about / command / [will] make	
12-04	人	9a	jên	one's / man's / a person's / human	
12-05	目	109	mu	eye / >inner eye [to become]	
12-06	盲 .	109	mang	blind / confuse / "darken"	
12-07	五	7	wu	five / the five / ~many / ~too many / ~all / ~the complete range of	
12-08	音	180	yin	notes / musical notes / tones / sounds }} hearing too many sounds	
12-09	令	9	ling	make / cause / bring about / command	
12-10	人	9a	jên	one's / a person's / people's / human	
12-11	耳	128	erh	ear [to become]	
12-12	聾 .	128	lung	deaf / deafen / "dull" / deaden	[2]
12-13	五	7	wu	five / the five	
12-14	味	30a	wei	tastes / flavors	
12-15	令	9	ling	make / cause / bring about / command	
12-16	人	9a	jên	one's / a person's / people's / human	
12-17	口	30	k'ou	mouth / palate / taste buds [to become]	
12-18	爽 .	89	shuang	dull / blunt / "jaded" // spoil[ed] / ruin / faulty / "cloy" / "weary"	
12-19	馳	187	ch'ih	chasing / racing about / galloping / horse-racing / the chase	
12-20	騁	187	ch'êng	too much / in excess	
12-21	畋	102b	t'ien	field / in a field / "cultivate" / (birds and beasts of the field)	
12-22	獵 。	94	lieh	hunting / chasing / the hunt	
12-23	令	9	ling	make[s] / cause / bring about / drive / command	
12-24	人	9a	jên	one's / a person's / people's / human	
12-25	心	61	hsin	heart / mind / heart-mind / (conduct)	
12-26	發	105	fa	go / become / turn / manifest as	
12-27	狂 .	94	k'uang	mad[ness] / madden / wild / excite[ment] / craze[d] / derange[d] / confound	
12-28	難	172	nan	difficult / hard	
12-29	得	60a	tê	to obtain / get / "come by"	
12-30	之	4	chih	of }}} rare / valuable / precious	
12-31	貨 。	154	huo	goods / products / things / treasures	
12-32	令	9	ling	make / cause / bring about / keep / command	
12-33	人	9a	jên	one's / a person's / people's / human	
12-34	行	144	hsing	activities / acting / actions / movement / conduct / "natural powers" / "right action"	

12-35	妨	38	fang	hinder / impede / impair / constrain / hold in check / limit // injure / harm / do wrong }} "on guard" / "awake at night" (Yutang) / "lead one astray" (Feng) [3][4]
12-36	是	72a	shih	(this)
12-37	以	9a	yi	(for) }} therefore / hence / for this reason / that is why
12-38	聖	128a	shêng	holy
12-39	人	9a	jên	man / human / person }} the sage
12-40	為	87	wei	attends to / cares for / works for / acts according to / concerned with / "guided by"
12-41	腹	130	fu	stomach / belly / "inner" / "middle" / "what he feels" / "needs" / ~inner self / ~inner powers
12-42	不	1	pu	not
12-43	為	87	wei	attends to / cares for / acts with / concerned with / provides for [the]
12-44	目	109	mu	eye / "outer" / ~senses / ~outer / "what he sees" / "pull of the senses" / ~external to the self
12-45	故	66	ku	therefore / thus / hence [he / she]
12-46	去	28	ch'ü	leave[s] / reject / discard / forgoes / dismiss / let go of / withdraw from
12-47	彼	60	pi	the latter / the one / this / that / (what is without) [and]
12-48	取	29	ch'ü	takes hold of / accepts / prefers / secures / chooses / abides in / receives / nurtures
12-49	此	76	tz'u	the former / the other / that / this / (what is within)

[1] **Wu shê** (the five colors) are green, yellow, red, white, and black; the five notes are the five notes of the Chinese musical scale; the five tastes are salty, sweet, bitter, sour, and pungent. These five-fold classifications resulted from the theory of the five elements or agents, namely water, fire, wood, metal, and earth. Figuratively, "the five colors" means all colors, and all things that can be seen. Colors do not cause blindness to the human eye; what this line implies is that too much involvement with the senses, too much looking outward, causes one's inner eye to become blind to the truth. (A similar meaning is also found in the next two lines.) Ould states that the five colors blind the eye "if unharmonized," but his meaning is unclear.

[2] "The five primary colours are apt to find the eyes blind to them; the five musical notes are apt to find the ears deaf to them. . . ." (Parker)

[3] **Fang** derives its meaning from a place where there is a woman; hence where one's actions are restrained or held in check.

[4] **Ling jên hsing fang**: "make people's actions harmful" (Chan); "causes mankind to do wrong" (Cheng); "entangle man's conduct" (Duy); "make a man run into harm" (Chalmers); "hinders one's progress" (Janwu); "are hobbles that slow walking feet" (Blakney)

VERSE 13

13-01	寵	40	ch'ung	Honor / praise / favor / glory / kindness / "inclination" / [when receiving] favor
13-02	辱	160	ju	dishonor / blame / disgrace / insult / humiliation / "disinclination"
13-03	若	140	jo	then / as / bring about / cause / sources of // seem / like[ly] / resemble / related to
13-04	驚	187	ching	fear / dread / apprehension / anxiety / trepidation / dismay // shock / surprise / startle / alarm / "pleasant surprise" / warning [1]
13-05	貴	154	kuei	esteem / honor / high rank / respect / "high status" // treasure / prize / value // regard / dignity / "regard seriously" / "highly regard" / > wei (be afraid)—HSK
13-06	大	37	ta	great / (highly)
13-07	患	61	huan	affliction / trouble / misfortune / calamity / suffering / sorrow / distress [2]
13-08	若	140	jo	like / as / then / to be / the same as / as one's / "are both bound up with" (Ould)
13-09	身	158	shên	self / body / person / "sense of self" }} "are within ourselves" (Yutang) [3]
13-10	何	9	ho	what is / why
13-11	謂	149	wei	implied by / means / say

13-12	寵	40	ch'ung	honor / praise / favor	
13-13	辱	160	ju	dishonor / disgrace / insult	
13-14	若	140	jo	then / as / to be / bring about // seem / are like[ly] [to cause] X Alt: omit—Okada	
13-15	驚 .	187	ching	fear / dread / anxiety // shock / surprise / startle / alarm [?] X Alt: omit—Okada	
13-16	寵	40	ch'ung	favor / honor / praise / kindness >Alt: *juh* (dishonor, disgrace)—HSK	
13-17	為	87	wei	makes / renders one // is / is [for the]	
13-18	下 .	1	hsia	lowly / inferior / depressed / below / "a base affair"	[4]
13-19	得	60a	tê	obtain / receive / get / [one] receives	
13-20	之	4	chih	it / them	
13-21	若	140	jo	is like / feels like / seems // causes / brings about / is likely [to cause] / as	
13-22	驚 .	187	ching	fear / apprehension // a shock / surprise	
13-23	失	37	shih	losing / loss	
13-24	之	4	chih	it / them	
13-25	若	140	jo	is like / feels like / seems // causes / then / brings about / is likely [to cause]	
13-26	驚	187	ching	fear / dread / apprehension // a shock / surprise	
13-27	是	72a	shih	this	
13-28	謂	149	wei	implies / means / suggests / is due to the fact [that]	
13-29	寵	40	ch'ung	favor / honor / praise [and]	
13-30	辱	160	ju	dishonor / disgrace / insult	
13-31	若	140	jo	is like / feels like / seems // causes / brings about / is likely [to cause]	
13-32	驚 .	187	ching	fear / dread / apprehension // a shock / surprise	
13-33	何	9	ho	what / why [is]	
13-34	謂	149	wei	implied by / means / say	
13-35	貴	154	kuei	esteem / honor / high rank // values / treasure / prize // regard	
13-36	大	37	ta	great	
13-37	患	61	huan	affliction / trouble / misfortune / anxiety / suffering / sorrow / distress	
13-38	若 .	140	jo	like / as / the same way as	
13-39	身	158	shên	self / body / person [?]	
13-40	吾	30	wu	I	
13-41	所	63	so	(____)	
13-42	以	9a	yi	therefore / thereby }} the reason why [I / we / you]	
13-43	有	74	yu	have	
13-44	大	37	ta	great / much	
13-45	患	61	huan	trouble / misfortune / affliction / anxiety / suffering / sorrow / distress	
13-46	者 。	125	chê	(the one) / that / > changes the preceding clause into a noun / (____)	
13-47	為	87	wei	act / claim / (identify oneself as) / "on that account" / "due to the fact that"	
13-48	吾	30	wu	I / me / my / we / you	
13-49	有	74	yu	have / (am) / "conscious of"	
13-50	身 .	158	shên	body / person / "self" / "limited sense of self" / "me and my selfishness" (Blakney)	
13-51	及	29	chi	"when" / reach / effect / > past tense >Alt: *jo* (if)	

13-52	吾	30	**wu**	I / we / you [am / are]
13-53	無	86	**wu**	without / don't have / have no / -less
13-54	身.	158	**shên**	a body / self / sense of self }} selfless
13-55	吾	30	**wu**	I / we / you
13-56	有	74	**yu**	have / bear
13-57	何.	9	**ho**	what
13-58	患.	61	**huan**	trouble / misfortune / suffering / sorrow / distress }}} what trouble could I have?
13-59	故	66	**ku**	therefore / thus [one who]
13-60	貴	154	**kuei**	value[s] / honors / treasures / regards
13-61	以	9a	**yi**	(thus) / (accordingly)
13-62	身	158	**shên**	himself / his person / body / "embody" / (his)
13-63	為	87	**wei**	act[ions][ing] / doing / serving // role / duty }}} his own actions as / specific duty
13-64	天	37	**t'ien**	Heaven
13-65	下	1	**hsia**	below }} the world / everyone
13-66	若	125	**chê**	(the one) / (oneself) / (he) / (those) +Alt: add *tseh* (then)
13-67	可	30	**k'o**	can / is able / is fit +Alt: add *yi* (thereby, accordingly)
13-68	寄	40b	**chi**	be trusted with / entrusted / [trusted to] care for / deliver / govern // draw to [5]
13-69	天	37	**t'ien**	Heaven
13-70	下.	1	**hsia**	below }} all below Heaven / the world / everyone }}} "care for the world" / "draw the world to them" (Cleary) +Alt: add *ku* (therefore) [6]
13-71	愛	61	**ai**	love[s] / cherishes / "takes care of"
13-72	以	9a	**yi**	(thus) / (accordingly)
13-73	身	158	**shên**	himself / his person / body / "embody" / (his)
13-74	為	87	**wei**	act[ions][ing] / doing / serving // role / duty }}} his own actions as / specific duty
13-75	天	37	**t'ien**	Heaven
13-76	下。	1	**hsia**	below }} the world / everyone
13-77	若	125	**chê**	(the one) / (oneself) / (he) / (those) +Alt: add *tseh* (then); or *nai* (but, doubtless)
13-78	可	30	**k'o**	can / is able / is fit [be][fit to] +Alt: add *yi* (thereby, accordingly)
13-79	託	149	**t'o**	entrusted with / care for / be guardian / trustee of / "given custody" / commission >Alt: *chi* (govern, trusted) [7]
13-80	天	37	**t'ien**	Heaven
13-81	下.	1	**hsia**	below }} "all below Heaven" / the world / everyone [8]

[1] ***Ch'ung ju jo ching***: (a) "accept honor and disgrace as a surprise / like a shock" (b) "be fearful / apprehensive when receiving praise or blame"

[2] ***Huan*** is made up of *ch'uan* (two objects pierced or strung together on a rod) and *hsin* (heart). It implies affliction, a series of troubles, continual suffering, "a heart pierced over and over again." ***Ta huan*** (great affliction) can be interpreted as the continual hardship of life, but perhaps more fittingly as the continual suffering that arises from the endless cycle of birth and death (*samsara*).

[3] ***Kuei ta huan jo shên***: "Value great disasters as your body." (Duy); "Accept misfortune as the human condition." (Feng); "High rank hurts keenly as our bodies hurt." (Waley); "Honor is great trouble if identified with the self." (Wei); "Honor this teaching: 'Great Sorrow (the cycle of birth and death) comes from identification with the body.' " (Janwu)

[4] >Alt: replace *ch'ung wei hsia* (favor makes low) with *ch'ung wei shang juh wei hsia* (favor makes high, disfavor makes low)

[5] **Chi**: from "roof" + (over) "great" + "ability" (holds a surplus of ability under his roof and can therefore be trusted to accomplish the task)

[6] **Ku kuei yi shên . . . t'ien hsia**: "Therefore he who values the world as his body may be entrusted with the empire." (Chan); "Therefore, one who honors his own duty (in the world) will win the trust of the world." (Janwu); "He who fulfills his own duty (with love) is a guardian of the world." (Ming); "Only he who can do it with love is worthy of being steward of the world." (Wu); "Surrender yourself humbly; then you can be trusted to care for all things. Love the world as your own self; then you can truly care for all things." (Feng); "If, for the sake of dignity, one seeks to make himself ruler of the world, he may be permitted, indeed, to rule it temporarily; But if, for love, one seeks to make himself ruler of the world, he may be entrusted with it forever." (Chalmers)

[7] **T'o**: from "words" + "stand next to" (true to one's word)

[8] Line 13.60–13.70 is virtually the same as the line below it (13.71–13.81) except that **kuei** (esteem, honor) is replaced by **ai** (love). Carus omits the second line as an interpolation that was "slipped into the text." One could preserve the meaning of both lines by combining kuei and ai: "One who honors and loves his own self as the universe can be trusted to care for the world."

VERSE 14

14-01	視	147	shih	Look[ing] / perceive / [we] look / try to see // consider [and]
14-02	之	4	chih	it / at it
14-03	不	1	pu	not / do not / not able / cannot
14-04	見	147	chien	seen / see / perceive [it] }}}} "what cannot be seen"
14-05	名	30a	ming	name
14-06	曰	73	yüeh	speak / call / say }} named / it is called / its name is
14-07	夷.	37	yi	[the] invisible / colorless // unobtrusive / elusive / extremely dim / evanescent
14-08	聽	128	t'ing	hearing / listening / [we] listen / try to hear
14-09	之	4	chih	it
14-10	不	1	pu	not / do not / not able / cannot
14-11	聞	128	wên	heard / hear
14-12	名	30a	ming	name
14-13	曰	73	yüeh	speak / call / say }} named / it is called
14-14	希.	50	hsi	soundless / inaudible / extremely faint / the Inaudible / rarefied
14-15	搏	64	po	touch / grasp / grab / try to touch
14-16	之	4	chih	it
14-17	不	1	pu	not / do no / not able / cannot
14-18	得	60a	tê	obtain / catch / get hold of / catch
14-19	名	30a	ming	name
14-20	曰	73	yüeh	speak / call / say }} named / it is called
14-21	微.	60	wei	formless / minute / diminished / extemely small / fading / subtle / bodiless
14-22	此	77	tz'u	these
14-23	三	1	san	three
14-24	者	125	chê	those / ~attributes, qualities, characteristics, properties
14-25	不	1	pu	not / are not
14-26	可	30	k'o	can / able }} cannot be / elude / evade
14-27	致	133b	chih	further / reach the end / (closer)
14-28	詰.	149	chieh	scrutiny / scrutinize / investigate / inquire / inquired into }} be comprehended / fathomed / defined }}}} indefinable / unfathomable

14-29	故	66	ku	the reason being / because / therefore / thus [they are / they]
14-30	混	85a	hun	merge[d] / blend / [inter]mingle / confused / joined / (together)
14-31	而	126	erh	and
14-32	為	87	wei	become / make / form / act as / (are fused into)
14-33	一 .	1	yi	one / a unity +Alt: add *yi che* (as to the one)—MWT
14-34	其	12	ch'i	its / (the One's)
14-35	上	1	shang	above / top part / upper side / surface // going up / rising / (revealed part)
14-36	不	1	pu	is not
14-37	皦	106	chiao	bright / light / dazzling / clear
14-38	其	12	ch'i	its
14-39	下	1	hsia	below / bottom / underside // sinking / setting / falling / (hidden part)
14-40	不	1	pu	is not
14-41	昧 .	72	mei	dark[ness] / dim / obscure
14-42	繩	120	shêng	continuous / unceasing / infinite / boundless / stretched out / (very) // unbroken thread / "twisted" / "dim" (a cord, a string) [1]
14-43	繩	120	shêng	continuous / infinite / stretched out }} "dimly visible" (Lau)
14-44	不	1	pu	not
14-45	可	30	k'o	able to / can
14-46	名 .	30a	ming	name[d] / given a name / define[d] / describe }}} unnameable / Nameless
14-47	復	60	fu	returns / reverts / "moves on"
14-48	歸	77	kuei	return / revert / restore back / again
14-49	於	70	yü	in / though / to become // to
14-50	無	86	wu	non- / without / "that which has no" / (beyond)
14-51	物 .	93	wu	existence / being / things / substance / realm of things }} nothing[ness] [2]
14-52	是	72a	shih	this is
14-53	謂	149	wei	called
14-54	無	86	wu	without
14-55	狀	94	chuang	form / shape / state
14-56	之	4	chih	's / of / of its own
14-57	狀 .	94	chuang	form / shape / state }}}} formless form / shape without shape
14-58	無	86	wu	without
14-59	物	93	wu	object / substance / existence / things >Alt: *hsiang* (form, image)
14-60	之	4	chih	of its own
14-61	象 .	152	hsiang	figure / form / image }}}} image without substance / "form of nothing"
14-62	是	72a	shih	this is
14-63	謂	149	wei	called
14-64	惚	61	hu	vague / obscure / abstruse / confusing / indistinct / illusory / blurred / indefinable
14-65	恍 .	61	huang	evasive / elusive / illusory / indistinct / shadowy / semblance / unimaginable }} "mental abstraction" (Cleary)
14-66	迎	162	ying	front // in the front / meet[ing] / going toward / encounter / confront / stand before

14-67	之	4	chih	it
14-68	不	1	pu	not / [you will] not / do not
14-69	見	147	chien	see / discover
14-70	其	12	ch'i	its
14-71	首.	185	shou	head / face / front / (beginning)
14-72	隨	170	sui	follow / follow behind / go after
14-73	之	4	chih	it
14-74	不	1	pu	not / [you will] not / do not
14-75	見	147	chien	see / discover
14-76	其	12	ch'i	its
14-77	後.	60	hou	back / rear / (end)
14-78	執	32	chih	hold / hold fast / grasp / seize / stay with // one who holds fast
14-79	古	30	ku	ancient / of old / the ancients / way of antiquity / "timeless"
14-80	之	4	chih	's / its
14-81	道.	162	tao	Tao / way }}} Tao of old / "ever-becoming Tao"
14-82	以	9a	yi	in order to / so as to / thereby / to
14-83	御	60	yü	master / manage / control / direct / govern / ride / "move with" / harness / apply
14-84	今	9	chin	the present / "here and now"
14-85	之	4	chih	(_____) / its
14-86	有.	74	yu	existence / realities / things / "realm" }}} here and now / "realm of today" (Lau)
14-87	能	130	nêng	able to / can / have the power to >Alt: yi (thus, accordingly)
14-88	知	111	chih	know / understand [its / it as]
14-89	古	30	ku	old / primeval / primitive / ancient / first
14-90	始.	38	shih	beginning / origin
14-91	是	72a	shih	this is
14-92	謂	149	wei	called / (is the clue to)
14-93	道	162	tao	Tao's
14-94	紀.	120	chi	main thread / "unbroken strand" / "strand running through" // lineage / tradition / continuity / "initiation" / discipline / "main body of tradition" [3]

[1] *Shêng* refers to a cord, string, or line. It can be a cord that is stretched taut and used to adjust a measurement, correct something out of line, or keep things in conformity with a single principle. It can also refer to an "unbroken thread" or something that is continuous or unending.

[2] *Shêng shêng pu k'o ming—fu kuei yü wu wu*: "An unbroken thread beyond description. / It returns to nothingness." (Feng); "Endless the series of things without name / On the way back to where there is nothing." (Waley); "Continually the Unnameable moves on, / Until it returns beyond the realm of things." (Wu); "It extends without end in both directions. How can it be captured in words?—Before you can name it, it disappears back into non-existence." (Ming)

[3] *Chi* (lit: "thread") denotes tradition, discipline, principle, order, essence, etc. It refers to a system, tradition, major principle, continuity, or set of beliefs that holds things together. It is translated as "major principle," "thread," "clue," "record," "essence," "unbroken strand" (Wei); "continuous thread" (Wing); "lineage" (Janwu); "initiation into Tao" (Wu); "bond of Tao" (Chan); "continuity of Tao" (Yutang); "basic cycle" (Cleary); "a part of the system" (Cheng); "(unwinding) the clue of Tao" (Legge); "key to Tao" (Maurer); "path to supreme Tao" (Au-Young)

				VERSE 15
15-01	古	30	ku	Ancient / old / antiquity
15-02	之	4	chih	of }} in olden times // the ancients [were]
15-03	善	30	shan	good / excellent / skilled / best / "well-versed" / adept // adepts
15-04	為	87	wei	practice of / cultivate / act / do / made
15-05	士	33	shih	masters / rulers / ruling / warriors / "military art" >Alt: *tao* (Tao)—Fu I
15-06	者	125	chê	(the ones) / those
15-07	微	60	wei	mysterious / subtle // discern / keen / penetrating / "minute[ly]"
15-08	妙	38	miao	mysterious / essence / spiritual / subtle // true nature }} "subtle wisdom" / discern their true nature / >v.1:32
15-09	玄	96	hsüan	deep[ly] / depth / profound / dark / mystery >Alt: *yüan* (origin, primal principle) }} "mysteriously powerful" (Cleary)
15-10	通	162	t'ung	penetrate[ing] / comprehend[sive] / "understand" / "beyond knowing" >Alt: *t'ung* (identification)—HSK >Alt: *yüan* (origin, primal principle)
15-11	深	85	shên	[too] profound / [so] deep / abstruse / intense
15-12	不	1	pu	not
15-13	可	30	k'o	able / fit / could
15-14	識	149	shih	understand / comprehend / know / recognize / fathom }}} "unrecognizable"
15-15	夫	37	fu	truly
15-16	唯	30b	wei	for this reason / exactly
15-17	不	1	pu	not
15-18	可	30	k'o	can / able / fit / could }} cannot / [we / one] cannot
15-19	識	149	shih	understand / know / comprehend / experience [them]
15-20	故	66	ku	therefore [make] [give]
15-21	強	57	ch'iang	a strong effort / try / force / "perforce" / "makeshift" (Lau) / (vaguely)
15-22	為	149	wei	make [a description of] / tell of / describe / do / act
15-23	之	4	chih	their / them
15-24	容	40	jung	appearance / attitude / outlook / demeanor
15-25	豫	152	yü	cautious / hesitant / careful / circumspect / wary / tentative / > once referred to a species of elephant known for its caution and deliberation
15-26	焉	86a	yen	make / act / do >Alt: *hsi* (!, oh) >Alt: *yen* (indeed, how)
15-27	若	140	jo	like / as / resembling [one]
15-28	冬	15	tung	winter
15-29	涉	85	shê	wading / fording / crossing
15-30	川	47	ch'uan	a river / stream / [a frozen] stream }}} crossing a river in winter / ~wading through icy water / walking over icy rocks / treading on thin ice
15-31	猶	94	yu	watchful / vigilant / alert // still / hesitant / cautious / timid / circumspect / "irresolute" / "being at a loss" / > originally referred to a species of wild monkey
15-32	兮	12	hsi	! / oh

15-33	若	140	jo	like / as / to be / resembling [one]
15-34	畏	102	wei	fearing / afraid of [danger]
15-35	四	31	ssu	four / (all)
15-36	鄰	163	lin	sides / quarters / directions // near / neighbor[s][ing] }} surrounded by
15-37	儼	9	yen	reserved / grave / reverent / dignified / formal / courteous / cautious
15-38	兮	12	hsi	! / oh
15-39	其	12	ch'i	they [were]
15-40	若	140	jo	like / as / resemble / to be
15-41	客	40	jung	a guest / visitor
15-42	渙	85	huan	yielding / supple / pliant // dissolving / falling apart / self-effacing // amiable / relaxed // "expansive" [1]
15-43	兮	12	hsi	! / oh
15-44	若	140	jo	like / as / resembling
15-45	冰	15	ping	ice
15-46	之	4	chih	which
15-47	將	41	chiang	is going to / about to / beginning to
15-48	釋	165	shih	melt / thaw }}} at the melting point [2]
15-49	敦	66	tun	thick[ness] / solid // simple / genuine / sincere // pure in nature / unspoiled / > as opposed to "thin"—cunning, overrefined, sophisticated, contrived [3]
15-50	兮	12	hsi	! / oh
15-51	其	12	ch'i	they
15-52	若	140	jo	resemble / [were] like
15-53	樸	75	p'u	uncut wood / the uncarved block / uncut jade // simplicity / (a peasant) [4]
15-54	曠	72	k'uang	open / empty / broad / wide / "open-minded" / "receptive" / vacant / hollow
15-55	兮	12	hsi	! / oh
15-56	其	12	ch'i	they [were]
15-57	若	140	jo	like / as / resemble
15-58	谷	150	ku	a valley / a mountain gorge // a cave / "a valley awaiting a guest" (Blakney)
15-59	混	85a	hun	obscure / opaque // merged / mixed / "mixing freely" / "undifferentiated" // chaotic / confused /turbid [5]
15-60	兮	12	hsi	! / oh
15-61	其	12	ch'i	they [were]
15-62	若	140	jo	like / as / resemble
15-63	濁	85	cho	muddy / murky / turbid [water / pools]
15-64	孰	39	shu	who
15-65	能	130	nêng	can / is able to [stop / make]
15-66	濁	85	cho	muddy / murky / turbid [water / pools]
15-67	以	9a	yi	by / through / (accordingly)
15-68	靜	174	ching	still[ness] / quiet[ude] / tranquil[ity] / calm / quieting down / being in repose
15-69	之	4	chih	it

15-70	徐	60	hsü	gradually / (slowly and steadily)
15-71	清	85	ch'ing	purify / becomes clear / > those aligned with Nature [?]
15-72	孰	39	shu	who / what
15-73	能	130	nêng	can / is able to [make]
15-74	安	40	an	still / quiet / content / inert / at rest
15-75	以	9a	yi	by / through
15-76	久	4	chiu	long-lasting / enduring X Alt: omit
15-77	動	19	tung	movement / activity / stirring / action
15-78	之	4	chih	them / he / it
15-79	徐	60	hsü	gradually / slowly
15-80	生	100	shêng	come to life / bring to life / living? [those who / whoever / one who] [6]
15-81	保	9	pao	embrace[s] / keep to / hold / (stay on) // maintain / conserve / "observers of"
15-82	此	77	tz'u	this
15-83	道	162	tao	Tao / path
15-84	者	125	chê	(the one) / (he) / (she) / it
15-85	不	1	pu	do not / does not
15-86	欲	76	yü	wish / want / long for / seek [to be] }} guards against
15-87	盈	108	ying	fullness / excess / being over full / "fill to overflow" // limit / extreme / fulfillment / ~fulfillment of personal ends
15-88	夫	37	fu	truly
15-89	唯	30b	wei	for this reason
15-90	不	1	pu	not
15-91	盈	108	ying	filled / full[ness] / excess / overflowing / "seeks to be [full]filled" }} empty [7]
15-92	故	66	ku	therefore [they / he]
15-93	能	130	nêng	can / is able to
15-94	蔽	140	pi	grow old / wear out / worn / (give in) // ruin / defeat / ~surrender [and] [8]
15-95	不	1	pu	not / not be / not [having to be] / (beyond) >Alt: erh (yet, but, and)
15-96	新	69	hsin	newly / renew / restore // improve / "increasingly"
15-97	成	62	ch'êng	made / accomplished / succeed / finished / fashioned / perfected }} reborn }}}} "beyond wearing out and renewal" / "they can wear out without renewal" (Duy)

[1] **Huan** . . . "like a melting block of ice," "Yielding," "supple," "pliant," "fluid" (Duy); "elusive" (Carus); "falling apart" (Lau); "dissolving" (Chen); "vanishing" (Chalmers); "self-effacing" (Yutang); "evanescent" (Legge) // "easygoing" (Wei); "relaxation" (Chan); "amiable" (Ku) // "expansive" (Tze)

[2] [25–48]: "They used the prudence of a man crossing rivers during winter, the caution of one dreading to give offense to his neighbors. They were deferential, as though dealing with unfamiliar visitors; and as compliant as ice, so to speak, which is just on the thaw." (Parker)

[3] **Tun** . . . "like a block of uncut wood": "Thick," "solid" (Duy); "staunch" (Tze) // "simple," "unpretentious" (Wei) // "genuine," "pure in nature," "unspoiled," "unadulterated," "rough" // "blank" (Waley)

[4] **P'u** refers to wood (or jade) which is uncarved, pure, virgin—in its original state. It is the famous Taoist symbol of the "uncarved block" which, like the "beginner's mind," represents unlimited possibilities.

[5] **Hun** relates to muddy (or stirred) water: "Chaotic," "confused" // "obscure," "inscrutable," "opaque (not recognizable)" // "merged," "mixing freely," "easygoing" (Yutang); "integrated" (Wing), (fitting in with all the rest) // "not particular" (Yutang), ~seeing all things as the same, ~having equal vision

[6] **Lines 64–80**: "Who can wait quietly while the mud settles? / Who can remain still until the moment of action?" (Feng); "Who is there that can take the turbid water, and, by stillness, make it gradually clear? / Who is there that can take what is at rest, and, by continuous motion make it gradually alive?" (Chalmers); "Like muddy water which naturally becomes clear, one who lives in accordance with Nature (Tao) becomes pure through the natural process of life." (Ming)

[7] **Ying**: "filled to the full" (Chen); "fill themselves to the brim" (Waley); "full (of themselves)" (Legge); "greedy" (Blakney); "self-satisfied" (Ku); "fulfillment" (Feng); "fulfillment of personal aims" (Wing); "go to the limit" (Wei); "reach an extreme" (Chung); "more than one's share" (Medhurst)

[8] **Pi** is variously translated as "defeated, distressed, reduced to extremities, deteriorated, worn out." It derives its meaning from "a piece of cloth with holes in it" (rip) + "a hand holding a rod" (to strike) + "folded hands" (suggesting the act of offering or discarding). The character could be symbolically interpreted as a master "striking" and "ripping to shreds" a disciple's ego while the disciple "folds his hands" and offers himself to the process. Hence it would suggest "giving in," "losing oneself," "submission," or "surrender."

VERSE 16

16-01	致	133b	chih	Attain / reach / cause / bring about / arrive at / (touch)	
16-02	虛	141	hsü	emptiness / vacuity / passivity / void / openness	
16-03	極	75b	chi	highest / utmost / ultimate / climax / summit // full / complete / goal / "the pole"	
16-04	守	40	shou	keep / hold / cling / hold firm // maintain / abide in / observe / preserve	
16-05	靜	174	ching	still[ness] / quiet[ude] / tranquil[ity] / "still-point" / peace / harmony / repose	
16-06	篤	118	tu	constant / firm / absolute / steadfast // essence / deepest level / genuine	[1]
16-07	萬	140	wan	ten thousand / myriad / all	
16-08	物	93	wu	things / creatures	
16-09	并	1	ping	together / in unison / united / alike / "with one impulse"	
16-10	作	9a	tso	arise / flourish / come into being / take form / grow // stir / stimulate	
16-11	吾	30	wu	I / we / (the Self) / "witness of the universe"	
16-12	以	9a	yi	thereby / thus [can]	
16-13	觀	147	kuan	see / perceive / recognize / discern / watch / observe / "contemplate" +Alt: add ch'i (their, them)	
16-14	復	60	fu	return / returning / "fall back" / "cyclic return"	
16-15	夫	37	fu	now // truly	
16-16	物	93	wu	things / (all things) / vegetation / creatures / (they)	
16-17	芸	140	yün	flourish / bloom / grow / (greatly)	
16-18	芸	140	yün	flourish / bloom / grow }} grow profusely / teeming / luxuriant	
16-19	各	30	ko	each one / each of them	
16-20	復	60	fu	returns / again X Alt: omit	
16-21	歸	77	kuei	returns / reverts back / restores / recovers }} "returns to the source"	
16-22	其	12	ch'i	to its / its / to be	
16-23	根	75	kên	root / source / origin / initial cause / (soil) / "from which it sprang" (Yutang)	
16-24	歸	77	kuei	return / returning / recover [to the]	
16-25	根	75	kên	root / source / origin	
16-26	曰	73	yüeh	is called / means / is to find / means	
16-27	靜	174	ching	still[ness] / tranquility / peace / quietude / repose / harmony / "supreme silence"	
16-28	是	72a	shih	it / this	

16-29	謂	149	**wei**	is called / is known as / means
16-30	復	60	**fu**	returning / the return / going back / restore / "the cycle of" / renewal [of][one's]
16-31	命	30b	**ming**	destiny / fate / life / original nature / law / decree / "one's nature" }} "the way of nature" (Feng)
16-32	復	60	**fu**	return / recover / restore / going back / the cycle of
16-33	命	30b	**ming**	destiny / fate / life / original nature
16-34	曰	73	**yüeh**	is called / is to be / is / is to find / "brings one in tune with" / means
16-35	常	50	**ch'ang**	eternal / everlasting / unchanging / constant / the Eternal [Law] / "ever-becoming"
16-36	知	111	**chih**	know / knowledge of / understand / to know [the]
16-37	常	50	**ch'ang**	eternal / unending / constant / constancy / immutable / unchanging
16-38	曰	73	**yüeh**	is called / is known as
16-39	明	72	**ming**	realization / enlightenment / insight / illumination / discernment
16-40	不	1	**pu**	not
16-41	知	111	**chih**	knowing / understanding [the]
16-42	常	50	**ch'ang**	eternal / constant / ~the one, constant, underlying reality [is / leads to]
16-43	妄	38	**wang**	error / falsehood / reckless / blind actions / "wanton behavior" [and]
16-44	作	9a	**tso**	brings about / results in / into / lead to
16-45	凶	17	**hsiung**	disaster / calamity / misfortune / misery / "unfortunate things"
16-46	知	111	**chih**	knowing / understanding [the] / [when you] know
16-47	常	50	**ch'ang**	eternal / constant / ~the unchanging, supreme reality [is][makes one][means][gives]
16-48	容	40	**jung**	all-encompassing / all-embracing / "all-containing" / broad / tolerant / "open-minded" / "having capacity" / "stature" / "perspective" (Cleary)
16-49	容	40	**jung**	all-encompassing / all-embracing
16-50	乃	4	**nai**	is / means / then / leads to
16-51	公	12a	**kung**	impartial / unprejudiced / just[ice] / righteous[ness] // broad / public / catholic
16-52	公	12a	**kung**	impartial / just // broad
16-53	乃	4	**nai**	means / is / then / leads to
16-54	王	95	**wang**	kingly / royal / noble / act royally / "highest nobility" >Alt: *chou* (universal, complete)—MHL; >Alt: *sheng* (to produce)
16-55	王	95	**wang**	kingly / royal / noble >Alt: *chou* (universal, complete)—MHL >Alt: *sheng* (to produce)
16-56	乃	4	**nai**	means / is / then / in accordance with / leads to
16-57	天	37	**t'ien**	Heaven / nature / divine / [union with] Heaven >Alt: *ta* (great)—MHL
16-58	天	37	**t'ien**	Heaven[ly] / nature / divinity >Alt: *ta* (great)—MHL
16-59	乃	4	**nai**	to / is / in accord with / one with
16-60	道	162	**tao**	Tao
16-61	道	162	**tao**	Tao / [being in accord with] Tao
16-62	乃	4	**nai**	means / is / then / one with / leads to
16-63	久	4	**chiu**	everlasting / eternal / "abide forever" / immortal / long-lasting [and]
16-64	殁	85	**mo**	the end / to lose
16-65	身	158	**shên**	self / life / body / personal existence }} till the end of life / throughout life

16-66	不	1	pu	free from / free of / without / is no
16-67	殆 。	78	tai	danger / peril // exhaustion / exhausted / wearing out / decay

[1] ***Chih hsü chi shou ching tu***: "Let limits be empty / the center be still." (Pine) / "Aim at extreme disinterestedness and maintain the utmost calm." (Parker) / "Abstraction complete, quiescence maintained unalloyed, the various forms arise within one accord." (Medhurst)

VERSE 17

17-01	太	37	t'ai	Great / best / most / highest in / superior / grand
17-02	上	1	shang	ruler[s] / leader // superior / excellent / virtue }} the best rulers
17-03	下	1	hsia	below / those below / the people >Alt: *pu* (not) +Alt: add *pu* (not)
17-04	知	111	chih	know[n] / aware
17-05	有	74	yu	existence / presence [of]
17-06	之 。	4	chih	him (ruler) / it (Tao) }}}}}} "the best rulers are barely known" / ~doesn't interfere with the lives of the people
17-07	其	12	ch'i	their / its / (the)
17-08	次	76	tz'u	next / second [best] [they have][rulers who are]
17-09	親	147	ch'in	love[d] / affection / sympathy / "attached to" [for]
17-10	而	126	erh	and / yet >Alt: *chi* (him, her, them)
17-11	譽	149	yü	praise[d] / honor
17-12	之 。	4	chih	him / her / them
17-13	其	12	ch'i	their / its / (the)
17-14	次	76	tz'u	next / next [best] [they]
17-15	畏	38	wei	in awe / fear[ed] / respect
17-16	之 。	4	chih	him / her / them
17-17	其	12	ch'i	their / its / (the)
17-18	次	76	tz'u	next >Alt: *hsia* (below, those below)—MWT
17-19	侮	9	wu	despise / revile / contempt / defy / scorn / "take liberties" (Lau)
17-20	之 。	4	chih	him / her / them +Alt: add *ku* (therefore)
17-21	信	9	hsin	faith / trust / integrity / belief [in oneself][in others]
17-22	不	1	pu	is not
17-23	足	157	tsu	adequate / enough / sufficient }} is lacking
17-24	焉 。	86a	yen	indeed / >particle of affirmation / [he / others]
17-25	有	74	yu	finds / has / have
17-26	不	1	pu	no / (not worthy of)
17-27	信	9	hsin	faith / trust [in others][in him]
17-28	焉 。	86a	yen	indeed / >v. 17:20–28 and v. 23:80–88 X Alt: omit
17-29	悠	61a	yu	relaxed / quiet >Alt: *yiu* (hesitant, "self-effacing," reluctant, cautious)
17-30	兮	12	hsi	! / indeed
17-31	其	12	ch'i	he / she / they / (sage / ruler) // [why should] we
17-32	貴	154	kuei	esteems / values / prizes // "carefully chooses" / "sparing of" [his / her]
17-33	言 。	149	yen	words / [his] word [?] [he / she] }}} "does not utter words lightly" (Wu) / "how invaluable are the words" (Cheng) }}}}} "Quiet, why value words" (Chen)

17-34	功	19	**kung**	completes / finishes / accomplishes
17-35	成	62	**ch'êng**	work / task / duty [and]
17-36	事	6	**shih**	deeds / work / affairs [of state] [are]
17-37	遂	162	**sui**	in order / complete / done / achieved
17-38	百	106b	**pai**	the hundred
17-39	姓	38	**hsing**	families }} everyone / the people
17-40	皆	106	**chieh**	all / together X Alt: omit *chieh*—MWT
17-41	謂	149	**wei**	say
17-42	我	62	**wo**	we [did] [acted]
17-43	自	132	**tzu**	self
17-44	然	86	**jan**	like / same }}} naturally / spontaneously / "did it ourselves" / "I am natural." (Chen) / "It happened to us naturally." (Lau)
			VERSE 18	
18-01	大	37	**ta**	Great / [when] the great
18-02	道	162	**tao**	Tao [is]
18-03	廢	53	**fei**	abandoned / forgotten / deserted / "falls into disuse" / neglected / lost / in decline / faded / rejected }}} > "When people do not hold to their inner truth"
18-04	有	74	**yu**	there is / arises / emerges / appears / arose [the doctrine of]
18-05	仁	9b	**jên**	humanity / benevolence / kindness / goodness / philanthropy [and]
18-06	義	123	**yi**	rectitude / morality / righteousness / justice / duty / >v. 19:10–16 [when] [1]
18-07	慧	61	**hui**	intellect / intelligence / wit / wiseness / strategies / shrewdness / "know-how"
18-08	智	72	**chih**	knowledge / cleverness / erudition / "street smarts" [and]
18-09	出	17	**ch'u**	appear / come forth / arise / emerge / are produced / are born }}} ~"When people's actions are no longer from the heart"
18-10	有	74	**yu**	there is / arises / emerges / appears / begins / "follows in its wake"
18-11	大	37	**ta**	great / the great / gross / much
18-12	偽	9	**wei**	hypocrisy / falsehood / duplicity / pretense / artifice / "lies" // hypocrites
18-13	六	12	**liu**	six / [when the] six
18-14	親	147	**ch'in**	relationships / degrees of kinship }} the entire family / the extended family
18-15	不	1	**pu**	not / fail [to be in] / are not it / no longer [live]
18-16	和	30b	**ho**	harmony / content / peace[ful] / friendly / in accord }} discordant / at variance }}}} ~"When natural love does not arise in the family"
18-17	有	74	**yu**	there is / arises / emerges / appears [praise of / preaching of]
18-18	孝	39	**hsiao**	filial piety / "duty and devotion" [and]
18-19	慈	61	**tz'u**	love / affection / parental love / devoted parents >Alt: *tzŭ* (sons, children) [2]
18-20	國	31	**kuo**	the state / country / nation / kingdom / [when] the state
18-21	家	40	**chia**	families / household / clans }} "national policy"
18-22	昏	72	**hun**	[in] disorder / confusion / disruption / chaos / darkness / benighted [and]
18-23	亂	5	**luan**	trouble / discord / anarchy / upheaval / strife / misrule / confusion
18-24	有	74	**yu**	there is / arises / emerges / appears [praise of]
18-25	忠	61	**chung**	loyal / devoted / patriotic / loyalty [and]

| 18-26 | 臣 | 131 | ch'ên | ministers / [royal] attendants / subjects   >Alt: *hsin* (faith, trustworthy, allegiance)—Okada
>Alt: *ch'eng* (virtue, upright)—Fu I |

[1] **Jên** (humanity) and **yi** (righteousness) refer to Confucian doctrines and codes of behavior. Taoism holds that these virtues are inherent within everyone and don't have to be cultivated—they will naturally emerge when one lives in accord with Tao. (See NOTES)

[2] **Hsiao tz'u**: "deep love for children" / "devotion to the family" / " 'kind parents' and 'filial sons' " (Yutang)

VERSE 19

19-01	絕	120	chüeh	Abandon / eliminate / banish / give up / forswear / spurn / sever / destroy / "get rid of" / "exterminate"
19-02	聖	128a	shêng	holiness / sageliness / sagacity / holy / the holy ones / "spiritual pride" / "wisdom" / "holier-than-thou attitude" }} "exterminate the sage" (Lau) / (>not recommended!)
19-03	棄	75	ch'i	discard / relinquish / abandon / put away / forsake / renounce / "put out"
19-04	智	72	chih	cleverness / wisdom / erudition / strategies / clever ones / "the professors" [and]
19-05	民	83	min	the people [will] / [for] everyone
19-06	利	18	li	benefit / profit / advance / gain / "be better off"
19-07	百	106b	pai	a hundred
19-08	倍	9	pei	times / -fold
19-09	絕	120	chüeh	abandon / eliminate / banish [the rules of][the doctrine of]
19-10	仁	9b	jên	benevolence / humanity / kindness / philanthropy [and]
19-11	棄	75	ch'i	discard / relinquish / put away [the rules of][the doctrine of]
19-12	義	123	yi	righteousness / justice / morality / duty / >v. 18:1–6 [and]
19-13	民	83	min	the people [will][will naturally]
19-14	復	60	fu	return to / recover / have again / again
19-15	孝	39	hsiao	filial piety / devotion [and]
19-16	慈	61	tz'u	parental love / love / deep love / affection / compassion }} love among the whole family / >opposite in meaning to v. 18:13–19
19-17	絕	120	chüeh	abandon / renounce / eliminate / banish / give up ^^Alt: move to v. 20:01
19-18	學	39	hsüeh	learnedness / academic knowledge / (outer knowledge) ^^Alt: move to v. 20:02
19-18a	棄	75	ch'i	discard / relinquish / renounce X Alt: omit—not found in any text
19-18b	禮	113	li	etiquette, propriety, rites, ceremony >Alt: *yi* (principle, order) >Alt: *yi* (usefulness) >Alt: *yi* (gain, benefit) X Alt: omit—not found in any text
19-18c	民	83	min	the people X Alt: omit—not found in any text
19-18d	有	74	yu	have / possess X Alt: omit—not found in any text
19-19	無	86	wu	no / nothing left of ^^Alt: move to v. 20:03
19-20	憂	61b	yu	sorrow / anxiety / distress ^^Alt: move to v. 20:04 [1]
19-21	絕	120	chüeh	abandon / eliminate / banish / discard / "root out"
19-22	巧	48	ch'iao	clever[ness] / craftiness / "clever schemes" / cunning / shrewdness / skill / artfulness / ingenuity / the clever ones / the artisans
19-23	棄	75	ch'i	discard / relinquish / renounce / banish [personal]
19-24	利	18	li	profit / profit-seeking / profiteers / gain / advantage / selfishness // sharpness
19-25	盜	108	tao	[then] thieves >Alt: *min* (the people)
19-26	賊	154b	tsê	robbers / bandits }} theft / stealing

19-27	無	86	**wu**	will not / not / dis-
19-28	有 .	74	**yu**	appear / exist }} will no longer exist / will disappear
19-29	此	77	**tz'u**	these
19-30	三	1	**san**	three >Alt: *ssu* (four)—only use if adding ll.19:17–20
19-31	者	125	**chê**	those / ~things, lessons
19-32	以	9a	**yi**	thus / (just) / (however)
19-33	為	87	**wei**	are / act as / touch / are considered / regarded as >Alt: *wei* (false, counterfeit)
19-34	文	67	**wên**	decoration[s] / adornment[s] / ornaments / embellishments / "icing on the cake" / externals / superficial / "outward forms" // cultural [teachings] / societal [lessons] [2]
19-35	不	1	**pu**	not / are not
19-36	足 。	157	**tsu**	enough / adequate / sufficient / essential / "the core" [teachings] / "central"
19-37	故	66	**ku**	therefore / hence
19-38	令	9	**ling**	let them // as a rule / (in general)
19-39	有	74	**yu**	have / possess
19-40	所	63	**so**	these / this / something / (these teachings) [to]
19-41	屬 .	44	**shu**	rely upon / depend on / attach to / follow / abide in [:]
19-42	見	147	**chien**	recognize / see / look to / discern // manifest / become / exhibit
19-43	素	120	**su**	simplicity / simple / plain[ness] / genuine / simple self / unadorned / "undyed silk"
19-44	抱	64	**pao**	embrace / hold on to / hold within / hold to / "realize"
19-45	樸 .	75	**p'u**	purity / simplicity / one's natural state / "uncarved wood" / "original nature" / "the primal" / "unspoiled"
19-46	少	42	**shao**	reduce / lessen / have little / check / "cast off" / attenuate
19-47	私	115	**ssu**	self-interest / ego / selfishness / self-concern / self-consciousness / sense of self
19-48	寡	40	**kua**	diminish / lessen / curb / curtail / restrain / temper / few / "don't give in to"
19-49	欲 .	76	**yü**	desires / wants / (pull of the senses) / (fickleness of the mind) }} ~be satisfied with what you have

[1] ***Chüeh hsüeh (+ ch'i + li + min + yu) wu yu***: *Chüeh hsüeh wu yu* is usually placed at the beginning of verse 20 where, most commentators agree, it is sadly out of place. In this rectification, we have added four characters—abandon, learning + ***ch'i*** (discard) + ***li*** (ceremony) + ***min*** (the people) + ***yu*** (have), no, sorrow—and placed this line in the third position of verse 19. (See NOTES for a full explanation of this rectification)

[2] ***Wên*** is "culture, literature, scholarship, arguments, superficiality, artificiality, grain, pattern" etc. (Chan). It is that which is "added unto" man. It has been variously translated as "externals" (Yutang); "civilization" (Hughes); "outward show" (Giles); and "criss-cross of Tao" (Wu). It connotes that which is on the surface, something outer, as opposed to the essence or core.

VERSE 20

20-01	唯	30b	**wei**	Yes / "yes sir" / "yea" / "eh" / ~a definite reply
20-02	之	4	**chih**	in its
20-03	與	134	**yü**	contrast with / addition to / "between"
20-04	阿 。	170	**a**	"no" / "nay" / "o" / (sign of disapproval) // "yeah" / "alright" / ~a hesitant reply
20-05	相	109	**hsiang**	together / mutually
20-06	去	28	**ch'ü**	differ / difference between

20-07	幾	52	chi	few / little / minute / nearly // subtle / hidden
20-08	何	9	ho	what / how }} how little? / how much? }}}} how much (little) difference is there? / what is the difference?
20-09	善	30	shan	good / virtuous
20-10	之	4	chih	in its
20-11	與	134	yü	contrast with / addition to / "between"
20-12	惡	61	wu	bad / evil
20-13	相	109	hsiang	together / mutual
20-14	去	28	ch'ü	differ
20-15	若	140	jo	alike / similar
20-16	何	9	ho	what / how }}}} how much alike?
20-17	人	9a	jên	people / men / others
20-18	之	4	chih	of
20-19	所	63	so	that which [they]
20-20	畏	102	wei	dread / fear }} what others fear
20-21	不	1	pu	not
20-22	可	30	k'o	can / able
20-23	不	1	pu	not / fail to
20-24	畏	102	wei	fear[ed] / dread }}}} one must also fear / must I also fear?
20-25	荒	140	huang	wilderness / desolation / barren / "uncultivated" >Alt: *huang* (hurried, confused, reckless, without restraint) >Alt: *kuang* (vast, expansive)
20-26	兮	12	hsi	! / oh / alas
20-27	其	12	ch'i	it
20-28	未	75	wei	has no[t] / without
20-29	央	37	yang	end / reached the end / limit / utmost // center / within me / "sunk in" // >lit: "dawn" / "dawn (of awakening)" (Yutang)
20-30	哉	30	tsai	! / indeed [1]
20-31	眾	143	chung	all
20-32	人	9a	jên	people / men }} the multitudes
20-33	熙	86	hsi	joyful / joyous / merry // busy / active / "lustily" / (very)
20-34	熙	86	hsi	joyful / merry // busy / active
20-35	如	38	ju	like / as if / as though / resembling
20-36	享	8	hsiang	enjoying / taking part in / celebrating / partaking / (feasting at)
20-37	太	37	ta	great / the great
20-38	牢	93	lao	feast / sacrificial feast / ox feast
20-39	如	38	ju	as if / like / as though
20-40	春	72	ch'un	spring / in springtime >Alt: reverse the order of *ch'un* and *têng*
20-41	登	104	têng	climbing / ascending / mounting / going up to / "taking in"
20-42	臺	133	t'ai	tower / lookout platform / terrace / "an outing" / the sights
20-43	我	62	wo	I / (a knower of Tao)
20-44	獨	94	tu	alone [remain]

20-45	泊	85	p'o	calm / steady / mild / placid / still / inactive / inert / unmoved // stop / rest / (to fasten a boat) / anchored / "anchored within myself"
20-46	兮	12	hsi	!
20-47	其	12	ch'i	as one
20-48	未	75	wei	not yet [seeing][showing][revealing] / [and] give no
20-49	兆	10	chao	sign / omen / sign of [desire] / "showing sentiment" // emerged / "employed" }} not given a sign / not yet emerged / "with no concern" (Jiyu)
20-50	如	38	ju	like / resembling / "into form"
20-51	嬰	39	ying	newborn
20-52	兒	10	erh	baby / child }} an infant
20-53	之	4	chih	who
20-54	未	75	wei	does not / has not yet / not yet [know / learned to]
20-55	孩	39	hai	smile[d]
20-56	儽	9	lei	wearied / exhausted / tired >Alt: ch'eng (forlorn, despondent)
20-57	儽	9	lei	wearied / exhausted >Alt: ch'eng (forlorn, "unattached," lost")
20-58	兮	12	hsi	! / indeed / oh
20-59	若	140	jo	like / as if / I seem to be
20-60	無	86	wu	without / not having
20-61	所	63	so	a place / a home }} nowhere
20-62	歸	77	kuei	to return to / to go back to / to belong }}} ~an aimless wanderer
20-63	眾	143	chung	all / most
20-64	人	9a	jên	people / men }} the multitudes
20-65	皆	106	chieh	all
20-66	有	74	yu	have / possess
20-67	餘	184	yü	an excess / a surplus / plenty / too much / more than enough / enough to spare
20-68	而	126	erh	but / yet
20-69	我	62	wo	I / (~a knower of Tao)
20-70	獨	94	tu	alone / solitary / single
20-71	若	140	jo	seem / like / appear as
20-72	遺	162	yi	wanting / deficient / "left out" / at a loss / insufficient / "possess nothing"
20-73	我	62	wo	I / me / mine
20-74	愚	61b	yü	foolish / ignorant / stupid / simple / rude
20-75	人	9a	jên	person / man
20-76	之	4	chih	in / of
20-77	心	61	hsin	mind / heart }} my mind is that of a fool
20-78	也	5	yeh	! / indeed
20-79	哉	30	tsai	! / indeed / ? / >a final particle
20-80	沌	85	t'un	confused / chaotic / turbid / ignorant / "unadulterated" / dull / muddled / (very)
20-81	沌	85	t'un	confused / chaotic / nebulous / "blank" (Lau) }}}}}}}}} "I am a fool, my mind is very confused"
20-82	兮	12	hsi	indeed / !

20-83	俗	9	su	worldly / common / "vulgar"
20-84	人	9a	jên	people / folks / men }} most people [are][try to be]
20-85	昭	72	chao	bright / brilliant / luminous / shine / displayed / knowing / clear / (very)
20-86	昭	72	chao	bright / brilliant / luminous / displayed / knowing / "out there" }} "clear and bright" / "know how to differentiate" (Lin)
20-87	我	62	wo	I / ~a knower of Tao
20-88	獨	94	tu	alone
20-89	昏	72	hun	dark / dim // confused >Alt: joh (resemble, is like, seem)
20-90	昏	72	hun	dark / dim // confounded
20-91	俗	9	su	worldly / common
20-92	人	9a	jên	people / men [are][try to be]
20-93	察	40	ch'a	sharp / alert / smart / clear-sighted / discern / "see differences" / clever / (very)
20-94	察	40	ch'a	sharp / clear-sighted / discerning / clear-cut / "self-assured"
20-95	我	62	wo	I ~a knower of Tao
20-96	獨	94	tu	alone [am]
20-97	悶	61	mên	dull / dejected / withdrawn / muddled / depressed / mum / unobtrusive / (very)
20-98	悶	61	mên	dull / dejected / withdrawn }} make no distinctions / "do not see differences" >>Etm: "mind" + "gate" (state when the mind is closed behind a gate)
20-99	澹	85b	tan	tranquil / placid / calm / "patient" / "bland" >Alt: hu (disturbed, confused, turbulent, desolate, "drifting")
20-100	兮	12	hsi	! / oh
20-101	其	12	ch'i	its / theirs X Alt: omit
20-102	若	140	jo	like / resembling / as the
20-103	海	85	hai	ocean / sea / "ocean depths" (Cleary) / "ocean waves"
20-104	飂	182	liu	whirlwind / gale / breeze / high winds / "wind blowing about" / "restless winds" >Alt: p'iao (float, drift on the waves, afloat)
20-105	兮	12	hsi	! / oh
20-106	若	140	jo	like / as / seemingly / [I] seem to be
20-107	無	86	wu	without / not having / "I never" +Alt: add so (a place, spot)
20-108	止	77	chih	stop / stand / anchor / ceasing / "destination" / "direction" }} aimless / drifting / blown about / without a place to stop
20-109	眾	143	chung	all / the many
20-110	人	9a	jên	people }} the masses / multitudes
20-111	皆	106	chieh	all / most
20-112	有	74	yu	have / possess
20-113	以	9a	yi	use / purpose / employment / something to do / "purposeful actions" / "ways and means" (Cleary) / "settle down in their grooves" (Wu)
20-114	而	126	erh	but / yet
20-115	我	62	wo	I / (a knower of Tao)
20-116	獨	94	tu	alone [am][seem to be][appear]
20-117	頑	181	wan	thickheaded / awkward / stubborn / foolish / "untamable" / obstinate / stupid / stubborn

20-118	似	9	ssu	like / similar / resembles / seem >Alt: *ts'ie* (and)
20-119	鄙	163	pi	rustic / unrefined / base / uncouth / "despicable" / "remain outside" / lowly material
20-120	我	62	wo	I / (a knower of Tao)
20-121	獨	94	tu	alone
20-122	異	102	yi	differ / am different / foreign / estranged / alien
20-123	於	70	yü	from
20-124	人	9a	jên	people / the people / others
20-125	而	126	erh	because / in that [I]
20-126	貴	154	kuei	value / honor / cherish / treasure +Alt: add *ch'iu* (seek, feed, draw, suck)
20-127	食	184	shih	food / nourishment / sustenance / milk / being fed by / "drawing sustenance from" [my / the] +Alt: add *yü* (from)
20-128	母	80	mu	Mother / great mother / mother's breast / (Tao)

[1] [1-30]

The difference between "ya" and "yes"—how great is it?
The difference between "you" and "me"—how great is it?
The difference between the real and the unreal—how great it is!
Must I see the differences that others do? Then alas, the end of my fear never comes!

VERSE 21

21-01	孔	39	k'ung	Vast / all-embracing / high[est] / great / grand / empty / >surname of Confucius: *K'ung Fu Tzu*
21-02	德	60b	tê	Te / virtue / power }} highest virtue / a man of great virtue / "the natural expression of Power" (Wing)
21-03	之	4	chih	's / its / (takes on its own)
21-04	容	40	jung	quality / manner / constitution / demeanor / nature of // appearance / features / face / expression / character / endure / capacity / development [1]
21-05	惟	61	wei	exactly / entirely / alone / exclusive[ly] / (only when)
21-06	道	162	tao	Tao
21-07	是	72a	shih	this / to be / (_____)
21-08	從	60	ts'ung	follow[ed] / comply with / (pursue) / live according to / comes from / proceed }}} follow alone (/entirely) from Tao
21-09	道	162	tao	Tao
21-10	之	4	chih	's / its
21-11	為	87	wei	being a / be / make / act[ion][s] / become / do / "constituting" X Alt: omit—MWT
21-12	物	93	wu	thing / something / an entity / being / concrete thing }}}} "the thing called Tao" / "what is Tao?"
21-13	惟	61	wei	entirely / exactly / only / utterly
21-14	恍	61	huang	elusive / Illusive / vague / abstruse / shadowy / nebulous / dreamlike / intangible / nebulous >Alt: *wang* (full moon)—MWT
21-15	惟	61	wei	only / entirely / exactly / (and)
21-16	惚	61	hu	indistinct / eluding / intangible / indefinite / evasive / hazy / ("to forget / to disregard")
21-17	惚	61	hu	indistinct / eluding / indefinite / evasive / "indeterminable" / "distracting"
21-18	兮	12	hsi	! / oh / (very) / (and)

21-19	恍	61	huang	vague / abstruse / elusive / shadowy / intangible >Alt: *wang* (full moon)—MWT
21-20	兮	12	hsi	! / oh / (very) X Alt: omit
21-21	其	12	ch'i	its
21-22	中	2	chung	within / middle / midst / center / inside / "latent in it" }} within itself
21-23	有	74	yu	has / contains
21-24	象	152	hsiang	form / substance / image / signs / a form / images
21-25	恍	61	huang	vague / abstruse / illusive / dim / "unsettled" / "uncertain" >Alt: *wang* (full moon)—MWT
21-26	兮	12	hsi	! / oh (very) / (and)
21-27	惚	61	hu	elusive / evasive / intangible / dark [yet]
21-28	兮	12	hsi	! / oh / (very) X Alt: omit
21-29	其	12	ch'i	its
21-30	中	2	chung	within / middle / midst / center / inside / ("latent") }} within itself
21-31	有	74	yu	has / contains
21-32	物	93	wu	things / substance / objects / being / (physical reality) / "thinghood" (Chen)
21-33	窈	116	yao	hidden / deep / profound / secret / impenetrable // dark / obscure / dim / shadowy / vague / distant
21-34	兮	12	hsi	oh / ! / (very)
21-35	冥	14	ming	obscure / dim / dark / vague / mysterious
21-36	兮	12	hsi	oh / ! / (very)
21-37	其	12	ch'i	its
21-38	中	2	chung	within / middle / midst / center / inside / ("latent in it") }} within itself
21-39	有	74	yu	has / contains / "there is"
21-40	精	119	ching	essence / spirit / life-force / "vitality" / intelligence / "core of vitality" (Wu) / "life-seed" (Chen)
21-41	其	12	ch'i	its
21-42	精	119	ching	essence / spirit / life-force [is]
21-43	甚	99	shên	very / quite
21-44	真	109	chên	real / genuine / true / rarefied
21-45	其	12	ch'i	its
21-46	中	2	chung	within / midst / middle / center / inside }} within itself / therein
21-47	有	74	yu	has / contains / (lies)
21-48	信	9	hsin	evidence[s] / proof / truth / sincerity / trust / faith // "growth power" / regularity / "a talisman" / "genuineness" (Ku) / "heart" (Pine) / "efficacious" (Waley) / >lit: a lamp wick [2]
21-49	自	132	tzu	from / since / (throughout)
21-50	古	30	ku	days of old / ancient times / antiquity >Alt: switch *ku* (v. 21:50) with *chin* (v. 21:52)—MWT
21-51	及	29	chi	until / to reach / > past tense
21-52	今	9	chin	now / the present }}}} throughout the ages / now, as it was long ago
21-53	其	12	ch'i	its / (Tao's)
21-54	名	30a	ming	name / name[d] / ~manifestations / effect / "life-giving words" (Waley) / >"charge," as in a battle cry (Waley) [has]
21-55	不	1	pu	not / never / not [been]

21-56	去	28	ch'ü	departed / gone away / been forgotten / ceased / deserted / abandoned / discarded / changed }} ever remains / been preserved
21-57	以	9a	yi	thereby / thus / so / by which / in order to / (serves as a means to) [it][we]
21-58	閲	169	yüeh	see / view / watch / discern / look at / survey / witness / inspect / recall / "passes" >Alt: *shun* (follow)—MWT >Alt: *shuo* (describe)—Duy [3]
21-59	衆	143	chung	all / everything / all things / the multitudes / common [its]
21-60	甫	101	fu	beginning / origin / creation / Creator / "beauties" (Cleary) >Alt: *fu* (father, men) }} the beginning (/creation) of all things / ~Tao creating all things
21-61	吾	30	wu	I
21-62	何	9	ho	how / what
21-63	以	9a	yi	accordingly / (by)
21-64	知	111	chih	know / know [the ways of]
21-65	衆	143	chung	all / everything / all things / the many
21-66	甫	101	fu	beginning / origin / creation // father / ~"the disposition of the origin" (Ku)
21-67	之	4	chih	its / 's
21-68	狀	86	jan	is so / is such
21-69	哉	30	tsai	(_____) / indeed [?]
21-70	以	9a	yi	by / through / because of / by means of / "use" / from
21-71	此	77	tz'u	this / these / it / this / "what is within me" (Wu) / ~Tao / ~manifestations / nature of Tao / ~"inward knowledge, intuition" (Waley)

[1] *Jung*: "outward manifestation" (Duy) // ~operation, disposition, capacity (Ku)

[2] *Ch'i chung yu hsin*: it can be tested / verified / "it has truth within" (Cleary) / "therein lies faith" (Feng)

[3] *Yüeh*, from "door / gate" + "issue forth." "To witness, inspect, or survey the coming out process of things" (Chen)

VERSE 22

22-01	曲	73	ch'ü	Bend / yield / give in / (surrender) / bow down / bowed / bend over / one who bends / "humbles himself" // crooked / crippled / the curved / hat which is curved // partial
22-02	則	18	tsê	then / thus / "to be" / "is to be" / "and you will be" / "becomes" / "means" / "it can be made"
22-03	全	11	ch'üan	perfect / whole / complete / all / preserved whole // (overcome)
22-04	枉	75	wang	crooked / distorted / warped / wronged / bent / bow / curl // (unjustly accused)
22-05	則	18	tsê	then / thus
22-06	直	109	chih	straight[en][ed] / rectified / made true / straight / (stand tall) // (vindicated) >Alt: *ting* (still)—MWTA >Alt: *cheng* (upright)—MWTB
22-07	窪	116	wa	empty / hollow / keep empty / being hollow / "deep" / low
22-08	則	18	tsê	then / thus
22-09	盈	108	ying	filled / full / excess / surplus / being full
22-10	敝	66	pi	worn out / old / grow old // abused / battered / defrauded / "shedding" / "exhausted"
22-11	則	18	tsê	then / thus
22-12	新	69	hsin	renew[ed] / refresh / rejuvenate / new / anew [have][be]
22-13	少	42	shao	little / few / economy / scanty / small / diminished
22-14	則	18	tsê	then / thus

22-15	得	60a	tê	obtain / gain / possess / benefit / receive / acquire / attain[able] / succeed / "content" [have][be]
22-16	多	36	to	much / plenty a lot / excess[ive] / increase // (exhibit / manifest / beautiful) // complex
22-17	則	18	tsê	then // this
22-18	惑	61	huo	confused / bewildered / perplexed / delusion / deluded / doubt / be deceived / misled / lose one's way
22-19	是	72a	shih	(this)
22-20	以	9a	yi	(for) }} therefore / thus / hence [the]
22-21	聖	128a	shêng	holy / saintly
22-22	人	9a	jên	man / men / person }} sage[s]
22-23	抱	64	pao	embraces / holds to / holds within / clings to
22-24	一	1	yi	unity / the One / "one thing" / (primal unity) / "the Absolute" [and]
22-25	為	87	wei	becomes / makes / does / acts as / "regard"
22-26	天	37	t'ien	Heaven
22-27	下	1	hsia	below }} the world / the empire / all under Heaven ['s]
22-28	式	56	shih	model / standard / pattern / example / measure // protector / master >Alt: mu (shepherd)—MWT }}} "takes care of the world" / "to use in guiding the world" (Pine)
22-29	不	1	pu	not / does not / is not
22-30	自	132	tzu	himself / themselves
22-31	見	147	chien	see[ing] / show / display // watch }}} is not self-seeing / does not show off / not focused on himself
22-32	故	66	ku	therefore / hence [he]
22-33	明	72	ming	shines / clear / shines forth / conspicuous / appears / (in the spotlight) / enlightened / clear-sighted / wise / discerning / illustrious / ~celebrated / ~renowned
22-34	不	1	pu	not
22-35	自	132	tzu	himself / self / themselves
22-36	是	72a	shih	right / correct / (righteous) / (assertive) / (justified) / (display) / to be }}} ~does not claim to be right
22-37	故	66	ku	therefore / thus [he is / he becomes]
22-38	彰	59	chang	distinguish[ed] / prominent / famous / outstanding / illustrious / recognition / shine / glory / flourishes // manifest / exhibit / "beautiful"
22-39	不	1	pu	not / does not
22-40	自	132	tzu	himself
22-41	伐	9	fa	boast / show off / brag / flatter / make claims / "indulge in self-praise" (Ku) // (cut down, chastise, destroy others)
22-42	故	66	ku	therefore / thus
22-43	有	74	yu	he has / (is given)
22-44	功	19	kung	merit / credit / succeed / success / achievements
22-45	不	1	pu	not
22-46	自	132	tzu	himself
22-47	矜	110	ching	brag / boast / self-approve / arrogant / proud / pride / parading / "wallow in self-conceit" (Ku) // complacent
22-48	故	66	ku	therefore / thus

22-49	長	168	ch'ang	endures / lasts a long time // leads / advance / chief / "chief among men"
22-50	夫	37	fu	to the extent that / it is because / to the fullest extent / truly
22-51	唯	30b	wei	only / exactly / precisely / indeed / (because)
22-52	不	1	pu	not
22-53	爭	87	chêng	go against / contend / strive / quarrel / compete / contentious / >lit: "two hands pulling in opposite directions"
22-54	故	66	ku	therefore / thus
22-55	天	37	t'ien	Heaven
22-56	下	1	hsia	below }} the world
22-57	莫	140	mo	none / not / no one
22-58	能	130	nêng	can / able
22-59	與	134	yü	with // (share, together, union)
22-60	之	4	chih	him
22-61	爭	87	chêng	go against / contend / strive / quarrel / compete / contentious
22-62	古	30	ku	old
22-63	之	4	chih	it / they }} of old / ancient / the ancients
22-64	所	63	so	it / that / who
22-65	謂	149	wei	said / saying }}} of old it was said / the ancients said / the ancient saying
22-66	曲	73	ch'ü	bend / yield / give in / crooked / (surrender)
22-67	則	18	tsê	then / thus
22-68	全	11	ch'üan	perfect / complete / be preserved / whole
22-69	者	125	chê	that
22-70	豈	151	ch'i	? / how / why
22-71	虛	141	hsü	empty / vacant / useless / false / weak / futile / idle / in vain
22-72	言	149	yen	words / saying / spoken / talk [?]
22-73	哉	30	tsai	? / indeed / (final particle) }}}} are these just empty words? / are these words in vain?
22-74	誠	149	ch'êng	truly / really / sincere / honest >Alt: ch'eng (become, be)
22-75	全	11	ch'üan	perfect[ion] / complete[ness] / preserved / wholeness / ~the perfection that results from humility
22-76	而	126	erh	and / then / by X Alt: omit—MWT
22-77	歸	77	kuei	return / restore / turn back / come back to / will come / ~belongs [to]
22-78	之	4	chih	him / them / It / ~Tao / ~everything / ~within / ~one's true nature [1]

[1] **Ch'êng ch'üan erh kuei chih**: "Truly it enables one to be preserved to the end." (Lau); "If you have really attained wholeness, everything will flock to you." (Wu); "True wholeness can be achieved by returning to the Tao." (Ming)

VERSE 23

23-01	希	50	hsi	Little / rare / few / seldom / "whimpered"
23-02	言	149	yen	speak / says / words / ~issuing commands
23-03	自	132	tzu	(of) }}} "to be brief of word" (Duy) / "be sparing of your talk" (Chalmers)
23-04	然	86	jan	(itself) }} Nature / natural / spontaneous / self-so / the natural way / in accordance with nature [1][2]

23-05	故	66	ku	therefore
23-06	飄	182	p'iao	violent / fierce / (whirl-)
23-07	風	182	fêng	wind[s] / squall }} a gale
23-08	不	1	pu	not / doesn't
23-09	終	120	chung	outlast / the end / last to the end / utmost
23-10	朝 .	74	chao	morning / dawn }}} last the whole morning
23-11	驟	187	chou	violent / torrential / (storm)
23-12	雨	173	yü	rain / downpour }} rainstorm / cloudburst
23-13	不	1	pu	not / does not
23-14	終	120	chung	outlast / the end / last to the end / utmost
23-15	日 .	72	jih	day
23-16	孰	39	shu	what / who / who [else]
23-17	為	87	wei	causes / makes / acts / produces / could make
23-18	此	77	tz'u	of / (_____)
23-19	者 。	125	chê	this / these / (the one) [?] }}}} "who is their author?" (Wu)
23-20	天	37	t'ien	Heaven [and]
23-21	地 .	32	ti	earth }} Nature
23-22	天	37	t'ien	Heaven [and]
23-23	地 .	32	ti	earth }} Nature
23-24	尚	42	shang	even / if // wish to / add to [these actions]
23-25	不	1	pu	not
23-26	能	130	nêng	can / able
23-27	久 .	4	chiu	last long / persist / ancient / go on forever
23-28	而	126	erh	(how) / then
23-29	況	85	k'uang	much less so
23-30	於	70	yü	for
23-31	人	9a	jên	man / humans / ~the works of man
23-32	乎 .	4	hu	? / indeed!
23-33	故	66	ku	therefore / thus [one who]
23-34	從	60	ts'ung	follows / pursues / complies with / cultivates / devotes
23-35	事	6	shih	daily activities / dealings / lifestyle / business }} deals / works / "in whatever we do"
23-36	於	70	yü	with / through / in / "let"
23-37	道	162	tao	Tao
23-38	者 .	125	chê	(he) / (him) / it / (the one)
23-39	道	162	tao	Tao X Alt: omit
23-40	者	125	chê	he / him / it / the one X Alt: omit
23-41	同	30	t'ung	identify[ies][ied] / together / alike / aligns / resemble / be of / becomes one / is one / "assimilate"
23-42	於	70	yü	with / through / in
23-43	道 .	162	tao	Tao }}}} "Let those on the way be one with the Way." (Pine) [3]

23-44	德	60b	**tê**	Te / virtue / power >Alt: *tê* (success, succeed, to obtain)—Fu I
23-45	者	125	**chê**	(he) / (him) / it / (the one)
23-46	同	30	**t'ung**	identifies / together / alike / aligns / resemble / be of / becomes one / is one
23-47	於	70	**yü**	with / through / in
23-48	德 .	60b	**tê**	Te / virtue / power [one who] >Alt: *tê* (success, succeed, to obtain)—Fu I [4]
23-49	失	37	**shih**	loss / failure / abandonment (of Tao) / renunciation >Alt: *t'ien* (Heaven, Nature)
23-50	者	125	**chê**	(the one)
23-51	同	30	**t'ung**	identifies / together / alike / aligns / resemble / be of / becomes one / is one
23-52	於	70	**yü**	with / through / in
23-53	失 .	37	**shih**	loss / failure / abandonment (of Tao) / renunciation >Alt: *t'ien* (Heaven, Nature)
23-54	同	30	**t'ung**	identifies / together / alike / aligns / resemble / be of / be one / becomes one / is one
23-55	於	70	**yü**	with
23-56	道	162	**tao**	Tao
23-57	者 。	125	**chê**	(he) / (him) / it / (the one)
23-58	道	162	**tao**	Tao
23-59	亦	8	**yi**	also / moreover
23-60	樂	75	**lo**	enjoys / joy / happily / glad / pleased
23-61	得	60a	**tê**	obtain / accept / (welcome)
23-62	之 .	4	**chih**	(he) / (him) / it / (the one)
23-63	同	30	**t'ung**	identifies / together / alike / aligns / resemble / bc of / becomes one / ls one
23-64	於	70	**yü**	with
23-65	德	60b	**tê**	Te >Alt: *tê* (success, succeed, obtain)—Fu I
23-66	者 .	125	**chê**	(he) / (him) / it / (the one)
23-67	德	60b	**tê**	Te >Alt: *tê* (success, succeed, obtain)—Fu I
23-68	亦	8	**yi**	also / moreover
23-69	樂	75	**lo**	enjoys / joy / happily / glad / pleased
23-70	得	60a	**tê**	obtain / accept / (welcome)
23-71	之 .	4	**chih**	(he) / (him) / it / (the one)
23-72	同	30	**t'ung**	identifies / together / alike / aligns / resemble / be of / becomes one / is one
23-73	於	70	**yü**	with
23-74	失	37	**shih**	loss / abandonment / renunciation >Alt: *t'ien* (Heaven, Nature)
23-75	者 。	125	**chê**	(he) / (him) / it / (the one)
23-76	失	37	**shih**	loss / abandonment / renunciation >Alt: *t'ien* (Heaven, Nature)
23-77	亦	8	**yi**	also
23-78	樂	75	**lo**	enjoys / joy / happily / glad / pleased
23-79	得	60a	**tê**	obtain / accept / (welcome)
23-80	之 .	4	**chih**	he / him / it / the one
23-81	信	9	**hsin**	faith / trust / credibility / honesty / belief XXX Alt: omit v. 23:81–88—MWT
23-82	不	1	**pu**	not / in-
23-83	足	157	**tsu**	sufficient / enough / adequate / (stand on its own) }} fails / lacks / is lacking

23-84	焉	86a	yen	indeed
23-85	有	74	yu	receive / have / has / finds / be
23-86	不	1	pu	no / not / dis- / lack of / (not worthy of)
23-87	信	9	hsin	faith / trust / credibility / honesty / belief
23-88	焉	86a	yen	indeed / how? / why? X Alt: omit—MWT }}}}}}} "Where honesty fails dishonesty prevails." (Pine) [5]

[1] **Tzu-jan** is a term meaning "of itself," naturally, spontaneous, etc. This is the natural and spontaneous state of one who is in harmony with himself and all of nature.

[2] **Hsi yen tzu jan**: Nature speaks little; speaking little is natural; "Sparing indeed is the nature of its talk." (Blakney); "To use words but rarely is to be natural." (Lau); "Only simple and quiet words will ripen of themselves." (Wu)

[3] +Alt: add ts'ung shi yü. Ts'ung (follows, pursues, complies with); shi (daily activities, dealings, lifestyle, business); yü (with, through, in)

[4] +Alt: add ts'ung shi yü. Ts'ung (follows, pursues, complies with); shi (daily activities, dealings, lifestyle, business); yü (with, through, in)

[5] Last 8 lines are also found in v. 17:21–28; v. 23:81–8.

VERSE 24

24-01	企	9	ch'i	On tiptoes / stand erect >Alt: ch'ui (to cook, to blow, "blow hot air," boast, brag)—MWT
24-02	者	125	chê	(the one) / (he) / it
24-03	不	1	pu	not / cannot / does not
24-04	立	117	li	stand / stand firm / stand steady / established
24-05	跨	157	k'ua	stride / stride forward / straddle / step across / astride / "protracts his stride" / "straddle-legged"
24-06	者	125	chê	(the one) / (he) / it
24-07	不	1	pu	not / cannot / does not
24-08	行	144	hsing	walk / go / go forward / walk [far] XXX Alt: omit v. 24:5–8—MWT
24-09	自	132	tzu	self- / himself
24-10	見	147	chien	display / show off / reveal // see }} make a show of himself
24-11	者	125	chê	(the one) / (he) / it
24-12	不	1	pu	not / cannot [be]
24-13	明	72	ming	bright / enlighten[ed] / shine / luminous / "flourish" / illustrious
24-14	自	132	tzu	self- / himself
24-15	是	72a	shih	right / correct / (righteous) / (assertive) / (approving) / to be }} hold one's ground / hold to being right >Alt: shih (watch)—MWT
24-16	者	125	chê	(the one) / (he) / it
24-17	不	1	pu	not / cannot / doesn't [be / become]
24-18	彰	59	chang	prominent / outstanding / distinguished / famous / illustrious / shine / beautiful / glory // exhibit / appear / to manifest
24-19	自	132	tzu	self-
24-20	伐	9	fa	approving / praise / show off // cut down / chastise
24-21	者	125	chê	(the one) / (he) / (his) / ~one's own deeds }} "boasts of his own abilities" (Wu)
24-22	無	86	wu	not / has no / without

24-23	功	19	**kung**	merit / accomplishment
24-24	自	132	**tzu**	self- / himself
24-25	矜	110	**ching**	praise / conceit }} "parades his own success" (Wu) / "wallows in self-conceit" (Ku)
24-26	者	125	**chê**	(the one) / (he)
24-27	不	1	**pu**	not / cannot
24-28	長	168	**ch'ang**	endure / last long // grow // lead
24-29	其	12	**ch'i**	he / she / it / their
24-30	在	32	**tsai**	to be / presence / existence [with] / in / at >Alt: *yü* (with, in, as, at, through)
24-31	道	162	**tao**	Tao }} from the point of view of Tao / in light of the Tao / "to a Taoist" / to those who know Tao
24-32	也	5	**yeh**	indeed
24-33	曰	73	**yüeh**	called
24-34	餘	184	**yü**	excess / remainder / surplus / too much / surplus / remnants / unwanted / leftovers / offal
24-35	食	184	**shih**	food / to eat }} "over-consumption" (Cleary)
24-36	贅	154	**chui**	extraneous / superfluous / excess / redundant / waste[ful] / useless // tumor[ous] / burdensome
24-37	行	144	**hsing**	actions / activity / to step / to go / pace >Alt: *hsing* (growth, form) }} "tumors of actions" (Chan) / "excrescences" }}}} "too much food and a tiring pace" (Pine) [1]
24-38	物	93	**wu**	beings / things / creatures / all things / all
24-39	或	62	**huo**	likely / perhaps / supposing
24-40	惡	61	**wu**	detest[ed] / loathe[d] / detest / disdain
24-41	之	4	**chih**	them / he / she / it
24-42	故	66	**ku**	therefore / thus
24-43	有	74	**yu**	has / to have / to be
24-44	道	162	**tao**	Tao >Alt: *yü* (desires)—MWT
24-45	者	125	**chê**	(the one) }} one who seeks the Tao / a man of Tao / one who knows Tao
24-46	不	1	**pu**	not / does not
24-47	處	141	**ch'u**	dwell / stay / stop / rest / abide / indulge / "set his heart upon" (Wu) +Alt: add *ye* (indeed / !) }} avoids / spurns / shuns / turns away from [2]

[1] ***Chui hsing*** can be translated as "redundant actions" or "tumorous growths."

[2] ***Yu tao chê pu ch'u***: "Therefore, one who has the Tao does not dwell in it (egotistical actions)." ***Yu yü chê pu ch'u***: "Therefore, one who has desires / limiting thoughts (*yü*), does not dwell in it (the Tao)."

V E R S E 2 5

25-01	有	74	**yu**	There is / there was // being / having
25-02	物	93	**wu**	thing / something / being
25-03	混	85a	**hun**	confused / nebulous / chaos / "blend" / undifferentiated // containing everything / (ocean) / "in a state of fusion" (Duy) / "heterogeneously formed" (Ku)
25-04	成	62	**ch'êng**	complete / whole / formed / finish / accomplish // existing
25-05	先	10	**hsien**	preceding / coming before / pre-dating
25-06	天	37	**t'ien**	Heaven [and]
25-07	地	32	**ti**	earth [were][in its]

25-08	生	100	shêng	born / birth / existing / come forth / live / formed
25-09	寂	40a	chi	tranquil / silent / soundless / calm // even / harmony
25-10	兮	12	hsi	oh / !
25-11	寥	40	liao	formless / void / bodiless / elusive // vast
25-12	兮	12	hsi	oh / !
25-13	獨	94	tu	alone / single / solitary / isolated / independent
25-14	立	117	li	stand / it stands / stand erect +Alt: add *erh* (and, yet)
25-15	不	1	pu	not / does not
25-16	改	66	kai	change / alter / waver[ing] / another
25-17	周	30	chou	complete / surround / everywhere / universal / all-pervading // a dynasty // cycle / revolving motion
25-18	行	144	hsing	go out / operates / goes around }} operates everywhere / "moving cyclically" (Chen) / revolves / "permeates universally" (Duy) [1]
25-19	而	126	erh	and
25-20	不	1	pu	not / without / free of [being / becoming]
25-21	殆	78	tai	tired / weary / exhausted / approaching (end) / pause // hinder[ed] / peril / harm / endangered / danger XXX Alt: omit v. 25:17–21—MWT
25-22	可	30	k'o	can / able / could
25-23	以	9a	yi	thereby
25-24	為	87	wei	be / become / make / act / "may be regarded" / considered
25-25	天	37	t'ien	Heaven
25-26	下	1	hsia	below }} the world / the universe / all / >Alt: *ti* (earth)—MWT
25-27	母	80	mu	mother / Mother
25-28	吾	30	wu	I
25-29	不	126	erh	do not / not
25-30	知	111	chih	know / knowledge
25-31	其	12	ch'i	its
25-32	名	30a	ming	name / characterize / "alias" / style / designate +Alt: add *ch'iang* (constrain, force, compel)
25-33	字	39	tzu	love / shelter / protect
25-34	之	4	chih	it / itself / I
25-35	曰	73	yüeh	call [it]
25-36	道	162	tao	Tao
25-37	強	57	ch'iang	forced / compelled / "with reluctance" / constrained
25-38	為	87	wei	to make / act / do / give / assign
25-39	之	4	chih	I / it
25-40	名	30a	ming	name / "picture it" }}} "for lack of a better word" (Feng) / "imposing on it a name" (Cleary)
25-41	曰	73	yüeh	call / say [it is] / [I would] call it
25-42	大	37	ta	great / Great
25-43	大	37	ta	great / Great
25-44	曰	73	yüeh	call / [further] described as / (means) / (implies)

25-45	逝	162	shih	functioning everywhere / far-reaching / ever-flowing / continuing // moving away / receding / pass away / passing / death
25-46	逝	162	shih	functioning everywhere / far-reaching // receding / pass away / depart
25-47	曰	73	yüeh	call / [further] described as / (means) / (implies)
25-48	遠	162	yüan	far away / far-reaching / to go far / distant / distance / removed
25-49	遠	162	yüan	far away / distant / removed
25-50	曰	73	yüeh	call / [further] described as // means / implies
25-51	反	29	fan	return[ing] / return to the root or original place / revert / turn back // opposite
25-52	故	66	ku	thus / therefore / hence
25-53	道	162	tao	Tao [is]
25-54	大	37	ta	great
25-55	天	37	t'ien	Heaven [is]
25-56	大	37	ta	great
25-57	地	32	ti	earth [is]
25-58	大	37	ta	great
25-59	王	95	wang	king / royalty / ~the highest aspect of man >Alt: *jan* (man, people, human)——Fu I
25-60	亦	8	yi	also
25-61	大	37	ta	great
25-62	域	32	yü	region / world / universe / realm // a limit >Alt: *kuo* (country)——MWT
25-63	中	2	chung	middle / within }} within the empire / in the universe / in the realm
25-64	有	74	yu	there are
25-65	四	31	ssu	four
25-66	大	37	ta	great[s] / greatness[es] / great ones
25-67	而	126	erh	and
25-68	王	95	wang	the king / royalty / >*wang* (king) implies *jan* (man) >Alt: *jan* (man, person)
25-69	居	44	chü	occupies / dwells / to be in / inhabits / counts on
25-70	其	12	ch'i	he / she / it
25-71	一	1	yi	one / unity
25-72	焉	86a	yen	there }}} is one of them
25-73	人	9a	jên	man / humans >Alt: *wang* (king)
25-74	法	85	fa	follows / imitates / takes after / models / patterns itself / emulates // the law / rules [after]
25-75	地	32	ti	earth
25-76	地	32	ti	earth
25-77	法	85	fa	follows / imitates / takes after / models / patterns itself / emulates // the law / rules [after]
25-78	天	37	t'ien	Heaven
25-79	天	37	t'ien	Heaven
25-80	法	85	fa	follows / imitates / takes after / models / patterns itself / emulates // the law / rules [after]
25-81	道	162	tao	Tao
25-82	道	162	tao	Tao
25-83	法	85	fa	follows / imitates / takes after / models / patterns itself / emulates // the law / rules [after]

25-84	自	132	tzu	self
25-85	然.	86	jan	same / like }} nature / Nature / itself / its own nature / "naturally so" / "self-becoming" / "its own way" / the Natural / natural to itself

[1] **Chou hsing**: "Universal going out" or "everywhere circulating" describes the way Tao operates. This can be interpreted as (a) "Circulating everywhere means that there is nowhere it does not reach" (Wang Pi Commentary), (b) Tao is all-pervasive and completes everything, or (c) Tao moves in a cyclical motion and completes everything by return.

VERSE 26

26-01	重	166	chung	Heavy / weighty / solid // genuine / real // gravity / substantial / important / (serious) / ~associated with the characteristics of generosity, stability, honesty
26-02	為	87	wei	is / makes / acts
26-03	輕	159	ch'ing	light[s] / lightness / frivolous / easy / flimsy / "not taken seriously"
26-04	根.	75	kên	root / origin / initial cause / foundation / support
26-05	靜	119	ching	tranquil / serene / quiet / still / repose
26-06	為	87	wei	is / make / act
26-07	躁	157	tsao	restless / agitated / agitation / rashness / hasty / moving / busy
26-08	君.	30	chün	master / lord / prince / ruler }} is master of the restless >Alt: *kan* (root, foundation)—Wang Pi Commentary
26-09	是	72a	shih	(this)
26-10	以	9a	yi	(for) }} therefore / thus
26-11	聖	128a	shêng	holy
26-12	人	9a	jên	man }} sage[s] >Alt: *chün tzu* (perfect man, superior man, nobleman, ruler)
26-13	終	120	chung	all
26-14	日	72	jih	day
26-15	行。	144	hsing	walks / steps / goes forward / travel[ing]
26-16	不	1	pu	does not / not / never
26-17	離	172	li	leave / depart / separate from / distance / part from / far from / abandon / ~let out of sight
26-18	輜	159	tzu	cart / wagon[s] / baggage-wagon
26-19	重.	166	chung	weight[y] / heavy // important / severe }} heavily-laden carts / supplies / "equipment" [1]
26-20	雖	172	sui	though / even though / even / although
26-21	有	74	yu	has / he has / in
26-22	榮	75	jung	magnificent / glorious / beautiful / splendor >Alt: *ying* (camp, hostel, palace, watchtower) >Alt: *huan* (guarded, protected)—MWT
26-23	觀.	147	kuan	sights / scenes / spectacles / view / to look / watch >Alt: *kuan* (camp, inn, palace) }}} "lives amidst luxury" (Ku) / "possesses gorgeous palaces" (Chalmers)
26-24	燕	86b	yen	calm / composed / peaceful / at ease // swallow / a feast
26-25	處	141	ch'u	sit / stop / stay / dwell / rest // nest }} >lit: "swallow's nest"—chamber of concubines / leisurely / rest peacefully / stay at ease
26-26	超	156	ch'ao	indifferent / undisturbed / aloof / "above worries" / unattached / unconcerned / avoid [2]
26-27	然.	86	jan	manner
26-28	奈	37	nai	(____) / "with what means?"
26-29	何	9	ho	(____) }} how / what / why / for what / how could [?]

26-30	萬	140	wan	ten thousand
26-31	乘	4	ch'êng	chariots }} ~a powerful country
26-32	之	4	chih	's / of
26-33	主	3	chu	master / ruler / lord }}}} ~ruler of a great nation
26-34	而	126	erh	yet
26-35	以	9a	yi	(as to) / (of)
26-36	身	158	shên	person / himself / his own person / his body / (in public) [behave / act]
26-37	輕	159	ch'ing	lighthearted / too light / lightly / frivolous / make light of }} display his lightness +Alt: add yu (than)
26-38	天	37	t'ien	Heaven
26-39	下	1	hsia	below }} the world / the empire / kingdom / everyone / all
26-40	輕	159	ch'ing	lighthearted / too light / lightly / frivolous / make light of / [acts] lightly / [to be] light
26-41	則	18	tsê	then
26-42	失	37	shih	lose / loses / lost / destroy / be separated from
26-43	本	75	pên	root / foundation / origin / base / support >Alt: ch'en (minister, subject) >Alt: ken (root, foundation)—Okada [3]
26-44	躁	157	tsao	restless / hasty action / rash / agitated / busy
26-45	則	18	tsê	then
26-46	失	37	shih	lose / lost / destroy / be separated from
26-47	君	30	chün	ruler / [lord / master[y][ship] / rulership / command / (the throne) [4]

[1] *Tzu chung*: "Baggage-wagon" implies a heavy load; may represent the inner treasure   >Alt: Ho Shang Kung says: *tzu* (baggage) = *ching* (tranquility). *Ching chung*: tranquility and sedateness / inner calm / composure / "peace within" (Ku)

[2] [20-27] "It is only when he is safely behind walls and watchtowers that he rests peacefully and is above worries." (Lau); "In the midst of honor and glory / He lives leisurely, undisturbed." (Yutang)

[3] *Ch'ing tsê shih pên*: "Lightness will lose the foundation." (Lin); "one who acts lightly loses his foundation." (Chen)

[4] *Tsao tsê shih chün*: "Rashness will lose the lord." (Lin); "In hasty action, self-mastery is lost." (Yutang); "To be restless is to lose one's control." (Feng)

VERSE 27

27-01	善	30	shan	Good / excellent / skillful / one adept at / well- / (*dharma*—"in accord with natural law")
27-02	行	144	hsing	traveler / walker / runner / to step / to go / traveling / walking / path }} "good works" (Cleary)
27-03	無	86	wu	no / without / [leaves] no
27-04	轍	159b	ch'ê	track / rut / wheel ruts
27-05	迹	162	chi	trace / footprints / hoofprints // vestiges / results
27-06	善	30	shan	good / excellent / skillful / one adept at
27-07	言	149	yen	speaker / speech / words / talking
27-08	無	86	wu	no / without / [leaves / makes / reveals] no
27-09	瑕	95	hsia	flaw / blemish / slip-ups / imperfection [for / for finding]
27-10	謫	149	chai	error / attack / reproach }} "grounds for blame"
27-11	善	30	shan	good / excellent / skillful
27-12	數	66	shu	count[ers][ing] / reckoner / accountant / calculation / analysis / plan >Alt: *chi* (counters) [uses / needs]

27-13	不	1	pu	no / not / without / does not
27-14	用	101	yung	use / utilize / make use of
27-15	籌	118	ch'ou	counting / tally / calculate / counter
27-16	策 .	118	ts'ê	bamboo slips / counting rods / calculator }} "schemes" (Wing)	[1]
27-17	善	30	shan	good / excellent / well-
27-18	閉	169	pi	shut door / shutting / lock / closing / safe [needs / uses]
27-19	無	86	wu	no / not / without / does not [use]
27-20	關	169	kuan	bolts / latches / ~horizontal bar on a gate [and]
27-21	楗	75	chien	bar / keys / ~vertical bar on a gate
27-22	而	126	erh	and / yet
27-23	不	1	pu	not / none / no one
27-24	可	30	k'o	can / able
27-25	開 .	169	k'ai	open / open [what he closes]
27-26	善	30	shan	good / excellent / dharmic / well-
27-27	結	120	chieh	bindings / tying / knots / tied knots [needs / uses]
27-28	無	86	wu	no / without / [uses / needs] no
27-29	繩	120	shêng	rope / cord
27-30	約	120	yo	string
27-31	而	126	erh	and / yet
27-32	不	1	pu	none / not / no [one]
27-33	可	30	k'o	can / able
27-34	解 .	148	chieh	loosen / unfasten / untie [it]
27-35	是	72a	shih	(this)
27-36	以	9a	yi	(for) }} therefore / hence / thus
27-37	聖	128a	shêng	holy
27-38	人	9a	jên	man }} the sage[s]
27-39	常	50	ch'ang	always / eternal
27-40	善	30	shan	good / goodness / excellent [at]
27-41	救	66	chiu	rescue / save / take care of / saving / rescuing [all / his]
27-42	人 。	9a	jên	people / men / humans / others
27-43	故	66	ku	for // cause / reason / purpose / therefore / hence
27-44	無	86	wu	no / without / no one
27-45	棄	75	ch'i	reject[s] / outcast / abandon / throw out / forsake / waste[d]
27-46	人 .	9a	jên	people / men / humans
27-47	常	50	ch'ang	always
27-48	善	30	shan	good / goodness / excellent / dharmic
27-49	救	66	chiu	rescue / save / take care of / saving / rescuing
27-50	物 .	93	wu	things / all things / beings / (the physical world)
27-51	故	66	ku	for / therefore // cause / reason / purpose / therefore / hence
27-52	無	86	wu	no / without / none

27-53	棄	75	ch'i	reject / abandon / outcast / throw out / forget / waste[d]
27-54	物	93	wu	things / all things / beings / (the physical world)
27-55	是	72a	shih	this is
27-56	謂	149	wei	called
27-57	襲	145	hsi	follow[ing] / practice // conceal[ed] / cloak / cover // penetrate / force / steal [2]
27-58	明	72	ming	light / the light / enlightenment / mystical vision / shine / luminous / illumined / brilliant // brilliance / insight / discernment / awareness / understanding / wisdom [3]
27-59	故	66	ku	for / therefore / hence // cause / reason / purpose >Alt: *erh* (and, yet)—MWT
27-60	善	30	shan	good / goodness / excellent / dharmic
27-61	人	9a	jên	man / person
27-62	者	125	chê	(he) / (the one) / it
27-63	不	1	pu	not / no / lacking
27-64	善	30	shan	good / goodness / excellent / dharmic }} bad
27-65	人	9a	jên	person / man / woman
27-66	之	4	chih	's / of / his / her
27-67	師	50b	shih	teacher / instructor / tutor / instruct / model // master / sage / leader
27-68	不	1	pu	not / no / lacking
27-69	善	30	shan	good / goodness / excellent / dharmic }} bad
27-70	人	9a	jên	person / man / woman
27-71	者	4	chih	's / of / his / her
27-72	善	30	shan	good / goodness / excellent / dharmic
27-73	人	9a	jên	person / man / woman
27-74	之	4	chih	's / of / his / her
27-75	資	154	tzu	material / lesson / resources / raw material / valuables / property / capital / "charge" / something that leads to gain (such as a lesson)
27-76	不	1	pu	not
27-77	貴	154	kuei	esteem / value / honor / revere
27-78	其	12	ch'i	one's / his / her
27-79	師	50b	shih	teacher / instructor / tutor / model // master / sage / leader
27-80	不	1	pu	not / no
27-81	愛	61	ai	care for / love / cherish // "be sparing of" (Duy)
27-82	其	12	ch'i	one's / his / her
27-83	資	154	tzu	material / lesson / resources / raw material / valuables / property
27-84	雖	172	sui	even though / although
27-85	智	72	chih	wise / clever / intelligent / knowledgeable / wisdom
27-86	大	37	ta	great / greatly
27-87	迷	162	mi	confused / deluded / perplexed / misguided / "utterly lost" / "on the wrong road"
27-88	是	72a	shih	this is
27-89	謂	149	wei	called
27-90	要	146	yao	essential / significant / crucial / important / crux / "chief" (Duy) // want / need / necessary / "distant" (Pine)

27-91	妙	38	miao	spiritual / mystery / secret / sublime / subtle / mysterious >Alt: *miao* (peer, look at)—MWT }}} "this is an essential tenet of Tao" (Wu) [4]

[1] **[1–16]**

A) The good (dharmic) traveler follows no set route. The good speaker harms no one with his words. The good strategist follows no set plan.

B) A true journey has no set route. A true word has no false meaning. A true plan has no calculation.

C) To follow the truth, abandon all set rules. To speak the truth, abandon all outer knowledge. To know the truth, abandon all preconceived ideas.

[2] *Hsi*: to enter or secure by deceptive or secretive means, thus connoting an invasion, attack at night, penetration, etc.

[3] *Hsi ming*: "following one's discernment" (Lau); "following the guidance of the inner light" (Wu); "stealing the Light" (Yutang); "inherited enlightenment" (Lin) (See INTRO, p. 4.)

[4] Last four lines are out of place and could be moved.

VERSE 28

28-01	知	111	chih	Know / to know / be aware of / recognize / he who knows / conscious of
28-02	其	12	ch'i	one's / his / her / the / (your) }} he who knows / one who understands
28-03	雄	172	hsiung	male / manhood / masculine [way] / virile / "strength of men" (Feng) // male bird / cock // "thrust of yang" (Ku) / ~things symbolized by the masculine—active, outward
28-04	守	40	shou	keep / by keeping / hold / cling / hold firm // maintain / abide in / observe / preserve / sustain
28-05	其	12	ch'i	one's / his / her / (what is)
28-06	雌	172	tz'u	female / feminine [way] / womanhood / "a woman's care" (Feng) // (yin) // ~things symbolized by the female—passive, inward
28-07	為	87	wei	act / make / be / becomes / role of }}}} keep to the role of the female
28-08	天	37	t'ien	Heaven
28-09	下	1	hsia	below }} the world / the empire
28-10	谿	150	ch'i	valley / ravine / river / stream / channel / canyon / ~feminine principle—receptive, passive, humble >Alt: *hsi* (maid, house servant)—Tunhuang
28-11	為	87	wei	act / make / be / become / being / [if] you are
28-12	天	37	t'ien	Heaven
28-13	下	1	hsia	below }} the world / the empire
28-14	谿	150	ch'i	valley / ravine / river / stream / channel / canyon / ~feminine principle—receptive, passive, humble >Alt: *hsi* (maid, house servant)—Tunhuang
28-15	常	50	ch'ang	eternal / everlasting / constant / ancient
28-16	德	60b	tê	Te / [path of] Te / power / virtue }} ~one's original character
28-17	不	1	pu	not / no / never / without / don't
28-18	離	172	li	depart[ing] / leave / desert / quit him / separate / lose / digress / swerve // cut up }} endure / prevail }}}} "ever true and unswerving" (Feng)
28-19	復	60	fu	revert / restore / return / come back
28-20	歸	77	kuei	return / send back / again
28-21	於	70	yü	to / as / to [the state of] / to
28-22	嬰	39	ying	infant
28-23	兒	10	erh	child / baby }} infancy / newborn / (innocence)
28-24	知	111	chih	know / be conscious of / aware of / recognize

28-25	其	12	ch'i	one's / his / her / the }} one who understands
28-26	白	106a	pai	white / whiteness / pure / ~bright / ~things symbolized by white
28-27	守	40	shou	keep / keeps to / hold / cling / hold firm // maintain / abide in / observe / preserve / sustain
28-28	其	12	ch'i	one's / his / her / the
28-29	黑	203	hei	black / blackness / "defiled" / ~dark / ~symbols of black
28-30	為	87	wei	acts / makes / becomes / role
28-31	天	37	t'ien	Heaven
28-32	下	1	hsia	below }} the world / the empire ['s]
28-33	式	56	shih	form / rule / model / pattern / measure / example / exemplar / "instrument"
28-34	為	87	wei	acts / makes / becomes / being / [if] you are / as
28-35	天	37	t'ien	Heaven
28-36	下	1	hsia	below }} the world / the empire ['s]
28-37	式	56	shih	form / rule / model / pattern / example
28-38	常	50	ch'ang	always / eternal / constant / everlasting / ancient / permanent
28-39	德	60b	tê	Te / power / virtue
28-40	不	1	pu	not / no / never / does not
28-41	忒	61	t'ê	fail / faulty / faulter / err / erring / deviate from / go awry / be wanting }} endure / prevail
28-42	復	60	fu	revert / restore / return / come back
28-43	歸	77	kuei	return / send back / again / [and you will] return
28-44	於	70	yü	to / as / to [the state of]
28-45	無	86	wu	without / no / none / non- / [where there are] no
28-46	極	75b	chi	limits / extreme / end / ultimate / extreme boundary // perfection }} infinite / unlimited / boundless
28-47	知	111	chih	know / aware / conscious of
28-48	其	12	ch'i	one's / his / her / (the) / what is }} one who understands
28-49	榮	75	jung	glory / honor / glorious / illustrious / beautiful / splendor [but]
28-50	守	40	shou	keep / hold / cling / hold firm // maintain / abide in / observe / preserve / familiar with
28-51	其	12	ch'i	one's / his / her / [to] role of
28-52	辱	160	ju	humility / lowly / lowness / obscurity // dishonor / disgrace / insult / shame / ignoble
28-53	為	87	wei	acts / makes / becomes / being / [and] be / [one will] become
28-54	天	37	t'ien	Heaven
28-55	下	1	hsia	below }} the world / the empire ['s]
28-56	谷	150	ku	valley / ravine / channel / canyon / "fountain" }}}} become the world's ravine / "be open to the world" (Cleary) [1]
28-57	為	87	wei	acts / makes / becomes / being
28-58	天	37	t'ien	Heaven
28-59	下	1	hsia	below }} the world / the empire ['s]
28-60	谷	150	ku	valley / ravine
28-61	常	50	ch'ang	always / eternal / everlasting / constant / permanent
28-62	德	60b	tê	Te / power / virtue

28-63	乃	4	nai	then / (being) / will be / is
28-64	足	157	tsu	enough / satisfied / suffice / sufficient / full / "proficient"
28-65	復	60	fu	revert / restore / return / come back
28-66	歸	77	kuei	return / send back / again
28-67	於	70	yü	to / as / to [the state of]
28-68	樸	75	p'u	purity / simplicity / one's natural state / genuineness / "uncarved block" / uncarved wood [2]
28-69	樸	75	p'u	purity / simplicity / one's natural state / "uncarved block"
28-70	散	66	san	scatter / disperse / separate / dismiss / split / broken up / shatter / break up / diversify / dissipate[d]
28-71	則	18	tsê	then [it]
28-72	為	87	wei	becomes / acts / makes / do / becomes useful / shaped into
28-73	器	30	ch'i	vessel[s] / utensil[s] / concrete thing / tools
28-74	聖	128a	shêng	holy
28-75	人	9a	jên	man }} sage
28-76	用	101	yung	uses / makes use of / is used / employs / utilizes / in the hands of
28-77	之	4	chih	them / he / she / it X Alt: omit—MWT
28-78	則	18	tsê	then
28-79	為	87	wei	acts / makes / makes use of [these] / becomes / [they] become
28-80	官	40	kuan	officers / an official / magistrates
28-81	長	168	ch'ang	endure / last long // leader / chief }} head official / long-lasting officers
28-82	故	66	ku	for / therefore / hence / thus
28-83	大	37	ta	great / greatest / master / best
28-84	制	18	chih	ruler / ruling / govern[or][ing][ment] / well-regulated // tailor / fashioner / carving / cutting
28-85	不	1	pu	not / no / does not / not done by
28-86	割	18	ko	injure / harm / mutilate // cut / cut up / cut into pieces / hack / divide / split / sever / carve // ~cut off people from their own heart [3]

[1] **Wei t'ien hsia ku**: "becomes the world's valley." One who understands his own glory, his own perfection, is naturally humble, and plays out his own role in the world. By this humility he becomes "Heaven's river," a conduit of grace, an instrument through which the virtue of Heaven can flow.

[2] **P'u**: "primal simplicity" / "Virginal Block" (Blakney) / "natural integrity of uncarved wood" (Yutang) / >"condition of nature untouched by culture" (Chen)

[3] **Ku ta chih pu ko**: "Hence, the greatest cutting does not sever." (Lau); "Therefore, the great ruler does not cut up." (Chan); "Therefore the great system will not be cut apart." (Lin); "Thus, 'A great tailor cuts little.'" (Feng); "Therefore a great institution does not mutilate." (Chen); "For, 'The Master himself does not carve.'" (Blakney); "Therefore the perfect government does not arise out of artificiality." (Jiyu); "The best administration accords with what is natural to things. Therefore, it does not divide, and each thing simply embraces its natural genuineness." —Kao Heng's Commentary (Ku)

(See NOTES)

VERSE 29

29-01	將	41	chiang	Take in hand / receive // will / if / when going to / (i.e., future action)
29-02	欲	76	yü	want / desire / tendencies / habits / ~general outlook
29-03	取	29	ch'ü	take / take over / take hold of / govern / conquer }}} "trying to govern" (Pine)

29-04	天	37	t'ien	Heaven
29-05	下	1	hsia	below }} the world / the empire / the state / (natural world) / (environment)
29-06	而	126	erh	and / but / (with)
29-07	為	87	wei	act / make / do / act upon / do anything to / ~use of force / ~"impose an order on things alien to their inner rhythm" (Chen)
29-08	之 。	4	chih	it / he / she / them
29-09	吾	30	wu	I
29-10	見	147	chien	recognize / perceive / discover / see / know / think
29-11	其	1?	ch'i	him / she / it
29-12	不	1	pu	not / no / cannot
29-13	得	60a	tê	succeed / success / achieve / obtain / gain / benefit / get / attain }} cannot be done / fail
29-14	已 。	49	yi	end / finish / goal // cease / decline / "that is all" }}} won't reach the end / won't finish [1][2]
29-15	天	37	t'ien	Heaven
29-16	下	1	hsia	below }} the world / the empire / (natural world)
29-17	神	113	shên	sacred / God's [own] / soul / spirit / something divine / transcendent / "most sublime" / mysterious / >lit: "extend" + "Heaven" ("the extension of Heaven")
29-18	器 。	30	ch'i	vessel / bowl / utensil / thing / entity / instrument }} spiritual thing / sacred vessel
29-19	不	1	pu	not / no / nothing
29-20	可	30	k'o	can / able / should }} should not be
29-21	為	87	wei	acted upon / done to it / tampered with / contrived / control / try to change / make / made / act }}} "it cannot be made (by human interference)" (Yutang) / "it cannot be forced" (Pine)
29-22	也 。	5	yeh	! / indeed +Alt: add pu k'o chih ye (it cannot be grasped / seized)
29-23	為	87	wei	acts upon / does anything to it / tampers / try to change / control / make
29-24	者	125	chê	it / (he) / (she) / (the one)
29-25	敗	66	pai	ruin[s] / destroy[s] / defect / mar / spoil / fail
29-26	之 。	4	chih	it / he / she
29-27	執	32	chih	holds / take hold of / grasp / seize // manage
29-28	者	125	chê	it / (he) / (she) / (the one)
29-29	失	37	shih	lose / loses / lost / destroy / be separated from
29-30	之	4	chih	it / he / she
29-31	故	66	ku	thus / therefore / hence / for / (~according to natural law)
29-32	物	93	wu	things / beings / all this
29-33	或	62	huo	some / sometimes / likely / perhaps / (either) / (a time for) / (a time to)
29-34	行	144	hsing	lead / go out / travel / ahead / go forward / move forward / step / operate
29-35	或	62	huo	some / other / sometimes / (or)
29-36	隨 。	170	sui	follow / follow behind / behind / imitate / comply with
29-37	或	62	huo	some / other / sometimes
29-38	歔	76	hsü	sigh / breathe out / blow hot / breathe gently / "breathe a sigh of relief" // make warm
29-39	或	62	huo	some / other / sometimes
29-40	吹 。	30	ch'ui	breathe in / blow cold / breathe hard / pant violently // make cold

29-41	或	62	huo	some / other / sometimes
29-42	強	57	ch'iang	forceful / strong / [get] stronger / strength / robust / [grow in] strength
29-43	或	62	huo	some / other / sometimes
29-44	羸	123	lei	weak / weakness / thin / emaciated / decay XXX Alt: omit *ch'iang huo lei*—MWTB
29-45	或	62	huo	some / other / sometimes
29-46	挫	64	ts'o	break / destroy / overcome / oppress / "carry on" / defeat / shock >Alt: *tsai* (succeed, fill up, expand, a lot, be up, support; begin, start)—MWT
29-47	或	62	huo	some / other / sometimes
29-48	隳	170	hui	fail / give in / succumb / fall / be down / "lose heart" / be destroyed / end / collapse
29-49	是	72a	shih	(this)
29-50	以	9a	yi	(for) }} therefore / that is why / thus / hence
29-51	聖	128a	shêng	holy
29-52	人	9a	jên	man }} sage
29-53	去	28	ch'ü	abandons / avoids / leaves / rejects / discards / spurns / gets rid of / withdraws from / eschews
29-54	甚	99	shên	excess / extremes / "pleasures" / "overdoing" / "too much emphasis" (Duy)
29-55	去	28	ch'ü	abandons / avoids / leaves / rejects / discards / gets rid of / withdraws from / casts off
29-56	奢	37	shê	extravagance / extravagant / elaborate / "sweeping judgments" (Blakney) / "gaiety"
29-57	去	28	ch'ü	abandons / leaves / rejects / discards
29-58	泰	85	t'ai	excess[ive] / indulgence / "a life of excess" / extremes / arrogance / pride / "grandeur"

[1] **Pu tê yi**: an idiomatic expression meaning "to find oneself in a position of constraint in which one has to do things one would rather not do" (Duy)

[2] **Chiang yü ch'ü . . . ch'i pu tê yi**: "Does anyone want to take the world and do what he wants with it? I do not see how he can succeed." (Wu); "Do you think you can take over the universe and improve it? I do not believe it can be done." (Feng); "Trying to control the world? . . . I see you won't succeed." (Addis)

VERSE 30

30-01	以	9a	yi	With / according to / (one in harmony with) / those who use
30-02	道	162	tao	Tao
30-03	佐	9b	tso	assist / aid / guide / "propose to help"
30-04	人	9a	jên	people[s] / men
30-05	主	3	chu	master / ruler / lord }} ruler / leader / lord of men }}} "use the Tao to help your king" (Pine)
30-06	者	125	chê	(he) / (she) / it / (the one)
30-07	不	1	pu	not / no / oppose / does not [intimidate]
30-08	以	9a	yi	use
30-09	兵	12	ping	arms / weapons / military / military conquests // soldiers
30-10	強	57	ch'iang	force / strength / rule / use of force }} show of arms / military might [1]
30-11	天	37	t'ien	Heaven
30-12	下	1	hsia	below }} the world }}}} "override the world with force of arms" (Wu) / "dominate the world with force"
30-13	其	12	ch'i	he / she / it / those
30-14	事	6	shih	actions / affairs / way of life / lifestyle / conduct // things

30-15	好	38	hao	usual / usually / liable to / apt to / wont to / certain to / likely to / invite / brings / "welcomes"
30-16	還	162	huan	return / requital / recoil / rebound / come back / [equal] results / reward / repayment / retaliation / turn against / recoil / "apt to backfire" // "resistance" / retribution // repeat
30-17	師	50b	shih	army / troops / legions
30-18	之	4	chih	's / its
30-19	所	63	so	place / position
30-20	處	141	ch'u	stop / stays with / dwells / occupies }} stationed }}}} where armies are camped
30-21	荊	140	ching	briars / brambles / stickers
30-22	棘	75a	chi	thorns }} thorny bushes
30-23	生	100	shêng	grow / spring up / arise / produce
30-24	焉	86a	yen	there / in that place / (where)
30-25	大	37	ta	great XXX Alt: omit v. 30:25–32—MWT
30-26	軍	159	chün	war / battle / campaign / "the army has passed"
30-27	之	4	chih	's / its
30-28	後	60	hou	aftermath / wake / follows / followed by / result / after / behind / then
30-29	必	61	pi	surely / invariably / (always)
30-30	有	74	yu	are / there is / arises / emerges / appears
30-31	凶	17	hsiung	misfortune / calamity / bad / lean
30-32	年	51	nien	crops / harvest / (years) }} famine / "year of dearth"
30-33	善	30	shan	good / excellent / skillful / [one who is] good / good [man] / good [general]
30-34	有	125	chê	(the one) / (he) / (she) / it }} ~commander >Alt: yu (to have)—Wang Pi Commentary
30-35	果	75	kuo	resolute / has resolution / be resolved / aims / effects / "achieves his purpose" / effective / "bring results" / "attains your purpose" / "get the fruits of your actions" [2]
30-36	而	126	erh	and / and then
30-37	已	49	yi	stops / cease / finish / decline / (only) / bring to a conclusion }} that is all
30-38	不	1	pu	not / no
30-39	敢	66	kan	dares / ventures / presumption
30-40	以	9a	yi	thereby / accordingly / thus / hence
30-41	取	29	ch'ü	take hold of / take / seize / accept / prefer / seek / rely upon / "take the path of"
30-42	強	57	ch'iang	force / by force / strength / dominate / the strong / }} intimidate [1]
30-43	果	75	kuo	resolute / have resolution / be resolved / "get results" / "attain your purpose"
30-44	而	126	erh	and
30-45	勿	20	wu	not
30-46	矜	110	ching	brag / boast / self-approve / arrogant / proud
30-47	果	75	kuo	resolute / have resolution / be resolved / "get results" / "attain your purpose"
30-48	而	126	erh	and / yet
30-49	勿	20	wu	not / without / do not
30-50	伐	9	fa	boast / show off / brag / exalt // (cut down, chastise, destroy others)
30-51	果	75	kuo	resolute / have resolution / be resolved / "get results" / "attain your purpose"
30-52	而	126	erh	and / yet

30-53	勿	20	wu	not [be]
30-54	驕.	187	chiao	proud / arrogant / haughty / [take] pride [in it]
30-55	果	75	kuo	resolute / have resolution / be resolved / "get results" / "attain your purpose"
30-56	而	126	erh	and / yet
30-57	不	1	pu	not / without / do not / un-
30-58	得	60a	tê	obtain / gain / possess / benefit / receive / get / attain }} with reluctance
30-59	已.	49	yi	!
30-60	果	75	kuo	resolute / have resolution / be resolved / "get results" / "attain your purpose"
30-61	而	126	erh	and / yet
30-62	勿	20	wu	not / without / does not
30-63	強.	57	ch'iang	dominate / overpower / use force / strong / compel / "violent" [1]
30-64	物	93	wu	things / beings
30-65	壯	33	chuang	flourish / reach prime / full-grown / overgrown / "overdeveloped" // "extending beyond what is natural" (Ming)
30-66	則	18	tsê	then
30-67	老	125	lao	decay / become old / grow old / age / [hasten] decay
30-68	是	72a	shih	this is
30-69	謂	149	wei	called / (means) / (known as)
30-70	不	1	pu	not / no / un- / without / contrary to / going against / not [following]
30-71	道.	162	tao	Tao
30-72	不	1	pu	not / no / un- / without / contrary to / going against / not [following]
30-73	道	162	tao	Tao
30-74	早	72	tsao	soon / early
30-75	已.	49	yi	end / comes to an end / cease / finish / decline / destruction / perish / > Compare v. 30:68–75 with v. 55:74–81 [3]

[1] **Chi'ang** ("force," "forceful means or actions"), as used in this context, refers to using one's power in a way that is unnatural; that is contrary to natural law (Tao). (See NOTES)

[2] **Kuo** is variously interpreted as *chi* (to help, to save) —Wang Pi Commentary; *ch'eng* (to complete)—Ssu-ma Kuang Commentary; *sheng* (to overcome)—Erh Ya Commentary (Ku)

[3] (See NOTES for additional translations of v. 30:64–75)

V E R S E   3 1

31-01	夫	37	fu	Even / because / truly / "of all things"
31-02	佳	9	chia	excellent / fine / elegant / beautiful / ornamental >Alt: *wei* (only) X Alt: omit—MWT
31-03	兵	12	ping	arms / soldiers / weapons [1]
31-04	者	125	chê	(the one) / (he) / it
31-05	不	1	pu	not / no / un-
31-06	祥	113	hsiang	good fortune / good omen / auspicious }} evil / ill omen / fear / "augur evil"
31-07	之	4	chih	it
31-08	器.	30	ch'i	tool / instrument / vessel / utensil / implement
31-09	物	93	wu	things / beings / creatures / men / [even] things

31-10	或	62	huo	likely / perhaps / some / therefore / seem to >Alt: *chiu* (forever) (Duy)
31-11	惡	61	wu	detest / hate / hated / loathe / detest / disdain / avoid >>Etm: "ugly" + "heart"
31-12	之 ●	4	chih	them / (by men)
31-13	故	66	ku	thus / therefore / hence
31-14	有	74	yu	has / to have / possess
31-15	道	162	tao	Tao }} one who possesses Tao / a man of Tao
31-16	者	125	chê	(he) / (she) / it / (the one)
31-17	不	1	pu	not / no
31-18	處 ●	141	ch'u	stop / rest / stay / dwell there / occupy / deal / "set his heart upon them" (Wu) }} turns away from / spurns / does not use them / avoids
31-19	君	30	chün	Master / ruler / lord / (good) >All that follows is likely a commentary mixed in with the text—(Duy)
31-20	子	39	tzu	philosopher / infant / ruler / (person) }} a wise ruler / a wise man / nobleman / "gentleman"
31-21	居	44	chü	[at] home / (inhabit) / (occupy) / (be in) / in dwelling / in ordinary life
31-22	則	18	tsê	then
31-23	貴	154	kuei	honors / values / esteems / favor / give preference to / precedence
31-24	左 ●	48	tso	left / the left side / ~passive, weak, feminine side
31-25	用	101	yung	use / makes use of / employ / utilize / uses / bear / [when] using
31-26	兵	12	ping	arms / weapons // war / fighting // soldiers }} [when] at war / military occasions
31-27	則	18	tsê	then
31-28	貴	154	kuei	honors / values / esteems / favor / give preference to / precedence
31-29	右 ●	30	yu	right / the right side / ~active, strong, masculine side
31-30	兵	12	ping	arms / weapons // soldiers
31-31	者	125	chê	it / this
31-32	不	1	pu	not
31-33	祥	113	hsiang	fortunate / good fortune }} evil / ill omen
31-34	之	4	chih	it / his / among / 's
31-35	器 ●	30	ch'i	instruments / tools / utensils / vessels }}}} instruments of evil
31-36	非	175	fei	not / oppose / go against
31-37	君	30	chün	master / ruler / lord / (good)
31-38	子	39	tzu	philosopher / infant }} wise ruler / wise man / nobleman
31-39	之	4	chih	his / its
31-40	器 ●	30	ch'i	instruments / tools / utensils / vessels
31-41	不	1	pu	not / un- / [when] not
31-42	得	60a	tê	obtain / gain / possess / benefit / receive / get / attain
31-43	已	49	yi	avoid / cease / finish / decline // excess }} unavoidable / only if necessary / when compelled / if forced
31-44	而	126	erh	and / but / to
31-45	用	101	yung	use[s] / put to use / utilizes / bears / [will he] use
31-46	之 ●	4	chih	them / it

31-47	恬	61	t'ien	peace / calm / tranquility
31-48	淡	85a	tan	quiet / state of being quiet / dull / flat / restraint / detached
31-49	為	87	wei	makes / acts / causes / uses / to do so
31-50	上.	1	shang	best / best [policy] / best [principle] / superior / exalted / highest
31-51	勝	19	shêng	conquer[s] / victory / victorious / outdo / sustain / [even in] victory
31-52	而	126	erh	and / but
31-53	不	1	pu	not / no
31-54	美	123	mei	enjoy / delight in / beautiful // [seek] glory / boast / praise / praiseworthy / admire
31-55	而	126	erh	and / but
31-56	美	123	mei	enjoy / delight in / find beauty // glory / boast
31-57	之	4	chih	it
31-58	者。	125	chê	it / (he) / (she) / (the one)
31-59	是	72a	shih	(this)
31-60	樂	75	lo	enjoys / rejoices in / joy / happy / glad / likes / is pleased by / relishes
31-61	殺	79	sha	slay[ing] / kill / slaughter / the killing of
31-62	人.	9a	jên	people / men
31-63	夫	37	fu	truly
31-64	樂	75	lo	enjoys / one who enjoys / rejoices in / joy / happy / glad / likes / is pleased by / relishes
31-65	殺	79	sha	slay[ing] / kill / slaughter / the killing of
31-66	人	9a	jên	people / men
31-67	者。	125	chê	(he) / (she) / it }}}} he who enjoys the slaying of men
31-68	則	18	tsê	then
31-69	不	1	pu	not / will not / never
31-70	可	30	k'o	able / can
31-71	以	9a	yi	thus / thereby
31-72	得	60a	tê	obtain / gain / possess / benefit / receive / get / attain / exercise [his]
31-73	志	61	chih	wishes / desire / will / what he wants / ambition [to rule] }} succeed / be successful / exercise his will / "cannot expect to thrive" (Wu)
31-74	於	70	yü	in
31-75	天	37	t'ien	Heaven
31-76	下	1	hsia	below }} the world / the empire
31-77	矣.	111	yi	!
31-78	吉	30	chi	Fortunate / lucky / auspicious / happy / joyful
31-79	事	6	shih	occasions / activities / affairs / events / ceremonies }} celebrations / festivities
31-80	尚	42	shang	honor / esteem / favor / prefer // to wish / to add
31-81	左.	48	tso	left / left side / the left
31-82	凶	17	hsiung	unfortunate / bad fortune / inauspicious / sorrowful / mournful / calamity >Alt: *sang* (mourn)—MWT
31-83	事	6	shih	occasions / activities / affairs / ceremonies }} funerals
31-84	尚	42	shang	honor / esteem / favor / prefer

31-85	右.	30	yu	right / right side / the right
31-86	偏	9	p'ien	assistant / second
31-87	將	41	chiang	army
31-88	軍	159	chün	leader }}} second in command / second general / lieutenant
31-89	居	44	chü	stands [on] / occupies / takes the place on / is placed on / sits
31-90	左.	48	tso	left / the left side
31-91	上	1	shang	superior
31-92	將	41	chiang	army
31-93	軍	159	chün	leader }}} general / commander in chief
31-94	居	44	chü	stands [on] / occupies / takes the place on / is placed on / sits
31-95	右.	30	yu	right / the right side
31-96	言	149	yen	speak / says / words / that is to say / this means [2]
31-97	以	9a	yi	is like / accordingly / [arranged] like / [celebrated] like / "on a par with"
31-98	喪	30	sang	funeral / mournful / mourning / die
31-99	禮	113	li	ceremony [ies] / rite
31-100	處	141	ch'u	stop / dwell / stay / occupy / manage
31-101	之.	4	chih	it
31-102	殺	79	sha	kill / slay / slaughter / killing
31-103	人	9a	jên	people / men
31-104	之	4	chih	's / theirs
31-105	眾	143	chung	all / everything / many / a lot / all things / multitudes
31-106	以	9a	yi	(with) / accordingly
31-107	哀	30	ai	lament / grieve / grief / bewailed [with]
31-108	悲	61	pei	sorrow >>Etm: "go against" + "heart" ("that which goes against the heart")
31-109	泣	85	ch'i	weep / cry / lamentation }}}} "let us weep with sorrow and grief" >Alt: li (stand, come, arrive)—MWT
31-110	之.	4	chih	he / she / it / them
31-111	戰	62	chan	war / battle // to fight / fear / tremble
31-112	勝	19	shêng	victory / overcome }} upon a victory in war
31-113	以	9a	yi	thus / accordingly / therefore
31-114	喪	30	sang	funeral / mourning
31-115	禮	113	li	ceremony / rite }} wake
31-116	處	141	ch'u	treated [like] / observed / celebrated [like] // stop / dwells / occupies / placed
31-117	之.	4	chih	he / she / it / they [3]

[1] *Fu chia ping* (See NOTES)

[2] +Alt: add *chü shang shih tsê* after *yen* [v. 31-96]. *Chü* (being in, occupying, standing in); *shang* (superior, supreme, exalted, highest); *shi* (position); *tsê* (then).

[3] **[111–117]** "When victorious in battle, mark the occasion with the rite of a funeral." (Chen); "Hence, even a victory is a funeral." (Wu) / "When you win a war, you celebrate by mourning." (Cleary)

NOTE: Many commentators feel that this verse is corrupted due to its inconsistent style and content and because Wang Pi offered no commentary on it. Either Wang Pi suspected that this verse was a forgery and refused to comment on it or Wang Pi's commentary somehow got mixed in with the original text.

VERSE 32

32-01	道	162	tao	Tao	
32-02	常	50	ch'ang	eternal / everlasting / forever / constant / always / endless / ~Absolute	
32-03	無	86	wu	not / without / void of / has no } never	
32-04	名	30a	ming	name / (manifestations) / (definitions) }} nameless / undefined }}}} "Tao never had a name"	[1]
32-05	樸	75	p'u	purity / simplicity / one's natural state / "uncarved block" / uncarved wood	
32-06	雖	172	sui	though / however / although	
32-07	小	42	hsiao	small / subtle / insignificant / [its manifestations are] subtle	
32-08	天	37	t'ien	Heaven	
32-09	下	1	hsia	below }} the world	
32-10	莫	140	mo	not / cannot }}} no one in the world	
32-11	能	130	nêng	can / able >Alt: kan (dare, venture, presume)	
32-12	臣	131	ch'ên	rule over / subject / minister / master [it] / employ / command / use / "harness it" / subjugate [it]	
32-13	也	5	yeh	! / indeed ^^Alt: move v. 32:05–13 to v. 36	
32-14	侯	9	hou	princes / barons / dukes	
32-15	王	95	wang	kings / lords }} rulers / a lord	
32-16	若	140	jo	if / when	
32-17	能	130	nêng	can / able / have the ability to / would	
32-18	守	40	shou	hold / uphold / keep / keep [in accordance with] / abide [in] / >as a law—obey its decree / (hold to their own pure nature) / "retain its potency for good" (Blakney)	
32-19	之	4	chih	it	
32-20	萬	140	wan	ten thousand / all	
32-21	物	93	wu	things }} everything / everything in the world / the world	
32-22	將	41	chiang	will / will become / going to / (future action)	
32-23	自	132	tzu	themselves / by themselves / of their own accord / naturally	
32-24	賓	154	pin	honor / [pay] homage / "honor like a guest in one's house" / be as guests / submit / yield [to them] / resort [to them] / "say yes to him" (Kwok)	
32-25	天	37	t'ien	Heaven [and]	
32-26	地	32	ti	earth	
32-27	相	109	hsiang	mutually / together / "symmetric"	
32-28	合	30a	ho	join[ed][s] / combined / united / match / meet / come together / unite / harmony / "make love"	
32-29	以	9a	yi	thereby / hence / accordingly	
32-30	降	170	chiang	drip / fall / descend / send down / come into this world / drop / "bestow"	
32-31	甘	99	kan	sweet	
32-32	露	173	lu	dew / rain	
32-33	民	83	min	the people	

32-34	莫	140	**mo**	none / without
32-35	之	4	**chih**	their / it / men's
32-36	令	9	**ling**	law / an order / command // commanders }}} without being ordered
32-37	而	126	**erh**	and / but
32-38	自	132	**tzu**	of themselves / naturally / "take their course"
32-39	均 .	32	**chün**	harmony / peace / "equal vision" / cooperate / impartiality / fairness / evenly / get along [with each other]
32-40	始	38	**shih**	beginning / begin / at first / only when / "as soon as there was"
32-41	制	85	**chih**	rules / regulations / orders / regulate / manage / institutions // "it is cut" / distinction
32-42	有	74	**yu**	have / exist / becomes / there are
32-43	名 .	30a	**ming**	name / names / nameable / ~naming of things / ~words
32-44	名	30a	**ming**	name / names / nameable / ~naming of things / ~words
32-45	亦	8	**yi**	also / again / moreover }} keep naming things / more differences
32-46	既	71	**chi**	since / already / when // to finish / finished / all / at the end / (exhausted)
32-47	有 .	74	**yu**	exists / have
32-48	夫	37	**fu**	truly / (the end result) / even / then
32-49	亦	8	**yi**	also / in turn
32-50	將	41	**chiang**	act // about to / is going to / (future action) // receive / take in hand
32-51	知	111	**chih**	know / realize / be aware of / knowing [when to]
32-52	止 .	77	**chih**	stop / stand / anchor / abide / where to stop // limit >Alt: *chih* (it)
32-53	知	111	**chih**	know / realize / be aware of / knowing [when to] }}} know where to stop
32-54	止	77	**chih**	stop / stand / anchor / where to stop // limit >Alt: *chih* (it)
32-55	可	63	**so**	place / postion // reason / that which
32-56	以	30	**k'o**	can / able }} is the reason why
32-57	不	1	**pu**	no / there is no / [one can be] free from
32-58	殆	78	**tai**	danger / trouble / peril // approaching / near / soon / exhausted
32-59	譬	149	**p'i**	to illustrate / thus / as an analogy / the relations of / to picture / in the same way
32-60	道	162	**tao**	Tao
32-61	之	4	**chih**	's / its
32-62	在	32	**tsai**	to be / being / exist / presence [in] / alive
32-63	天	37	**t'ien**	Heaven
32-64	下 .	1	**hsia**	below }} the world
32-65	猶	94	**yu**	resembles / [may be] compared to / is to / is like / "imagine"
32-66	川	47	**ch'uan**	rivers / rivulets
32-67	谷	150	**ku**	streams
32-68	之	4	**chih**	them / it / (running)
32-69	於	70	**yü**	to / in / at / into
32-70	江	85	**chiang**	great rivers / river [and]
32-71	海 .	85	**hai**	ocean / the sea +Alt: add *ye* (!, indeed)

[1] *Tao ch'ang wu ming*: "The Tao of the Absolute has no name." (Wing); "The Tao has never had a name." (Pine)

VERSE 33				
33-01	知	111	chih	Know / understand / realize / aware / [he who / one who] knows
33-02	人	9a	jên	others / people / men
33-03	者	125	chê	(he) / (she) / it / (the one)
33-04	智.	72	chih	wise / intelligent / has wisdom / clever / learned / perceptive / knowing / ~knowledge of the outer world
33-05	自	132	tzu	self / himself / of himself / his person
33-06	知	111	chih	know / understand / realize / aware / [he who / one who] knows
33-07	者	125	chê	(he) / (she) / it / (the one)
33-08	明.	72	ming	enlightened / illumined / discernment / "with light" / wise / insight
33-09	勝	19	shêng	conquer / victorious / outdo / overcome / vanquish[es]
33-10	人	9a	jên	others / people / men
33-11	者	125	chê	(he) / (she) / it / (the one)
33-12	有	74	yu	has / possesses
33-13	力.	19	li	strength / physical strength / force[ful] / power }} requires force
33-14	自	132	tzu	self / himself / of himself
33-15	勝	19	shêng	conquer / victorious / outdo / overcome
33-16	者	125	chê	(he) / (she) / it / (the one)
33-17	強.	57	ch'iang	mighty / strong / powerful / good [1]
33-18	知	111	chih	know / understand / realize / aware / [he who / one who] knows
33-19	足	157	tsu	content[ment] / enough / sufficient / satisfied where one is / when he has enough
33-20	者	125	chê	(he) / (she) / it / (the one)
33-21	富.	40	fu	rich / abundant / wealthy / (has everything)
33-22	強	57	ch'iang	strong effort / force / strength >Alt: *ch'in* (perseverance, determination, vigor, diligence) [1]
33-23	行	144	hsing	act / go out }} acts with vigor / "forges ahead" / "boldly goes"
33-24	者	125	chê	(he) / (she) / it / (the one)
33-25	有	74	yu	has / is / possesses / ~is a sign of
33-26	志.	61	chih	resolution / will / willpower / "inner resolve" / "steady purpose" }} "succeeds"
33-27	不	1	pu	not
33-28	失	37	shih	loses / lost / be separated from / departs from
33-29	其	12	ch'i	his / her / its / their
33-30	所	63	so	position / place / station / center / "where one belongs" / place [with Tao] / "allotted place" / ~dharma }}}} "stays where he is" / "accepts his lot in life"
33-31	者	125	chê	(he) / (she) / it / (the one)
33-32	久.	4	chiu	lasts long / endures / will endure
33-33	死	78	ssu	dies / [he who] dies
33-34	而	126	erh	yet / still / then / yet [his power]
33-35	不	1	pu	not / does not
33-36	亡	61	wang	die / perish / cease >Alt: *wang* (forget, is forgotten)—MWT

33-37	者	125	chê	(he) / (she) / it / (the one) [has / enjoys]
33-38	壽 .	33	shou	lives long / lives on / longevity / immortal

[1] **Ch'iang** is usually used in a negative sense, meaning stiff and rigid (v. 76) or "forcing things," which means going against nature. Here, and in v. 52:57, it is used in a positive sense, meaning strength. (See NOTES, v. 30.)

VERSE 34

34-01	大	37	ta	Great / greatest
34-02	道	162	tao	Tao
34-03	氾	85	fan	all-pervading / flows everywhere / universal / broad / overflows / expansive / floods over / ~like the ocean / "drifts" / "floats and drifts" / "ambiguous" (Duy) [1]
34-04	兮	12	hsi	! / oh
34-05	其	12	ch'i	it / he / she
34-06	可	30	k'o	can / able / can [go] / (reach) / able [to move] / "how can it be turned . . ." (Wu)
34-07	左	48	tso	left / to the left
34-08	右 .	30	yu	right / to the right }}} "reaches in all directions"
34-09	萬	140	wan	ten thousand / all
34-10	物	93	wu	things / beings }} everything in the universe
34-11	恃	61	shih	rely upon / depend upon / trust >Alt: *shih* (help, wait upon)
34-12	之	4	chih	it
34-13	而	126	erh	thus / hence / thereby / for
34-14	生	100	shêng	life / produces / gives life / gives birth / born / bear / come forth / live
34-15	而	126	erh	and / yet
34-16	不	1	pu	not
34-17	辭 .	160	tz'u	refuse / deny / decline / reject / turn away from // dominate / claim authority / their master }} "holds nothing back" (Feng) XXX Alt: omit: v. 34:9–17—MWT
34-18	功	19	kung	merit / credit / success / work / task
34-19	成	62	ch'êng	finish / complete / accomplish / become / succeed / fulfillment / conclusion }} does its work / accomplishes its task / fulfills its purpose / when work is complete
34-20	不	1	pu	not / makes no [claim to it] / lays no [claim to it] / does not [appropriate]
34-21	名	30a	ming	name / (wanting a name or recognition) / (claiming credit / merit) X Alt: omit (Duy)
34-22	有 .	74	yu	it / to have / to be
34-23	衣	145	yi	clothe >Alt: *ai* (love, like, adore)—HSK
34-24	養	184	yang	nourish[es] / feed[s] / rear / bring up >Alt: *pei* (blanket, to cover) —Fu I
34-25	萬	140	wan	ten thousand / all
34-26	物	93	wu	things / beings }} everything in the universe
34-27	而	126	erh	and / yet
34-28	不	1	pu	not / no / without
34-29	為	87	wei	act / make / do / become / being / (claim) / (wanting to be)
34-30	主 .	3	chu	ruler / lord / owner / master over [them]
34-31	常	50	ch'ang	eternal / constantly / always / forever

34-32	無	86	wu	without / has no / free of
34-33	欲	76	yü	tendencies / desires / wants / needs / thought constructs / "mind or passion" >Alt: *wei* (action)—Kao Heng XXX Alt: omit v. 34:31–33
34-34	可	30	k'o	can / able / "allows"
34-35	名	30a	ming	name / named / be called / ~considered
34-36	於	70	yü	with / in / at / to
34-37	小	42	hsiao	small / the small / subtle / insignificant / the little
34-38	萬	140	wan	ten thousand / all
34-39	物	93	wu	things / beings }} everything in the universe
34-40	歸	77	kuei	return / revert / restore / again / come [to it]
34-41	焉	86a	yen	there / in that place / thereto }}}} "being the home of all things" (Yutang) / "return to it as their home" (Wu)
34-42	而	126	erh	and / but
34-43	不	1	pu	not
34-44	為	87	wei	act / make / do / become / makes [no claim to being]
34-45	主	3	chu	ruler / lord / owner / master / lord over [them]
34-46	可	30	k'o	can / able
34-47	名	30a	ming	name / named / be called / (considered)
34-48	為	87	wei	act / make / do / as / being
34-49	大	37	ta	great / the great
34-50	以	9a	yi	for / thereby / thus / accordingly / (it is because)
34-51	其	12	ch'i	he / it >Alt: *sheng jen* (holy man, sage)—HSK
34-52	終	120	chung	to the end / utmost / the last / fully / (because)
34-53	不	1	pu	not
34-54	自	132	tzu	self / personal / for himself
34-55	為	87	wei	act / make / do / become / strive / claim / (wish to be)
34-56	大	37	ta	great
34-57	故	66	ku	thus / hence / therefore / thereby
34-58	能	130	nêng	can / able
34-59	成	62	ch'êng	success / accomplish / achieve / realize / "fully realized" / to become
34-60	其	12	ch'i	his / her / its / the one
34-61	大	37	ta	great / greatness [2]

[1] *Fan*, from "water" + "cyclical"

[2] *Chung pu tzu wei ta ku nêng ch'eng ch'i ta*: Most interpreters suggest a causality here, whereby the sage or the Tao
becomes "great," or achieves "greatness," by not acting great. However, the sage and Tao are already great, their greatness has
already been achieved—that is why they do not need to act great.
Subject = Tao: "It is because it never attempts to be great that it succeeds in being great." (Lau); "By not making itself great, it can
do great things." (Addis)
Subject = Sage: "Just because the sage would never regard himself as great, he is able to attain his own greatness." (Lin); "(The
wise man) will never make a show of being great: And that is how his greatness is achieved." (Blakney)
Subject = You: "The highest end is reached through humility: through this you will come to know your own greatness." (Janwu);
"Follow the path to the end: don't act great—be great!" (Ming)

		VERSE 35		
35-01	執	32	**chih**	Take hold of / grasp / hold / "have in your hand" / manage / one who holds
35-02	大	37	**ta**	great / the great
35-03	象	152	**hsiang**	form / figure / image / symbol / idea / "the image without image" // elephant }} ~Tao [1]
35-04	天	37	**t'ien**	Heaven
35-05	下	1	**hsia**	below }} the world / the empire / all below Heaven / all things
35-06	往	60	**wang**	follow / will come / resort to / attract / flock / those who resort to // go / go on >>Etm: "walk" + "field"
35-07	往	60	**wang**	follow / will come / attract / flock // go / go on
35-08	而	126	**erh**	and / but
35-09	不	1	**pu**	not / without / ~beyond
35-10	害	40	**hai**	harm / injury / hurt / offend / damage / encounter harm / suffer harm / "collapse"
35-11	安	40	**an**	content[ment] / enjoy / satisfy / happiness
35-12	平	51	**p'ing**	peace / peaceful / serene / in harmony / concord // even / equal
35-13	泰	85	**t'ai**	in abundance / health / good health >Alt: *t'ai* (rest, comfort, security)
35-14	樂	75	**lo**	music / [when there is] music / song
35-15	與	134	**yü**	with / and
35-16	餌	184	**erh**	cake / pastries / food / tasty food / fine food
35-17	過	162	**kuo**	pass / pass by / passing / passersby
35-18	客	40	**k'o**	strangers / people / guests }} travelers / those passing by
35-19	止	77	**chih**	stop / stay / [cause to / will] stop / pause / delay
35-20	道	162	**tao**	Tao
35-21	之	4	**chih**	's / its
35-22	出	17	**ch'u**	go out / give out / go forth / (uttered by) / (spoken by)
35-23	口	30	**k'ou**	mouth }} words / speaks >Alt: *yen* (words)—Fu I }}}} word spoken about Tao
35-24	淡	85a	**tan**	tasteless / flat / insipid
35-25	乎	4	**hu**	! / oh
35-26	其	12	**ch'i**	it
35-27	無	86	**wu**	without / void of / no
35-28	味	30a	**wei**	taste / flavor / (*rasa*: sweetness) }} bland / tasteless
35-29	視	147	**shih**	looked at / [we] look at >>Etm: "from Heaven" + "seeing"
35-30	之	4	**chih**	it
35-31	不	1	**pu**	not
35-32	足	157	**tsu**	sufficient / enough / satisfied with
35-33	見	147	**chien**	to see / to visit / to appear / to be seen }}}} imperceptible / it cannot be seen / "not worth seeing" (Duy)
35-34	聽	128	**t'ing**	listened to // a court / a tribunal
35-35	之	4	**chih**	it
35-36	不	1	**pu**	not

35-37	足	157	tsu	sufficient / enough / satisfied with	
35-38	聞 .	128	wên	heard / to be heard }}}} inaudible / "not worth hearing" (Duy)	[2]
35-39	用	101	yung	use / use of / make use of / employ / utilize / applied	
35-40	之	4	chih	it	
35-41	不	1	pu	not / never / without	
35-42	足	157	tsu	can / could	
35-43	既 .	71	chi	exhausted / finish / fail / end }}}} inexhaustible / unfailing	

[1] **Chi ta hsiang** (See NOTES)

[2] Compare v. 35:29–38 with v. 14:01–11

V E R S E   3 6

36-01	將	41	chiang	If / about to / going to / (future action) // receive / take in hand	
36-02	欲	76	yü	want / wish / desire / tendencies }} "what you would" / "in order to"	
36-03	歙	76	hsi	contract / shrink / dwindle / reduce / deplete / shut it / shorten // "gather up"	
36-04	之 。	4	chih	it / itself / (something) / "any creature"	
36-05	必	61	pi	must / surely / truthful >>Etm: "hand" + (over) "heart" ("by one's heart")	
36-06	固	31	ku	necessary / therefore / thoroughly / strong / assuredly }} quite surely >Alt: *ku* (for the time being)—MHL	
36-07	張	57	chang	expand / stretch / open / extend / weaken / spread out // to draw a bow	[1]
36-08	之 .	4	chih	it / itself / (something)	
36-09	將	41	chiang	if / about to / going to / (future action)	
36-10	欲	76	yü	want / wish / desire / tendencies }} "in order to"	
36-11	弱	57	jo	weak[en] / weakened / feeble	
36-12	之 。	4	chih	it / itself / (something)	
36-13	必	61	pi	surely / truthful / swear	
36-14	固	31	ku	necessary / therefore / thoroughly / strong / assuredly	
36-15	強	57	ch'iang	strong / strength / strengthen / power / force	
36-16	之 .	4	chih	it / itself / (something)	
36-17	將	41	chiang	if / about to / going to / (future action)	
36-18	欲	76	yü	want / wish / desire / tendencies / thought constructs	
36-19	廢	53	fei	abandon / reject / forget / give up / lay aside / abolish / throw away / lay low // neglect / ruin / destroy / topple >Alt: *ch'ü* (leave, desert)—MWT	
36-20	之 。	4	chih	it / itself / (something)	
36-21	必	61	pi	surely / truthful / swear	
36-22	固	31	ku	necessary / therefore / assuredly	
36-23	興	134	hsing	raise / raise up / uplift / elevate / promote / set it up / exalt / made strong / establish / "set on high" / rouse >Alt: *yü* (share, work closely)—MWT	
36-24	之 .	4	chih	it / itself / (something)	
36-25	將	41	chiang	if / about to / going to / (future action)	
36-26	欲	76	yü	want / wish / desire / tendencies / thought constructs	
36-27	奪	37	to	deprive / grasp / take / seize / despoil >Alt: *ch'ü* (take)—MWT	

36-28	之	4	chih	it / itself / (something)	
36-29	必	61	pi	surely / truthful / swear	
36-30	固	31	ku	necessary / therefore / assuredly	
36-31	與	134	yü	endow / "richly endow" / give / give to it // join / union / to share / together	
36-32	之	4	chih	it / itself / (something)	
36-33	是	72a	shih	this is	
36-34	謂	149	wei	called	
36-35	微	60	wei	mystery / secret / subtle / hidden // obscure / dark // minute / fading away / formless	
36-36	明	72	ming	enlightenment / illumination / light / discernment / vision	[2]
36-37	柔	75	jou	tender / submissive / gentle / gentleness / soft / flexible	
36-38	弱	57	jo	weak / yielding	
36-39	勝	19	shêng	victory / conquer / overcome / outdo / subdue	
36-40	剛	18	kang	hard / stiff / unyielding / adamant / "brittle"	
36-41	強	57	ch'iang	strong / forceful / "coerciveness"	
36-42	魚	195	yü	fish	
36-43	不	1	pu	not / must not	
36-44	可	30	k'o	can / able / should }} cannot / should not	
36-45	脫	130	t'o	be taken from / take / leave / be separated // escape / allowed to leave / (~survive)	
36-46	於	70	yü	from / with / in / away from / out of	
36-47	淵	85	yüan	deep / deep water / abyss / the deep / depth	
36-48	國	31	kuo	empire / country / state / [ruler] of empire / state	
36-49	之	4	chih	's / its	
36-50	利	18	li	profit[able] / benefit / advantage / gain / sharp / ~useful / (harvest) / (power) >> Etm: "grain" + "cutting instrument"	
36-51	器	30	ch'i	weapons / tools / instruments / vessels	[3]
36-52	不	1	pu	not	
36-53	可	30	k'o	can / able / should	
36-54	以	9a	yi	thus / thereby	
36-55	示	113	shih	show[n] / reveal[ed] / display	
36-56	人	9a	jên	people / others / to the people	

[1] *Chiang yü hsi chih pi ku chang*: "If you would have a thing shrink, you must first stretch it." (Lau); "About to shrink, let it first be opened." (Lin); "That which shrinks must first expand." (Feng); "Should you want to contain something, you must deliberately let it expand." (Cleary)

[2] *Shi wei wei ming* (See NOTES)

[3] *Li ch'i*: "sharp tools" / arms / "instruments of power" (Lau); "greatest tool" (Pine); "useful instruments" (Duy); ~ruler's power to reward and punish

VERSE 37

37-01	道	162	tao	Tao
37-02	常	50	ch'ang	always / eternal / constant[ly] / everlasting / invariable
37-03	無	86	wu	without / non- / nothing / no }} never

37-04	為	87	wei	action / act / make / do / doing / become / being }} non-action / never acts / never does / inactive >Alt: *ming* (name)—MWT
37-05	而	126	erh	and / but / yet
37-06	無	86	wu	nothing / without
37-07	不	1	pu	not / un-
37-08	為	87	wei	action / act / make / do / doing / become / being }} it doesn't do / remains undone / >v. 48:16–23 [1]
37-09	侯	9	hou	prince / baron / duke
37-10	王	95	wang	king[s] }} rulers / leaders
37-11	若	140	jo	if / when
37-12	能	130	nêng	can / able / have the ability to
37-13	守	40	shou	hold to / uphold / keep / cling to / hold fast / abide by / keep in accordance with
37-14	之	4	chih	it / this / ~Tao
37-15	萬	140	wan	ten thousand / all
37-16	物	93	wu	things }} everything / everything in the world
37-17	將	41	chiang	will / would
37-18	自	132	tzu	naturally / of themselves / spontaneously / of their own accord
37-19	化	21	hua	transform / be transformed / evolve / change / reform / "turn around" / grow / develop [2]
37-20	化	21	hua	transformation / be transformed / evolve / change / reform / "turn around" / grow / develop [if after]
37-21	而	126	erh	and / but
37-22	欲	76	yü	desires / tendencies / old habits
37-23	作	9a	tso	move / stir / make a stir / "come up" / arise / be active / emerge / rise to action / "raise its head"
37-24	吾	30	wu	I / he
37-25	將	41	chiang	will / could / would
37-26	鎮	157	chên	restrain / suppress / subdue / press it down / protect / keep / "make still"
37-27	之	4	chih	them / it
37-28	以	9a	yi	by / with / through / with [the weight of / the aid of]
37-29	無	86	wu	without / not / void of / un- / no
37-30	名	30a	ming	name / nameable }} nameless
37-31	之	4	chih	's / its
37-32	樸	75	p'u	purity / simplicity / one's natural state / "uncarved block of wood" / uncut jade / "pristine simplicity" }}}} the nameless uncarved block / simplicity of the nameless [3]
37-33	無	86	wu	without / not / void of / un-
37-34	名	30a	ming	name / nameable }} the nameless
37-35	之	4	chih	's / its
37-36	樸	75	p'u	purity / simplicity / natural state / "uncarved block"
37-37	夫	37	fu	truly / "now" / (what follows is true)
37-38	亦	8	yi	in turn / again / moreover / also
37-39	將	41	chiang	will / is / is [but]
37-40	無	86	wu	without / not / void of / [make them] without / free them of

37-41	欲 .	76	**yü**	desires / tendencies / old habits >Alt: *ju* (shame, disgrace)—MWT
37-42	不	1	**pu**	not / [being] free of / [and if I] cease to >Alt: *wu* (without)—Tang Dynasty Inscription
37-43	欲	76	**yü**	desires / tendencies / old habits >Alt: *ju* (shame, disgrace)—MWT
37-44	以	9a	**yi**	thus / thereby [it has / it is]
37-45	靜 。	174	**ching**	still[ness] / quietude / tranquil[ity] / peace / harmony / repose / "interior peace" [is achieved]
37-46	天	37	**t'ien**	Heaven
37-47	下	1	**hsia**	below }} the world >Alt: *ti* (earth)—MWT
37-48	將	41	**chiang**	will
37-49	自	132	**tzu**	of itself / naturally / spontaneously / of its own accord [be]
37-50	定 .	40	**ting**	settled / fix[ed] / anchor[ed] / stabilize / certain / secure // peace / calm / >lit: "stone used as an anchor" >Alt: *cheng* (correct, upright, order)—MWT [4]

[1] *Tao ch'ang wu wei erh wu pu wei*: "The way never acts, yet nothing is left undone." (Lau); "The Tao never does, yet through it everything is done." (Yutang); "The Way is always uncontrived, yet there's nothing it doesn't do." (Cleary); "Tao abides in non-action . . ." (Feng); "Tao is always inactive. . . ." (Lin)

[2] *Tzu hua*: *Tzu* (of itself, naturally); *hua* (change, transform, "turn around"). *Hua* comes from "a man" + "a man turning around," implying a complete change, transformation, or "turnaround" in one's view or approach. In this case, it may mean a turning from an exterior existence to an interior one; a turning from the outer expression to one's own nature. *Tzu hua* implies a transformation that is natural and spontaneous, which comes about when a person is aligned with Tao (the power of the universe).

"All things will transform spontaneously." (Chan); "Each thing would develop in accordance with its own nature." (Bahm); "All those will be transformed from within." (Au-Young)

[3] +Alt: add *chen chi yi* (restrain them with) after *p'u*—MWT

[4] *Pu yü yi ching t'ien hsia chiang tzu ting*: "And if I cease to desire and remain still, the empire will be at peace of its own accord." (Lau); "By stripping of desire quiescence is achieved . . ." (Yutang); "When the desires of men are curbed, there will be peace, and the world will settle down of its own accord." (Wu)

VERSE 38

38-01	上	1	**shang**	Superior / high[est] / supreme / best // [a person of] superior / [one with the] highest
38-02	德	60b	**tê**	Te / power / virtue / character
38-03	不	1	**pu**	not / un- / not [conscious of] / does not [display / keep to]
38-04	德 。	60b	**tê**	Te / power / virtue / virtuous / [acting] virtuous / ~rules of virtue / character / "goodness"
38-05	是	72a	**shih**	(this)
38-06	以	9a	**yi**	(for) }} thus / therefore / hence / in that way / that is why
38-07	有	74	**yu**	has / possesses / [he really] possesses
38-08	德 。	60b	**tê**	Te / power / virtue
38-09	下	1	**hsia**	inferior / low / lower / lowest // [one of] inferior
38-10	德	60b	**tê**	Te / power / virtue
38-11	不	1	**pu**	not / un-
38-12	失	37	**shih**	lose / lost / loses [sight of] / be separated from / stray from / let go of / forget about
38-13	德 。	60b	**tê**	Te / power / virtue / [acting] virtuous / "reward"
38-14	是	72a	**shih**	(this)
38-15	以	9a	**yi**	(for) }} therefore / thus / hence / in that way / that is why
38-16	無	86	**wu**	without / not / void of / un- / no / (loses)

38-17	德。	60b	tê	Te / power / virtue
38-18	上	1	shang	superior / high[est][er] / supreme / best
38-19	德	60b	tê	Te / power / virtue
38-20	無	86	wu	without / not / void of / un- / no / take no
38-21	為。	87	wei	action / act / make / do / doing / become / being / effort / pretension / (~ulterior motive)
38-22	而	126	erh	and / but / yet
38-23	無	86	wu	without / not / void of / un- / no / has no
38-24	以	9a	yi	in order to / thereby / "brings about" / makes // ~deliberate >Alt: *pu* (not)—Fu I
38-25	為.	87	wei	action / acting / do / become / being / effort [1]
38-26	下	1	hsia	inferior / low / man of inferior
38-27	德	60b	tê	Te / power / virtue
38-28	為	87	wei	action / acts / makes / does / becomes / effort / being / "is created" / "pretensions"
38-29	之。	4	chih	itself / (____)
38-30	而	126	erh	and / but
38-31	有	74	yu	has / possess / possesses
38-32	以	9a	yi	in order to / thereby / "brings about' / "makes"
38-33	為.	87	wei	action / act / make / do / doing / become / being }} ulterior motives / intent XX Alt: omit v. 38:26–33—MWT
38-34	上	1	shang	superior / high[er][est] / supreme / highest / best / man of superior
38-35	仁	9b	jên	benevolence / kindness / kindheartedness / humanity / "compassion" }} "compassion at its best" (Blakney)
38-36	為	87	wei	action / acts / makes / does / becomes / being / effort / is created
38-37	之。	4	chih	itself / (____)
38-38	而	126	erh	and / but
38-39	無	86	wu	without / not / void of / un- / no
38-40	以	9a	yi	in order to / thereby / "brings about" / "makes"
38-41	為.	87	wei	action / act / make / do / doing / become / being }} ulterior motives / intent
38-42	上	1	shang	superior / high[er][est] / supreme / best
38-43	義	123	yi	virtue / righteousness / justice / morality / rectitude / "duty"
38-44	為	87	wei	action / acts / take action / to act / makes / does / doing / becomes / being
38-45	之。	4	chih	itself / (____)
38-46	而	126	erh	and / but
38-47	有	74	yu	has / possesses
38-48	以	9a	yi	in order to / thereby / "brings about" / "makes"
38-49	為.	87	wei	action / act / make / does / doing / become / being }} ulterior motives / intent
38-50	上	1	shang	superior / high / supreme / highest / best / man of superior
38-51	禮	113	li	propriety / ritual / ceremony / rites / rules of behavior / principles of conduct >Confucian doctrine
38-52	為	87	wei	action / act / make / do / doing / become / being / does something
38-53	之.	4	chih	itself / himself / (____)

38-54	而	126	erh	and / but / (when)
38-55	莫	140	mo	no one / no / not
38-56	之	4	chih	itself / people / (_____)
38-57	應.	61	ying	answers / responds / response // fulfills [expectations]
38-58	則	18	tsê	then
38-59	攘	64	jang	seize / stretch / stretch out / bare // reject
38-60	臂	130	pi	arms / [his] arms }} "rolls up his sleeves" (Lau)
38-61	而	126	erh	and / but
38-62	扔	64	jêng	forces / enforces / apply force / "throw a rope"
38-63	之.	4	chih	it / itself / it [on them] / (order)
38-64	故	66	ku	hence / thus / therefore
38-65	失	37	shih	lose / lost / loss / failing / be separated from / omit
38-66	道	162	tao	Tao / way }} when Tao is lost
38-67	而	126	erh	and / yet / still
38-68	後	60	hou	then / after / arise / followed by / result / comes after / "one must cultivate" / "man resorts to"
38-69	德.	60b	tê	Te / power / virtue / [rules of] virtue
38-70	失	37	shih	lose / lost / failing / be separated from / [when one] loses
38-71	德	60b	tê	Te / power / virtue
38-72	而	126	erh	and / yet
38-73	後	60	hou	then / after / arise / followed by / result / comes after
38-74	仁.	9b	jên	humanity / benevolence / kindheartedness / rules of benevolence
38-75	失	37	shih	lose / lost / failing / be separated from / [when one] loses
38-76	仁	9b	jên	humanity / benevolence / kindheartedness / rules of benevolence
38-77	而	126	erh	and / but
38-78	後	60	hou	then / after / arise / followed by / result / comes after
38-79	義	123	yi	righteousness / justice / morality / rules of righteousness
38-80	失	37	shih	lose / lost / failing / be separated from / [when one] loses
38-81	義.	123	yi	righteousness / justice / morality / rules of righteousness
38-82	而	126	erh	and / yet
38-83	後	60	hou	then / after / arise / followed by / result / comes after
38-84	禮.	113	li	propriety / ceremony / rites / rituals / ritualized conduct
38-85	夫	37	fu	truly / "now" / (what follows is true)
38-86	禮	113	li	propriety // ceremony / rites / rituals
38-87	者	125	chê	it / (things)
38-88	忠	61	chung	loyalty / loyal / devoted / faithful / sincere / patriotic >>Etm: "center" + (over) "heart"
38-89	信	9	hsin	faith / faithful / faithfulness / sincere / truthful / "honesty of heart" / belief >>Etm: "man" + "words" ("true to his word")
38-90	之	4	chih	their / its / his / her
38-91	薄	140	pao	thin[ness] / thinning out / wearing thin / waning / "shabby" // husk / "merest husk of" / veneer / superficial

38-92	而	126	erh	and / but	
38-93	亂	5	luan	trouble / discord / disorder / anarchy / chaos / confusion	
38-94	之	4	chih	's / their / its / his / her	
38-95	首	185	shou	beginning }} beginning of	
38-96	前	18	ch'ien	before / preceding / "premature"	
38-97	識	149	shih	knowledge / understand / comprehend / know	[2]
38-98	者	125	chê	it / that	
38-99	道	162	tao	Tao	
38-100	之	4	chih	's / its / their / (have)	
38-101	華	140	hua	flower / flowery / blossom / embellishments / flowery trappings / luster / ornament / ~exterior	
38-102	而	126	erh	and / yet	
38-103	愚	61b	yü	foolish / folly / ignorant / ignorance / stupid / delusion / stupidity / unaware of / simple	
38-104	之	4	chih	its / their / 's	
38-105	始	38	shih	beginning / origin / beginning of / starting point of }}} "the beginning of folly" (Duy)	
38-106	是	72a	shih	(this)	
38-107	以	9a	yi	(for) }} hence / thus / therefore / for this reason	
38-108	大	37	ta	great	
38-109	丈	1	chang	large / > a term of respect—reverence	
38-110	夫	37	fu	master / "organizer" / "man of affairs" }} "full-grown man" (Wu) / "great people"	
38-111	處	141	ch'u	stop / stays / dwells / abides / ~can enter }}}} "those with the greatest endurance" (Wing)	
38-112	其	12	ch'i	in its / [on] what is	
38-113	厚	27	hou	solid / solidness / thick / heavy / real / substance / substantial / the base / ~internal / ~inner	
38-114	不	1	pu	not / does not	
38-115	居	44	chü	inhabit / occupy / be in / dwell / rest / keeps	
38-116	其	12	ch'i	in its / in the / what is / ~Tao's	
38-117	薄	140	pao	thin / thinness / thinning / flimsy // on the surface / the husk / superficial / shell / shallowness / shadow / ~exterior / ~outer	
38-118	處	141	ch'u	stop / stay / dwell / ~can enter	
38-119	其	12	ch'i	in its / in the	
38-120	實	37	shih	fruit / full / fullness / fill / solidness / substance / kernel / ~inner / ~reality	
38-121	不	1	pu	not / does not	
38-122	居	44	chü	inhabit / occupy / be in / dwell / rest	
38-123	其	12	ch'i	in its / in the	
38-124	華	140	hua	flower / embellishments / ornament / blossom / luster / flowery [expression] / ~outer	
38-125	故	66	ku	hence / thus / therefore	
38-126	去	28	ch'ü	leaves / rejects / discards / abandons / avoids	
38-127	彼	60	pi	the latter / the one / that / "what is without" (Wu)	
38-128	取	29	ch'ü	takes hold of / accepts / receive	
38-129	此	76	tz'u	the former / the other / that / this / "what is within" (Wu) / > v. 12; v. 72	

[1] **Yi-wei**: ulterior motives / "Private ends to serve." (Wu); "Higher virtue lacks efforts and the thought of effort." (Pine); "superior virtue neither acts nor aims." (Duy)

[2] **Ch'ien shih**: those who are first // foreknowledge / "Swift Apprehension" / "first to know" / foresight // prejudice / having one's mind made up beforehand // knowing the future / "one who knows the future" (Wing)

VERSE 39

39-01	昔	72	hsi	Old / ancient
39-02	之	4	chih	's / its }} of old / in ancient times / long ago / those of old
39-03	得	60a	tê	obtain / attain / gain / possess / possessed / benefit / receive / [those who] attained [is]
39-04	一	1	yi	unity / the one / whole / wholeness / oneness [with Tao]
39-05	者	125	chê	(he) / (she) / it / (the one) / (the One)
39-06	天	37	t'ien	Heaven / sky
39-07	得	60a	tê	obtain[ed] / attain / gain / possess / receive / "in virtue of" (Lau) / "in harmony with" (Wing) / >In ancient China, tê (obtain, attain) and tê (Te, virtue) were interchangeable.
39-08	一	1	yi	unity / the one / whole / wholeness / oneness [with Tao]
39-09	以	9a	yi	thus / hence / thereby / "brings about" / "becomes"
39-10	清	85	ch'ing	clear / pure
39-11	地	32	ti	earth
39-12	得	60a	tê	obtain[ed] / attained / gain / possess / benefit / receive
39-13	一	1	yi	unity / the one / whole / wholeness / oneness [with Tao]
39-14	以	9a	yi	thus / hence / thereby / "brings about" / "becomes"
39-15	寧	40	ning	peace[ful][fulness] / rest / repose / serene / tranquil // settled / stabilized / firm
39-16	神	113	shên	spirits / spiritual beings / gods / "mind" (Wing) // soul / sacred
39-17	得	60a	tê	obtain[ed] / attain / gain / possess / benefit / receive
39-18	一	1	yi	unity / the one / whole / wholeness / oneness [with Tao]
39-19	以	9a	yi	thus / hence / thereby / "brings about" / "becomes"
39-20	靈	173	ling	divine / [charged with] spiritual power / spiritualized / "inspired" / energized / potent / animated
39-21	谷	150	ku	valley[s] / ravine / ~what is empty, like a valley // fountain / stream
39-22	得	60a	tê	obtain[ed] / attain / gain / [came to] possess / benefit / receive
39-23	一	1	yi	unity / the one
39-24	以	9a	yi	thus / hence / thereby / "brings about" / "becomes"
39-25	盈	108	ying	full / fullness / fulfillment / filled / replenish / excess / abundance
39-26	萬	140	wan	ten thousand / all / myriad
39-27	物	93	wu	things / beings }} all things / all the creatures of the world / everything
39-28	得	60a	tê	obtained / attained / gained / possess / benefit / receive
39-29	一	1	yi	unity / the one
39-30	以	9a	yi	thus / hence / thereby / "brings about" / "becomes"
39-31	生	100	shêng	alive / life / have life / "live and grow" / born / exist / produce[d] / come forth / creative XXX Alt: omit v. 39:26–31—MWT
39-32	侯	9	hou	prince / duke / baron

39-33	王	95	**wang**	king / lord }} rulers
39-34	得	60a	**tê**	obtain[ed] / attain / gain / possess / benefit / receive
39-35	一	1	**yi**	unity / the one >Alt: *wei* (imply, suggest, it would mean)—MWT
39-36	以	9a	**yi**	thus / hence / thereby / "brings about" / "becomes"
39-37	為	87	**wei**	become / make / action / "ruled"
39-38	天	37	**t'ien**	Heaven
39-39	下	1	**hsia**	below }} the world / the empire
39-40	貞.	154	**chên**	pure / virtue / chaste >Alt: *cheng* (correct, upright, just, standard, rectitude, ruler)
39-41	其	12	**ch'i**	that which
39-42	致	133b	**chih**	cause / bring about / produces / made it so // "arrive at" (Henricks) / "extreme" (Henricks)
39-43	之.	4	**chih**	it / these +Alt: add *yi* (unity, the one) +Alt: add *ye* (!, indeed)
39-44	天	37	**t'ien**	Heaven / sky / [if] Heaven
39-45	無	86	**wu**	without / had not / were not [with it]
39-46	以	9a	**yi**	thus / hence / thereby / "becomes" / "by this means" >Alt: *yi* (stop, completion, finally)—MWT [1]
39-47	清	85	**ch'ing**	clear / pure / clarity [it]
39-48	將	41	**chiang**	would / could / might // avoid / (future action)
39-49	恐	61	**k'ung**	(____) / fear // "I fear" / "presumably" }} "I'm afraid it would" / fear that it would
39-50	裂.	145	**lieh**	split open / crack / "fall to pieces" / disrupt / burst [2]
39-51	地	32	**ti**	earth / [if] earth
39-52	無	86	**wu**	without / had not / were not [with it]
39-53	以	9a	**yi**	thus / hence / thereby / "becomes" / "by this means" >Alt: *yi* (stop, completion, finally)—MWT
39-54	寧	40	**ning**	peace / steadiness / tranquil[ity] // repose / steadfast / firmness
39-55	將	41	**chiang**	would / could / might // avoid / (future action)
39-56	恐	61	**k'ung**	(____) / fear / "I fear"
39-57	發.	105	**fa**	shake / be shaken / quake / break down / sink / explode / "burst into pieces" / collapse / crumble
39-58	神	113	**shên**	spirits / spiritual beings / gods
39-59	無	86	**wu**	without / had not / were not [with it]
39-60	以	9a	**yi**	thus / hence / thereby / "becomes" / "by this means" >Alt: *yi* (stop, completion, finally)—MWT
39-61	靈	173	**ling**	divine / [gained / charged with] spiritual power / spiritualized / energized / potent
39-62	將	41	**chiang**	would / could / might // avoid / (future action)
39-63	恐	61	**k'ung**	(____) / fear / "I fear"
39-64	歇.	76	**hsieh**	give out / end / dissolve / wither away / "cease from being" / stop
39-65	谷	150	**ku**	valley / ravine / fountains
39-66	無	86	**wu**	without / had not / were not [with it]
39-67	以	9a	**yi**	thus / hence / thereby / "becomes" / "by this means" >Alt: *yi* (stop, completion, finally)—MWT
39-68	盈	108	**ying**	full / fullness / fulfillment / replenish / excess / abundance
39-69	將	41	**chiang**	would / could / might // avoid / (future action)

39-70	恐	61	k'ung	(___) / fear / "I fear"
39-71	竭	117	chieh	utmost / reach its end / be exhausted
39-72	萬	140	wan	ten thousand / all
39-73	物	93	wu	things / beings }} all things / all the creatures of the world / everything
39-74	無	86	wu	without / not
39-75	以	9a	yi	thus / hence / thereby
39-76	生	100	shêng	life / existence / arise / grow / growth / "lived and grown"
39-77	將	41	chiang	would / could / might // avoid / (future action)
39-78	恐	61	k'ung	(___) / fear / "I fear"
39-79	滅	85	mieh	die / be destroyed / perish[ing] / exterminated / "become extinct" XXX Alt: omit v. 39:72–79—MWT
39-80	侯	9	hou	prince / duke
39-81	王	95	wang	king / lord }} rulers
39-82	無	86	wu	without / not / ~did not follow
39-83	以	9a	yi	thus / hence / thereby +Alt: add *cheng-erh*: *cheng* (upright, standard, ruler); *erh* (and, but)
39-84	貴	154	kuei	esteem / value / honor / honorable / dignity / revere / treasure [themselves]
39-85	高	189	kao	high / superior / lofty // noble / eminent / high position / exalted
39-86	將	41	chiang	would / could / might // avoid / (future action)
39-87	恐	61	k'ung	(___) / fear / "I fear"
39-88	蹶	157	chüeh	fall / be toppled / trip / stumble and fall / "lose their kingdoms"
39-89	故	66	ku	hence / thus / therefore / for
39-90	貴	154	kuei	esteem / value / honor / treasure / [the] noble / nobility / basis of honor // (superior)
39-91	以	9a	yi	thus / hence / thereby
39-92	賤	154	chien	low / humility / humble // common man / commoners // (inferior) / (vile)
39-93	為	87	wei	action / act / acting as / make / do / doing / become / being / "take"
39-94	本	75	pên	root / foundation / support / rooted in
39-95	高	189	kao	high / superior / lofty / noble / eminent / distinction / exalted / exalted ones / nobility
39-96	以	9a	yi	thus / hence / thereby
39-97	下	1	hsia	low / lowly / lowliness
39-98	為	87	wei	action / act / make / do / doing / become / being / "take as"
39-99	基	32	chi	foundation / base / based on
39-100	是	72a	shih	(this)
39-101	以	9a	yi	(for) }} thus / hence / therefore / for this reason
39-102	侯	9	hou	prince / duke
39-103	王	95	wang	king / lord }} rulers
39-104	自	132	tzu	themselves
39-105	謂	149	wei	call / refer
39-106	孤	39	ku	orphans / alone / "solitary" / "helpless" / "the Orphan"
39-107	寡	40	kua	widowers / lacking / "little" / "desolate" / "the Lonely One"

39-108	不	1	pu	not / un-
39-109	穀	115	ku	worthy }} worthless / starving / "hapless" / "the Destitute One"
39-110	此	77	tz'u	this / (because)
39-111	非	175	fei	not
39-112	以	9a	yi	thus / hence / thereby / accordingly / (from)
39-113	賤	154	chien	low / humility / humble // common man / commoners // (inferior) / (vile)
39-114	為	87	wei	action / act / make / do / doing / become / being / "have"
39-115	本	75	pên	root / origin / base / rooted
39-116	耶	163	hsieh	? / (a question)
39-117	非	175	fei	not so / oppose
39-118	乎	4	hu	? / (a question) }} is it not so? / is it not?
39-119	故	66	ku	Hence / thus / therefore / (truly)
39-120	致	133b	chih	highest / supreme / reach the end / too much / "repeated" // bring about / cause
39-121	數	66	shu	count / reckoning / plan
39-122	輿	159	yü	carriage / wheel >Alt: ch'e (carriage, wheel) >Alt: yü (praise, praiseworthy, prestige, honor; success, name)
39-123	無	86	wu	without / needs no / has no / there is no
39-124	輿	159	yü	praise / praiseworthy / prestige / honor / success / fame >Alt: ch'e (carriage, wheel) [3]
39-125	不	1	pu	not / do not
39-126	欲	76	yü	want / wish / desire / tendencies / thought constructs
39-127	琭	95	lu	(shine / respect)
39-128	琭	95	lu	(shine / respect) }} jingle / tinkle / rare as // noble
39-129	如	38	ju	like / also / so
39-130	玉	95	yü	a gem / jade }}}} "rather than jingle like jade" (Chen)
39-131	珞	95	lo	(let down)
39-132	珞	95	lo	(let down) }} clatter / rumble / chime / resound // humble
39-133	如	38	ju	like / as
39-134	石	112	shih	stone / rock }}}} "rumble like the rocks" (Chen)

[1] **Wu-yi**: without means, unable to be. **Wu-yi**: without stop, without completion, always—MWT
[2] **T'ien wu yi ch'ing chiang k'ung lieh**: "Heaven would crack if it were always clear." (Pine); "It implies that, if Heaven were ever pure, it would be likely to rend." (Mair)
[3] **Shu yü wu yü pu**: "counting a carriage as no carriage at all" (Pine); "counting their fame as no fame at all" (Pine); "Supreme honour attained is without honour." (Duy)
(See NOTES for a related story by Chuang-tsu)

VERSE 40

40-01	反	29	fan	Return / reverse / turn back / revert / reversion / returning / return to the root / circulating // opposite [1]
40-02	者	125	chê	that / is
40-03	道	162	tao	Tao
40-04	之	4	chih	's / its

40-05	動.	19	tung	motion / movement / moves / action }}}}} "Tao moves the other way." (Pine)
40-06	弱	57	jo	tender[ness] / weak / gentle / yielding / soft / fragile / "receptivity" (Wing) >>Etm: "wing of a bird" + "wing of a bird"
40-07	者	125	chê	that
40-08	道	162	tao	Tao
40-09	之	4	chih	's / its
40-10	用.	101	yung	use / utility / function / purpose / employ / method / way / "works through" [2]
40-11	天	37	t'ien	Heaven
40-12	下	1	hsia	below }} the world >Alt: ti (earth)—Kao Heng Commentary
40-13	萬	140	wan	ten thousand / all X Alt: omit—MWT
40-14	物	93	wu	things / beings }} all things / all the creatures of the world / everything
40-15	生	100	shêng	live / exist / grows from / produce[d] / come / are born / engender
40-16	於	70	yü	from / of
40-17	有.	74	yu	existence / being / Being / something / "the corporeal" / the manifest / the physical / "what-is" / what one has
40-18	有	74	yu	existence / being / Being / something
40-19	生	100	shêng	live / exist / grows from / produce[d]
40-20	於	70	yü	from
40-21	無.	86	wu	nothingness / non-existence / nothing / non-being / "incorporeal" / "what-is-not"

[1] *Fan* (return) comes from "the motion of a hand" + "turning something over." This "return" is most often associated with the cyclical process of nature, wherein things return to their source. (See verses 14, 16, 25, 28, 30, and 52.) It can also mean a "turning within" and a return to one's true nature. Duyvendak sees it as "the constant alternation between being and non-being."

[2] *Fan chê tao chih tung jo chê tao chih yung*: The action of Tao is to return. The function of Tao is to be receptive. / "Return—that is Tao's movement. Weakness—that is Tao's strength."

VERSE 41

41-01	上	1	shang	Superior / supreme / highest / best / great / "top grade" / (wise)
41-02	士	33	shih	scholar / student / class of person / people / man / officer / man of learning / ~leader
41-03	聞	128	wên	hear[s][ing] / hears about / listening to
41-04	道。	162	tao	Tao / [teachings of] Tao
41-05	勤	19	ch'in	diligent / diligence / attentive / earnest[ly] / work / puts forth effort / devotion / "try hard to"
41-06	而	126	erh	and / to >Alt: neng (can, able)—MWTB
41-07	行	144	hsing	practice / [put into] action / follow / "carry it out" / work / live in accordance with / [uses his] "natural powers"
41-08	之.	4	chih	it }}}} practices with diligence
41-09	中	2	chung	middle / center / average / mediocre / "middle grade"
41-10	士	33	shih	scholar / student / class of person / officer / man
41-11	聞	128	wên	hear[s][ing] / hears about / listening to
41-12	道。	162	tao	Tao
41-13	若	140	jo	sometimes // resembles / like / one moment / follow
41-14	存	39	ts'un	keeps / to preserve / retain / "believe" / here / "aware"
41-15	若	140	jo	sometimes // resembles / like / one moment / follow

41-16	亡 。	8	**wang**	lose / loses [it] / gone // unaware / doubt / "disbelieve" }}}} "half believe in it" / unsure
41-17	下	1	**hsia**	inferior / low / lowest / below [average] / lesser / "worthless"
41-18	士	33	**shih**	scholar / student / class of person / type of man / man
41-19	聞	128	**wên**	hear[s][ing] / hears about / listening to
41-20	道 。	162	**tao**	Tao
41-21	大	37	**ta**	greatly / ~heartily / ~out loud
41-22	笑	118	**hsiao**	laughs / ridicules / belittles / laughs [at] }} laughs out loud
41-23	之 .	4	**chih**	it
41-24	不	1	**pu**	not / [if they did] not / [if he did] not
41-25	笑 。	118	**hsiao**	laugh / ridicules / belittle
41-26	不	1	**pu**	not
41-27	足	157	**tsu**	could / would } it couldn't be / it wouldn't be
41-28	以	9a	**yi**	thus / thereby
41-29	為	87	**wei**	be / act / make / do / become / "be worthy of" / be regarded as
41-30	道 .	162	**tao**	Tao
41-31	故	66	**ku**	thus / therefore / hence [there is]
41-32	建	54	**chien**	establish / [an] established / set / "constructive"
41-33	言	149	**yen**	saying / words / maxim
41-34	有	125	**chê**	it / (the one) +Alt: add *yu* (says)
41-35	之 .	4	**chih**	that / the following [:]
41-36	明	72	**ming**	bright[est] / luminous / illumination / light / enlightened
41-37	道	162	**tao**	Tao / path / way }} "Tao which is light" / "the way of illumination" (Cleary) / "who understands Tao" (Yutang)
41-38	若	140	**jo**	is like / seems like / resembles / appears / looks like // (follows) / (akin to)
41-39	昧 .	72	**mei**	dark / dim / obscure / dull
41-40	進	162	**chin**	advance[ment] / advancing / moving forward / leading forward / "progressive" / "quickest"
41-41	道 .	162	**tao**	Tao / path / way / "on the path of Tao"
41-42	若	140	**jo**	is like / seems like / resembles / appears / looks like
41-43	退	162	**t'ui**	retreat / retreating / draw back / fall backward / slow / "retrograde" // refuse
41-44	夷	37	**yi**	straight / level / even / plain // easy / smooth
41-45	道	162	**tao**	Tao / path / way
41-46	若	140	**jo**	is like / seems like / resembles / appears / looks
41-47	纇 .	120b	**lei**	rugged / rough / uneven / "move up and down" // difficult
41-48	上	1	**shang**	high[est] / superior / supreme / exalted / lofty
41-49	德	60b	**tê**	Te / power / virtue
41-50	若	140	**jo**	is like / seems like / appears / resembles / looks like
41-51	谷 .	150	**ku**	valley / ravine / abyss / chasm // empty / hollow / emptiness
41-52	大	37	**ta**	great / perfect / (purest) / (sheerest)
41-53	白	106a	**pai**	white / whiteness / ~quality of white—clarity, purity, innocence
41-54	若	140	**jo**	is like / seems like / resembles / appears / looks like

41-55	辱	160	ju	sullied / opaque / tarnished / blackened / "spotted" // insult / disgrace / shame >Alt: *ju* (pitch-black)—Fu I
41-56	廣	53	kuang	large / broad / broadest / liberal / abundant / vast / ample / greatest / far-reaching / "a wealth of" / "most magnificent" / "all-inclusive"
41-57	德	60b	tê	Te / power / virtue
41-58	若	140	jo	is like / seems like / resembles / appears / looks like
41-59	不	1	pu	not
41-60	足	157	tsu	enough / sufficient / full / adequate / satisfied with }} insignificant / defective / wanting / lacking
41-61	建	54	chien	established / solid / firmly established / staunchest / steadfast / "vigorous" / "strength of"
41-62	德	60b	tê	Te / power / virtue / "goodness"
41-63	若	140	jo	is like / seems like / resembles / appears / looks like
41-64	偷	9	t'ou	unsteady / frail / flimsy / "shabby" / infirm // fraudulent / remiss / steal / stolen // clandestine / "secretive" >Alt: *ju* (timid)—Kao Heng Commentary [1]
41-65	質	154	chih	substantial / substance / real / genuine / solid / "the substratum" // simple / plain / "indolent"
41-66	真	109	chên	real / reality / true / pure / genuine / truth / purity / virtue / worth / "pure worth" >Alt: *tê* (te, virtue)
41-67	若	140	jo	is like / seems like / resembles / appears / looks like
41-68	渝	85	yü	unsteady / changing / changeable / uncertain / fickle / fluid / spurious / "melted" / "shifting tides" (Blakney) // soiled / contaminated // faded, as in faded colors
41-69	大	37	ta	great / the greatest / perfect / the Great
41-70	方	70	fang	square / squareness // place / region / space / range // method
41-71	無	86	wu	has no / without / lacks
41-72	隅	170	yü	corners / boundaries / angles }} ~cannot be limited, cannot be contained
41-73	大	37	ta	great / the greatest / perfect
41-74	器	30	ch'i	vessel / implement / "talent" / tool
41-75	晚	72	wan	not yet / late / slow to // the evening
41-76	成	62	ch'êng	complete / completion / finish / accomplish / succeed / "mature" }} ripens late / takes long to mature / slow to finish / "does nothing"
41-77	大	37	ta	great / the greatest / perfect / (highest)
41-78	音	180	yin	music / sound / musical note / tone / sound
41-79	希	50	hsi	without / void of / "soft" / "rarefied"
41-80	聲	128b	shêng	sound / music / tone }} Is faint / hard to hear / silent / "is hushed"
41-81	大	37	ta	great / greatest / perfect
41-82	象	152	hsiang	form / image / figure // elephant
41-83	無	86	wu	without / has no
41-84	形	59	hsing	shape / form / material / body / substance / contour
41-85	道	162	tao	Tao
41-86	隱	170b	yin	hidden / concealed / in the background >Alt: *pao* (great)—MWTB
41-87	無	86	wu	without / not [having]
41-88	名	30a	ming	name / [parts that can be] named / (manifestations) }} nameless

41-89	夫	37	**fu**	yet / above all / forasmuch / truly
41-90	唯	30b	**wei**	exactly / for this exact reason / alone / only / it is / just because
41-91	道	162	**tao**	Tao
41-92	善	30	**shan**	good / good at / is good / excellent / virtuous / can / skillful / adept at / "knows how to" / "is able" (Duy)
41-93	貸	154	**tai**	give[s] / giving / bestow / provide / support / lending [its power / help] / nourishes / "enhance" >Alt: *shih* (begin, start)—MWTB
41-94	且	1	**ch'ieh**	and +Alt: add *shan* (good, skillful)—MWTB
41-95	成	62	**ch'êng**	complete / completing / completion / bringing fulfillment / fulfilling [all] / accomplish / finish / succeed / perfect / "bring to perfection" }}}} "skilled investor" (Blakney)

[1] *T'ou* originally referred to the pulling or forcing open of a door. Hence we arrive at two definitions: (a) frail, flimsy—that which is able to be forced open, and (b) one who forces open a door, i.e., a thief, one who steals, "a forcer of doors"—and by extension: "secret," "clandestine."

VERSE 42

42-01	道	162	**tao**	Tao X Alt: omit—Duy
42-02	生	100	**shêng**	begets / begot / produce[s][d] / gives birth to / gives life to X Alt: omit—Duy
42-03	一	1	**yi**	the one / unity / oneness / one X Alt: omit—Duy
42-04	一	1	**yi**	the one / unity / oneness / one / ~Tao
42-05	生	100	**shêng**	begets / produce[s][d] / gives birth to / gives life to
42-06	二	7	**erh**	two / the two / duality / ~yin and yang
42-07	二	7	**erh**	two / the two / duality
42-08	生	100	**shêng**	begets / produce[s][d] / gives birth to / gives life to
42-09	三	1	**san**	three / the three / trinity
42-10	三	1	**san**	three / the three / trinity
42-11	生	100	**shêng**	begets / produce[s][d] / gives birth to / gives life to
42-12	萬	140	**wan**	ten thousand / all
42-13	物	93	**wu**	things / beings }} everything in the universe / all physical things
42-14	萬	140	**wan**	ten thousand / all
42-15	物	93	**wu**	things / beings
42-16	負	154	**fu**	carry / "carry on their backs" // revert / return / repeat
42-17	陰	170a	**yin**	yin / "shade" / ~negative, female principle / >complement of *yang*
42-18	而	126	**erh**	and / but
42-19	抱	64	**pao**	embrace / enfold / carry in their arms / carry in front // conceal / envelop / contain >>Etm: "foetus" + (wrapped in) "womb" + "hand"
42-20	陽	170	**yang**	yang / "sun" / ~positive / ~male principle / >complement of *yin*
42-21	沖	85	**ch'ung**	blend / merge / union / combine / coalesce // empty / vacant / ~still-point >Alt: *chung* (between)—MWT >>Etm: "center" + "water / ice" ("in the middle of water / ice")
42-22	氣	84	**ch'i**	*chi* / vital force / vital breath / life-force / vital energy / breath
42-23	以	9a	**yi**	thus / thereby / ~what follows
42-24	為	87	**wei**	cause / make / produce / act / achieve / attain

42-25	和 。	30b	ho	harmony / harmonious / content / peaceful / balance / equilibrium >> Etm: "grain" + "mouth" [1]
42-26	人	9a	jên	people / men
42-27	之	4	chih	's / its / theirs
42-28	所	63	so	that which
42-29	惡	61	wu	detest / loathe / hate / despise / disdain / >lit: "ugly-hearted"
42-30	唯	30b	wei	exactly / for this exact reason / only // consent / to be
42-31	孤	39	ku	orphans / "solitary" / ~alone
42-32	寡	40	kua	widowers / "desolate" / ~lonely
42-33	不	1	pu	not / un-
42-34	穀 。	115	ku	worthy }} without food to eat / hungry / "hapless" / unfavored
42-35	而	126	erh	and / but / and yet
42-36	王	95	wang	kings / noblemen
42-37	公	12a	kung	lords
42-38	以	9a	yi	thus / thereby
42-39	為	87	wei	make / act / take / use
42-40	稱 。	115	ch'êng	titles / refer / call }}} refer to themselves by these names
42-41	故	66	ku	thus / hence / therefore
42-42	物	93	wu	sometimes / likely / perhaps
42-43	或	62	huo	things / beings
42-44	損	64	sun	lose / decrease / diminish / take away // harm / injure / suffer
42-45	之	4	chih	it / itself / (something) / (a thing)
42-46	而	126	erh	and / but
42-47	益 。	108	yi	gain / benefit / increase / augment / add to / more and more
42-48	或	62	huo	sometimes / likely / perhaps
42-49	益	108	yi	gain / benefit / increase / augment / add to / more and more
42-50	之	4	chih	it / itself / (something) / (a thing)
42-51	而	126	erh	and / but
42-52	損 。	64	sun	lose / harm / injure / diminish / suffer / decrease +Alt: add ku (thus)—MWTA
42-53	人	9a	jên	people / others / men / other men
42-54	之	4	chih	's / theirs
42-55	所	63	so	that which
42-56	教 。	66	chiao	taught / teachings / lessons / doctrines / teach }}}} what others teach
42-57	我	62	wo	I
42-58	亦	8	yi	also
42-59	教	66	chiao	teach / teachings / lessons / doctrines
42-60	之 。	4	chih	it [:] +Alt: add ku (thus)—MWTA
42-61	強	57	ch'iang	forceful / strong / violent
42-62	梁	75	liang	aggressive / fierce / violent }} "those who are forceful and aggressive" / "tyrants"
42-63	者	125	chê	(they) / (he) / (she) / it / (the ones)

42-64	不	1	**pu**	not / do not / cannot
42-65	得	60a	**tê**	obtain / receive / gain / possess / benefit / (die)
42-66	其	12	**ch'i**	their / his / her / its
42-67	死	78	**ssu**	death / ~natural death / ~die young / [a good] death }}} die a natural death }}}}}}} "Tyrants never choose their deaths." (Pine) [2]
42-68	吾	30	**wu**	I
42-69	將	41	**chiang**	take in hand / receive
42-70	以	9a	**yi**	thus / thereby
42-71	為	87	**wei**	make / act / use / becomes / make [this]
42-72	教	66	**chiao**	teaching / lesson / doctrine >Alt: *hsüen* (studies)—MWT
42-73	父	88	**fu**	father / chief / beginning / precept / basis / ~foundation / ~fundamental teaching [3]

[1] **[12–25]:** The ten thousand things carry (on their backs) *yin* and hold *yang* in front. It is at the empty part of the breath—where the inner and outer breath merge, the frozen center between the breathing in and the breathing out—where they (*yin* and *yang*) blend in perfect harmony.

[2] This line reflects the notion of karma, "as you sow, so you shall reap"; "as you live, so you will die."

[3] *Fu*, originally meaning a "wooden bell," was accordingly struck to announce the arrival of an elder or a teacher. *Fu*, in this context, refers to the foundation, underlying principle, or essence upon which other teachings are built. "I will make this the basis of my teachings." (Legge)

VERSE 43

43-01	天	37	**t'ien**	Heaven
43-02	下	1	**hsia**	below }} the world / the empire
43-03	之	4	**chih**	's / its
43-04	至	133a	**chih**	most
43-05	柔	75	**jou**	soft / yielding / tender / weak / submissive }} softest / softest substance
43-06	馳	187	**ch'ih**	gallop[s] / race
43-07	騁	187	**ch'êng**	on horseback }} courses over / overcomes / jumps over / overrides / dashes against // ~excel /~surpass
43-08	天	37	**t'ien**	Heaven
43-09	下	1	**hsia**	below
43-10	之	4	**chih**	's / its }}} the world's
43-11	至	133a	**chih**	most / utmost
43-12	堅	32	**chien**	hard / solid / strong }} hardest thing
43-13	無	86	**wu**	without / not having / non- / that which has no
43-14	有	74	**yu**	existence / being / to be / substance / form }} nothing / nothingness
43-15	入	11	**ju**	enters / penetrates / can enter / "finds room"
43-16	無	86	**wu**	without / not having / non-
43-17	間	169	**chien**	crevice / space / "penetrable" / "room" / "seam"
43-18	吾	30	**wu**	I
43-19	是	72a	**shih**	(this)
43-20	以	9a	**yi**	(for) }} therefore / through this / from this

43-21	知	111	chih	know / understand / realize / know [the value of]
43-22	無	86	wu	without / not / non-
43-23	為	87	wei	action / doing / making / becoming / "ado" } doing nothing / not acting
43-24	之	4	chih	's / its
43-25	有	74	yu	have / possess // to be / exist
43-26	益.	108	yi	benefit / increase / advantage / profit / "success"
43-27	不	1	pu	not / non-
43-28	言	149	yen	speaking / words }} wordless
43-29	之	4	chih	's / Its
43-30	教.	66	chiao	teachings / doctrine / philosophy / "guidance"
43-31	無	86	wu	without / not having / non- }}}} silent teaching / teaching without words
43-32	為	87	wei	act / make / do / become / being
43-33	之	4	chih	's / its
43-34	益	108	yi	benefit / increase / advantage / succeed
43-35	天	37	t'ien	Heaven
43-36	下	1	hsia	below }} the world / the empire
43-37	希	50	hsi	few / rare / seldom
43-38	及	29	chi	reach / put into effect / obtain / can obtain [an understanding of] / (understand) / (comprehend) / "put into practice" / "can equal"
43-39	之.	4	chih	it / its / itself / he / she / them / this

V E R S E 4 4

44-01	名	30a	ming	Name / fame
44-02	與	134	yü	and / with / together / union / or
44-03	身	158	shên	person / oneself / body / own life / (position)
44-04	孰	39	shu	which / who / what [is]
44-05	親.	147	ch'in	close / closer / near / dearer / nearer to one's heart / affinity / love [more] [?]
44-06	身	158	shên	person / oneself / body / own life / (position)
44-07	與	134	yü	and / or
44-08	貨	154	huo	wealth / goods / merchandise / treasure
44-09	孰	39	shu	which / who / what [is]
44-10	多.	36	to	more / worth more / more abundant [?]
44-11	得	60a	tê	gain / obtain / worth / benefit / receive / "precious"
44-12	與	134	yü	and / or
44-13	亡	8	wang	lose / loss // die / cease [?]
44-14	孰	39	shu	which / who / what [is]
44-15	病.	104	ping	worse / more harmful, painful, distressing, destructive / a greater bane, evil // sickness / illness [?]
44-16	是	72a	shih	(____) / this X Alt: omit
44-17	故	66	ku	therefore X Alt: omit

44-18	甚	99	shên	excessive / extreme / lavish / ~deep
44-19	愛	61	ai	love / conditional love / affection / fondness / desires >Alt: "meanness" }} "the stronger the attachment"
44-20	必	61	pi	must / surely / incurs
44-21	大	37	ta	great[er][ly] / "too much" / higher
44-22	費	154	fei	waste / overuse / cost / expense / spend / cost / ~suffer }} "spend extravagantly" / spends most
44-23	多	36	to	more / most / much / bigger
44-24	藏	140	ts'ang	hoards / pile up / hide / [he who] hoards / "treasure"
44-25	必	61	pi	must / surely [brings] / sure to end in
44-26	厚	27	hou	much / immense / intense / heavily / [suffers] a heavy / greater
44-27	亡	8	wang	loss / lose // die / cease
44-28	知	111	chih	knows / [one who] knows
44-29	足	157	tsu	contentment / satisfaction / enough / sufficient / satisfied with }} a contented man	[1]
44-30	不	1	pu	not / does not / "is immune to" / "suffers no"
44-31	辱	160	ju	dishonor / disgrace / shame / insult / disappointment
44-32	知	111	chih	knows / [he who] knows
44-33	止	77	chih	stop / stand / when to stop / restraint // limit
44-34	不	1	pu	not / does not / if free from / [encounters] no
44-35	殆	78	tai	danger / peril / trouble // exhausted
44-36	可	30	k'o	can / able
44-37	以	9a	yi	thus / thereby
44-38	長	168	ch'ang	last / last a long time / forever / constantly / ~live
44-39	久	4	chiu	long / ancient / continue / endure }} "forever safe" (Feng) / "live long"

[1] *Tsu* is from "foot" + "standing still," meaning "content where one is," "not wanting to go to another place."

VERSE 45

45-01	大	37	ta	Great / most / (highest) / greatest
45-02	成	62	ch'êng	perfection / perfect / flawless // complete / completion / finish / accomplish[ment] / achievement
45-03	若	140	jo	seems / appears / seems to be
45-04	缺	121	ch'üeh	imperfect / broken / defective / incomplete / lacking / "chipped"
45-05	其	12	ch'i	its / but its / yet
45-06	用	101	yung	use / function / utility / usefulness
45-07	不	1	pu	not / does not / un-
45-08	弊	55	pi	exhausted / worn-out / wear out / impaired / grow old / end / outlive / impaired	[1]
45-09	大	37	ta	great / most / greatest
45-10	盈	108	ying	fullness / full / abundance / surplus
45-11	若	140	jo	seems / appears / seems to be
45-12	沖	85	ch'ung	empty / void / "meager"
45-13	其	12	ch'i	its / but its

45-14	用	101	**yung**	use / function / utility / usefulness
45-15	不	1	**pu**	not / never / un-
45-16	窮 •	116	**ch'iung**	exhausted / reach the end / limit / drain / fail / "forced into a corner" / "run dry" [2]
45-17	大	37	**ta**	great / most / greatest
45-18	直	109	**chih**	truth / justice / correctness / straight / straightness / "directness" }} "the straightest thing" (Pine)
45-19	若	140	**jo**	seems / appears
45-20	屈 •	73	**ch'ü**	bent / crooked / awkward / twisted // unjust / wrong
45-21	大	37	**ta**	great / most / greatest
45-22	巧	48	**ch'iao**	skill / artful / intelligence / ingenuity / clever
45-23	若	140	**jo**	seems / appears
45-24	拙 •	64	**cho**	unskilled / clumsy / stupid / crude / inept
45-25	大	37	**ta**	great / most / greatest
45-26	辯	160	**pien**	eloquence / oratory >Alt: *fu* (riches, wealth, surplus)
45-27	若	140	**jo**	seems / appears / seems to be
45-28	訥 •	149a	**no**	stutter / stammer / awkward / inarticulate / "tongue-tied" / hesitant >Alt: *ch'u* (poor, lacking)—MWTB [3]
45-29	躁	157	**tsao**	movement / motion / quick movement / activity / restless / hastiness / "agitation" / "quick on your feet"
45-30	勝	19	**shêng**	overcomes / conquers / outdoes
45-31	寒 •	40	**han**	cold / shiver
45-32	靜	174	**ching**	stillness / still / repose / tranquility / serenity / calm / keeping still
45-33	勝	19	**shêng**	overcomes / conquers / outdoes
45-34	熱 •	86	**jê**	heat / warm / the hot
45-35	清	85	**ch'ing**	peaceful / calm / still // pure / clear / clarity / one who is clear >>Etm: "water" + "green" (hue of growing plants)
45-36	靜	174	**ching**	serene / quiet / tranquil / stillness // clear / pure / spotless / immaculate / to wash }} "he who is perfectly still" (Pine) +Alt: add *ko-yi* (can thus)—MWTA
45-37	為	87	**wei**	make / act / become / by being / one can become / set / put
45-38	天	37	**t'ien**	Heaven
45-39	下	1	**hsia**	below }} the world / the universe
45-40	正 •	77	**chêng**	standard / order / rectitude / right mode / norm // ruler / guide }}}} "govern the world" [4]

[1] ***Ta chêng jo ch'üeh ch'i yung pu pi:*** "Treat the most flawless (vase) as cracked, and it will not wear out in use." (Duy)

[2] *Ch'iung*, from "to bend one's body so that the spine sticks out" (crouch down) + "cavern." "Driven into a corner," confined, captive, limits, misery

[3] **Lines 25–28** may be a combination of two lines: (a) "Great eloquence seems like stammering," and (b) "Great surplus seems lacking." "Great surplus seems like stammering" is a corruption found in some texts.

[4] ***Ch'ing ching wei t'ien hsia chêng***: "Peace and quiet is the true path in the world." (Cheng); "Purity and stillness are the world's measuring gauge." (Wei); "Stillness and tranquility set things in order in the universe." (Feng); Only through purity and quietude can the world be ruled." (Ta-Kao) (See NOTES)

46-01	天	37	t'ien	Heaven
46-02	下	1	hsia	below }} the world / universe
46-03	有	74	yu	has / possesses / is with / practices / "lives in accord with" / "is present" / "prevails"
46-04	道	162	tao	Tao }} when Tao prevails in the world
46-05	卻	26	ch'üeh	curb / turn back / draw back / reject >Alt: hsieh (put in a stable)—Kao Heng Commentary
46-06	走	156	tsou	race / galloping / fast / racing
46-07	馬	187	ma	horses
46-08	以	9a	yi	used for / (then)
46-09	糞	119	fên	dung / hauling / "haul manure" / "plough the fields" / "fertilize fields with their manure" >Alt: po (to sow, plant)—Fu I
46-10	天	37	t'ien	Heaven
46-11	下	1	hsia	below }} the world
46-12	無	86	wu	without / no / ~fails
46-13	道	162	tao	Tao
46-14	戎	62	jung	war / army / soldiers
46-15	馬	187	ma	horses }} cavalry
46-16	生	100	shêng	thrive / breed / are bred / are raised
46-17	於	70	yü	in / on
46-18	郊	163	chiao	the countryside / outside the city / "suburbs" / common // border // sacred mound outside the city [1][2]
46-19	禍	113	huo	calamity / misfortune / curse / disaster / wrong // guilt
46-20	莫	140	mo	none / not one / [there] is none
46-21	大	37	ta	great / greater
46-22	於	70	yü	than
46-23	不	1	pu	not
46-24	知	111	chih	know[ing]
46-25	足	157	tsu	contentment / satisfaction / enough / (one's resting place) / (one's own nature) / satisfied where one is / satisfied with what one has }}} discontentment
46-26	咎	30	chiu	calamity / disaster / curse / misfortune / evil / fault / blame
46-27	莫	140	mo	none / not one / [there] is none
46-28	大	37	ta	great / greater / ~crueler
46-29	於	70	yü	than
46-30	欲	76	yü	want / wish / desire / desire for / longing for / tendencies
46-31	得	60a	tê	obtain / gain / possess / benefit / attain }} greed / covetousness / "wanting something for oneself" / "getting what you want" (Pine) [3]
46-32	故	66	ku	hence / thus / therefore
46-33	知	111	chih	knows / understands / [he who] knows
46-34	足	157	tsu	contentment / satisfaction / enough / "in his place" / (where he wants to be)
46-35	之	4	chih	's / its / (one's portion) }} satisfied with what one has

46-36	足	157	**tsu**	contentment / satisfaction / enough }} [when] enough is enough
46-37	常	50	**ch'ang**	always / constantly / eternal / the Eternal
46-38	足	157	**tsu**	content / satisfied / enough / has enough
46-39	矣	111	**yi**	! / indeed [4]

[1] According to Waley, the mound on the outskirts of the city refers to a sacred site that is associated with peace. It was an insult to the town, and considered sacrilegious, to let weeds grow on this sacred mound. It would be a double insult to let warhorses (the antithesis of peace) breed on this mound.
[2] ++Alt: add *tsui mo ta yü k'o yü* (sin, none, greater, than, having, desires) after *chiao*.
[3] "There are two tragedies in life: one is not getting what you want, and the other is getting what you want. The latter being the worse of the two." (Oscar Wilde)
[4] ***Chih tsu chih tsu ch'ang tsu yi***: "To know that enough is enough is to always have enough." (Duy); One who knows contentment will always have enough; Know that contentment is enough; the Eternal [is found] in your contentment.

VERSE 47

47-01	不	1	**pu**	Not / without
47-02	出	17	**ch'u**	going out / going forth / going through / going beyond // stepping out
47-03	戶	63	**hu**	door }} going out into the world
47-04	知	111	**chih**	know / [one][he] can know / understand / know [what is happening] >Alt: *chih* (arrives)—MHL
47-05	天	37	**t'ien**	Heaven
47-06	下	1	**hsia**	below }} the world / everything in the world / all below Heaven
47-07	不	1	**pu**	not / without
47-08	闚	169	**k'uei**	look[ing] / watch / see out
47-09	牖	91	**yu**	window
47-10	見	147	**chien**	see / perceive / [one can / they can] see / ~knows
47-11	天	37	**t'ien**	Heaven / sky['s] [1]
47-12	道	162	**tao**	Tao / way }} the way of Heaven / "the sky and its pattern" (Cleary)
47-13	其	12	**ch'i**	one
47-14	出	17	**ch'u**	go out / go forth / venture out
47-15	彌	57	**mi**	very much / full / complete / more and more / further
47-16	遠	162	**yüan**	distance / remove / "far from one's home" }}} the further one goes
47-17	其	12	**ch'i**	one's
47-18	知	111	**chih**	know / knowledge / be aware of / realize
47-19	彌	57	**mi**	very much / full / complete / more and more
47-20	少	42	**shao**	diminishes / few / little }} the less one knows >>Etm: "cut back on" + "small" ("to cut back what is already small")
47-21	是	72a	**shih**	(this)
47-22	以	9a	**yi**	(for) }} therefore / thus
47-23	聖	128a	**shêng**	holy / saintly
47-24	人	9a	**jên**	man }} sage
47-25	不	1	**pu**	not / "without"
47-26	行	144	**hsing**	go out / go about / go forward / walk / travel

47-27	而	126	erh	and / yet
47-28	知	111	chih	knows / [he knows] / knowledge
47-29	不	1	pu	not
47-30	見	147	chien	look[s] / see / observe / looks out
47-31	而	126	erh	and / yet
47-32	名	30a	ming	name / names / ~understands, comprehends, sees, "identifies with") >Alt: *ming* (perceive, understand)—Fu I
47-33	不	1	pu	not / "without"
47-34	為	87	wei	do / does / doing / make / act / action / work / strive / try
47-35	而	126	erh	and / yet
47-36	成	62	ch'êng	completes / finishes / accomplishes / succeeds / perfects / "works"

[1] These first two lines reflect the dictum "as above, so below" and imply that everything found outside can also be found within. (See NOTES, Verse 2: *wu-wei*)

VERSE 48

48-01	為	87	wei	Seek[s] / attend to / the pursuit of / ~student of / ~one's goal // do / does / make / act / action
48-02	學	39	hsüeh	knowledge / learning / school
48-03	日	72	jih	every day / daily / day after day
48-04	益	108	yi	gains / acquires / increase / know more / accumulate / (something is acquired) / [aims at] learning
48-05	為	87	wei	seek[s] / attend to / the pursuit of / ~student of / ~one's goal // do / make / act >Alt: *wen* (hear, heard)—MWT
48-06	道	162	tao	Tao
48-07	日	72	jih	every day / daily
48-08	損	64	sun	lose / diminish / decrease / does less / [something is] dropped / [aims at] losing
48-09	損	64	sun	lose / diminish / decrease / less / does less
48-10	之	4	chih	itself / it / him / her
48-11	又	29	yu	and / (again)
48-12	損	64	sun	lose / diminish / decrease / less / does less
48-13	以	9a	yi	(until) / thus / hence / thereby
48-14	至	133a	chih	reach / to go / attains
48-15	於	70	yü	to / through / of / until
48-16	無	86	wu	without / not / void of / non- / (empty)
48-17	為	87	wei	action / acting / make / do / become / being }} non-action / "one does nothing at all"
48-18	無	86	wu	without / non- / not / void of
48-19	為	87	wei	action / acting / make / do / become / being
48-20	而	126	erh	and / but
48-21	無	86	wu	without / non- / not / void of
48-22	不	1	pu	not / un-
48-23	為	87	wei	done / action / acting / make / do / become / being +Alt: add *chiang-yü* (when someone wants to)—Fu I
48-24	取	29	ch'ü	take hold of / capture / win / control / conquer // rely upon / "take the path of"

48-25	天	37	t'ien	Heaven
48-26	下	1	hsia	below }} the world / the empire
48-27	常	50	ch'ang	always / constantly / forever / eternal / (often)
48-28	以	9a	yi	thus / thereby / accordingly / ~according to principles
48-29	無	86	wu	without / non- / not / void of / by not / ~renouncing / "unconcerned with"
48-30	事	6	shih	interfering / meddling / affairs / busy-ness / activity / overmanaging / "trying" / tampering / "trying to change" / personal or ego-motivated action
48-31	及	12	ch'l	he / she / it / them
48-32	其	29	chi	until / "when" / >past tense
48-33	有	74	yu	have / one has / possess / (use) / (undertake)
48-34	事	6	shih	interfering / meddling / busy-ness / business / affairs / activity / overmanaging / "trying" [1]
48-35	不	1	pu	not / never
48-36	足	157	tsu	enough / sufficient / satisfied / content // "fit" / qualified / able
48-37	以	9a	yi	thus / thereby / accordingly
48-38	取	29	ch'ü	take hold of / capture / win / conquer // rule / govern
48-39	天	37	t'ien	Heaven
48-40	下	1	hsia	below }} the world / the empire

[1] [32–40] "When one is impelled to do something, the world is already beyond conquering." (Yutang); "As for activity, it is insufficient to capture the world." (Lin); "If one still has private ends to serve, one will not be able to win the world." (Wu)

V E R S E   4 9

49-01	聖	128a	shêng	Holy / saintly
49-02	人	9a	jên	man }} sage
49-03	無	86	wu	without / non- / not / void of / has no
49-04	常	50	ch'ang	constant / fixed / "decided"
49-05	心	61	hsin	heart / mind / heart-mind / ~ideas / ~opinions and feelings }}} "no interests of his own" (Lau) [1]
49-06	以	9a	yi	thus / thereby / accordingly
49-07	百	106b	pai	the hundred
49-08	姓	38	hsing	families }} everyone / the people +Alt: add chi ('s, its, theirs)
49-09	心	61	hsin	heart / mind / heart-mind / ~ideas / ~opinions and feelings
49-10	為	87	wei	act / make / do / become / being
49-11	心	61	hsin	heart / mind / heart-mind / ~ideas / ~opinions and feelings
49-12	善	30	shan	good / excellent
49-13	者	125	chê	(the ones)
49-14	吾	30	wu	I / they
49-15	善	30	shan	good / excellent / [treat with] goodness / [regard as / declare as] good
49-16	之	4	chih	he / she / it / them
49-17	不	1	pu	not / without
49-18	善	30	shan	good / excellent
49-19	者	125	chê	(the ones)

49-20	吾	30	wu	I / they
49-21	亦	8	yi	also / in turn
49-22	善 .	30	shan	good / excellent / [treat with] goodness / [regard as] good
49-23	之 .	4	chih	he / she / it / them
49-24	德	60b	tê	Te / virtue / power >Alt: *tê* (get, attain, obtain // until)—Fu I
49-25	善 .	30	shan	good / excellent / [is] good }} goodness of virtue / goodness is attained / I gain in goodness
49-26	信	9	hsin	truthful / loyal / faithful / honest / trust / trustworthy >>Etm: "stand by" + "word" ("those who stand by their word")
49-27	者	125	chê	(the ones)
49-28	吾	30	wu	I / they
49-29	信	9	hsin	truthful / loyal / faithful / honest / trust / trustworthy / [treat with] truth / [regard as] truthful
49-30	之 .	4	chih	he / she / it / them
49-31	不	1	pu	not
49-32	信	9	hsin	truthful / loyal / faithful / honest / trustworthy
49-33	者	125	chê	(the ones)
49-34	吾	30	wu	I / they
49-35	亦	8	yi	also
49-36	信	9	hsin	truthful / loyal / faithful / honest / trustworthy / [treat with] truth / [regard as] truthful
49-37	之 .	4	chih	he / she / it / them
49-38	德	60b	tê	Te / virtue / power >Alt: *tê* (get, attain, obtain // until)—Fu I
49-39	信 .	9	hsin	truthful / loyal / faithful / honest / trustworthy / [is] truthful }} faith of virtue / truth is attained
49-40	聖	128a	shêng	holy / saintly
49-41	人	9a	jên	man }} sage
49-42	在	32	tsai	lives / exist / is present / alive / presence in / "in the midst of" // (govern) / (in governing)
49-43	天	37	t'ien	Heaven
49-44	下	1	hsia	below }} the world / the empire
49-45	歙	76	hsi	unite / harmony / harmoniously >Alt: *tieh* (peaceful, shy, with reserve, humble, self-effacing)
49-46	歙	76	hsi	unite / harmony }} "he is one" >Alt: *tieh* (peaceful, shy, timid, cautious) +Alt: add *yen* (on him)—MWT
49-47	為	87	wei	action / acting / make / do / become / being
49-48	天	37	t'ien	Heaven
49-49	下	1	hsia	below }} the world / people of the world
49-50	渾	85b	hun	universal / ocean-like / harmonious whole / "community" // mixed / undifferentiated / nebulous / clouded
49-51	其	12	ch'i	his / its
49-52	心 .	61	hsin	heart / mind / heart-mind [2]
49-53	聖	128a	shêng	holy / saintly
49-54	人	9a	jên	man }} sage / sages
49-55	皆	106	chieh	all / everyone / together / [regards them, treats them, sees them] all as // [is fully] like a

| 49-56 | 孩 | 39 | hai | children / infants / [his] children / (innocent) // child   >Alt: ai (obstruct, cover) |
| 49-57 | 之 . | 4 | chih | he / she / them / his | [3] |

[1] **Wu ch'ang hsin** (without, fixed, heart-mind) is similar to Chuang-tsu's idea of *ch'eng hsin* (predisposed mind). *Wu ch'ang hsin* refers to a heart-mind that is totally free, without likes or dislikes. It is a mind "impartial" (Au), "not prejudiced" (Tze), "without decided opinions and feelings" (Yutang), and "without an interest of his own" (Wu). *Wu ch'ang hsin* is akin to the thought-free state of mind (*ch'ang wu yü*), mentioned in verse 1, which enables one to perceive the "essence," the true nature of the universe.

[2] Some texts add seven characters after *hsin* [49:52]: (hundred, families, all, focus, their, ears, eyes, [on him]) MWT has eight characters by adding *yen* (on him)—MWT (See: Lin, p. xiv)

[3] **Shêng jên chieh hai chih**: "to the sage, all are children". / "he behaves like a little child" (Feng) / "and sages renders them innocent" (Cleary) / "people open their ears and eyes, the sage covers them up" (Pine).

VERSE 50

50-01	出	17	ch'u	Go out / come out / out of / "going one way" / "appearing" [means]
50-02	生 。	100	shêng	life / live / exist
50-03	入	11	ju	go in / come in / going back / enter / "going the other way" / "disappearing" [means]
50-04	死 .	78	ssu	death }} "between birth and death" (Feng) / "out of life, death enters" (Yutang)
50-05	生	100	shêng	life / live / exist
50-06	之	4	chih	's / its
50-07	徒	60	t'u	companion / comrade / disciple / (go on foot with) / pursuers
50-08	十	24	shih	ten
50-09	有	74	yu	have / possess / are
50-10	三 .	1	san	three }}} three in ten / one-third / "about one-third" / thirteen / ~about one in three
50-11	死	78	ssu	death
50-12	之	4	chih	's / its
50-13	徒	60	t'u	companion / comrade / disciple / (go on foot with) / pursuers
50-14	十	24	shih	ten
50-15	有	74	yu	have / possess / are
50-16	三 .	1	san	three }}} three in ten / "about one-third"
50-17	人	9a	jên	people / men
50-18	之	4	chih	their / his / her / its
50-19	生	100	shêng	life / lives
50-20	動	19	tung	move / movement / moving to / "passing through" / just passing }} "living to live" (Pine)
50-21	之	4	chih	their / his / her / its
50-22	死	78	ssu	death
50-23	地	32	ti	place / realm
50-24	亦	8	yi	also
50-25	十	24	shih	ten
50-26	有	74	yu	have / possess / are
50-27	三 .	1	san	three }}} three in ten
50-28	夫	37	fu	truly / (what follows is true)
50-29	何	9	ho	what

50-30	故	66	ku	reason / cause [?]
50-31	以	9a	yi	because / therefore / hence
50-32	其	12	ch'i	they / he / she / it / man's
50-33	生	100	shêng	life / live / exist
50-34	生	100	shêng	life / live / exist }} "live their lives" / "live to live"
50-35	之	4	chih	's / its
50-36	厚	27	hou	too much / surplus / abundance / intense / intensely / too heavily / seriousness / "on gross level"
50-37	蓋	140	kai	indeed }}}}} "intense striving after life" / "set too much store by life" (Lau)
50-38	聞	128	wên	hear / I hear / have heard // said / [it is] said
50-39	善	30	shan	good / excellent / skillful / able / excels // one who is good / one who excels [in]
50-40	攝	64	shê	living / preserving / [safe]guarding / sustaining / taking care of / nourishing / maintaining >Alt: *chih* (hold, grasp)—MWT [1]
50-41	生	100	shêng	life / [his] life
50-42	者	125	chê	(he) / (she) / (the one)
50-43	陸	170	lu	on land / dry land >Alt: *ling* (hills)—MWT
50-44	行	144	hsing	travel / go out / go forth / [when] traveling / walk }} walk abroad
50-45	不	1	pu	not / does not / without
50-46	遇	162	yü	meet with / encounter / (fear) / [fear of] meeting with / ~harmed by >Alt: *pi* (avoid)—MWT
50-47	兕	141	hu	rhinoceros / wild buffalo
50-48	虎	10	ssu	tigers
50-49	入	11	ju	enter / come in / [when] entering / coming among
50-50	軍	159	chün	battlefield / middle of battle / soldiers / fighting
50-51	不	1	pu	not
50-52	被	145	pei	wear / cover with // suffer >Alt: *pi* (flee from, try to escape; avoid, shun)
50-53	甲	102	chia	armor / protective plates / "arms"
50-54	兵	12	ping	arms / weapons / sharp weapons // war / fighting / battle // soldiers }}}}} "will not be wounded in battle" (Feng) / "not injured by soldiers" (Pine)
50-55	兕	10	ssu	rhinoceros / wild buffalo
50-56	無	86	wu	without / has no / cannot
50-57	所	63	so	place / position / pitch / "mark"
50-58	投	64	t'ou	butt / thrust / throw / place upon >Alt: *ch'uai* (probe, sink)—MWT
50-59	其	12	ch'i	its / his
50-60	角	148	chiao	horn / horn [against him]
50-61	虎	141	hu	tigers
50-62	無	86	wu	without / no / cannot
50-63	所	63	so	place
50-64	措	64	ts'u	put / place / attach / fix / sink / "use"
50-65	其	12	ch'i	its / their
50-66	爪	87	chao	claw / claws / claw [in him]
50-67	兵	12	ping	soldiers / weapons of war

50-68	無	86	**wu**	without / no
50-69	所	63	**so**	place
50-70	容	40	**jung**	enter / let enter / thrust / lodge / pierce / admit / insert / sink
50-71	其	12	**ch'i**	their / its
50-72	刃	18	**jên**	blades / sword / point
50-73	夫	37	**fu**	truly / "now" / (what follows is true)
50-74	何	9	**ho**	what / why
50-75	故	66	**ku**	reason / cause / [is the] reason / so [?]
50-76	以	9a	**yi**	because / thereby / accordingly
50-77	其	12	**ch'i**	he / she
50-78	無	86	**wu**	without / has no
50-79	死	78	**ssu**	death / dying / death's
50-80	地	32	**ti**	place / realm / ground / land / room / spot }} room for death / "grounds for death"

[1] **Shan shê**: "knows how to live" / "has a firm purchase on life" (Duy); "one whose life is based on goodness" (Carus); "one possessing the secret of life" (Parker); "one who knows how to maintain his vital powers" (Alexander)

V E R S E 5 1

51-01	道	162	**tao**	Tao
51-02	生	100	**shêng**	life / live / gives life to / produces / begets / birth / brings forth
51-03	之	4	**chih**	them / it / he / she / (_____) }}} "all things arise from Tao" (Feng)
51-04	德	60b	**tê**	Te / virtue / power
51-05	畜	102	**hsü**	nourishes / feeds / nurses / fosters / rears / nurtures // keeps / keeps safe
51-06	之	4	**chih**	them / it / he / she / (_____)
51-07	物	93	**wu**	things / concrete things / matter / material world / things of this world
51-08	形	59	**hsing**	shape / form / physical form / material
51-09	之	4	**chih**	them / (_____) }} give them shape / give them physical form }}} "They receive their forms according to the nature of each." (Legge)
51-10	勢	19	**shih**	circumstances [and tendencies] / environment // ~forces // opposites >Alt: *chi* (usage, "talents," "unique capacity")—MWT
51-11	成	62	**ch'êng**	complete[s] / perfect / make perfect / bring to maturity
51-12	之	4	**chih**	them / (_____)
51-13	是	72a	**shih**	(this)
51-14	以	9a	**yi**	(for) }} therefore / hence / thus
51-15	萬	140	**wan**	ten thousand / all
51-16	物	93	**wu**	things }} everything / all things in the world
51-17	莫	140	**mo**	none / no / no one X Alt: omit
51-18	不	1	**pu**	not / does not X Alt: omit
51-19	尊	41	**tsun**	esteem / honor / worship / revere / respect
51-20	道	162	**tao**	Tao
51-21	而	126	**erh**	and
51-22	貴	154	**kuei**	honor / esteem / prize / hold dear / exalt[ed] / glorify

51-23	德	60b	tê	Te / virtue / power
51-24	道	162	tao	Tao
51-25	之	4	chih	's / its
51-26	尊	41	tsun	esteem / honor / worship / revere / treasure / do homage to / "honorableness"
51-27	德	60b	tê	Te / virtue / power
51-28	之	4	chih	's / its
51-29	貴	154	kuei	esteem[ed] / prize / honor / hold dear / exalt / glory / "esteemableness"
51-30	夫	37	fu	"yet" / above all / forasmuch / "because" / truly / (what follows is true)
51-31	莫	140	mo	none / no one / without / not by
51-32	之	4	chih	it / it being / anyone's
51-33	命	30b	ming	command[ed] / order / decree / behest / demanded // fate / destiny >Alt: *chüeh* (reward, give noble rank) [1]
51-34	而	126	erh	and / yet / but
51-35	常	50	ch'ang	always / constantly / they always come
51-36	自	132	tzu	self
51-37	然	86	jan	so }} spontaneous / spontaneity / naturally / of themselves / of their own accord / "natural for them" / "in the nature of things" / "because by nature it is so" (Blakney)
51-38	故	66	ku	hence / thus / therefore X Alt: omit
51-39	道	162	tao	Tao
51-40	生	100	shêng	life / live / gives life / "gives birth to them" / begets / produces / birth / "arise from"
51-41	之	4	chih	them / (_____)
51-42	德	60b	tê	Te / virtue / power X Alt: omit
51-43	畜	17	ch'u	nourishes / feeds / nurses / fosters / rears / nurtures / keeps
51-44	之	4	chih	them / (_____)
51-45	長	168	ch'ang	raises / grows / rears / matures / "makes them grow" / "grows old with them" / brings them up / ripens
51-46	之	4	chih	them / (_____)
51-47	育	130	yü	nurtures / bring up / rear / develop / nourish / nurses / educate / accomplishes
51-48	之	4	chih	them / (_____)
51-49	亭	8	t'ing	covers / protects / shelters >Alt: *ch'ing* (complete / finish / perfect / accomplish / succeed)
51-50	之	4	chih	them / (_____)
51-51	毒	80	tu	matures / prepares / ripen >Alt: *tu* (provide for, mature, adjust, rest)
51-52	之	4	chih	them / (_____)
51-53	養	184	yang	rear / nourish / feed / nurture / sustain / support >Alt: *kai* (cover)—Tang Inscription
51-54	之	4	chih	them / (_____)
51-55	覆	146	fu	protect / guard / cover / shelter / house / bury / "cover them under her wing" (Wu)
51-56	之	4	chih	them / (_____) }}}} "build them up, break them down"
51-57	生	100	shêng	live / life / give life / produce / [Tao] produces them / begets / give birth
51-58	而	126	erh	and / yet / but
51-59	不	1	pu	not / without

51-60	有	74	yu	have / own / owning them / possess[ing] / claim possession / take possession of them
51-61	為	87	wei	act / do / make / (benefit) / (help)
51-62	而	126	erh	and / yet
51-63	不	1	pu	not / without
51-64	恃	61	shih	claim / rely upon / presume / expect / "appropriate" / assert / hold on to / "presuming" / "exact gratitude" / "set no store by it"
51-65	長	168	ch'ang	develop / foster growth / raises // is superior / "the steward"
51-66	而	126	erh	and / yet
51-67	不	1	pu	not
51-68	宰	40	tsai	rule [over] / lord over / dominate / control / master / "exercise authority" / "butcher"
51-69	是	72a	shih	this is
51-70	謂	149	wei	called
51-71	玄	96	hsüan	secret / obscure / hidden / deep / profound / dark / mysterious >Alt: yuan (primal)
51-72	德	60b	tê	Te / virtue / power

[1] *Mo chih ming*: "not granted by anyone" / "not due to a decree" / "without anyone commanding it" / "not conferred"

VERSE 52

52-01	天	37	t'ien	Heaven
52-02	下	1	hsia	below }} the world / the universe
52-03	有	74	yu	has / possesses / takes / (there was) / (had)
52-04	始	38	shih	beginning / a beginning / origin / first / cause / common beginning / genesis // maiden
52-05	以	9a	yi	thus / (which may)
52-06	為	87	wei	become / make / do / was / is / (can be called) / (can be regarded as)
52-07	天	37	t'ien	Heaven
52-08	下	1	hsia	below }} the world / the universe
52-09	母	80	mu	mother / Mother
52-10	既	71	chi	when
52-11	得	60a	tê	obtain / attain >Alt: chih (know, understand)
52-12	其	12	ch'i	one's / the
52-13	母	80	mu	mother
52-14	以	9a	yi	thereby / thus >Alt: fu (return, in turn)
52-15	知	111	chih	know / having known / [one] knows / aware of / understand / "reached"
52-16	其	12	ch'i	her / the / its
52-17	子	39	tzu	child / son / children / progeny / offspring / (manifestations)
52-18	既	71	chi	when / after
52-19	知	111	chih	know / having known / [one] knows / aware of / understand / "reached"
52-20	其	12	ch'i	her / the / its
52-21	子	39	tzu	child / son / children / progeny / offspring
52-22	復	60	fu	in turn / return / still / go back to / "remain"
52-23	守	40	shou	hold / keep / keep close / keep safe / stay with / abide in / keep hold of / "keep in touch with"
52-24	其	12	ch'i	its / (the)

52-25	母	80	mu	mother
52-26	沒	85	mo	end / till the end / throughout / fully / disappear
52-27	身	158	shên	one's life / person / body
52-28	不	1	pu	not / free of / without / freedom from / "preserved from"
52-29	殆	78	tai	danger / peril / harm / injury / risk / "fear of death" / perishing // exhaustion
52-30	塞	32	sai	close / stop / cork / block
52-31	其	12	ch'i	the / your / his
52-32	兌	10	tui	mouth / opening / passages / apertures / holes / "senses"
52-33	閉	169	pi	shut / close / bolt / "guard"
52-34	其	12	ch'i	the / your / his
52-35	門	169	mên	gate / door / "sense-gate" / "senses" / "doors (of cunning and desire)" (Chan)
52-36	終	120	chung	last / to the end
52-37	身	158	shên	of life / one's life / person / body }} all your life / throughout life
52-38	不	1	pu	not / do not / with / out / there will be no
52-39	勤	19	ch'in	toil / work / labor / troubled // worn-out / exhausted }} "peace" / "ever full" / "not run dry"
52-40	開	169	k'ai	open / "unblock"
52-41	其	12	ch'i	the / your / his
52-42	兌	10	tui	mouth / opening / passages
52-43	濟	85	chi	meddle / be busy / crowd / engages / "multiply" / "carry out" / "insist"
52-44	其	12	ch'i	with / to / your
52-45	事	6	shih	affairs / activities / meddling / busy-ness / "trying to control everything" // "troubles"
52-46	終	120	chung	end / to the end of / utmost
52-47	身	158	shên	one's life / person / of life / your days
52-48	不	1	pu	not / there will be no / (beyond)
52-49	救	66	chiu	rescue / saving / salvation / redemption / cure / hope / help
52-50	見	147	chien	see / perceive / seeing / discern
52-51	小	42	hsiao	small / smallness / the small / what is small / insignificant / diminish
52-52	曰	73	yüeh	called / is called / is / ~has
52-53	明	72	ming	light / illumination / enlightenment / bright / insight // clarity / discernment / "clear-sighted" / "vision"
52-54	守	40	shou	hold / keep to / keeping / stay with / abide by / guard / protect / preserve
52-55	柔	75	jou	tender[ness] / weak / soft / yielding / pliant / gentle[ness] / flexible / "submissive"
52-56	曰	73	yüeh	called / is
52-57	強	57	ch'iang	strong / strength
52-58	用	101	yung	use[s] / make[s] use of / using / employ[s] / utilize
52-59	其	12	ch'i	its / the
52-60	光	10	kuang	light / bright / bright light / brightness / "shining radiance" / "Tao's light"
52-61	復	60	fu	revert / return / send back / restore
52-62	歸	77	kuei	return / restore / send back / "go home to" / again
52-63	其	12	ch'i	its / he / she / to

52-64	明	72	ming	light / illumination / enlightenment / insight
52-65	無	86	wu	without / not / does not / do not
52-66	遺	162	yi	expose / let / surrender / transmit to }} avoid
52-67	身	158	shên	oneself / one's life [to]
52-68	殃	78	yang	misfortune / calamity / danger / distress / peril / "perdition"
52-69	是	72a	shih	this is
52-70	謂	149	wei	called / is to }} such is to
52-71	習	124	hsi	practice [of] / practicing / usage / custom / following / entering / learning / cultivating / rest // hidden >Alt: *hsi* (inherit, accord with)—Fu I
52-72	常	50	ch'ang	eternal / everlasting / [the] constant / consistency / the Absolute / the Eternal [1]

[1] *Hsi ch'ang*: "Practice of the Eternal"; "Following the Eternal (Light)"; "Following the Eternal (Tao)" (Ta-Kao); "Returning to the nature of one's origin" (Wai-Tao); "Being clothed with immortality" (Parker); "The eternal heritage" (Mears); "Resorting to the always-so" (Waley)

VERSE 53

53-01	使	9b	shih	If
53-02	我	62	wo	I / ~rulers / ~kings
53-03	介	9	chieh	little / insignificant / small / subtle
53-04	然	86	jan	manner / natural }} "least scrap of" (Waley)
53-05	有	74	yu	have / possess / had
53-06	知	111	chih	knowledge / understanding / sense
53-07	行	144	hsing	walk / travel / to walk / follow / [I would] follow
53-08	於	70	yü	in / with / through / on
53-09	大	37	ta	great / greatest / broad / main
53-10	道	162	tao	path / way / road / Tao
53-11	唯	30b	wei	only / alone / for this reason / exactly / I alone
53-12	施	70	shih	stray // to do / act / give / use / shall / "application" [1]
53-13	是	72a	shih	this
53-14	畏	102	wei	fear / dread / afraid of / danger / "demand care"
53-15	大	37	ta	great / greatest / broad / main
53-16	道	162	tao	path / way / road / Tao
53-17	甚	99	shên	very / excess / extreme
53-18	夷	37	yi	even / level / smooth / flat / steady / straight / easy [to walk on]
53-19	而	126	erh	and / but / yet
53-20	民	83	min	the people / others >Alt: *jên* (men, ~rulers)
53-21	好	38	hao	like / prefer / are fond of / love / "welcome" / want to [use, take]
53-22	徑	60	ching	by-paths / side roads / deviations / to be sidetracked / "devious paths" / ~symbolism for the "by-roads" of the mind—too many thoughts [2]
53-23	朝	74	chao	palace / seat of government / courts / royal court
53-24	甚	99	shên	very / excess / extreme / exceedingly / "rank with" / (arranged in)
53-25	除	170	ch'u	splendid / splendor / well-kept // immaculate

53-26	田	102a	t'ien	fields / [while the] fields
53-27	甚	99	shên	very / excess / extreme / exceedingly / full of / (overgrown with)
53-28	蕪	140	wu	weeds / weedy / poor / "without producing" / "go untilled"
53-29	倉	9	ts'ang	granaries
53-30	甚	99	shên	very / extremely / exceedingly / (all but)
53-31	虛	141	hsü	empty / bare / vacant
53-32	服	74	fu	clothed in / dressed in / clad in / wear / clothes
53-33	文	67	wên	elegant / embroidered / gorgeous / ornaments
53-34	綵	120	ts'ai	clothes / gown / colors }} finery
53-35	帶	50	tai	carry / carrying / "at their side"
53-36	利	18	li	sharp / fine
53-37	劍	18	chien	weapons / swords
53-38	厭	27	yen	excessive / extreme / beyond limit / filled / satisfied with / gorged / "indulge in"
53-39	飲	184	yin	drinks / drinking X Alt: omit—MWT
53-40	食	184	shih	food / eating
53-41	財	154	ts'ai	wealth
53-42	貨	154	huo	possessions / goods / merchandise / treasure
53-43	有	74	yu	have / are / possess / "accumulated in"
53-44	餘	184	yü	surplus / excess / abundance / too much / "more than they can use" / "splitting with"
53-45	是	72a	shih	this is
53-46	謂	149	wei	called / known as
53-47	盜	108	tao	robber / thief / robbery / larceny / brigandage / robber's
53-48	夸	37	k'ua	pride / grand / "showing off" / boastfulness / vanity / extravagance / exaggeration >Alt: *hsi* (its, 's) [3]
53-49	非	175	fei	not / anti- / opposing / opposite / goes against / far from / not following +Alt: add *tao-hsi* (robbery, thievery)——Fu I
53-50	道	162	tao	Tao
53-51	也	5	yeh	! / indeed X Alt: omit
53-52	哉	30	tsai	! / indeed / really

[1] **Shih** derives its meaning from "the raising of a banner," which implies a claim to individuality and name. Thus, *shih* is associated with personal or ego-motivated action and is the opposite of *wu-wei*, non-action. Acting individually—seeing your action in a limited context—is a by-road, a path leading away from the truth.

[2] **Ching** ("Side-roads") (See NOTES)

[3] **Tao-k'ua** (robber pride, "stealing and exaggeration"). **Tao-hsi** (robbery, thievery). This is a pun on the similar pronunciation of tao (Tao, the Way) and tao (rob). One variation reads: "This is called tao (robbery), and tao (robbery) is certainly not tao (the Way)."

VERSE 54

54-01	善	30	shan	Good / well- / excellent / (firmly) // [one who is / that which is] good
54-02	建	54	chien	rooted / plant / planted / established / set // built / constructions / "with foundation"
54-03	者	125	chê	it / (the thing) / [in Tao]
54-04	不	1	pu	not / cannot be / does not

54-05	拔 •	64	pa	uprooted / eradicated / pulled up / pulled out // toppled / fall down / "easily shaken"
54-06	善	30	shan	good / well / excellent / (firm) / (tight)
54-07	抱	64	pao	grasp / hold / held / held fast / "carry in their arms" // conceal / contain / embrace
54-08	者	125	chê	it / (the thing) / (of Tao)
54-09	不	1	pu	not / cannot be
54-10	脱 •	130	t'o	taken away / separated / slip / slip loose / let go // escape / stolen [from it]
54-11	子	39	tzu	children / sons
54-12	孫	39	sun	grandchildren / grandsons }} for generations / your descendants / their heirs
54-13	以	9a	yi	thereby / thus
54-14	祭	113	chi	offering / worship / honor
54-15	祀	113	ssu	sacrifice / sacrifice to ancestors
54-16	不	1	pu	not / will not / shall not
54-17	輟 •	159	cho	cease / end / finish / stop / be suspended }} never end / continue without fail
54-18	修	9	hsiu	cultivate[s][d] / practice / [when one] cultivates
54-19	之	4	chih	it
54-20	於	70	yü	to / at / through / in
54-21	身 •	158	shên	person / oneself / one's life / your self / individual / [his] person / "the inner self"
54-22	其	12	ch'i	his / it / its
54-23	德	60b	tê	Te / virtue / power / character
54-24	乃	4	nai	then / thus / precisely / thereupon [it becomes] [will be]
54-25	真 •	109	chên	real / true / genuine
54-26	修	9	hsiu	cultivate / practice / adorn / [one who] cultivates
54-27	之	4	chih	it
54-28	於	70	yü	in / through
54-29	家 •	40	chia	family / the family / [his] family
54-30	其	12	ch'i	his / it
54-31	德	60b	tê	Te / virtue / power
54-32	乃	4	nai	then
54-33	餘 •	184	yü	surplus / excess / overflow[ing] / multiplies / "more than sufficient"
54-34	修	9	hsiu	cultivate / practice / [when on] cultivates
54-35	之	4	chih	it
54-36	於	70	yü	in / through / with [one's]
54-37	鄉 •	163	hsiang	village / district / town / local area / community
54-38	其	12	ch'i	it / his
54-39	德	60b	tê	Te / virtue / power
54-40	乃	4	nai	then / hence / thereupon
54-41	長 •	168	ch'ang	lasts / lasting / long time / endure / "increase"
54-42	修	9	hsiu	cultivate / practice / adorn / [when one] practices
54-43	之	4	chih	it
54-44	於	70	yü	in / with / through

54-45	國 .	31	kuo	country / nation / state
54-46	其	12	ch'i	his / its
54-47	德	60b	tê	Te / virtue / power
54-48	乃	4	nai	then / hence
54-49	豐 .	151	fêng	abundant / abound / copious / prolific / prosper
54-50	修	9	hsiu	cultivate / practice / adorn / [one who] practices
54-51	之	4	chih	it
54-52	於	70	yü	in / with / through
54-53	天	37	t'ien	Heaven
54-54	下 .	1	hsia	below }} the world / universe / everywhere
54-55	其	12	ch'i	his / it
54-56	德	60b	tê	Te / virtue / power
54-57	乃	4	nai	then
54-58	普 .	72	p'u	universal / grand / large / everywhere / pervasive / abounds / "good" (Lin)
54-59	故	66	ku	therefore X Alt: omit—MWT
54-60	以	9a	yi	(by) / (with) / (through) / therefore / according to / (as)
54-61	身	158	shên	the person / yourself / oneself / one's life / individual / the self
54-62	觀	147	kuan	view[ed] / truly see / judge / "test" / consider / examine / look at
54-63	身 .	158	shên	the person / persons / yourself / oneself / one's life / individual / the self
54-64	以	9a	yi	(by) / (with) / (through) / (as) / thus
54-65	家	40	chia	family / home
54-66	觀	147	kuan	view[ed] / judge / "test" / consider / examine / look at / "conceive"
54-67	家 .	40	chia	family / home
54-68	以	9a	yi	(by) / (with) / (through) / (as) / thus
54-69	鄉	163	hsiang	village / district / town / local area
54-70	觀	147	kuan	view[ed] / judge / "test" / consider / examine / look at
54-71	鄉 .	163	hsiang	village / district / town / local area / community
54-72	以	9a	yi	(by) / (with) / (through) / (as) / thus
54-73	國	31	kuo	country / nation / state
54-74	觀	147	kuan	view[ed] / judge / "test" / consider / examine / look at
54-75	國 .	31	kuo	country / nation / state
54-76	以	9a	yi	(by) / (with) / (through) / (as) / thus
54-77	天	37	t'ien	Heaven
54-78	下	1	hsia	below }} the world / all below Heaven
54-79	觀	147	kuan	view[ed] / judge / "test" / consider / examine / look at
54-80	天	37	t'ien	Heaven
54-81	下 .	1	hsia	below }} the world / all below Heaven
54-82	吾	30	wu	I
54-83	何	9	ho	what / why / how
54-84	以	9a	yi	(by) / (with) / (through) / thus

54-85	知	111	chih	know / understand / realize
54-86	天	37	t'ien	Heaven
54-87	下	1	hsia	below　+Alt: add *chih* (its, 's)　}} the world / the universe / "the way of the world"
54-88	然	86	jan	so / being so / is so / as such / "as it is" / "this to be the case"
54-89	哉.	30	tsai	? / (question)
54-90	以	9a	yi	(by) / (through) / (by means of)
54-91	此.	77	tz'u	this / ~cultivation of virtue / "what is within me"

VERSE 55

55-01	含	30	han	Possess / contain / embody / hold / maintain / one who possesses
55-02	德	60b	tê	Te / virtue / power / character
55-03	之	4	chih	it / in / its
55-04	厚.	27	hou	fullness / full / filled with / abundance / richness / generous / thick / "steeped in"
55-05	比	81	pi	the One / that
55-06	於	70	yü	to / comparable to / is like / resembles
55-07	赤	155	ch'ih	infant / newborn
55-08	子.	39	tzu	baby / child
55-09	蜂	142	fêng	bee / wasp / hornet
55-10	蠆	142	ch'ai	scorpion
55-11	虺	142	hui	serpent / cobra / snake
55-12	蛇	142	shê	snake / serpent　}}}} >Alt: replace v. 55:09–12 with *tu ch'ung* (poisonous insects)
55-13	不	1	pu	not / will not
55-14	螫.	142	shih	sting [him / it]
55-15	猛	94	mêng	wild / fierce / ferocious
55-16	獸	94	shou	beasts / animals
55-17	不	1	pu	not / will not
55-18	據.	64	chü	seize / pounce / attack / claw　[him / it]
55-19	攫	64	chüeh	carnivorous / prey / predatory
55-20	鳥	196	niao	birds　}} birds of prey
55-21	不	1	pu	not / will not
55-22	搏.	64	po	strike / grasp / seize / pounce / attack / "carry off" / maul / "swoop down on"　[him / it]
55-23	骨	188	ku	bones / [his] bones
55-24	弱	57	jo	weak / flexible / yielding
55-25	筋	118	chin	muscles / sinews / tendons
55-26	柔	75	jou	tender / soft / gentle / pliant / weak
55-27	而	126	erh	and / yet / but
55-28	握	64	wo	grasp / hold
55-29	固.	31	ku	firm / strong / lasting
55-30	未	75	wei	not / does not / has not
55-31	知	111	chih	know / understand / yet experienced

55-32	牝	93	p'in	female / the female
55-33	牡	93	mu	male / the male
55-34	之	4	chih	their
55-35	合	30a	ho	union / join / meet / relation / mating }} union of the sexes
55-36	而	126	erh	and / yet
55-37	全	11	ch'üan	complete / whole / fully formed / perfect >Alt: *tsui* (organ / male genitalia)
55-38	作.	9a	tso	arise / aroused / erect / stirs / ~hard
55-39	精	119	ching	life-force / essence / essential part / vigor / virility / "manhood"
55-40	之	4	chih	its / [grows to] its
55-41	至	133a	chih	utmost / at its height / zenith / epitome / "strong" / full / perfection / "unspoiled"
55-42	也.	5	yeh	! / indeed
55-43	終	120	chung	all / to the end / full
55-44	日	72	jih	day
55-45	號	141	hao	cries / wails +Alt: add *yi* (sobs, weeps, screams)
55-46	而	126	erh	and
55-47	不	1	pu	not / does not [get]
55-48	嗄.	30	sha	hoarse / become hoarse
55-49	和	30b	ho	harmony / content / peace / equilibrium / harmony
55-50	之	4	chih	its / his / is
55-51	至	133a	chih	utmost / perfection / at its height / zenith / epitome / highest expression
55-52	也.	5	yeh	! / indeed
55-53	知	111	chih	know / to know / understand / perceive / realize
55-54	和	30b	ho	harmony / contentment / peacefulness / equilibrium / harmonious
55-55	曰	73	yüeh	called / is called / (means) / to be in accord with
55-56	常.	50	ch'ang	[the] eternal / everlasting / constant / unchanging
55-57	知	111	chih	know / to know / understand / perceive / realize / "be in accord with"
55-58	常	50	ch'ang	eternal / everlasting / constant / unchanging
55-59	曰	73	yüeh	called / is called / means
55-60	明.	72	ming	light / brilliant / luminous / enlightenment / discernment / [to be] enlightened
55-61	益	108	yi	increase / gain / benefit // "force growth of" / "add to" / "help along" / "improve"
55-62	生	100	shêng	life / one's life / one's vitality
55-63	曰	73	yüeh	called / is called / means / is / portends
55-64	祥.	113	hsiang	blessing / good omen / propitious // ill omen / ominous / ill-fated / ill-portend }}}} "A full life—it is your blessing." [1]
55-65	心	61	hsin	heart / mind / heart-mind / ("impulse")
55-66	使	9b	shih	direct / directing / order / control / master[ing] / employ / "let go" / "egg on"
55-67	氣	84	ch'i	*chi* / vital force / vital breath / life-force / vital energy / spirit / "vigor"
55-68	曰	73	yüeh	called / is called / means / is to be
55-69	強.	57	ch'iang	strength / strong // violence / violent / overstrain / assertive / "stark" }}}}} "A loving heart—it is your strength."

55-70	物	93	wu	things / creatures
55-71	壯	33	chuang	strong / robust / fully grown / overgrown / "too much energy used" / "climax in power"
55-72	則	18	tsê	then >Alt: *tsiang* (going to / about to / will soon)
55-73	老	125	lao	grow old / become old / decay / exhaustion
55-74	謂	149	wei	call / this is called / we call
55-75	之	4	chih	it
55-76	不	1	pu	not
55-77	道	162	tao	Tao
55-78	不	1	pu	not / [whatever is] not
55-79	道	162	tao	Tao
55-80	知	72	tsao	soon
55-81	已	49	yi	ends / ceases / comes to an end / >v. 55:70–81 = v. 30:64–75

[1] **Hsiang**, meaning "blessings," can also mean "misfortune": (A) "To increase life is called a blessing." (Carus); "That which is beneficial to life is auspicious." (Cheng); "Improvement in health is a good omen." (Wei), and (B) "To force the growth of things means ill omen." (Chan); "To hasten the growth of life is ominous." (Wu); "To benefit one's own life is ill-fated." (Lin)

VERSE 56

56-01	知	111	chih	Know[s] / understand[s] / realize[s]
56-02	者	125	chê	(the one) / (he) }} one who knows // one who is wise
56-03	不	1	pu	not / does not
56-04	言	149	yen	speak[s] / talk[s] / ~give political decrees
56-05	言	149	yen	speak[s] / talk[s] / ~give political decrees
56-06	者	125	chê	(the one) / (he)
56-07	不	1	pu	not / does not
56-08	知	111	chih	know[s] / understand[s] / realize[s]
56-09	塞	32	sai	shut / close / secure / seal / block / fill / "put a lid on"
56-10	其	12	ch'i	the / his / its
56-11	兌	10	tui	mouth / openings / apertures
56-12	閉	169	pi	shut / close / lock
56-13	其	12	ch'i	the / his / its
56-14	門	169	mên	gates / doors / "sense-gates" / "gates to the senses"
56-15	挫	64	ts'o	blunt / break / dull / temper
56-16	其	12	ch'i	the / your / its / his
56-17	銳	167	jui	sharpness / sharp / point / edge[s] / acute
56-18	解	148	chieh	unravel / untie / untangle / (simplify) / (resolve)
56-19	其	12	ch'i	the / yours / its / his
56-20	紛	120	fên	tangles / knots / (problems) / (complications)
56-21	和	30b	ho	harmony / harmonizes / dim / soften / blend with / temper / mask
56-22	其	12	ch'l	the / yours / its / his
56-23	光	10	kuang	brilliance / light / brightness / glare / glory
56-24	同	30	t'ung	identify / join / unite / make identical / become one with // subdue / assimilate / "submerge"

56-25	其	12	ch'i	the / yours / its / oneself [with]
56-26	塵	32	ch'ên	[the] dust / lowest / worldly / dusty world / dust of the earth / "turmoil"
56-27	是	72a	shih	this is
56-28	謂	149	wei	called
56-29	玄	96	hsüan	profound / mysterious / secret / hidden / dark / deep / obscure >Alt: *yüan* (primal)
56-30	同	30	t'ung	identification / identity / union / whole / unity / harmony / sameness / alike / blending / merging / alliance / level / equal }}}} "this is called the mystery of unity" [1][2]
56-31	故	66	ku	hence / therefore
56-32	不	1	pu	not
56-33	可	30	k'o	can / able / possible
56-34	得	60a	tê	obtain / attain / gain / possess / benefit
56-35	而	126	erh	and / yet
56-36	親	147	ch'in	attachment / love / be loved // approach / affinity / "be close" / "touch" / "intimate" / kindred +Alt: add *yi* (and) [3]
56-37	不	1	pu	not
56-38	可	30	k'o	can / able / can be
56-39	得	60a	tê	obtain / attain / gain / possess / benefit / "touch him"
56-40	而	126	erh	and
56-41	疏	103	shu	aversion / hate / shun / abandon / far / distant / estrange / indifferent / far from / repel [3]
56-42	不	1	pu	not
56-43	可	30	k'o	can / able
56-44	得	60a	tê	obtain / attain / gain / possess / benefit / "reach him"
56-45	而	126	erh	and / yet
56-46	利	18	li	profit / benefit / advantage / gain / help / "good" / advantage / enrichment // sharp [4]
56-47	不	1	pu	not
56-48	可	30	k'o	can / able
56-49	得	60a	tê	obtain / be obtained / attain / gain / possess / benefit
56-50	而	126	erh	and / yet
56-51	害	40	hai	loss // injure / hurt / harm / damage / offend / disadvantage / calamity [4]
56-52	不	1	pu	not
56-53	可	30	k'o	can / able / can he / is he able to
56-54	得	60a	tê	obtain / be obtained / attain / gain / possess / benefit / "affect him"
56-55	而	126	erh	and / yet
56-56	貴	154	kuei	honor / esteem / treasure / value / exalt / cherish / ennoble / exalt +Alt: add *yi* (and) [5]
56-57	不	1	pu	not
56-58	可	30	k'o	can / able / can he / is he able to
56-59	得	60a	tê	obtain / be obtained / attain / gain / possess / benefit
56-60	而	126	erh	and / yet
56-61	賤	154	chien	disgrace / debase / despise / humiliate / demean // mutilate [5]

56-62	故	66	ku	thus / therefore / for this reason
56-63	為	87	wei	make / do / becomes / he is
56-64	天	37	t'ien	Heaven
56-65	下	1	hsia	below / under }} the world ['s]
56-66	貴	154	kuei	honor / esteem / treasure / value / cherish / precious / prize / dear / highest }}} "highest state of man" (Feng)

[1] **Shih wei hsüan t'ung**: This is called . . ."Profound identification" (Chan); "Mystic Unity" (Yutang); "Mystic Whole" (Wu); "Mystic Agreement" (Legge); "Mystic Assimilation" (Wei); "Mysterious leveling" (Waley); "primal oneness"; "Primal Union" (Feng); "Original oneness" (Maurer).

[2] Compare *shih wei hsüan t'ung* ("this," "is called," "mysterious," "oneness") with *t'ung wei chih hsüan* ("oneness," "is called," "its," "mystery.")—v. 1:48–51.

[3] **Ch'in** and **shu** are usually translated as a pair of opposites, such as: close–far / love–hate / intimate and close–distant and indifferent / court after–shun / made familiar–estranged / affection-estrangement (Blakney) / friends-enemies (Feng).

[4] **Li** (profit) and **hai** (loss) are posited as opposites.

[5] **Kuei** (honor) and **chien** (disgrace) are posited as opposites.

VERSE 57

57-01	以	9a	yi	Use / employ / (with)
57-02	正	77	chêng	righteousness / straightforward / justice / correct behavior / upright / rectitude / normality / "direction" [1]
57-03	治	85	chih	govern / rule / administer
57-04	國	31	kuo	the empire / the state / country
57-05	以	9a	yi	use / employ / (with)
57-06	奇	37a	ch'i	strange / surprise tactics / abnormal / "abnormal tactics" / cunning / surprise / deceit / trickery / crafty / strategy / extraordinary / unorthodox / bizarre [2]
57-07	用	101	yung	use / put to use / utilizes / direct / operate / conduct / wage / ~fight
57-08	兵	12	ping	the army / war / military / a war
57-09	以	9a	yi	(with)
57-10	無	86	wu	non- / nothing
57-11	事	6	shih	interfere[ing] / meddle / doing / busy-ness / activity / "trying to control everything" / "striving" / involvement / business }} inaction
57-12	取	29	ch'ü	take hold of / capture / win / conquer // rule / govern / administer / become master of
57-13	天	37	t'ien	Heaven
57-14	下	1	hsia	below / under }} the world / the empire / all below Heaven / universe
57-15	吾	30	wu	I
57-16	何	9	ho	what / how
57-17	以	9a	yi	thus / thereby / accordingly }} by what
57-18	知	111	chih	know / understand / realize
57-19	其	12	ch'i	its / this
57-20	然	86	jan	so / being so / is so / as such / "as it is"
57-21	哉	30	tsai	! / indeed [?]
57-22	以	9a	yi	(by) / through / according to / by [reason of] X Alt: omit—MWT

57-23	此	77	tz'u	this / "what is within me" X Alt: omit—MWT	[3]
57-24	天	37	t'ien	Heaven	
57-25	下	1	hsia	below / under }} the world / the empire / all below Heaven	
57-26	多	36	to	more / many / much / plenty / a lot / excess / greater	
57-27	忌	61	chi	restrictions / fear / "confinement of the heart" >>Etm: "confine" (surround) + (over) "heart"	
57-28	諱	149	hui	prohibitions / conceal / taboo / to shun	
57-29	而	126	erh	and / yet / (_____)	
57-30	民	83	min	the people / common / multitudes / populace	
57-31	彌	57	mi	increase / complete / full / more	
57-32	貧	154	p'in	impoverished / poor / become poor }} poorer	
57-33	民	83	min	the people >Alt: *ch'ao* (the court)	
57-34	多	36	to	more / many / much / plenty / a lot / excess	
57-35	利	18	li	sharp / profit }} sharper	
57-36	器	30	ch'i	weapons	
57-37	國	31	kuo	country / nation / state	
57-38	家	40	chia	(_____) }} country / nation / state	
57-39	滋	85	tzu	more and more / greater / great	
57-40	昏	72	hun	confused / troubled / chaos / disorder / dark / darkness / obscure / benighted	
57-41	人	9a	jên	the people / man	
57-42	多	36	to	more / many / much / plenty / a lot / excess / abound in	
57-43	伎	9	chi	artful / skill / crafty / clever	
57-44	巧	48	ch'iao	skillful / crafty / technique / schemes / ingenious / ingenuity / cunning }} "crafts people have"	
57-45	奇	37a	ch'i	abnormal / rare / extraordinary / non-commonplace / trickery / strange / exotic / vicious	
57-46	物	93	wu	things	
57-47	滋	85	tzu	more and more / multiply / greater number	
57-48	起	156	ch'i	arise / occur / begin to happen / appear / produced / "articulate" }}}} "the stranger the outcome" (Pine)	
57-49	法	85	fa	laws / rules >Alt: *fa* (fine)—MWT	
57-50	令	9	ling	order / law / command / edicts / statutes >Alt: *wu* (things, ~treasure)—MWT	
57-51	滋	85	tzu	more and more / increase / greater number	
57-52	彰	59	chang	manifest / arise / exhibited / prominent / promulgated / "conspicuous"	
57-53	盜	108	tao	robbers / highwaymen / brigands	
57-54	賊	154b	tsê	thieves }} criminals	
57-55	多	36	to	more / many / much / plenty	
57-56	有	74	yu	are / appear / exist / there will be }} "the thicker the thieves" (Pine)	
57-57	故	66	ku	thus / hence / therefore / (cause) / (reason)	
57-58	聖	128a	shêng	holy	
57-59	人	9a	jên	man	
57-60	云	7	yün	says / speak[s] [:]	
57-61	我	62	wo	I [do, practice]	

57-62	無	86	wu	without / non- / nothing / [take] no
57-63	為	87	wei	action / doing }} do nothing
57-64	而	126	erh	and / yet
57-65	民	83	min	the people
57-66	自	132	tzu	naturally / spontaneously / of themselves
57-67	化	21	hua	transform / change / reform / "touched" / "civilized by moral influence" (Yutang)
57-68	我	62	wo	I / they
57-69	好	38	hao	welcome / good / right / love / prefer / enjoy / [regard as] good
57-70	靜	174	ching	quiet / quietude / peace / stillness / repose / tranquility }} stay quiet
57-71	而	126	erh	and
57-72	民	83	min	the people
57-73	自	132	tzu	naturally / spontaneously / of themselves [become]
57-74	正	77	chêng	righteous / upright / correct / "adjust" / "civilized" / just / honest / fair [with each other] / "settle down into their regular grooves" (Wu) [1]
57-75	我	62	wo	I [do, practice, engage in]
57-76	無	86	wu	non- / without / no / don't
57-77	事	6	shih	interfering / meddling / busy-ness / activity / over-managing / "trying" / business
57-78	而	126	erh	and
57-79	民	83	min	the people
57-80	自	132	tzu	naturally / spontaneously / of themselves [become, grow]
57-81	富	40	fu	wealthy / rich / abundant / prosper / enriched / "a house which is full"
57-82	我	62	wo	I [do, practice, engage in] +Alt: add yü (desire, want)—MWT
57-83	無	86	wu	not / without / no / don't
57-84	欲	76	yü	desires / having desires / wants / desiring [results] / (expectations)
57-85	而	126	erh	and
57-86	民	83	min	the people
57-87	自	132	tzu	naturally / spontaneously / of themselves [become]
57-88	樸	75	p'u	pure / simple / honest / one's natural state / "uncarved block" }} "return to the good and simple life" (Feng)

[1] **Chêng**, from "Heaven" + "earth" + "a man standing in between." Implies actions that are in accord with Heaven's will, that which connects Heaven and earth. Actions that are virtuous, righteous, fair, etc.

[2] **Ch'i** connotes the extraordinary that deviates from the correct and good—the opposite of cheng.

[3] Compare v. 57:15–23 with v. 21:61–71 and v. 52:82–91.

VERSE 58

58-01	其	12	ch'i	One's / one / [when] one's
58-02	政	66	chêng	government / administration / governing / politics / rule [is]
58-03	悶	61	mên	dull / unobtrusive / muddled / subdued / "mum" / sluggish / "non-discriminative" / "a light hand" >>Etm: "gate" + "heart" ("a heart behind a gate")
58-04	悶	61	mên	dull / "holds the heart behind a gate" }} very dull / doubly dull / does not interfere / "stands aloof" (Pine)

58-05	其	12	ch'i	the / one's
58-06	民	83	min	people
58-07	淳	85	shun	simple / pure / wholesome / honest / sincere >Alt: shun (pure, genuine)
58-08	淳	85	shun	simple / pure / wholesome / "pure like lambs" }} very simple / doubly simple
58-09	其	12	ch'i	the / one's
58-10	政	66	chêng	government / administration / governing
58-11	察	40	ch'a	searching / prying / discriminative / sharp / "exacting" / "alert" / "efficient" / "severity"
58-12	察 ○	40	ch'a	searching / prying }} very prying / ~interferes with the people's lives
58-13	其	12	ch'i	the / one's
58-14	民	83	min	people
58-15	缺	121	ch'üeh	needy / wanting / deficient / disappointed / contentious / restless / "wily" / "cunning"
58-16	缺 .	121	ch'üeh	needy / wanting }} very needy / destitute / "slip away" (Pine)
58-17	禍	113	huo	terrible fate / misery / calamity / misfortune / disaster >>Etm: "will of Heaven" + "physical defect" (cleft palate)
58-18	兮	12	hsi	! / alas [upon which]
58-19	福	113	fu	happiness / luck / blessings / good fortune [1]
58-20	之	4	chih	's / its / (_____)
58-21	所	63	so	place / place of / position / home
58-22	倚	9b	yi	support / lean upon / trust }} depends on / "rests upon" / "rooted in" / "perch" / "avenue"
58-23	福	113	fu	happiness / luck / blessings / good fortune
58-24	兮	12	hsi	! / alas / [upon which]
58-25	禍	113	huo	terrible fate / misery / calamity / misfortune / disaster / misery [1]
58-26	之	4	chih	's / its
58-27	所	63	so	place / place of / position / home
58-28	伏 .	9	fu	conceal[ment] / hide / beneath / subdue / "lie in ambush" }} latent / "lurks beneath"
58-29	孰	39	shu	who / who [would be able to]
58-30	知	111	chih	know[s] / understands / perceives
58-31	其	12	ch'i	the / its / their / when [its]
58-32	極	75b	chi	limit[s] / extreme / end / highest / "ultimate result" / "turning point" / "what the future holds"
58-33	其	12	ch'i	it
58-34	無	86	wu	without / not / there is no
58-35	正 .	77	chêng	correct / standard / right / normal / upright / just / honest / "direction" }}} "is there no right or wrong?" (Waley) [2]
58-36	正	77	chêng	standard / normal / upright / just / straightforward
58-37	復	60	fu	in turn / return / turn to / revert / again
58-38	為	87	wei	become / make / do / does }} "changes into" / "turns into"
58-39	奇 .	37a	ch'i	abnormal / dishonest / deceitful / perverse / surprise / crafty / >v. 57:06
58-40	善	30	shan	[the] good / goodness / skill / excellence / "auspicious" / "orthodox"
58-41	復	60	fu	in turn / return / turn to / revert / again
58-42	為	87	wei	become / becomes / make / do }} "changes into" / "turns into"

58-43	妖	38	yao	unlucky / unpropitious / witchcraft / "spooked" // evil / monstrous / ominous / sinister
58-44	人	9a	jên	the people
58-45	之	4	chih	's [are, become, have become]
58-46	迷	162	mi	confused / confusion / deluded / "bewitched" / perplexed / misguided / deceived / lost / "gone astray" [3]
58-47	其	12	ch'i	it / it [is so]
58-48	日	72	jih	every day / daily / day after day
58-49	固	31	ku	assuredly / strong / firm / definite
58-50	久	4	chiu	lasting / for a long time }}} for a long time
58-51	是	72a	shih	(this)
58-52	以	9a	yi	(for) }} thus / hence / therefore
58-53	聖	128a	shêng	holy X Alt: omit—MWT
58-54	人	9a	jên	man }} the sage [is] X Alt: omit—MWT
58-55	方	70	fang	sharp / "pointed" / square / upright // "square-edged" / ~has firm principles / ~solid / "four-square"
58-56	而	126	erh	and / yet / but
58-57	不	1	pu	not / does not / is not / does not [cause]
58-58	割	18	ko	injure / injury / cut / cutting / pierce / scrape / divide }}}}} "sharp but not cutting" / "squares but does not cut" [4]
58-59	廉	53	lien	angular / corners / pointed / "acute as a knife" / carves / honest / "has integrity"
58-60	而	126	erh	and / yet / but
58-61	不	1	pu	not / does not
58-62	劌	18	k'uei	hurt / hurting / pierce / injure / "disfiguring" / "to behead"
58-63	直	109	chih	straight / true / "straight as a line" / a line / straightforward / direct / honest / consistent / "does not deviate"
58-64	而	126	erh	and / yet / but
58-65	不	1	pu	not / does not
58-66	肆	129	ssu	extend / "overreach" / severe / straining / "unrestrained" / "tactless" / "bully" / "high-handed" (Yutang) / "at the expense of others" (Lau) [5]
58-67	光	10	kuang	bright / brilliant / shines / illumined / enlightened / a light / bright as a light
58-68	而	126	erh	and / yet / but
58-69	不	1	pu	not / does not
58-70	燿	86	yao	shining / luminous / bright / brilliant / blind / flashy / dazzle / dazzling [6]

[1] *Huo* (bad fortune) and *fu* (good fortune) have the same root word, *shih*, which means "comes from Heaven." Both good fortune and bad fortune are decrees of Heaven, or fated. *Huo* is "from Heaven" + "a child born with a cleft palate"; *fu* is "from heaven" + "fullness."

[2] >Alt: *chi*: (cease, stop)   +Alt: add *hsieh* (bad, wrong, perverse)

[3] *Mi* shares the same roots as tao, both comprised of "foot" + "head" = path. *Mi*, however, adds "grains of rice," which represents "many paths," or "many different views." This could literally translate as "the path of rice"; of seeing the world as divided, as being made up of many different things—like many grains of rice. This vision leads one astray from the true nature of things.

[4] *Fang erh pu ko*: Wang Pi says: "Lead the people with the pointed square, and remove their evil, but do not use the pointed square to pierce things." This is what is meant by the saying, "The great square has no corners." The square can be seen as an equal-

sided geometric shape, representing equal vision. Squaring without cutting can mean using one's discrimination to see all things equally and not using the sharpness of the intellect to cut up or divide the world into differences.

[5] **Chih erh pu ssu**: "Straightens without stretching" might mean aligning one's actions with Heaven naturally, without forcing things.

[6] **Kuang erh pu yao**: "Bright without dazzling" can mean that the Sage shows people their own inner light—and they are guided by that light. He does not shine the light on himself.

VERSE 59

59-01	治	85	chih	Govern / in governing / rule / lead / order / manage / care for
59-02	人	9a	jên	the people / others / humanity
59-03	事	6	shih	serve / serving / attending to / caring for // affairs / give and take / involvement with
59-04	天	37	t'ien	Heaven / divine / "God" / Nature
59-05	莫	140	mo	nothing / there is nothing / no [rule]
59-06	若	140	jo	surpass[es] / better than / compares with // follow / be in sympathy with
59-07	嗇	30	sê	moderation / thrift[iness] / economy / sparing / frugal / "restraint" / saving / the harvest >Alt: *shih* (pattern) [1]
59-08	夫	37	fu	truly / "now" / (what follows is true)
59-09	唯	30b	wei	by being / only through // consider / ponder / think about
59-10	嗇	30	sê	moderation / thrift / economy / frugality / saving / the harvest
59-11	是	72a	shih	this / to be / X Alt: omit—MWT
59-12	謂	149	wei	called / means / is / [can one] >Alt: *ku* (therefore)—MWT
59-13	早	72	tsao	early / morning / quick
59-14	服	74	fu	recover / acquire / adhere / habit / submit // plan / subdue [2][3]
59-15	早	72	tsao	early / morning
59-16	服	74	fu	recovery / acquisition // subdue / plan
59-17	謂	149	wei	called / means / "depends on"
59-18	之	4	chih	its / one's
59-19	重	166	chung	heavy / heaviness / weight / important // gather / heap / be prepared
59-20	積	115c	chi	accumulate / accumulation of / build up of }} "a double reserve of"
59-21	德	60b	tê	Te / virtue / power }}} "garner a double (harvest of) Virtue" (Duy)
59-22	重	166	chung	heavy / heaviness / weight / important // gather / heap / be prepared
59-23	積	115c	chi	accumulate / accumulation of / buildup of }} "a double reserve of"
59-24	德	60b	tê	Te / virtue / power }}} "if there is a good store of Virtue" (Feng)
59-25	則	18	tsê	then / means
59-26	無	86	wu	nothing / nothingness / without
59-27	不	1	pu	not
59-28	克	10	k'o	overcome / subdue / master / (possible) }}} "overcoming everything"
59-29	無	86	wu	nothing / nothingness / without
59-30	不	1	pu	not
59-31	克	10	k'o	overcome / subdue
59-32	則	18	tsê	then / means

59-33	莫	140	**mo**	no / no one / not
59-34	知	111	**chih**	knows / knowledge
59-35	其	12	**ch'i**	the / its / his
59-36	極	75b	**chi**	limit / extreme / boundary / end / zenith / highest point }}}} "have infinite capacity" (Yutang) / "there are no limits" / "reach an invisible height" (Wu)
59-37	莫	140	**mo**	no / no one / not
59-38	知	111	**chih**	knows
59-39	其	12	**ch'i**	the / its / his
59-40	極	75b	**chi**	limit / extreme
59-41	可	30	**k'o**	one can / is able / is fit
59-42	以	9a	**yi**	thus / thereby
59-43	有	74	**yu**	have / hold / possess / rule / maintain / guard
59-44	國	31	**kuo**	the state / country / nation / the realm
59-45	有	74	**yu**	to have / possess / guard
59-46	國	31	**kuo**	the state / country / nation
59-47	之	4	**chih**	its / 's
59-48	母	80	**mu**	mother / "matrix"
59-49	可	30	**k'o**	can / able / he can
59-50	以	9a	**yi**	thereby / (will)
59-51	長	168	**ch'ang**	last / endure / be lasting
59-52	久	4	**chiu**	endure }} last long / live long
59-53	是	72a	**shih**	this is
59-54	謂	149	**wei**	called / ~means
59-55	深	85	**shên**	deep / firm / abstruse
59-56	根	75	**kên**	roots / rooted
59-57	固	31	**ku**	sturdy / firm / staunch / solid
59-58	柢	75	**ti**	stem / stalk / trunk / planted // basis / foundation
59-59	長	168	**ch'ang**	long / lasting / [the way to] long
59-60	生	100	**shêng**	life }} immortality
59-61	久	4	**chiu**	lasting / everlasting / enduring / eternal
59-62	視	147	**shih**	insight / perception / vision / perceive / consider
59-63	之	4	**chih**	's / its
59-64	道	162	**tao**	Tao / way / path

[1] **Shê** comes from "corn" + "grange," referring to a grange filled with corn, the harvest, or the abundance that comes after a harvest. It is a reserve, or "laying up a store." *Shê* can also mean moderation or thrift, which is what one needs to protect, and use sparingly, that which one has acquired—so that it will last till the next harvest.

[2] **Fu** is derived from "two hands holding a scepter" and can mean "obey" or "yield."

[3] **Tsao fu**: "forestall"; "return before straying"; "applying oneself early" (Duy); "yielding early" (Wing); "planning ahead" (Pine)

60-01	治	85	chih	Govern / rule / ruling
60-02	大	37	ta	great / a great / big / large
60-03	國	31	kuo	state / nation / country
60-04	若	140	jo	as / like
60-05	烹	86	p'êng	fry / frying / cooking / boiling
60-06	小	42	hsiao	small
60-07	鮮	195	hsien	fish / >i.e., "Don't overdo it."
60-08	以	9a	yi	use / (with) / (in accord with)
60-09	道	162	tao	Tao / (a man of Tao)
60-10	莅	140	li	govern / rule / oversee / approach / "is employed to rule" / ~present [in]
60-11	天	37	t'ien	Heaven
60-12	下	1	hsia	below / under }} the empire / the world / the universe
60-13	其	12	ch'i	its
60-14	鬼	194	kuei	dark spirits / evil spirits / demons / ghosts / spirits // cunning // ~evil or deceptive thoughts [1]
60-15	不	1	pu	not / will not have / (lose)
60-16	神	113	shên	power / spiritual power / potency / godliness / transcendence / spirit / mysterious / "sanction as divinities" (Blakney) }}} "the cunning are not mysterious" (Wing) [2]
60-17	非	175	fei	not / not only / not that
60-18	其	12	ch'i	they / its
60-19	鬼	194	kuei	dark spirits / demons / ghosts
60-20	不	1	pu	not / will not have / (lose)
60-21	神	113	shên	power / spiritual power / potency
60-22	其	12	ch'i	its / but / their
60-23	神	113	shên	power / spiritual power / potency
60-24	不	1	pu	not / cannot / (no longer can) / (ceases)
60-25	傷	9	shang	harm / injure / wound / cause distress [3]
60-26	人	9a	jên	the people / others
60-27	非	175	fei	not / not only
60-28	其	12	ch'i	their / its
60-29	神	113	shên	power / spiritual power / potency
60-30	不	1	pu	not
60-31	傷	9	shang	harm / injure / wound / cause distress
60-32	人	9a	jên	the people / men
60-33	聖	128a	shêng	holy
60-34	人	9a	jên	man }} the sage
60-35	亦	8	yi	also
60-36	不	1	pu	not
60-37	傷	9	shang	harm / injure / wound / cause distress }}} "will also be protected" (Feng)

60-38	人	9a	jên	the people / men / them
60-39	夫	37	fu	truly / "now" / "since" / "when" / (what follows is true)
60-40	兩	1	liang	both of them / the two
60-41	不	1	pu	not / do not
60-42	相	109	hsiang	together / each other }} neither
60-43	傷	9	shang	harm / injure / wound / cause distress
60-44	故	66	ku	thus / therefore
60-45	德	60b	tê	Te / virtue / power / "original character"
60-46	交	8	chiao	united / unified / combined / integrated / accumulated
60-47	歸	77	kuei	returns / send back / restore / refreshes
60-48	焉	86a	yen	there / in that place / thereto / (to both) }} is restored / converge

[1] **Kuei**, spirits of the dead, are thought of not so much as being malicious or evil but as tricky and deceptive—spirits that can lead a person astray. Kuei is derived from "a man standing in a field," someone who is lost, without direction.

[2] **Shên**: "from heaven" + "two hands"

[3] **Shang**, from "arrow"—"wound with an arrow," "enter like an arrow." This could apply to actual spirits or deceptive thoughts entering the mind and leading a person astray.

VERSE 61

61-01	大	37	ta	Great / large / big
61-02	國	31	kuo	state / country / nation
61-03	者	125	chê	(one) / (one that) / (is like) / "may be compared with" / "should be like"
61-04	下	1	hsia	below / under / lower part of / lowland / low regions / "down-"
61-05	流	85	liu	river / delta / "stream" // flows / spreads }} "should flow downward" (Wing)
61-06	天	37	t'ien	Heaven
61-07	下	1	hsia	below / under }} the world / the empire / the universe
61-08	之	4	chih	's }}} the world's / [becomes the] world's
61-09	交	8	chiao	union / converging point / concourse / focus point / meeting ground / intercourse / confluence
61-10	天	37	t'ien	Heaven
61-11	下	1	hsia	below / under }} the world / the empire
61-12	之	4	chih	's }}} the world's / [becomes the] world's
61-13	牝	93	p'in	female / woman
61-14	牝	93	p'in	female / woman
61-15	常	50	ch'ang	constantly / always
61-16	以	9a	yi	(by) / (through)
61-17	靜	174	ching	still / stillness / quiet / quietude / tranquility / peace / repose
61-18	勝	19	shêng	overcomes / conquers / outdoes / "gets the better of"
61-19	牡	93	mu	male / the male
61-20	以	9a	yi	(by) / (with) / (through) / "in order to be"
61-21	靜	174	ching	still / stillness / quiet / quietude / tranquility / peace / repose
61-22	為	87	wei	makes / does / acts / takes / achieves / makes [herself]
61-23	下	1	hsia	low / below / underneath / lower position / lying low

61-24	故	66	ku	thus / therefore
61-25	大	37	ta	great / big
61-26	國	31	kuo	state / country / nation
61-27	以	9a	yi	therefore / thus / accordingly
61-28	下	1	hsia	below / under / lower / [puts itself] below / take lower position / "gives way to" / "bows to"
61-29	小	42	hsiao	small / smaller / a small
61-30	國.	31	kuo	state / country / nation
61-31	則	18	tsê	then / and so / accordingly / on that account / by that means / it will
61-32	取	29	ch'ü	win / win over / capture / conquer / overcome / take over / acquire / join / "absorb"
61-33	小	42	hsiao	small / smaller / a small
61-34	國.	31	kuo	state / country / nation
61-35	小	42	hsiao	small / smaller / a small
61-36	國	31	kuo	state / country / nation
61-37	以	9a	yi	thus / (by)
61-38	下	1	hsia	below / under / lower / [putting itself] below / submit / taking the lower position
61-39	大	37	ta	great
61-40	國。	31	kuo	state / country / nation
61-41	則	18	tsê	then / and so / accordingly / it can
61-42	取	29	ch'ü	win / win over / capture / conquer / overcome / take over / acquire / join / "absorb"
61-43	大	37	ta	great
61-44	國.	31	kuo	state / country / nation
61-45	故	66	ku	thus / therefore
61-46	或	62	huo	some
61-47	下	1	hsia	below / under / lower / [putting themselves] below
61-48	以	9a	yi	thus / (in order to) / (can)
61-49	取.	29	ch'ü	win / win over / capture / conquer / rule / govern
61-50	或	62	huo	some / others
61-51	下	1	hsia	below / under / [by putting themselves] below / "by naturally being below"
61-52	而	126	erh	and / as well / also / in order to
61-53	取.	29	ch'ü	win / take hold of / capture / conquer / rule / govern / ~other states / ~others
61-54	大	37	ta	great / big
61-55	國	31	kuo	state / country / nation
61-56	不	1	pu	not
61-57	過	162	kuo	more / pass / pass by / "overstepping its boundaries"
61-58	欲	76	yü	want / wish / need / desire }} wants nothing more / all it wants
61-59	兼	12	chien	unite / bring together / join / annex
61-60	畜	102	hsü	feed / care for / herd }} "take under its wing"
61-61	人	9a	jên	the people / others / the other }} gain more people / embrace more people
61-62	小	42	hsiao	small / smaller
61-63	國	31	kuo	state / country / nation

61-64	不	1	pu	not
61-65	過	162	kuo	more / pass / pass by / "overstepping its boundaries"
61-66	欲	76	yü	want / wish / need / desire
61-67	入	11	ju	enter / come in
61-68	事	6	shih	serve / "serve its patron" / "have its service accepted" // be involved with / take a part in
61-69	人.	9a	jên	the people / others
61-70	夫	37	fu	truly / "now" / "since" / (what follows is true)
61-71	兩	1	liang	both / the two
61-72	者	125	chê	(the ones)
61-73	各	30	ko	each
61-74	得	60a	tê	obtain / get / attain / "are granted"
61-75	其	12	ch'i	they
61-76	所	63	so	that which / what / (~relative pronoun)
61-77	欲.	76	yü	wish / want / need / desire }}}} get what they want (from being low)
61-78	大	37	ta	great / greater / [but the] greater / big [state]
61-79	者	125	chê	(the one)
61-80	宜	40	yi	rightly / should / properly / ought to / is fitting / behooves / must
61-81	為	87	wei	make / act / become / place itself / attempt / (stay)
61-82	下.	1	hsia	low / lower / below / (humble) }} "yield"
VERSE 62				
62-01	道	162	tao	Tao
62-02	者	125	chê	it / (the one) / (man) }} "man of Tao"
62-03	萬	140	wan	ten thousand / all
62-04	物	93	wu	things / beings }} creation
62-05	之	4	chih	their
62-06	奧.	37	ao	storehouse / "hidden reservoir" / source / refuge "hidden secret" / "shrine in the house" / "sanctuary" (Pine) >Alt: *chu* (flow, the way things flow, tendency; chief)—MWT [1][2]
62-07	善	30	shan	good / excellent / dharmic
62-08	人	9a	jên	man / person
62-09	之	4	chih	's / it / his / their
62-10	寶.	40	pao	treasure / protect / refuge / hold fast to / guarantee / "shield" / "safeguard"
62-11	不	1	pu	not
62-12	善	30	shan	good / excellent / dharmic }} bad
62-13	人	9a	jên	man / person
62-14	之	4	chih	's / it / his / their
62-15	所	63	so	that which / (_____)
62-16	保.	9	pao	protect[ion] / safeguard / shield / preserve / refuge / guarantee / hold fast to
62-17	美	123	mei	beautiful / pleasing / fine / good / fair
62-18	言	149	yen	words / speech / saying

62-19	可	30	k'o	can / able
62-20	以	9a	yi	thus / accordingly
62-21	市	50a	shih	sell / buy / a market / "the price" / "buy and sell" / "sell at the market" / "find its own market" / "win in return"
62-22	尊	41	tsun	honorable / noble / honor / high rank / good +Alt: add: *mei* (fine, beautiful)
62-23	行	144	hsing	actions / acts / deeds / conduct // to step / to go
62-24	可	30	k'o	can / one can / permits
62-25	以	9a	yi	thus / accordingly
62-26	加	19	chia	add / accomplish / confer upon / gain respect / raise above / surpass >Alt: *ho* (give, present as a gift)
62-27	人	9a	jên	the people / to others }} raise a man above others
62-28	人	9a	jên	people / man / others
62-29	之	4	chih	's / for its / for his
62-30	不	1	pu	non- / "lack of"
62-31	善	30	shan	good / goodness / dharma }}} if a man is bad // "if straying from the right path" (Wu)
62-32	何	9	ho	why / what / for what
62-33	棄	75	ch'i	discard / throw away / abandon / reject / forsake / cast away
62-34	之	4	chih	his / its / (him, them)
62-35	有	74	yu	is [?]	[3]
62-36	故	66	ku	thus / therefore / hence / (on the occasion of)
62-37	立	19	li	crowning / installation / enthronement
62-38	天	37	t'ien	Heaven ['s]
62-39	子	39	tzu	son / child }} the emperor / king / "Son of Heaven"
62-40	置	122	chih	appointment / arrange / installing of
62-41	三	1	san	three / the three
62-42	公	12a	kung	ministers / officers / officials / dukes / "ducal ministers"	[4]
62-43	雖	172	sui	though / although / even if / rather than
62-44	有	74	yu	have / present / offer / send
62-45	拱	64	kung	precious / priceless / "disks of" / "tributes of" / "bowing" / "hold near one's heart" >>Etm: lit.: "holding reverently with both hands"
62-46	璧	98	pi	jade / a gem / >jade disks were worn over the heart
62-47	以	9a	yi	(thus) / (thereby)
62-48	先	10	hsien	preceded by / preceding / coming before // followed by
62-49	駟	187	ssu	four / a team of four
62-50	馬	187	ma	horses
62-51	不	1	pu	not / it does not
62-52	如	38	ju	equal / like / as good as / ~rival }} it is not better / preferable
62-53	坐	32	tso	sitting down / kneeling / remaining still / sitting still / calmly // one who sits
62-54	進	162	chin	offer / give [as a gift] / present / make a present of / send / bring as a tribute // advance / make progress
62-55	此	77	tz'u	this / the / on this

62-56	道	162	tao	Tao / Way X Alt: omit—MWT
62-57	古	30	ku	old / ancient / those of old / the ancients
62-58	之	4	chih	their / its
62-59	所	63	so	reason
62-60	以	9a	yi	(thus) / (as to why)
62-61	貴	154	kuei	honor / esteem / treasure / prize / hold dear / value / exalted
62-62	此	77	tz'u	this / it
62-63	道	162	tao	Tao X Alt: omit—MWT
62-64	者	125	chê	that is
62-65	何	9	ho	what / why +Alt: add *yeh* (indeed)
62-66	不	1	pu	not / is it not / was it not
62-67	曰	73	yüeh	say / said }} did they not say
62-68	以	9a	yi	thus / accordingly
62-69	求	85	ch'iu	seek / those who seek / seeker / sought / beg / aim for
62-70	得	60a	tê	obtained / obtain / get / receive / attain
62-71	有	74	yu	have / possess / he who has
62-72	罪	122	tsui	sin / crime / faults / wrong[doers] / guilty / offend / sinner / "sinners who find" / "criminal" >>Etm: "eye" + "against / opposing" ("that which goes against the eye")
62-73	以	9a	yi	thus / thereby / (shall be)
62-74	免	10	mien	save[d] / free / spare / forgiven / released
62-75	邪	163	hsieh	?
62-76	故	66	ku	thus / therefore / for this reason
62-77	為	87	wei	become / make / act / is / [Tao] is
62-78	天	37	t'ien	Heaven
62-79	下	1	hsia	below / under }} the world / the world's
62-80	貴	154	kuei	honor / esteem / exalt / treasure / prize / hold dear / valued / "held above everything else"

[1] **Ao**: "Mysterious Sanctuary" (Au); "hiding place" (Erkes); "hidden reservoir" (Wu); "most honored place" (Legge)

[2] **Tao chê wan wu chih chu**: "The Way is that toward which all things flow." (Henricks)

[3] (See NOTES)

[4] The "three ministers" refers to the grand tutor, grand preceptor, and grand protector. As part of the ritual installment of the emperor, or the three ministers, a precious jade disk was presented.

VERSE 63

63-01	為	87	wei	Act / do / make / become / practice / accomplish
63-02	無	86	wu	without / non- / nothing
63-03	為	87	wei	action / doing / making / do
63-04	事	6	shih	be busy with / practice / do / pursue / attend / work / "serve"
63-05	無	86	wu	without / not / non- / no / by not
63-06	事	6	shih	being busy / practice / doing / meddling / affairs / work
63-07	味	30a	wei	taste / savor / flavor
63-08	無	86	wu	non- / not / without / by not

63-09	味	30a	wei	taste / tasting / flavor }} tasteless / flavorless
63-10	大	37	ta	great / make great / big / make big / "magnify"
63-11	小	42	hsiao	small / the small
63-12	多	36	to	many / much / increase / make many
63-13	少	42	shao	few / the few / to lessen
63-14	報	32	pao	requite / respond with / return / repay / reward
63-15	怨	61	yüan	hatred / ill-treatment / injury / malice / enmity / "bitterness" / wrong
63-16	以	9a	yi	with
63-17	德	60b	tê	Te / virtue / goodness / doing good / care / kindness
63-18	圖	31	t'u	plan / plan for / prepare / arrange for / deal with / tackle / contemplate
63-19	難	172	nan	difficult / difficulty / hard
63-20	於	70	yü	while
63-21	其	12	ch'i	it [is]
63-22	易	72	yi	easy / still easy }} before it becomes difficult
63-23	為	87	wei	make / act / do / manage / take care of / deal with / achieve / employ
63-24	大	37	ta	great / great thing / big
63-25	於	70	yü	while / "by attending to"
63-26	其	12	ch'i	it / their
63-27	細	120	hsi	small / minute / [while still] small / small [beginnings]
63-28	天	37	t'ien	Heaven
63-29	下	1	hsia	below / under }} the world
63-30	難	172	nan	difficult
63-31	事	6	shih	affairs / activities / undertakings / (problems)
63-32	必	61	pi	surely / always / must / must needs
63-33	作	9a	tso	arise / will arise / originate / start / begin / "have their beginnings" / "be dealt with" (Yutang)
63-34	於	70	yü	from / through / in / when
63-35	易	72	yi	easiness / easy / the easy / what is easy // change / transform
63-36	天	37	t'ien	Heaven
63-37	下	1	hsia	below / under }} the world / the world's
63-38	大	37	ta	great
63-39	事	6	shih	affairs / activities / undertakings / (problems)
63-40	必	61	pi	surely / always / must / must needs
63-41	作	9a	tso	arise / will arise / originate / start / begin
63-42	於	70	yü	from / with / in / while
63-43	細	120	hsi	small / the small / smallness / small [deeds]
63-44	是	72a	shih	(this)
63-45	以	9a	yi	(for) }} therefore / thus
63-46	聖	128a	shêng	holy / saintly
63-47	人	9a	jên	man }} the sage
63-48	終	120	chung	to the end / utmost

63-49	不	1	pu	not
63-50	為	87	wei	act / makes / plays / to be / strives }} never attempts
63-51	大。	37	ta	great / the great / to be great / for the great
63-52	故	66	ku	hence / therefore / thereby
63-53	能	130	nêng	can / able / he can / has the ability to
63-54	成	62	ch'êng	accomplish / finish / succeed / achieve / fulfill / complete / perfect
63-55	其	12	ch'i	his / the / [in becoming] / their
63-56	大.	37	ta	great / greatness / great [deeds]
63-57	夫	37	fu	truly / "now" / "as" / (what follows is true)
63-58	輕	159	ch'ing	frivolous[ly] / light / too lightly / rash / [to take, one who takes] lightly
63-59	諾	149b	no	promises / agreements / agree / commit
63-60	必	61	pi	surely / (results in)
63-61	寡	40	kua	lack[s] / little / "hard to keep" }} rarely keeps
63-62	信.	9	hsin	truth / faith / sincerity / confidence / "his word" }} "inspires little trust"
63-63	多	36	to	too / very / many
63-64	易	72	yi	easy / light[ly]
63-65	必	61	pi	surely / surely results in
63-66	多	36	to	many / many things / much / often / great / [encounter] great
63-67	難.	172	nan	difficult[y] / will be difficult
63-68	是	72a	shih	(this)
63-69	以	9a	yi	(for) }} thus / therefore / for this reason / because
63-70	聖	128a	shêng	holy
63-71	人	9a	jên	man }} the sage
63-72	猶	94	yu	accepts / regards [things as] / treats / "through" / "choosing" / "confronts"
63-73	難	172	nan	difficult / difficulty // (seriously)
63-74	之.	4	chih	it / things
63-75	故	66	ku	thus / therefore / for this reason
63-76	終	120	chung	to the end / ultimate / limit / end up / in the end are
63-77	無	86	wu	without / not / has no / is without / [encounters] no }} never meets with
63-78	難	172	nan	difficulty / difficult / hard / problems }}} "no difficulty can get the better of him"
63-79	矣.	111	yi	! / indeed
		VERSE 64		
64-01	其	12	ch'i	That / that [which is] / what
64-02	安	40	an	rest / at rest / content / peaceful / remains still / secure / equilibrium
64-03	易	72	yi	easy / easily
64-04	持.	64	ch'ih	hold / grasp / manage / hold / maintain / rule
64-05	其	12	ch'i	that / it / what
64-06	未	75	wei	not yet
64-07	兆	10	chao	appear / manifest / begun / given a sign / emerged / an omen / "symptoms develop"

64-08	易	72	yi	easy / easily / is easy to
64-09	謀 .	149	mou	prevent / plan for
64-10	其	12	ch'i	that / that [which is] / what / things that are
64-11	脆	130	ts'ui	brittle / fragile / crisp / thin
64-12	易	72	yi	easy / easily / is easy to
64-13	泮 .	85	p'an	melt / dissolve >Alt: p'o (break, broken, crack, shatter; defeat, ruin) }} fragile
64-14	其	12	ch'i	that / that [which is] / what is
64-15	微	60	wei	small / minute / fading / hidden / vague
64-16	易	72	yi	easy / easily / easy to
64-17	散 .	66	san	disperse / scatter / separate / dispel / dissolve / dismiss
64-18	為	87	wei	make / do / act / treat / deal with / manage / tackle
64-19	之	4	chih	them / it / things
64-20	於	70	yü	while
64-21	未	75	wei	not / not yet }} before [they]
64-22	有 .	74	yu	exist / existence / being / come into being / emerge / something / ~here / ~appear
64-23	治	85	chih	govern / rule / administer / manage / set things in order / "cultivate peace and order"
64-24	之	4	chih	them / it
64-25	於	70	yü	while
64-26	未	75	wei	not / not yet }} before
64-27	亂 .	5	luan	trouble / disorder / discord / confusion / rebellion / anarchy / chaos [arises, set in]
64-28	合	30a	ho	join / unite / together / a pair
64-29	抱	64	pao	hold in both arms / hold in front / embrace / hold / grasp
64-30	之	4	chih	(____) / 's
64-31	木 ○	75	mu	tree }}} a tree as big as one's embrace / a tree that can fill a man's arms / a giant tree
64-32	生	100	shêng	grows / springs / emerges / grows / originates >Alt: tso (starts out as)——MWT
64-33	於	70	yü	from
64-34	毫	82	hao	tiny / small / tiniest
64-35	末 .	75	mo	seed / rootlet / shoot / sprout / root
64-36	九	5	chiu	nine
64-37	層	44	ts'êng	stories / levels
64-38	之	4	chih	's
64-39	臺 ○	133	t'ai	a tower / terrace
64-40	起	156	ch'i	rises / high
64-41	於	70	yü	from
64-42	累	120a	lei	accumulating / heaping / a heap of / pile of / "hodfuls of" >Alt: lei (basket)——MWT
64-43	土	32	t'u	earth / clay / bricks / dirt
64-44	千	24	ch'ien	thousand / very many
64-45	里	166	li	li / unit of measurement / >approx. one-third of a mile / Chinese mile
64-46	之	4	chih	(____) / 's

64-47	行。	144	hsing	journey / go forth }}}} a very long journey
64-48	始	38	shih	begins
64-49	於	70	yü	with / from
64-50	足	157	tsu	a foot / feet / one's feet
64-51	下.	1	hsia	underneath / below / beneath }} a step / "from where one stands"
64-52	為	87	wei	make / act / do / [he who] acts / takes action / does anything / those who act +Alt: add: *chih* (it)—MWT
64-53	者	125	chê	(he) / (the) one / it / (means to)
64-54	敗	66	pai	fail[s] / ruin[s] / destroy / spoil / mars / defeat / "defeats his own purpose" (Feng)
64-55	之.	4	chih	it / he who
64-56	執	32	chih	seize / hold / take hold of / grasp // manage / control / "insist" / "fusses over"
64-57	者	125	chê	it / (things) / (the one) / (he)
64-58	失	37	shih	loss / loses / will lose / lets slip / fail[s]
64-59	之.	4	chih	it / them
64-60	是	72a	shih	(this)
64-61	以	9a	yi	(for) }} therefore / thus
64-62	聖	128a	shêng	holy
64-63	人	9a	jên	man }} the sage
64-64	無	86	wu	without / not / does not / takes no
64-65	為	87	wei	make / act / action / do
64-66	故	66	ku	thus / therefore / because
64-67	無	86	wu	not / does not
64-68	敗.	66	pai	fail / ruin / spoil / destroy / mar / defeat
64-69	無	86	wu	without / not / does not
64-70	執	32	chih	seize / hold / take hold of / grasp // manage / control / "insist"
64-71	故	66	ku	thus / therefore
64-72	無	86	wu	not / does not
64-73	失.	37	shih	loss / loses / fail / lose anything / let slip
64-74	民	83	min	the people / of men
64-75	之	4	chih	their / in their
64-76	從	60	ts'ung	follow / following of / pursue / pursuit of / handling of
64-77	事。	6	shih	affairs / busy-ness / worldly activities / projects / enterprise
64-78	常	50	ch'ang	constantly / always / often
64-79	於	70	yü	at
64-80	幾	52	chi	near / almost / approach / verge of / "within an ace of" (Yutang)
64-81	成	62	ch'êng	success / completion / finish / the end
64-82	而	126	erh	and / yet
64-83	敗	66	pai	fail / defeat / meet with failure / ruin / spoil / "make a mess"
64-84	之.	4	chih	in it / if one [remains, is as]

64-85	慎	61	**shên**	careful / cautious / "heedful and patient"
64-86	終	120	**chung**	to the end / at the end / utmost
64-87	如	38	**ju**	as / as at / as he was / also / like / as well as
64-88	始 。	38	**shih**	the beginning / onset / begin
64-89	則	18	**tsê**	then
64-90	無	86	**wu**	not / there will be no / avert
64-91	敗	66	**pai**	fail / failure / ruin / being ruined
64-92	事 .	6	**shih**	in activities / business / enterprise
64-93	是	72a	**shih**	(this)
64-94	以	9a	**yi**	(for) }} thus / therefore
64-95	聖	128a	**shêng**	holy
64-96	人	9a	**jên**	man }} the sage
64-97	欲	76	**yü**	wants / desires / seeks
64-98	不	1	**pu**	not / [to have] no / freedom from
64-99	欲 。	76	**yü**	wants / desires
64-100	不	1	**pu**	not / does no
64-101	貴	154	**kuei**	honor / esteem / treasure / value / "collect"
64-102	難	172	**nan**	difficult
64-103	得	60a	**tê**	obtain / to get / attain }} rare / hard to come by
64-104	之	4	**chih**	's
64-105	貨 .	154	**huo**	treasures / good / merchandise / "precious things"
64-106	學	39	**hsüeh**	learns / studies / "in the school of"
64-107	不	1	**pu**	no / not / non- / (to be without) / (not hold on to)
64-108	學 。	39	**hsüeh**	learning / studying / school / ideas / what he has learned }}} "learns not to learn" }}} "learns to unlearn his learning" (Wu) / "studies what others neglect" (Blakney)
64-109	復	60	**fu**	returns / restores / reverses / recovers / "makes good"
64-110	眾	143	**chung**	all / to all
64-111	人	9a	**jên**	the people / other
64-112	之	4	**chih**	's / its
64-113	所	63	**so**	what they / their
64-114	過 。	162	**kuo**	missed / passed by / fault / mistakes / transgressions / excesses
64-115	以	9a	**yi**	therefore / accordingly / (in order to) / (his object is to)
64-116	輔	159a	**fu**	helps / assists / ministers / support / help / restore
64-117	萬	140	**wan**	ten thousand / all
64-118	物	93	**wu**	things / beings
64-119	之	4	**chih**	their / in their / [find] their
64-120	自	132	**tzu**	self
64-121	然	86	**jan**	so }} naturally / naturalness / natural development / own nature / self-becoming / natural state / course of nature
64-122	而	126	**erh**	and / yet

64-123	不	1	pu	not / (refrain from) >Alt: *fu* (not)—MWT	[1]
64-124	敢	66	kan	dare / venture / presume / daring to	
64-125	為 。	87	wei	act / action / do / make / take any action > interfere / "lead them by the nose" (Wu)	

[1] With the character ***pu***, the last line would read: "dare not act" or "dare not do"; with ***fu***, the last line would read: "dare not do it."

VERSE 65

65-01	古	30	ku	Ancient / the ancient[s] / those of old / ancient times / the past / in the beginning	
65-02	之	4	chih	's [who were]	
65-03	善	30	shan	good / well / excellent / excelled / skillful / "knew how to" / "well-versed" X Alt: omit—MWT	
65-04	為	87	wei	practice / follow / pursuit of / action / do	
65-05	道	162	tao	Tao / way	
65-06	者	125	chê	it / (the ones) / (they)	
65-07	非	175	fei	did not / oppose	
65-08	以	9a	yi	thereby / accordingly [seek to][aim to][use it to]	
65-09	明	72	ming	illumine / enlighten / "teach with intelligence"	
65-10	民 。	83	min	the people / others	
65-11	將	41	chiang	act / take in hand / will [but][keep them][make them]	
65-12	以	9a	yi	thus [a state of]	
65-13	愚	61b	yü	simple[-hearted] / ignorant / ignorance / unsophisticated / "hidden" / "hoodwinked"	
65-14	之 。	4	chih	them / it	[1]
65-15	民	83	min	the people	
65-16	之	4	chih	their / are	
65-17	難	172	nan	difficult / being difficult / hard [to]	
65-18	治 。	85	chih	govern / rule / control / "live in peace" }} unruly	
65-19	以	9a	yi	accordingly / because / the reason / hence	
65-20	其	12	ch'i	they [are][have][use]	
65-21	智	72	chih	clever[ness] / know[ledge] / sophisticated / "know-it-all-ness" / "outer knowledge"	[2]
65-22	多 。	36	to	much / many / often / too much X Alt: omit—MWT	
65-23	故	66	ku	therefore / hence	
65-24	以	9a	yi	accordingly [with][using][those who use]	
65-25	智	72	chih	cleverness / knowledge / "outer knowledge"	
65-26	治	85	chih	to rule / govern	
65-27	國 。	31	kuo	country / nation / state [is] [is to be] [they] [he]	
65-28	國	31	kuo	country / nation / state	
65-29	之	4	chih	's / its	
65-30	賊 。	154b	tsê	ruin / curse / detriment / "hold it back" / thief / robber / cheat / "malefactor" }}} robs the nation / cheats the country	
65-31	不	1	pu	not >Alt: *yi* (with)—MWT	
65-32	以	9a	yi	with / (from) >Alt: *pu* (not)—MWT	

65-33	智	72	chih	cleverness / knowledge / "outer knowledge" }}} ~from the heart // "with non-knowing"—MWT
65-34	治	85	chih	govern / rule
65-35	國	31	kuo	country / nation / state
65-36	國	31	kuo	country / nation / state
65-37	之	4	chih	's / its / (brings)
65-38	福	113	fu	blessing / treasure / luck / happiness / good fortune / boon / "benefactor" >Alt: *tê* (virtue)—MWT +Alt: add: *heng* (constantly, always)—MWT
65-39	知	111	chih	know / who knows
65-40	此	77	tz'u	these
65-41	兩	1	liang	two / both / pair / >> Etm: "an ancient balance scale"
65-42	者	125	chê	those / (things) / (principles) / (alternatives)
65-43	亦	8	yi	also / (is to possess) / (means)
65-44	稽	115b	chi	standard / model / pattern / rule / norm >Alt: *ch'i* (to know, scrutinize)
65-45	式	56	shih	pattern / model / rule / form / measure / "Heaven's rule" / ~model set up for imitation
65-46	常	50	ch'ang	constant / always
65-47	知	111	chih	know / to know
65-48	稽	115b	chi	standard / model / rule
65-49	式	56	shih	pattern / model / mode / measure
65-50	是	72a	shih	this is
65-51	謂	149	wei	called / ~means
65-52	玄	96	hsüan	profound / deep / hidden / mystic >Alt: *yüan* (primal, origin)
65-53	德	60b	tê	Te / virtue / power
65-54	玄	96	hsüan	profound / deep / hidden / mystic >Alt: *yüan* (primal, origin)
65-55	德	60b	tê	Te / virtue / power
65-56	深	85	shên	deep / goes deep / abstruse >Alt: *ch'ing* (clear, clarifies)
65-57	矣	111	yi	! / indeed [and]
65-58	遠	162	yüan	distant / far / far-reaching / far away / removed
65-59	矣	111	yi	! / indeed
65-60	與	134	yü	to / to give / with it / share / resemble / compare / fit for / hence
65-61	物	61	wu	things / all things
65-62	反	29	fan	revert / turn back / lead back / "return to the source" // contrary / oppose / "in contrast (to ordinary people)" (Cleary)　　　　[3]
65-63	矣	111	yi	indeed
65-64	然	86	jan	so X Alt: omit
65-65	後	60	hou	then / after / behind / keep behind X Alt: omit
65-66	乃	4	nai	thus / "only when it is"
65-67	至	133a	chih	obtain[ed] / reach[ed] / attain / realized / arrives / utmost
65-68	大	37	ta	great / grand / the Great / "complete"
65-69	順	181	shun	harmony / oneness / conformity / compliance // follow / accord / obey / "norm" / "discipleship" / (submissive)

[1] [**Lines 1–14**]: In ancient times, those who excelled in the practice of Tao did not thereby enlighten others, but kept them simple-hearted. / In ancient times, those who excelled in the practice of Tao did not (teach others about) enlightenment, but about holding to their own simplicity. / The ancients who excelled in the practice of Tao did not appear luminous to others, but simple in their actions. / Those of old, whose actions were in accordance with the Tao, did not appear enlightened, but ignorant. / The old masters did not seem enlightened, but simple in their ways.

[2] *Chih*: (a) knowledge learned from books—as opposed to direct knowledge or experience; (b) mentally, from the mind, according to the rules—without compassion or heart.

[3] *Fan*, return, is the primal impulse that drives a person to return to his own source, his own perfection, his own Self which is God. This is divine longing. Every action, by every creature, is to some measure an action of return, an action that leads to unity with God. "Every natural thing, in its own way, longs for the divine and desires to share in the divine life to the fullest extent it can" (Aristotle). "Whether you like it or not, whether you know it or not, secretly all nature seeks God and works toward him" (Eckehart). "All that exists desires and aspires toward the Supreme by a necessity of nature" (Plotinus).

VERSE 66

66-01	江	85	**chiang**	Rivers / great rivers	
66-02	海	85	**hai**	seas	
66-03	所	63	**so**	that which	
66-04	以	9a	**yi**	thus / for }} the reason why	
66-05	能	130	**nêng**	can / able / ability / power	
66-06	為	87	**wei**	be / become / act / do	
66-07	百	106b	**pai**	hundred / of the hundred	
66-08	谷	150	**ku**	valleys / ravines	
66-09	王	95	**wang**	the king / their king / lord	[1]
66-10	者	125	**chê**	that	
66-11	以	9a	**yi**	because / (thus)	
66-12	其	12	**ch'i**	they [are]	
66-13	善	30	**shan**	good at / can / skillful / skillfully [staying][keeping][taking]	
66-14	下	1	**hsia**	low[er] / beneath / below / the lower position / "flowing downward"	
66-15	之	4	**chih**	it / they / themselves	
66-16	故	66	**ku**	thus / therefore / hence	
66-17	能	130	**nêng**	can / able to / ability	
66-18	為	87	**wei**	be / become / do / act	
66-19	百	106b	**pai**	hundred	
66-20	谷	150	**ku**	valley / ravine	
66-21	王	95	**wang**	king / lord	
66-22	是	72a	**shih**	(this)	
66-23	以	9a	**yi**	(for) }} therefore +Alt: add: *sheng jen chih* (the holy man's)	
66-24	欲	76	**yü**	want[ing] / wishing / desire [he who / one who] wants [to be]	
66-25	上	1	**shang**	above / higher / superior / rule over / chief among / "guide"	
66-26	民	83	**min**	the people / others	
66-27	必	61	**pi**	surely / must / one must	
66-28	以	9a	**yi**	for / therefore	

66-29	言	149	yen	words / speech / speak like / [his / your] words [keep][place himself]
66-30	下	1	hsia	below / under / lower / humble oneself / reach down / inferior position [to]
66-31	之	4	chih	them }}}} "serve them with humility" (Feng)
66-32	欲	76	yü	want[ing] / wishing / desire / "if one would" / "in order to be"
66-33	先	10	hsien	be ahead / lead / precede / foremost among // feed / nourish
66-34	民	83	min	the people / others / them
66-35	必	61	pi	surely / must / one must
66-36	以	9a	yi	with / (through) / thereby
66-37	身	158	shên	himself / his person / bodily / his life [walks][keeps]
66-38	後	60	hou	behind / follow / come after / "go after them in status" (Cleary)
66-39	之	4	chih	them
66-40	是	72a	shih	(this)
66-41	以	9a	yi	(for) }} therefore / in this way
66-42	聖	128a	shêng	holy X Alt: omit
66-43	人	9a	jên	man }} the sage[s] X Alt: omit
66-44	處	141	ch'u	stop[s] / stay[s] / rest / dwell / place / "takes his place" [yourself][himself]
66-45	上	1	shang	above / higher / over
66-46	而	126	erh	and / yet / "causes"
66-47	民	83	min	the people
66-48	不	1	pu	not / no [feel][take] [his]
66-49	重	166	chung	heavy / [the] weight / weighed down / burdened / oppressed / "hindrance" / "gravely"
66-50	處	141	ch'u	[he] stop[s] / stay / rest / dwell / places [himself] / takes his place / "walks" / "stands"
66-51	前	18	ch'ien	first / in front / ahead / before [them] // leader / chief
66-52	而	126	erh	and / but / yet / causes
66-53	民	83	min	the people
66-54	不	1	pu	not / no / do not / are not / do not [wish him][consider him]
66-55	害	40	hai	injure / harm[ful] / suffer harm / offend / obstruction / attack [him / them]
66-56	是	72a	shih	(this)
66-57	以	9a	yi	(for) }} therefore / that is why
66-58	天	37	t'ien	Heaven
66-59	下	1	hsia	below / under }} the world
66-60	樂	75	lo	joy / rejoice[s] / joyfully / are glad to
66-61	推	64	t'ui	exalt / praise // support / uphold / push forward [him]
66-62	而	126	erh	and / but
66-63	不	1	pu	not / never / without
66-64	厭	27	yen	tire / reach limit / tiring / [being] tired of it
66-65	以	9a	yi	because / (precisely because) / the reason being
66-66	其	12	ch'i	he
66-67	不	1	pu	not / does not

66-68	爭	87	chêng	compete / contend / quarrel / resist / "go against the flow"
66-69	故	66	ku	therefore
66-70	天	37	t'ien	Heaven
66-71	下	1	hsia	below / under }} the world
66-72	莫	140	mo	none / no one
66-73	能	130	nêng	can / able / has the ability to / power / "is in a position" }} cannot
66-74	與	134	yü	with / against
66-75	之	4	chih	him
66-76	爭 .	87	chêng	contend / quarrel / resist / "go against" / >v. 22:50–62

[1] **Wang** means "king." According to the ancient Shao Wen Dictionary, *wang* is the one "to whom the empire turns and flocks to," and this may be the intended meaning.

VERSE 67

67-01	天	37	t'ien	Heaven
67-02	下	1	hsia	below / under }} the world
67-03	皆	106	chieh	all
67-04	謂	149	wei	call / name / say[s] / say that
67-05	我	62	wo	me / I / my
67-06	道	162	tao	Tao / (teaching about the Tao) X Alt: omit—MWT
67-07	大	37	ta	great / the greatest / is great / vast +Alt: add: *ta* (great)—MWT
67-08	似	9	ssu	like / similar to / resemble[s]
67-09	不	1	pu	not / no / un-
67-10	肖 .	130	hsiao	resemble / like anything / seeming / distinguished / described // small // worthy [1]
67-11	夫	37	fu	truly / "now" / (what follows is true)
67-12	唯	30b	wei	only / precisely / because it is
67-13	大 。	37	ta	great / one is great
67-14	故	66	ku	because / therefore
67-15	似	9	ssu	like / similar / resemble / it resembles / seems
67-16	不	1	pu	not / un-
67-17	肖 .	130	hsiao	resemble / to be like / seeming // "worthy" }} unlike / different / useless
67-18	若	140	jo	like / resembling [if it / one were / did]
67-19	肖	130	hsiao	resemble / to be like / seeming / "something" }} like something / "worthy" / "useful" / "orthodox"
67-20	久	4	chiu	long / long before / "from the beginning" / how long
67-21	矣	111	yi	indeed / (_____)
67-22	其	12	ch'i	it / his [would become][would have become]
67-23	細	120	hsi	small / petty / vanish / disappear / "a small and petty thing" (Blakney) / "trivialized" (Cleary)
67-24	也	5	yeh	! / indeed
67-25	夫 .	37	fu	truly / "now" / (what I'm about to say is true)
67-26	我	62	wo	I
67-27	有	74	yu	have

67-28	三	1	san	three
67-29	寶	40	pao	treasures / ~"virtues which constitute a man's worth" (Carus) [that I]
67-30	持	64	ch'ih	hold / keep / hold fast / guard / preserve
67-31	而	126	erh	and
67-32	保	9	pao	protect / guard / guarantee / cherish / keep safe / "watch over closely" // treasure
67-33	之	4	chih	them
67-34	一	1	yi	one / the first
67-35	曰	73	yüeh	is called / "is" / is known as
67-36	慈	61	tz'u	love / deep love / great love / motherly love / affection / compassion / unconditional love / mercy / "tolerance" / "love that protects and nurtures"
67-37	二	7	erh	two / the second
67-38	曰	73	yüeh	is called / "is" / is known as
67-39	儉	9	chien	frugal[ity] / thrift[iness] / economy / sparing / moderation / "never too much" (Yutang) / "proper use of everything" / "not waste anything" [2]
67-40	三	1	san	three / the third
67-41	曰	73	yüeh	is called / "is" / is known as
67-42	不	1	pu	not / never
67-43	敢	66	kan	dare / daring / venture / presume
67-44	為	87	wei	do / make / to be / to take / be
67-45	天	37	t'ien	Heaven
67-46	下	1	hsia	below / under }} the world
67-47	先	10	hsien	first / in front of / ahead of / "the lead" / leader / foremost }} first in the world
67-48	慈	61	tz'u	loving / affectionate / compassionate / merciful
67-49	故	66	ku	therefore
67-50	能	130	nêng	can / able / has the power to / can be / can afford to be
67-51	勇	19	yung	brave / daring / courageous / fearless
67-52	儉	9	chien	frugal / sparing / economical / moderation / "not wasteful" / "not doing too much"
67-53	故	66	ku	therefore
67-54	能	130	nêng	can / able / has the power to / can be / can afford to be
67-55	廣	53	kuang	generous / giving / broad / expansive / "wide-reaching" / "amplitude" / liberal / "extend one's territory" (Lau) / "reserve power"
67-56	不	1	pu	not / one who does not / [because of] not
67-57	敢	66	kan	dare / daring / venture / presume
67-58	為	87	wei	be / [one can] become
67-59	天	37	t'ien	Heaven
67-60	下	1	hsia	below / under }} the world
67-61	先	10	hsien	first / foremost / ahead / leader / ruler
67-62	故	66	ku	therefore
67-63	能	130	nêng	can / able / has the power to / [one] can
67-64	成	62	ch'êng	finish / accomplish / succeed / make / develop / perfect / full // "master" / "chief"

67-65	器	30	ch'i	vessel / utensil // [one's] "talent" / "potential"
67-66	長	168	ch'ang	endure / last long / grow / [and let it] mature / profit }}} "lord over the vessels" / "grow to a full vessel" (Chen) / "make your potential last" (Cleary) [3]
67-67	今	9	chin	now / nowadays [if you][people]
67-68	舍	135	shê	discard / renounce / forsake / shun
67-69	慈	61	tz'u	love / deep love / affection / compassion / mercy
67-70	且	1	ch'ieh	and / but [remain][try to be][for][to be]
67-71	勇	19	yung	brave / daring / courage[ous] / fearless[ness]
67-72	舍	135	shê	[if you] discard / renounce / forsake / shun
67-73	儉	9	chien	frugal[ity] / thriftiness / economy / restraint }} are wasteful
67-74	且	1	ch'ieh	and
67-75	廣	53	kuang	broad / generous / giving / expansive
67-76	舍	135	shê	[if you] discard / renounce / forsake / shun / [men] shun
67-77	後	60	hou	following / coming after / being behind / "the rear" / "humility"
67-78	且	1	ch'ieh	and [to be][for]
67-79	先	10	hsien	first / foremost / ahead / leader [one][one is][it is][one meets with]
67-80	死	78	ssu	die[s] / death / fatal / doomed / "courting death" (Wu)
67-81	矣	111	yi	indeed / certain / "sure to end in"
67-82	夫	37	fu	now / however / truly [if][for][through][with]
67-83	慈	61	tz'u	love / deep love / loving / affection[ate] / compassion[ate] / merciful
67-84	以	9a	yi	thereby [during][in]
67-85	戰	62	chan	fight[ing] / battle / attack
67-86	則	18	tsê	then [they will] / will bring
67-87	勝	19	shêng	conquer / victorious / win / outdo / overcome / triumph }} "win in a war"
67-88	以	9a	yi	thus / thereby
67-89	守	40	shou	defend / in defense / keep away / ward off
67-90	則	18	tsê	then [they will] / will
67-91	固	66	ku	lasting / strong / strength / firm / hold firm / "impregnable" / "invulnerable"
67-92	天	37	t'ien	Heaven
67-93	將	41	chiang	about to / act / give / side with / is to / wills / comes to
67-94	救	66	chiu	rescue / save / help / succor / "arms" >Alt: chien (create, establish)—MWT
67-95	之	4	chih	them / him / a man / a person / a people
67-96	以	9a	yi	with / by using }} those who have
67-97	慈	61	tz'u	love / deep love / affection / compassion [it][Heaven][Heaven will]
67-98	衛	144	wei	guard[s] / protect[s] / save[s] >Alt: huan (surround with a wall, wall in)—MWT
67-99	之	4	chih	them / him

[1] **Ssu pu hsiao**: (a) lack of convention or tradition, (b) resembling nothing / indescribable / different / "beyond compare" (Cleary); "not like anything concrete" (Jiyu); "not resembling the ordinary", (c) "seems useless" / unworthy / folly / degenerate / moral or physical decline

[2] **Chien** was "originally associated with p'u, purity, one's original, unspoiled state . . . and stands for the economy of nature that does not waste anything. When applied to moral life, it stands for simplicity of desire." (Chen)

| [3] *Ch'êng ch'i ch'ang*: "Be a vessel of the highest honor" (Legge) / "complete the duration of the vessel" (Erkes) / "be chief of all vessels" (Wu) / "chief of the ministers" (Waley) / "leader of the world" (Wang) |

VERSE 68

68-01	善	30	shan	Good / well / skillful / excel / (brave)
68-02	為	87	wei	act / action / make / do
68-03	士	33	shih	warrior / soldier / officer // leader of troops / captain / general / military leader }}} one who acts as a good warrior
68-04	者	125	chê	(the one) / (he)
68-05	不	1	pu	not
68-06	武	77	wu	warlike / violent / aggressive / "appear formidable" / "arm" / "exhibit his martial prowess" (Chen) / "oppressive with military strength" (Chan)
68-07	善	30	shan	good / well / skillful / excel / [one who] excels in
68-08	戰	62	chan	fight[er][ing] / battle
68-09	者	125	chê	(the one) / (he)
68-10	不	1	pu	not / does not [become / give in to] / never [aroused in]
68-11	怒	61	nu	angry / wrath[ful] / furious / rage / mad / lose his temper / "resort to his rage" (Jiyu)
68-12	善	30	shan	good / well / skillful / excel
68-13	勝	19	shêng	defeat / outdo / conquer[or] of / sustain
68-14	敵	66	ti	enemy / enemies / opponent }}} conqueror / winner / champion
68-15	者	125	chê	(the one) / (he)
68-16	不	1	pu	not / does not >Alt: *fu* (not)—MWT [1]
68-17	與	134	yü	engage / union / "join issue" / help / give / resemble >Alt: *cheng* (compete, go against) / "instigate a combat" (Chen) / "vengeful" / "wrestle"
68-18	善	30	shan	good / well / skillful / best way
68-19	用	101	yung	to use / employ / utilize / put to use / manage / user of / employer[s]
68-20	人	9a	jên	the people / others / men / (workers)
68-21	者	125	chê	(the one) / (he)
68-22	為	87	wei	makes / acts / puts / places
68-23	之	4	chih	it / itself / himself
68-24	下	1	hsia	below / under / lower than [others] }} humble / humbles himself / serve them
68-25	是	72a	shih	this is
68-26	謂	149	wei	called / ~means / ~known as
68-27	不	1	pu	not / non-
68-28	爭	87	chêng	contend[ing] / quarreling / striving / "going against the flow of nature" (Ming) }} "harmonious living"
68-29	之	4	chih	its / 's
68-30	德	60b	tê	Te / virtue / power }}}} the virtue of not contending
68-31	是	72a	shih	this is
68-32	謂	149	wei	called / ~means / ~known as
68-33	用	101	yung	use / employ / utilize / put to use / making use of / "ability to handle"

68-34	人	9a	jên	people / men / others
68-35	之	4	chih	's X Alt:omit—MWT
68-36	力	19	li	strength / abilities / capacity / physical strength / force / power / efforts X Alt: omit—MWT }}}} "mastery of men" / "the strength to use others"
68-37	是	72a	shih	this is
68-38	謂	149	wei	called / ~means / ~known as
68-39	配	164	p'ei	comply / pair / mate[d] to / match[ing] / unity / "being wedded to" / "living in accord with"
68-40	天	37	t'ien	Heaven
68-41	古	30	ku	ancient / of old / the ancients X Alt: omit
68-42	之	4	chih	's / its
68-43	極	75b	chi	perfect[ion] / highest [point / principle] / extreme / ultimate / sublimity / pristine / "reaching the ultimate" / "height of being" (Yutang) [2]

[1] (a) **pu yü** (does not engage), (b) **fu yü** (does not engage him)

[2] **Shih wei p'ei t'ien ku chih chi:** This is called . . . complying with Heaven's highest (principle); the sublime union with Heaven; uniting with Heaven's perfection; matching with Heaven, the highest (attainment) of the ancients.

VERSE 69

69-01	用	101	yung	Use / employ / utilize / [when] using / one who can use / expert in use
69-02	兵	12	ping	arms / warfare / war strategy / military / soldier / weaponry }} strategist / commander
69-03	有	74	yu	has / it is
69-04	言	149	yen	a saying / words / said / maxim }} say [:]
69-05	吾	30	wu	I
69-06	不	1	pu	not
69-07	敢	66	kan	dare / venture / presume
69-08	為	87	wei	be / act as / become
69-09	主	3	chu	host }} "take the offensive" / "attack first" / "make the first move"
69-10	而	126	erh	but
69-11	為	87	wei	be / act as / become
69-12	客	40	k'o	guest }} "take the defense / "rather be invaded"
69-13	不	1	pu	not / I do not
69-14	敢	66	kan	dare / venture / presume
69-15	進	162	chin	advance / make progress / move ahead / move forward / press forward
69-16	寸	41	ts'un	an inch
69-17	而	126	erh	but
69-18	退	162	t'ui	retreat / withdraw / draw back
69-19	尺	44	ch'ih	a foot
69-20	是	72a	shih	this is
69-21	謂	149	wei	called / ~means / ~known as
69-22	行	144	hsing	step / go forward / proceed / advance / march / march forward
69-23	無	86	wu	without / when there is no / without [appearing]
69-24	行	144	hsing	step / going forward / proceed / moving / advancing }}} "march without formation" / "marching forward without a road"

69-25	攘	64	jang	seize / grab / stretch out the arms / "roll up one's sleeves"
69-26	無	86	wu	without / when there is no
69-27	臂	130	pi	arms / "bearing one's arms"
69-28	扔	64	jêng	force[ing] / charge[ing] / confront / face / capture / "throw a rope" [the opponent / enemy]
69-29	無	86	wu	without
69-30	敵.	66	ti	enemy / opponent / attack[ing] / adversary / "frontal attack" / hostility
69-31	執	32	chih	seize / hold / grasp / carry / "take up arms" // manage / control [weapons]
69-32	無	86	wu	without / when there is no
69-33	兵.	12	ping	arms / weapons / "baring one's arms" / soldiers
69-34	禍	113	huo	calamity / misfortune / disaster / catastrophe / bad fate / evil / ~"tactical error that leads to a terrible defeat"
69-35	莫	140	mo	none / no / no thing
69-36	大	37	ta	greater / (worse)
69-37	於	70	yü	than
69-38	輕	159	ch'ing	lightness [toward] / making light of / frivolous / underestimating / "helpless" >Alt: wu (without, no)—MWT
69-39	敵.	66	ti	enemy / enemies / opponent / adversary [1]
69-40	輕	85	ch'ing	lightness [toward] / making light of / taking too lightly / underestimating / "making fun of"
69-41	敵	66	ti	enemy / opponent / ~inner enemies, i.e., greed, anger, etc.
69-42	幾	52	chi	will nearly / close / risk / "might entail"
69-43	喪	30	sang	losing / loss of / lose / ruin / destroy // death of
69-44	吾	30	wu	I / our / my
69-45	寶.	40	pao	treasure[s] / "what I value" / "ones' life"—HSK / ~"three treasures" / ~inner repose, access to our inner treasure, the self, what is within
69-46	故	66	ku	therefore
69-47	抗	64	k'ang	matched / opposing / two sides / equal / equally matched
69-48	兵	12	ping	armies / soldier / warrior / battle
69-49	相	109	hsiang	both / mutually / each other / even
69-50	加.	19	chia	encounter / face each other / meet / join / engage in battle / "raise arms" / fight >Alt: jo (matched, well-matched)—Fu I
69-51	哀	30	ai	weaker / compassionate / "underdog" // sorry / grieving side / sorrowful / "with pity" >Alt: hsiang (to yield) >Alt: shuai (wear away, fade away, ruin)
69-52	者	125	chê	that / it / (the one) / (he) / (they) / (man) / (party) }} "man of sorrow"
69-53	勝	19	shêng	wins / will win / conquer / sustain / outdo
69-54	矣.	111	yi	! / indeed [2][3]

| [1] **Ch'ing ti**: regarding your enemy too lightly, underestimating your enemy; **Wu ti**: not [knowing, recognizing] your enemy; [thinking, believing] you have no enemy |

| [2] **[47–54]** When two opponents meet, the one who has faded (who has no ego) will win. / The one who yields will win. / The one who has compassion will conquer. |

| [3] (See NOTES) |

70-01	吾	30	**wu**	My / I
70-02	言	149	**yen**	words / teachings / doctrines
70-03	甚	99	**shên**	very / are very
70-04	易	72	**yi**	easy [to]
70-05	知	111	**chih**	understand / know [and]
70-06	甚	99	**shên**	very
70-07	易	72	**yi**	easy [to]
70-08	行	144	**hsing**	practice / put into practice / perform / move forward
70-09	天	37	**t'ien**	Heaven
70-10	下	1	**hsia**	below / under }} [in] the world / the people of the world
70-11	莫	140	**mo**	no one / none
70-12	能	130	**nêng**	can / able / has the ability to
70-13	知	111	**chih**	understand / know
70-14	莫	140	**mo**	no one / none
70-15	能	130	**nêng**	can / able / has the ability to
70-16	行	144	**hsing**	practice / put into practice
70-17	言	149	**yen**	words / [my] words / teachings
70-18	有	74	**yu**	have / (there is)
70-19	宗	40	**tsung**	ancestor / source / root / "progenitor" / "ancient beginning" (Feng) / Ancestor // "system" (Duy) / "buildup of power through the ages"
70-20	事	6	**shih**	deeds / actions / affairs / dealings / activities / events / business / "affairs of men"
70-21	有	74	**yu**	have / (there is)
70-22	君	30	**chün**	ruler / master / lord / sovereign / governor / "a system" / (ultimate authority) / "disciplined"
70-23	夫	37	**fu**	truly / "now" / (what follows is true)
70-24	惟	30b	**wei**	only }} just as / it is because
70-25	無	86	**wu**	not / [he is / it is] not / [the people do] not
70-26	知	111	**chih**	know[n] / knowing / understand / aware of [this] }} the people are ignorant
70-27	是	72a	**shih**	(this)
70-28	以	9a	**yi**	(for) }} therefore / for this reason
70-29	不	1	**pu**	not / [they do] not
70-30	我	30	**wu**	I / me
70-31	知	111	**chih**	know[n] / knowing / understand / aware of / imitate
70-32	知	111	**chih**	know / understand / aware of
70-33	我	30	**wu**	me / I / (my teachings)
70-34	者	125	**chê**	(the ones) / (he)
70-35	希	50	**hsi**	rare / few [those who]
70-36	則	18	**tsê**	follow / imitate / emulate // "abuse" (Feng) // then / on that account / accordingly
70-37	我	30	**wu**	I am / me / (my teachings / my ways / my path)

70-38	者	125	chê	(the one) / (he)
70-39	貴	154	kuei	treasured / honored / highly valued / rare / noble[r] / "distinguished" / "reach their inner treasure" (Ming)
70-40	是	72a	shih	(this)
70-41	以	9a	yi	(for) }} therefore / hence
70-42	聖	128a	shêng	holy
70-43	人	9a	jên	man }} the sage
70-44	被	145	pei	wears / covers / dresses] / clad [himself with][in]
70-45	褐	145	ho	coarse clothes / wool / "poor man's garb" / "homespun" / "haircloth" / "plainly"
70-46	懷	61	huai	hides inside / holds / cherish / conceal / bear[s] / carry[ing]
70-47	玉	95	yü	gem[s] / jade / jewel[s] / "what is precious" [within][within his bosom][underneath] [on his person][near his breast][in his heart] [1]
[1] (See NOTES)				

V E R S E 7 1

71-01	知	111	chih	Know / understand / aware of / to know / [he who] knows / "from knowing to"
71-02	不	1	pu	un- / not / don't / does not }} unconsciously
71-03	知	111	chih	know[n][ing] / understand / aware of [is] [1]
71-04	上	1	shang	highest / superior / best / "transcend"
71-05	不	1	pu	not
71-06	知	111	chih	know / understand / aware of +Alt: add pu (not)—MWT
71-07	知	111	chih	know[able] / understand[able] / [yet to think] you know [will lead to]
71-08	病	104	ping	sickness / illness / disease / affliction // sick-minded / mental sickness // pain / difficulty / disaster / flaw / defect / fault [2]
71-09	夫	37	fu	truly / "now" / "when" / (what follows is true)
71-10	惟	30b	wei	only / exactly
71-11	病	104	ping	sick [of] / affliction / sick-minded / pain / difficulty / flaw / [one who recognizes this] disease as
71-12	病	104	ping	sick[ness] / disease [3]
71-13	是	72a	shih	(this)
71-14	以	9a	yi	(for) }} therefore / thus / the reason why
71-15	不	1	pu	not / free of / avoid
71-16	病	104	ping	sick[ness] / disease / difficulty / pain / afflicted
71-17	聖	128a	shêng	holy
71-18	人	9a	jên	man }} the sage
71-19	不	1	pu	not / free of / meets with no
71-20	病	104	ping	sick[ness] / sick-mindedness / pain / difficulty / affliction
71-21	以	9a	yi	because / since / it is because
71-22	其	12	ch'i	he is [recognizes]
71-23	病	104	ping	sick[ness] / disease / difficulty / pain / sick of
71-24	病	104	ping	sick[ness] / disease / difficulty / pain / being sick
71-25	是	72a	shih	(this)

71-26	以	9a	yi	(for) }} therefore / for that reason
71-27	不	1	pu	not / free of
71-28	病 .	104	ping	sick[ness] / disease / difficulty / pain }} "this is the secret of health" (Wu)

[1] **Chih pu chih**: "to know yet think you do not know"; "to know without knowing you know"; "unaware of knowing"; (blissfully ignorant)

[2] **Ping**: derived from "in bed" + "fire in the house" (fever). (See NOTES)

[3] **Wei ping ping**: "being alive to sickness" (Lau) / sick-sick / very difficult / "only when you pain the pain" (work through the pain)

VERSE 72

72-01	民	83	min	[When] the people / men
72-02	不	1	pu	not / are not / do not / lack / lack [sense of]
72-03	畏	102	wei	fear / dread / afraid of / power
72-04	威 .	38	wei	threats / punishment / force / "death sentence" // authority / imposition of authority / awe / "awe-inspiring" / military force / power / "God"
72-05	則	18	tsê	then / what follows
72-06	大	37	ta	the great / a greater
72-07	威	38	wei	dreadful / force / power / "God's anger" / (disaster)
72-08	至 .	133a	chih	arrive / will come / reach / descend [upon them] / appear / attained / "there will be" }} "awful visitation" (Lau) [1]
72-09	無	86	wu	do not
72-10	狎	94	hsia	squeeze / make narrow / restrict / reduce / cramp / cage / constrict—HSK >Alt: hsia (abuse, disturb, interfere, intrude, despise)—Wang Pi Commentary
72-11	其	12	ch'i	their / its / people's
72-12	所	63	so	place
72-13	居	44	chü	dwell / inhabit / live / home }} living space / quarters
72-14	無	86	wu	do not
72-15	厭	27	yen	oppress / press down on / repress / burden / make weary / disrupt / disturb / harass / dislike
72-16	其	12	ch'i	their
72-17	所	63	so	place / (means of)
72-18	生 .	100	shêng	dwell / inhabit / live / livelihood }} lives / how they live / "children" / "progeny" [2]
72-19	夫	37	fu	truly / "now" / (what follows is true)
72-20	唯	30b	wei	only when / just because / it is because
72-21	不	1	pu	not / do not / one does not / you do not / cease >Alt: fu (not) or fu yen (does not oppress them)
72-22	厭 .	27	yen	oppress / repress / burden / exhaust / disrupt / disturb
72-23	是	72a	shih	(this)
72-24	以	9a	yi	(for) }} therefore / thereby / for this reason
72-25	不	1	pu	not
72-26	厭 .	27	yen	oppress[ed] / burden[ed] // weary of / tiresome / "fed up" / annoyed [by them] // protest
72-27	是	72a	shih	(this)
72-28	以	9a	yi	(for) }} therefore / thus / hence

72-29	聖	128a	**shêng**	holy
72-30	人	9a	**jên**	man }} the sage[s]
72-31	自	132	**tzu**	himself / themselves
72-32	知	111	**chih**	know[s] / aware of
72-33	不	1	**pu**	not / but does not
72-34	自	132	**tzu**	himself
72-35	見.	147	**chien**	see / regard // show / display }} boastful / parade himself / "arrogant"
72-36	自	132	**tzu**	himself
72-37	愛	61	**ai**	love / cherish / adore / "take care of"
72-38	不	1	**pu**	not / but not
72-39	自	132	**tzu**	himself
72-40	貴.	154	**kuei**	treasure / exalt / "distinguish" [himself]
72-41	故	66	**ku**	therefore [he]
72-42	去	28	**ch'ü**	discard[s] / leave / let go of
72-43	彼	60	**pi**	the one / this / that / the latter / (his own view) / (the outer)
72-44	取	29	**ch'ü**	chooses / take hold of / accept / prefer[s] / rely upon
72-45	此.	76	**tz'u**	the other / that / this / the former / (the inner) [3]

[1] **Chih** implies something that descends from Heaven, such as something fated. This character is based on "a bird flying down to earth, as if sent by Heaven."

[2] **[09–18]** These lines are usually seen as advice to a ruler, telling him not to oppress the people and not to "narrow their living space." Su-Che (a Chinese commentator of the tenth century) and others see this as a metaphor for the body, suggesting that a person does not "confine" his own living space by limiting the identification of himself to his body. HSK and others see the "dwelling place" as one's heart, and this passage could mean "do not limit your heart," "do not withhold your love and humanity from others." It could also mean "do not limit your heart with conditional love—love all people equally."

[3] Verse 72:41–45 is the same as v. 12:45–49 and v. 38:125–29.

VERSE 73

73-01	勇	19	**yung**	Courage[ous] / brave[ry] / daring / bold[ness] / fearless / being brave >>Etm: "blooming of flowers" + "manly vigor" ("brave, rushing forth, bursting forth")
73-02	於	70	**yü**	to / carried to / in / out of
73-03	敢	66	**kan**	daring / risk taking / fearless[ness] / presumptuous / "passionate"
73-04	則	18	**tsê**	then / leads to / will meet with / is to be / is
73-05	殺.	79	**sha**	death / killed / [you will be] killed
73-06	勇	19	**yung**	courage / bravery / daring / boldness / fearless
73-07	於	70	**yü**	to / carried to / in / out of
73-08	不	1	**pu**	not
73-09	敢	66	**kan**	daring / risk taking / presumptuous / fearless
73-10	則	18	**tsê**	then / leads to [you][you will]
73-11	活.	85	**huo**	life / live / survive / preserve life / let live +Alt: add *chih* (to know)
73-12	此	77	**tz'u**	these / of these
73-13	兩	1	**liang**	two / both

73-14	者	125	chê	these / (things)
73-15	或	62	huo	some / sometimes / at times / likely / perhaps / one / "leads to" / (this is)
73-16	利	18	li	benefit / advantage[ous] / gain / good / profit
73-17	或	62	huo	some / sometimes / at times / likely / perhaps / one / "brings" / (this is)
73-18	害	40	hai	injure / injury / harm[ful] / hurt / offend / loss / disadvantage }}}} one brings benefit, the other harm / are either beneficial or harmful
73-19	天	37	t'ien	Heaven
73-20	之	4	chih	's / its
73-21	所	63	so	what it
73-22	惡	61	wu	hate[s][d] / reject / despise / detest / dislikes / "not favored"
73-23	孰	39	shu	who / what
73-24	知	111	chih	know[s] / understand[s]
73-25	其	12	ch'i	its / (the)
73-26	故	66	ku	cause / reason / reason why [?]
73-27	是	72a	shih	(this) }}}}}}}} "Who knows the real reason for Heaven's hatred?" (Lin)
73-28	以	9a	yi	(for) }} therefore / even X Alt: omit—MWT
73-29	聖	128a	shêng	holy X Alt: omit—MWT
73-30	人	9a	jên	man }} the sage X Alt: omit—MWT
73-31	猶	94	yu	still / like / "considers" / "treats some things as" X Alt: omit—MWT
73-32	難	172	nan	difficult / (problems) X Alt: omit—MWT
73-33	之	4	chih	it / this / (this question) / (to explain) }} unsure of / baffled by X Alt: omit—MWT
73-34	天	37	t'ien	Heaven
73-35	之	4	chih	's / its
73-36	道	162	tao	Tao / way
73-37	不	1	pu	not / does not
73-38	爭	87	chêng	contend / compete / strive / contest / "go against anything"
73-39	而	126	erh	yet / and
73-40	善	30	shan	well / good / excels / skill[fully] / in a good way
73-41	勝	19	shêng	conquer[s] / victory / overcome / win / sustain / outdo
73-42	不	1	pu	not / it does not
73-43	言	149	yen	speak / [use] words / speech
73-44	而	126	erh	and / yet
73-45	善	30	shan	good / well / excels / in a good way
73-46	應	61	ying	responds / answers / corresponds / "sends messages" / "gets responses" / "reward"
73-47	不	1	pu	not / it does not
73-48	召	30	chao	call / summon / ask / invitation / "being beckoned"
73-49	而	126	erh	and / yet
73-50	自	132	tzu	itself / of its own accord / naturally / [things] on their own / of themselves
73-51	來	9	lai	come[s] / "appear" / attracts }} "supplied with all its needs" (Feng)
73-52	繟	120	ch'an	slow / patient / calm

73-53	然	86	jan	manner / being so / behavior }} relaxed / not anxious / "appears slack" / unhurried / "no aim" / "without haste" (Wu)
73-54	而	126	erh	and / yet / but
73-55	善	30	shan	good / good at / well / (very)
73-56	謀	149	mou	plans / laying plans / in planning / "designs" / "resourceful"
73-57	天	37	t'ien	Heaven ['s]
73-58	網	120	wang	net
73-59	恢	61	k'uei	vast / wide / cast wide
73-60	恢	61	k'uei	vast / wide
73-61	疏	103	shu	space / open / "meshed" }} "sparse-meshed" (Wu) / "holes are large" (Cleary)
73-62	而	126	erh	and / yet / but [lets]
73-63	不	1	pu	not / "nothing" / "none" / "nothing ever" / don't
73-64	失	37	shih	slip[s] by / slip through / miss[es][ing] / loses / loss / omit / escape
VERSE 74				
				+Alt: add *jo* (if)—MWT
74-01	民	83	min	The people >Alt: *cheng* (always, constantly)
74-02	不	1	pu	not
74-03	畏	102	wei	fear / dread / afraid of
74-04	死	78	ssu	death
74-05	奈	37	nai	with what means / in what way
74-06	何	9	ho	how }} wherefore
74-07	以	9a	yi	with / using
74-08	死	78	ssu	death >Alt: *sha* (killing, execution)—MWT
74-09	懼	61	chü	threaten / scare / frighten / fear / "specter"
74-10	之	4	chih	them [with it] [?]
74-11	若	140	jo	if / suppose / were
74-12	使	9b	shih	cause / make / (it was that)
74-13	民	83	min	people
74-14	常	50	ch'ang	constant[ly] / always
74-15	畏	102	wei	fear / dread / afraid of
74-16	死	78	ssu	death
74-17	而	126	erh	but / if / and
74-18	為	87	wei	make / do / act / makers of / [those who] use / [someone] makes
74-19	奇	37a	ch'i	abnormal / dishonest / bizarre / deceitful / perverse / innovations / "vicious" }} lawbreakers / unruly / evildoers / one who does strange things / acts oddly
74-20	者	125	chê	(the ones) / (those who are)
74-21	吾	30	wu	we / I
74-22	得	60a	tê	get / take / obtain
74-23	執	32	chih	seize / hold / grasp }} arrest
74-24	而	126	erh	and

74-25	殺	79	sha	kill / put to death
74-26	之。	4	chih	him / them
74-27	孰	39	shu	who
74-28	敢。	66	kan	dare[s] / would dare / venture / presume [do so][take that position][?] }} (a) > who would dare kill them? (b) > who would dare break the law?
74-29	常	50	ch'ang	always / constant / "regular"
74-30	有	74	yu	there is
74-31	司	30	ssu	master / official / officer / one in charge
74-32	殺	79	sha	kill / one who kills / executioner }} "Great Executioner" / "Heaven" / "Lord of Death" / "Fate" / (a natural death)
74-33	者	125	chê	(one) / (those) [who][whose charge it is] X Alt: omit—MWT
74-34	殺。	79	sha	kills / to kill }} to do the killing X Alt: omit—MWT
74-35	夫	37	fu	truly / "now" / (what follows is true)
74-36	代	9	tai	on behalf of / for / instead of / substitute / take the place of / "undertake the executions of"
74-37	司	30	ssu	master / official / officer
74-38	殺	79	sha	kill / one who kills / executioner
74-39	者	125	chê	(one) / (those)
74-40	殺。	79	sha	who kills
74-41	是	72a	shih	this is
74-42	謂	149	wei	called / described as / ~resembles / ~means X Alt: omit—MWT
74-43	代	9	tai	take the place of / substitute / (cutting wood for) / "handle the hatchet of" (Yutang)
74-44	大	37	ta	great / master
74-45	匠	22	chiang	artisan / workman
74-46	斲。	69	cho	[who] hews / cuts / carves }}} wood-carver / carver / carpenter
74-47	夫	37	fu	truly / "now" / (what follows is true)
74-48	代	9	tai	taking the place of / substituting for / (cutting wood for)
74-49	大	37	ta	great / master
74-50	匠	22	chiang	artisan / workman
74-51	斲	69	cho	[who] hews / cuts / carves }}} wood-carver / carver / carpenter
74-52	者。	125	chê	(he) / (the one) / ~whoever does this
74-53	希	50	hsi	rare / few / seldom
74-54	有	74	yu	is / (escapes)
74-55	不	1	pu	not
74-56	傷	9	shang	injure / wound / cut[ting] / injuring / hurting
74-57	其	12	ch'i	his
74-58	手	64	shou	his own hands
74-59	矣。	111	yi	! / indeed / (final particle)
			VERSE 75	
75-01	民	83	min	The people / [why are] the people
75-02	之	4	chih	's / (they are)

75-03	饑 。	184	chi	starve / starving / hungry / famine / dearth
75-04	以	9a	yi	because
75-05	其	12	ch'i	their / they
75-06	上	1	shang	superior[s] / ruler[s] / those in authority / "man on top" X Alt: omit—MWT
75-07	食	184	shih	eat[s] / consume[s] / eat up / eat too much / devours / "swallowed up"
75-08	稅	115	shui	tax / tax-grain / tax money / duty on merchandise
75-09	之	4	chih	's / its
75-10	多 。	36	to	much / high / too high / often / many / too much }}}} "eat up the money in taxes" (Feng)
75-11	是	72a	shih	(this)
75-12	以	9a	yi	(for) }} therefore / for this reason
75-13	饑 .	184	chi	starving / hungry / famine
75-14	民	83	min	the people
75-15	之	4	chih	's / (they) [are]
75-16	難	172	nan	difficult to / hard to >Alt: pu (not, cannot be)—MWT
75-17	治 。	85	chih	govern / rule / manage / control }} unruly / rebellious
75-18	以	9a	yi	because
75-19	其	12	ch'i	their / they
75-20	上	1	shang	superior[s] / ruler[s] / those in authority
75-21	之	4	chih	's / its / theirs }} belonging to the superiors
75-22	有	74	yu	being / are / are fond of / have +Alt: add yi (reason for)—MWT
75-23	為 。	87	wei	activity / taking action / interfering / meddlesome / "contrivances" / "hands on everything"
75-24	是	72a	shih	(this)
75-25	以	9a	yi	(for) }} therefore / for this reason
75-26	難	172	nan	difficult / hard >Alt: pu (not, cannot be)—MWT
75-27	治 .	85	chih	govern / rule / manage
75-28	民	83	min	the people
75-29	之	4	chih	's / its / they / }} belonging to the people
75-30	輕	159	ch'ing	lightness / take lightly / make light of / frivolous / not take seriously / slight / not afraid of
75-31	死 。	78	ssu	death }} "anxious to make a living" (Yutang) / "do not consider the gravity of death" (Ming)
75-32	以	9a	yi	because
75-33	其	12	ch'i	their / they are / those +Alt: add shang (superiors)
75-34	求	85	ch'iu	seek[ing] / aiming for / strives for / pursuit / demand >Alt: sheng (life, live)
75-35	生	100	shêng	life / living }} strive for life / live life
75-36	之	4	chih	's / its [too]
75-37	厚 。	27	hou	thick[ness] / rich / much / intensity / vigorous[ly] / anxious / "much store" }}}} "in thick pursuit of life" (Chen) / "make too much of life" (Wu) / >v. 50:36
75-38	是	72a	shih	(this)
75-39	以	9a	yi	(for) }} therefore / this is why
75-40	輕	159	ch'ing	lightness / taking lightly / make light of / not take seriously
75-41	死 .	78	ssu	death

75-42	夫	37	fu	truly / "now" / (what follows is true)
75-43	唯	30b	wei	only / only [he who is]
75-44	無	86	wu	not / without / nothing
75-45	以	9a	yi	for
75-46	生	100	shêng	life / living
75-47	為	87	wei	act / make / pursue / do / seek after / "use" / "make a fuss over"
75-48	者。	125	chê	(the one)
75-49	是	72a	shih	this one / to be / is
75-50	賢	154	hsien	worthy / good / virtuous / moral / excels / "wise[r]"
75-51	於	70	yü	than / in / at / through / in making
75-52	貴	154	kuei	esteem / honor / value[able] / exalting / the one who values
75-53	生。	100	shêng	life / living [1]

[1] "It is only those who do not seek after life that excel in making life valuable." (Wing); "Therefore, it is better to do nothing for one's life than to value it." (Lin); "Truly, not acting for life's sake is wiser than valuing life." (Duy); "Now he who lays stress on life is worthier than he who values life." (Erkes); "The people have simply nothing to live upon! They know better than to value such a life!" (Wu)

VERSE 76

76-01	人	9a	jên	Man / person
76-02	之	4	chih	his / in his
76-03	生	100	shêng	life / growing / when born / at birth
76-04	也	5	yeh	is indeed / (final particle)
76-05	柔	75	jou	tender / soft / pliant / yielding / supple
76-06	弱。	57	jo	weak / gentle[ness] / tender / "filled up with sap" (Feng)
76-07	其	12	ch'i	he / she
76-08	死	78	ssu	dies / at death
76-09	也	5	yeh	is indeed / (final particle) +Alt: add: "end up stretched out"—MWTA
76-10	堅	32	chien	hard / firm / stiff / rigid
76-11	強。	57	ch'iang	unyielding / stiff / forceful / hard / strong / "stark"
76-12	萬	140	wan	ten thousand / all X Alt: omit—Fu I
76-13	物	93	wu	things / beings [such as][including] X Alt: omit—Fu I
76-14	草	140	ts'ao	grass
76-15	木	75	mu	trees
76-16	之	4	chih	in their
76-17	生	100	shêng	life / growing / while alive
76-18	也	5	yeh	are indeed / (~final particle)
76-19	柔	75	jou	tender /soft / pliant / yielding / supple
76-20	脆。	130	ts'ui	delicate / supple / frail
76-21	其	12	ch'i	they / when they
76-22	死	78	ssu	die / death / dead
76-23	也	5	yeh	are indeed / (~final particle)

76-24	枯	75	k'u	rigid / decayed / withered / dry / brittle
76-25	槁	75	kao	dry / rotten / decayed / shriveled
76-26	故	66	ku	therefore / this +Alt: add *yueh* (it is said)—MWT
76-27	堅	32	chien	hardness / firm / stiff
76-28	強	57	ch'iang	unyielding / stiff / forceful
76-29	者	125	chê	it / that / (those) / (they) [are]
76-30	死	78	ssu	death
76-31	之	4	chih	's }} belonging to death
76-32	徒	60	t'u	companion[s] / follower[s] / company of / comrade / disciple / >v. 50:13
76-33	柔	75	jou	tender / soft / pliant / yielding
76-34	弱	57	jo	weak / gentle[ness]
76-35	者	125	chê	it / that / (those) / (they) [are]
76-36	生	100	shêng	life
76-37	之	4	chih	's }} belonging to life
76-38	徒	60	t'u	companion[s] / follower[s] / company of / comrade / disciple / >v. 50:07
76-39	是	72a	shih	(this)
76-40	以	9a	yi	(for) }} therefore / so we see
76-41	兵	12	ping	army / arms / soldiers / weapons
76-42	強	57	ch'iang	unyielding / stiff / forceful / unbending / headstrong / strong / "uses its strength" / "unable to change plans"
76-43	則	18	tsê	then / thus
76-44	不	1	pu	not / will not / cannot
76-45	滅	19	shêng	win / victor[y] / conquer / overcome / vanquish }} is destroyed / will lose [in battle]
76-46	木	75	mu	tree
76-47	強	57	ch'iang	unyielding / stiff / forceful / unable to bend / strong / hard / stands firm
76-48	則	18	tsê	then
76-49	折	12	ping	weapon / arms / army // be felled / cut down / "struck down with a weapon" (Chen) / "suffer the axe" (Lau) [1]
76-50	強	57	ch'iang	unyielding / stiff / forceful / strong
76-51	大	37	ta	great / big / mighty
76-52	處	141	ch'u	stay / stop / rest / dwell / place themselves / take / "belong"
76-53	下	1	hsia	below / lower position / under / underneath }} inferior / subordinate / will fall / "will be laid low" (Wu) / "topple from their places" (Blakney)
76-54	柔	75	jou	tender / soft / pliant / yielding / gentle / (humble)
76-55	弱	57	jo	weak
76-56	處	141	ch'u	stay / rest / (belong) / (rise)
76-57	上	1	shang	above / higher position / on top / at the top / to the top }} superior / "will overcome" / "will be exalted" (Wu)

[1] >Alt: *che* (break, crack, snap)   >Alt: *kung* (share in common, together)—Fu I   >Alt: *keng* (end, come to its end)—MWTA
>Alt: *ching* (complete)—MWTB

77-01	天	37	t'ien	Heaven
77-02	之	4	chih	's / its
77-03	道。	162	tao	Tao / way }}} the way of Heaven
77-04	其	12	ch'i	it
77-05	猶	94	yu	is like / similar / resembles
77-06	張	57	chang	stretching / draw[ing] / bending / flexing / "stringing" [of]
77-07	弓	57	kung	a bow
77-08	歟。	134	yü	resemble / compare / and // give
77-09	高	189	kao	high[er] / top / when high
77-10	者	125	chê	(the one) / it
77-11	抑	64	yi	brings down / presses down / lower / pull down
77-12	之。	4	chih	it
77-13	下	1	hsia	when low / lower / low / under / "bottom end"
77-14	者	125	chê	(the one) / it
77-15	舉	134	chü	raise[s] / lift[s] up / goes up / promote / lifted
77-16	之。	4	chih	it
77-17	有	74	yu	have / possess / has
77-18	餘	184	yü	abundance / surplus / excess / too much / "extra" / "long" }} when there is an excess
77-19	者	125	chê	(the one) / it
77-20	損	64	sun	diminish / decrease / less[en] / reduce[s][d] / takes from / take away / "shorten"
77-21	之。	4	chih	them / it
77-22	不	1	pu	not / when not
77-23	足	157	tsu	enough / adequate / sufficient }} deficient / "short"
77-24	者	125	chê	(the one) / it
77-25	補	145	pu	complete / supplement / adds to / replenish / expand / "lengthen" >Alt: yü (give, unite, join)
77-26	之。	4	chih	them / it +Alt: add ku (therefore)—MWT
77-27	天	37	t'ien	Heaven +Alt: add chih (its, 's)
77-28	道	162	tao	Tao / way
77-29	損	64	sun	diminish / decrease / less[en] / reduce[s][d] / takes from
77-30	有	74	yu	have / possess / [what] has / [that which] has
77-31	餘	184	yü	abundance / surplus / excess[ive] / too much / too long
77-32	而	126	erh	and / yet
77-33	補	145	pu	add on / supplement / complete / replenish / mend / "make good" >Alt: yi (increase)—MWT
77-34	不	1	pu	not / [those who] do not have
77-35	足。	157	tsu	enough / adequate [supply] / sufficient }} is deficient / "short"
77-36	人	9a	jên	man / human / people
77-37	之	4	chih	's / their
77-38	道	162	tao	Tao / way }}} the way of man
77-39	則	18	tsê	is / then

77-40	不	1	pu	not
77-41	然 .	86	jan	so / as is / like this }} otherwise / different / the other way
77-42	損	64	sun	loss / lose / diminish / decrease / less[en] / reduce / take from
77-43	不	1	pu	not / [those] not [having]
77-44	足	157	tsu	enough / adequate [supply] / sufficient }} in want / deficient
77-45	以	9a	yi	thereby / thus
77-46	奉	37	fêng	offer[s] / give[s] to / supplies / serve / pay respects to / "gives as a tribute" [to those]
77-47	有	74	yu	have / possess
77-48	餘 .	184	yü	abundance / surplus / excess / too much }} the excessive
77-49	孰	39	shu	who / which / what
77-50	能	130	nêng	can / is able to / has the power to
77-51	有	74	yu	have / possess / take [what he has in]
77-52	餘	184	yü	abundance / surplus / excess / too much / "more than enough"
77-53	以	9a	yi	thereby / use / (to) / (for the purpose of) / (in order to) > Alt: *erh* (and)—MWT
77-54	奉	37	fêng	offer[s] / give[s] to / supplies / serve / pay respects to / "receive with both hands"
77-55	天	37	t'ien	Heaven
77-56	下 .	1	hsia	below / underneath }} the world X Alt: omit—MWT >Alt: *wu* (those with nothing)—Henricks
77-57	唯	30b	wei	only
77-58	有	74	yu	have / has / possess
77-59	道	162	tao	Tao
77-60	者 .	125	chê	it / (he) / (person) / (one) / (man) }}}} only the man of Tao / (sage)
77-61	是	72a	shih	(this)
77-62	以	9a	yi	(for) }} therefore / thus
77-63	聖	128a	shêng	holy
77-64	人	9a	jên	man }} the sage
77-65	為	87	wei	acts / does / makes / works
77-66	而	126	erh	and / yet
77-67	不	1	pu	not / without
77-68	恃 .	61	shih	claim / rely upon / presume / expect / exalting / assert / hold onto / "exact gratitude"
77-69	功	19	kung	merit / credit / success / his own ability / "fruits of his actions" / "his own efforts" }} possess[ing] / "seeking recognition" / "holding on to it"
77-70	成	62	ch'êng	accomplishes / completes / succeeds / finish / achieves [what needs to be done][task]
77-71	而	126	erh	and / yet
77-72	不	1	pu	not / does not / without
77-73	處 .	141	ch'u	stop / stay / dwell [on it] / "claim credit for" / "attachment" / "lay claim to merit" (Lau)
77-74	其	12	ch'i	he / he has / [it is because] he
77-75	不	1	pu	not / no / does not
77-76	欲	76	yü	want / wish / desire / (tries) [to]
77-77	見	147	chien	see / be seen / to seem / be considered // show / display / "flaunt" [his] }}} hides

77-78	賢	154	hsien	worth[iness] / virtue / goodness / excellence / superior / skill / "better than others" / "his knowledge" (Feng) / "his merits" (Wu) +Alt: add *ye* (?, eh?, no?, does he?)
			VERSE 78	
78-01	天	37	t'ien	Heaven
78-02	下	1	hsia	below / under }} the world / in the world
78-03	莫	140	mo	none / nothing
78-04	柔	75	jou	soft / pliant / yielding / tender[ness] / weak / submissive
78-05	弱	57	jo	weak[ness] / weaker
78-06	於	70	yü	than
78-07	水	85	shui	water [1]
78-08	而	126	erh	and / yet
78-09	攻	66	kung	attack / assault
78-10	堅	32	chien	hard / firm
78-11	強	57	ch'iang	unyielding / stiff / forceful / strong
78-12	者	125	chê	it / (the ones) / (they)
78-13	莫	140	mo	none / no one
78-14	之	4	chih	them
78-15	能	130	nêng	can / is able to / has the power to
78-16	勝	19	shêng	surpass / conquer / overcome / outdo / "compare with it" +Alt: add *yi* (accordingly) }} there is nothing better
78-17	其	12	ch'i	it / things / among all things
78-18	無	86	wu	none / nothing / [there is] none
78-19	以	9a	yi	accordingly / for this reason / (can)
78-20	易	72	yi	replace / takes the place / substitute [for] / change places with / exchange places / change // alter // "vanquish"
78-21	之	4	chih	it }}}} "for which there is no substitute"
78-22	弱	57	jo	weak / the weak / flexible / use weakness
78-23	之	4	chih	it / the ones [to]
78-24	勝	19	shêng	surpass / conquer / overcome / outdo / sustain
78-25	強	57	ch'iang	unyielding / stiff / adamant / inflexible // forceful / strong / strength
78-26	柔	75	jou	tender / soft / yielding / submissive / [use] softness
78-27	之	4	chih	it / ones [to]
78-28	勝	19	shêng	surpass[es] / conquer / overcome / outdo / sustain
78-29	剛	18	kang	stiff / hard[ness] / unyielding / rigid[ity] / forceful
78-30	天	37	t'ien	Heaven
78-31	下	1	hsia	below / under }} the world
78-32	莫	140	mo	none / there is no one
78-33	不	1	pu	not
78-34	知	111	chih	know[s] / understand [this]
78-35	莫	140	mo	no one / none / [yet] none

78-36	能	130	nêng	can / able / has the power to
78-37	行.	144	hsing	practice [it] / follow / move forward / "put this knowledge into practice"
78-38	是	72a	shih	(this)
78-39	以	9a	yi	(for) }} therefore / thus
78-40	聖	128a	shêng	holy
78-41	人	9a	jên	man }} the sage[s]
78-42	云	7	yün	say[s] / declares [he who can]
78-43	受	29	shou	hold / keep to / stay / guard / receive / protect / preserve // suffer / bear
78-44	國	31	kuo	country / nation / state
78-45	之	4	chih	's / its
78-46	垢○	32	kou	dishonor / disgrace / humiliation // immorality / sin / calumny / dirt / "filth"
78-47	是	72a	shih	this is
78-48	謂	149	wei	called / ~to be
78-49	社	113	shê	alter / shrine / sacrifice / "local shrine"
78-50	稷	115a	chi	soil / grain / millet / earth / land
78-51	主.	3	chu	master / lord / gods / "preserver" [he] [2]
78-52	受	29	shou	hold / keep to / stay / guard / receive // suffer[s] / bear / shoulders / "take unto himself"
78-53	國	31	kuo	nation / country / state ['s]
78-54	不	1	pu	un- / not
78-55	祥○	113	hsiang	blessing / fortune / good omen / auspicious }} curse / disaster / sins / evil / misfortune / calamity / ill fate
78-56	是	72a	shih	this is
78-57	謂	149	wei	called / known as / becomes / "deserves to be"
78-58	天	37	t'ien	Heaven
78-59	下	1	hsia	below / under }} the world / the empire / the universe
78-60	王.	95	wang	king
78-61	正	77	chêng	true / correct / straight / straightforward / upright / "positive"
78-62	言	149	yen	words
78-63	若	140	jo	seem / appear / (sound)
78-64	反.	29	fan	the opposite / paradoxical / to return / crooked / "negative" / "upside-down" }} "this is a paradox" (Blakney) [3]

[1] **Shui** ("water") (See NOTES)

[2] **Shê chi chu**: "lord of the community"; "gods of millet and earth" (Lau); "Master of the Altar of Soil and Grain" (Chen); "lord of its soil shrines" (Wu)

[3] The last four lines (*chêng yen jo fan*) seem out of place here, and interpreters have eliminated this line or moved it to verse 41 or 45.

VERSE 79

79-01	和	30b	ho	Harmony / harmonize / make peace / equilibrium / reconcile / settlement of / "patch up"
79-02	大	37	ta	great / (bitter)
79-03	怨	61	yüan	hatred / enmity / injury / grudge / resentment / enemies
79-04	必	61	pi	surely / sure to be

79-05	有	74	**yu**	there is / there will
79-06	餘	184	**yü**	surplus / remain[ing] / excess / residue[al] / some left / linger / "undispelled"
79-07	怨	61	**yüan**	hatred / enmity / injury / grudge / resentment / enemies
79-08	安	40	**an**	how? / "how can this be?" / where? / what? // still / rest
79-09	可	30	**k'o**	can / able / has the power to
79-10	以	9a	**yi**	thereby / (by) / accordingly
79-11	為	87	**wei**	make / made / do / act / (regard[ed]) / (consider[ed]) / be made
79-12	善	30	**shan**	good / satisfactory / "perfect" [?] }} remedied / "can be done about it"
79-13	是	72a	**shih**	(this)
79-14	以	9a	**yi**	(for) }} therefore / thus
79-15	聖	128a	**shêng**	holy
79-16	人	9a	**jên**	man }} the sage[s]
79-17	執	32	**chih**	hold[s] / grasp / keep / manage
79-18	左	48	**tso**	left side / left-hand portion / left stub / (creditor) / (debt owed) / (side of obligation)
79-19	契	37b	**ch'i**	contract / agreement / deed / tally / deed }}} inferior position / "keeps their faith" (Cleary) [1][2]
79-20	而	126	**erh**	and
79-21	不	1	**pu**	not / does not
79-22	責	154a	**tsê**	make claim / "exact his due" / pressure // blame / punish / chastise / "put guilt"
79-23	於	70	**yü**	from / upon / on
79-24	人	9a	**jên**	others / the people / the other party
79-25	有	74	**yu**	have / has / possess
79-26	德	60b	**tê**	Te / virtue / power }} one of virtue / virtuous people
79-27	司	30	**ssu**	keep / attend / hold to / take charge of / control [their]
79-28	契	37b	**ch'i**	contract[s] / obligation[s] / promises / tally }} does his part / "see to their promises" (Cleary)
79-29	無	86	**wu**	without / lacking / [those] without
79-30	德	60b	**tê**	Te / virtue
79-31	司	30	**ssu**	keep / attend / hold to / take charge of / control / insist on [their]
79-32	徹	60	**ch'ê**	claim / payment / "exaction" / "fixing guilt" (Yutang) / "other people's mistakes" / "the tax"
79-33	天	37	**t'ien**	Heaven ['s]
79-34	道	162	**tao**	Tao / way
79-35	無	86	**wu**	without / has no
79-36	親	147	**ch'in**	preference / favorItes / favoritism / partiality / "private affections" / nepotism [yet]
79-37	常	50	**ch'ang**	always / constantly / all the time / (only)
79-38	與	134	**yü**	with / on the side of / sides with / for / stay with / help / give / join with / accord with
79-39	善	30	**shan**	good / the good / virtuous / righteous / dharma
79-40	人	9a	**jên**	man / person / people }} one who follows dharma—the natural laws of the universe [3]

[1] In ancient China, when a loan of money was made, the figures were drawn on a bamboo stick and that stick was broken in half lengthwise—this created two pieces that interlocked with each other. The left side was the "inferior" side, the side of the debtor; the right side was the "superior" side, the side of the creditor. (See NOTES)

				[2] **Chih tso ch'i**: "takes the position of owing" / "keeps his half of the bargain" (Feng) / "gives but does not seek anything in return" (Ming)
				[3] (See NOTES)

V E R S E   80

80-01	小	42	hsiao	Small / [let there be] a small / reduce the size of
80-02	國	31	kuo	country / state
80-03	寡	40	kua	[with] few / small
80-04	民 .	83	min	people / citizens / population
80-05	使	9b	shih	let / "even if they"
80-06	有	74	yu	have / possess
80-07	什	9a	shih	ten times / tenfold / troop of ten
80-08	伯	9	po	a hundred / hundred times / hundredfold / batallion of one hundred [men] +Alt: add *jen* (man, men)
80-09	之	4	chih	their
80-10	器	30	ch'i	implements / utensils / "weapons" / supplies / vessels / "machines" / "people with talent" [1]
80-11	而	126	erh	and / yet
80-12	不	1	pu	not
80-13	用 .	101	yung	use [them] / employ / utilize / "needed" / use their [power, skill]
80-14	使	9b	shih	let / even if
80-15	民	83	min	the people
80-16	重	166	chung	take seriously / give weight to / heed / weigh heavily / "mind"
80-17	死	78	ssu	death }} "value their lives"
80-18	而	126	erh	and
80-19	不	1	pu	not / (have no desires to) / [such that they] do not X Alt: omit—MWT
80-20	遠	162	yüan	far away / distant / remove
80-21	徙 .	60	hsi	move / move away / migrate / (travel)
80-22	雖	172	sui	although / though / even though / even if they
80-23	有	74	yu	have / possess / (there are)
80-24	舟	137	chou	boats / ships / vessels
80-25	輿	159	yü	carriages / carts
80-26	無	86	wu	without / [they have] no / [there will be] no
80-27	所	63	so	place[s] / spot / "occasion"
80-28	乘	4	ch'êng	to ride
80-29	之 .	4	chih	in them
80-30	雖	172	sui	although / though / even though / even if they
80-31	有	74	yu	have / possess / (there are)
80-32	甲	102	chia	armor / "arrows"
80-33	兵	12	ping	weapons
80-34	無	86	wu	without / [they have] no
80-35	所	63	so	place / spot / "occasion"

80-36	陳	170	ch'ên	wear / don / display / exhibit
80-37	之.	4	chih	them
80-38	使	9b	shih	let
80-39	人	9a	jên	men / the people
80-40	復	60	fu	return / go back to / restore / once again
80-41	結	120	chieh	knot / knotted
80-42	繩	120	shêng	cords / ropes
80-43	而	126	erh	and
80-44	用	101	yung	use / employ
80-45	之.	4	chih	them [for reckoning][as memory aids][in place of writing][for communicating]
80-46	甘	99	kan	enjoy / delight in / relish
80-47	其	12	ch'i	in their
80-48	食.	184	shih	food
80-49	美	123	mei	beautiful / beautify / have beautiful / well-kept / appreciate / pleased with
80-50	其	12	ch'i	their
80-51	服	74	fu	clothes / clothing
80-52	安	40	an	content / satisfied / at peace / tranquil / harmony / "feel secure"
80-53	其	12	ch'i	their / with their
80-54	居.	44	chü	homes / dwellings / where they live / abode / occupy / inhabit
80-55	樂	75	lo	find joy in / rejoice in / delight joyfully / happily / "inured to"
80-56	其	12	ch'i	their
80-57	俗.	9	su	everyday life / "the way they live" / practices / customs / "simple way of living" (Wu)
80-58	鄰	163	lin	neighboring / nearby
80-59	國	31	kuo	communities / villages / country / state
80-60	相	109	hsiang	both / mutually / one another
80-61	望.	74	wang	see / overlook / can see / in sight of [each other][one another]
80-62	雞	172	chi	roosters / cocks
80-63	犬	94	ch'üan	dogs
80-64	之	4	chih	their
80-65	聲	128b	shêng	sound / (barking) / (crowing)
80-66	相	109	hsiang	both / mutually
80-67	聞.	128	wên	hear / can hear / in earshot of [each other]
80-68	民	83	min	the people
80-69	至	133a	chih	will reach / until they reach
80-70	老	125	lao	old age / grow old
80-71	死	78	ssu	and die }}} till the end of their days / until their death
80-72	不	1	pu	not / without / without having / never
80-73	相	109	hsiang	both / one another
80-74	往	74	wang	visit[ed] / (see) [each other]
80-75	來.	9	lai	gone to / go outside / come and go / back and forth }}} going to visit one another / "been outside their city" (Yutang)

				VERSE 81
81-01	信	9	hsin	Sincere / true / truthful / faithful / confident / "that inspire confidence"
81-02	言	149	yen	words
81-03	不	1	pu	are not
81-04	美	123	mei	beautiful / pleasing / fine / good / kind / sweet / fine-sounding / showy
81-05	美	123	mei	beautiful / pleasing / fine / good / kind / sweet / fine-sounding / showy
81-06	言	149	yen	words
81-07	不	1	pu	are not
81-08	信	9	hsin	sincere / true / truthful / faithful / confident / "inspire confidence"
81-09	善	30	shan	good / righteous / dharmic
81-10	者	125	chê	it / (the ones) / (man)
81-11	不	1	pu	not
81-12	辯	160	pien	dispute / quarrel / debate / argue / persuasive
81-13	辯	160	pien	[those who][one who] dispute[s] / quarrel / debate / argue
81-14	者	125	chê	it / (the ones) / (man)
81-15	不	1	pu	not
81-16	善	30	shan	good / righteous / dharmic
81-17	知	111	chih	know[ing] / aware / wise
81-18	者	125	chê	it / (the ones) / (man)
81-19	不	1	pu	not / is not / does not / do not [have]
81-20	博	24	po	learned / wide learning / "erudite" / universal in their knowledge / ample / "knowledge from books" / "knowledge without experience" / "a know-it-all"
81-21	博	24	po	learned / wide learning / "erudite" / universal in their knowledge / ample
81-22	者	125	chê	(the ones)
81-23	不	1	pu	not
81-24	知	111	chih	know[ing]
81-25	聖	128a	shêng	holy
81-26	人	9a	jên	man }} the sage
81-27	不	1	pu	not / does not
81-28	積	115c	chi	hoard / gather up / store up / accumulate [for himself]
81-29	既	71	chi	having / since
81-30	以	9a	yi	thereby [the more he]
81-31	為	87	wei	act[s] / work[s] / does / (uses) / gives / bestows / uses for / lives
81-32	人	9a	jên	for others / to others
81-33	己	49	chi	he himself / he has
81-34	愈	61a	yü	more / further / more and more / excess
81-35	有	74	yu	have / has himself / acquire
81-36	既	71	chi	having / since

81-37	以	9a	**yi**	thereby	
81-38	與	134	**yü**	give[n] / share / unite / given [all he has] / "devote himself"	
81-39	人	9a	**jên**	people / to the people / to others	
81-40	己	49	**chi**	he himself / he is	
81-41	愈	61a	**yü**	more / further / more and more / excess / greater	
81-42	多 .	36	**to**	more / many / much / abundant / a lot / excess / rich }} grows richer	
81-43	天	37	**t'ien**	Heaven	
81-44	之	4	**chih**	's / its	
81-45	道	162	**tao**	way / path / Tao [is to]	
81-46	利	18	**li**	benefit[s] / advantage / gives / helps / gain // pointed / sharp	
81-47	而	126	**erh**	and / yet	
81-48	不	1	**pu**	not / does not / nothing	
81-49	害 .	40	**hai**	injure / hurt / damage / offend / harm	[1]
81-50	聖	128a	**shêng**	holy	
81-51	人	9a	**jên**	man }} the sage	
81-52	之	4	**chih**	's / his	
81-53	道 .	162	**tao**	Tao / way	
81-54	為	87	**wei**	act / make / do / work / do his duty / accomplish[es] / "gives" / "bountiful" / "serve"	
81-55	而	126	**erh**	and / but	
81-56	不	1	**pu**	not >Alt: *fu* (not)—MWT	[2]
81-57	爭 .	87	**chêng**	contend / compete / contest / strive / go against / "go against the flow of " }} be In harmony [with others][Heaven][Nature]	

[1] ***T'ien chih tao li erh pu hai***: "The way of Heaven is to benefit and do no harm." / "The way of Heaven is to sharpen without cutting." (Waley); "With all the sharpness of the Way of Heaven, It injures not." (Legge)

[2] ***Pu chêng*** translates as "does not compete"; ***fu chêng*** translates as "does not compete with them."

NOTES

Verse 2 *Sheng jên* refers to one who perfectly embodies Tao. *Jên* means "man," "woman," or "person." *Sheng* means "holy" or "saintly" and is made up of three characters: (a) a mouth (*wei*), (b) an ear (*erh*), and (c) a person standing or sitting firmly on the ground (*t'ing*). The ear positioned next to the mouth (and positioned above the person) suggests a direct hearing, without interference, between the holy man and the Absolute. The holy man hears the pure voice of Tao; the holy man acts in perfect harmony with the universe.

Sheng jên has been translated in various ways: (a) "Holy man, Sacred person." These terms suggest some spiritual attainment, but not necessarily enlightenment. (b) "Sage, Ideal Sage, Perfected Sage." These terms generally refer to one who is a seer, one who penetrates the mysteries of the universe, one who is sagacious. Using a capital letter or adding the modifying words "Ideal" or "Perfected" suggests an enlightened sage and comes closer to the meaning of *sheng jen*. (c) "Enlightened Being, Perfect Being, Perfect Man, Realized Being, Saint, Master, *Siddha*." All these terms refer to one who has reached the highest state of consciousness, one who has realized his inseparable unity with God. "Perfect Man" is a term that most often means one who has perfect morality. Here it means one who has attained perfection. "Saint" has been used by some translators, and although it is an accurate translation, it has an inescapable Christian association. *Siddha* (from Sanskrit), meaning "perfect," "one who is perfect," or "one who has realized his own perfection," is a perfect translation but is too strongly associated with the Indian tradition. (d) "Man of Calling," "Evolved Individuals." Neither of these terms conveys the lofty state of enlightenment. "Evolved Individuals" is perhaps the most politically correct term but the most defective and cumbersome.

Wu-wei. The following quotation from the thirteenth-century Indian saint Jnaneshwar beautifully explicates the Chinese concept of *wu-wei* (non-action):

> Action is that natural activity which makes possible the manifestation of the universe. First understand this thoroughly. . . . When the sun rises and sets, it seems to move although it is actually motionless. In the same way, realize that freedom from action lies in action. Such a person seems like other people, but he is not affected by human nature, like the sun which cannot be drowned in water. He sees the world without seeing it, does everything without doing it, enjoys all the pleasures without being involved in them. Though he is seated in one place, he travels everywhere, for even while in this body he has become the universe. . . . The walking of his feet, the speaking of his mouth, and all his other actions are the Supreme moving through him. Furthermore, he sees the whole universe as not different from himself. Then how can action affect him? . . . He is free in every way and, even though he acts, he is free from action. Though he possesses attributes, he is beyond all attributes. There is no doubt about this.
>
> —*Jnaneshwar's Gita*, 4:88, 98–101, 110, 111, 113 (Kripananda)

The Chinese word *jên* is defined by the ancient *Shao Wen* dictionary as "near," or **Verse 5** "akin," and was probably first used to mean the way one treats his own family. Later, the term was adopted by Confucius to mean "humanity," or "treat others with the same love as you would those in your own family." Hence this is an impartial type of love, a call to love all people as you would your own family. This "impartiality" or "dispassion" of the Sage does not imply a disregard for people, but a disregard to judgment and all those things that divide people. The Sage welcomes everyone equally, as his own Self.

There is not a dint of partiality in him, friend and foe are regarded alike. A lamp spreads light to every house, not just its own. A tree gives shade to the one who has planted it and also to the one who cuts it down. A sugar-cane is sweet to the one who cultivates it, and to the one who crushes it.

—The Philosophy of Jnanadeva, 12:197–199 (Bahirat)

The Sage is merciful, kind, and enduring of all. He is pure-hearted and the essence of truth. He is the same to all and beneficent to all.

—*Avadhuta Gita*, 8:4 (Ashokananda)

Verse 6   *Spanda shakti* is the perfect, pure "I"-consciousness. . . . In Shiva, She manifests in infinite shapes and appears as the innumerable and unique forms of the universe. . . . She vibrates eternally. . . . This vibrating Shakti is the Supreme Reality. Because it is the Supreme Reality, it has the freedom to perform any action. It gives birth to every visible object that exists in the world.

—MUKTANANDA, *Secret of the Siddhas*, p. 156

Kundalini is Shakti, supreme energy, whom the sages of India worship as the mother of the universe. . . . She is the active aspect of the formless, attributeless Absolute . . . [For devotees] she becomes the object of their love. Enlightened men of knowledge perceive Her in all forms and objects in the universe, and seeing everything as one in That, they merge in That. There is nothing higher, nothing greater, nothing more sublime and beautiful than Shakti. Dwelling within the center of the heart, She shines with all the colors of the morning sun, and when She is awakened within us, we can see Her there, blazing in all Her effulgence. . . . She is the supreme creative power of the Absolute Being. . . . She is Brahman in the form of sound, the sound vibration of the Absolute, which manifested as the universe. . . . She becomes the sun, the moon, the stars. . . . She becomes the breath, the vital force to keep all creatures alive. To quench our thirst, She becomes water. To satisfy our hunger, She becomes food. Whatever we see or don't see, whatever exists, right from the earth to the sky, is nothing but Chiti, nothing but Kundalini. It is that supreme energy which moves and animates all creatures, from the elephant to the tiniest ant. She enters each and every creature and thing that She creates, yet never loses Her identity or Her immaculate purity. . . . It is very difficult to know the supreme principle. Even though it does everything, it does not identify itself as the doer. . . . When the Self is limitless, unborn and eternal, how can it be known? Only through the medium of Shakti can we gain entry to the Self. Shakti is the pathway to God. Shakti is the face of Shiva. When we look at someone's face we know who he is; and in the same way, when we perceive the Shakti working within, we come to know God.

—MUKTANANDA, *Kundalini*, pp. 13–17

An alternate rendering:

Verse 8

> What is the best way to live? Be like water
> Water benefits all things
> it does not struggle up a hill
> but flows without resistance
>
> Where is the best place to live? Level ground
> What is the best personal trait? Serenity
> Who are the best friends? The kindhearted
> What is the right way to speak? With sincerity
> What makes a good leader? Good order
> What is proper work? Effectiveness
> What is good action? The right moment
>
> Above all, do not strive against others
> and no one will resist you
>
> —MITCH HOROWITZ
> *(from an unpublished manuscript)*

Te. The Chinese character *te* (pronounced "duh"), which is found in the title of the *Tao Te Ching*, has been variously translated as "virtue," "power," "character," "moral force," "truth," and "integrity." Each of these words reflects some aspect of Te, and the combination of them all suggests a fuller meaning of this mysterious principle. When the Absolute, formless principle of the universe (Tao) operates in one place, through one particular form, it becomes Te. All the virtues of the universe are manifest through this form or this action. The ancient

Verse 10

Taoist sage Han Fei Tzu writes, "Te is the perfection of personality." It is the fullest expression of life, which naturally reveals itself as moral excellence, generosity, kindness, unconditional love, selfless action, and spontaneity. Te is embodied in the Sage and his actions.

The Chinese pictograph for Te is comprised of three symbols. The first is a picture of "ten eyes and a curve" (*chih*). This character means "flawless," "perfect," "not curved in the least," or "without deviation." The explanation is that if ten eyes look at something and find no curve or fault, the observed thing must be perfect.

The second pictograph is that of the human heart (*hsin*). It translates as "heart" or "mind," and represents the higher human feelings. When *chih* and *hsin* are combined, the sense is "perfect-heartedness," "moral rectitude," or "one who does not deviate from the truth." To make the character Te complete, a pictograph of "the foot taking a step forward" (*ch'ih*) is added. This means "to go" or "to walk," and signifies action, movement, or expression. So, Te is not so much "perfect-heartedness" but its *expression* and the action that gives rise to it. Te literally reads "perfect-hearted action," "action which does not deviate from the heart," "the flawless expression of the heart," or "perfect action based on love."

Although Te is a Chinese character, the principle it symbolizes is universal. In one regard, Te is similar to the Indian concept of *dharma*, action in harmony with the natural laws of the universe; it shares some qualities with the Judaic ideal of *sedeq*, righteousness; and in regard to the Christian outlook of the world it can be seen as "grace," or the power that comes to one who follows the Will of God. Saint Augustine once said, "First love, then do what you will." This captures one aspect of Te: When there is love, one's actions reflect those of the universe itself—one's actions are virtuous, righteous, noble, perfect, and always in harmony with the Truth.

Te is also the inherent power which gives each thing its unique characteristic—it is that which makes a thing what it is and a person what he is. It can be seen as the manifestation of the universal power, inseparable from Tao. The Sanskrit scripture, the *Yoga Vasistha*, describes this same power:

It is by that power that the nature of every object in the universe is ordained. That power (*chit shakti*) is also known as *Mahasatta* (the great existence), *Mahachiti* (the great intelligence), *Mahashakti* (the great power), *Mahadrishti* (the great vision), *Mahakriya* (the great doer or doing), *Mahabhava* (the great becoming), and *Mahaspanda* (the great vibration). It is this power that endows everything with its characteristic quality. But this power is not different from, or independent of, the absolute Brahman (God).

—*Yoga Vasistha*, p. 73 (Venkatesananda)

This fictional account by the Taoist sage Chuang-tsu outlines a major difference **Verse 18** between the philosophies of Confucius and Lao-tzu: Confucius holds that virtues must be cultivated; Lao-tzu holds that virtues will naturally appear when a person gets in touch with his own perfect nature. In this account, Confucius visits Lao-tzu to ask him questions about rules and proper conduct. He receives this reply:

If when winnowing chaff, the dust blows in your eyes, how can you find true direction? If a swarm of mosquitoes is biting you in the night, how are you to get any sleep? So let me tell you, all this talk of "benevolence" and "goodness to one's neighbor" is nothing but an annoyance which confuses the mind and keeps people up at night. Just let the world hold to its own nature. Let the wind blow as it may. And you—just follow your own nature. Surely these virtues you talk about will come and establish themselves. Wherefore this self-defeating effort, as if searching for a runaway son while beating on a loud drum?

The swan is white without a daily bath; the crow is black without the need to color itself. Can we argue whether white is fitting for the swan or black the crow? Can fame or the learning of proper conduct add anything to the greatness that a man already possesses? When the water dries up, the fish are left on the ground with nothing but the spittle from their mouths to moisten each other—tell me, can this compare to leaving them in their own native rivers and lakes?

Alas then—be off! You are disturbing the nature of man with all your talk! —STAR, *The Inner Treasure*, p. 45

Verse 19   *Chüeh hsüeh (ch'i li min yu) wu yu*

abandon learning (+ discard + etiquette + the people + have) no sorrow

In ancient times, the last word of this phrase (*yu*) rhymed with the last line of verse 19 (*yü*), and for this reason some scholars have placed these four characters (*chüeh hsüeh wu yu*) at the end of verse 19. Yet, due to the similarity in structure with the first three lines of verse 19 (all beginning with *chüeh*, "abandon"), many scholars have placed this line at the beginning of verse 19. Due to the rhyme between *yu* (appear) and *yu* (sorrow) and other considerations—such as similar structure and meaning—we have placed these characters after the second line of verse 19. In order for it to make any sense, however, and to share the same structure with the two preceding lines, we have added four characters. Here is the logic we used in our addition and placement of these characters: The fourth characters in lines 1, 2, and 4 are *chi*, *yi*, and *li*. Hence, the fourth character of the rectified line (line 3) should (a) rhyme with the fourth character of the other lines, (b) be related to learnedness (and the ideas expressed in the previous lines), and (c) be related to "sorrow" among the people. The character *li* (etiquette, rites, ceremony) (38-084); *yi* (increase, gain) (48-04); *yi* (use, usefulness, purpose) (20-112); *li* (principle, order, the reasoning principle, reason) (found in Wang Pi's commentary but not in the Tao Te Ching text); *chih* (knowing, cunning, cleverness, sophistication); *chih* (correctness, uprightness, rules); and *chih* (will, willfulness) are possible choices for the missing character. To complete the rectification and preserve the structure, we added the characters *min* (the people) and *yu* (have).

Tao (thieves, highwaymen)—which is a different character than *tao* (Tao, path, highway)—appearing in line 4, is out of place both in terms of the line structure and the meaning of the character. The line would be made a better fit by using the character *min* (the people), which is found in the fifth position in the other lines. Also, *tao* (thieves) has the same meaning as the following character, *tsê*, which makes the use of *tao* in this context somewhat redundant. Thus, using the character *min*, line 4 would read: "Abandon cleverness, discard profit, and the people will not become thieves" or "Abandon cleverness, discard profit, and thieves will not appear among the people."

In this rectification, four characters were added and four characters were moved from verse 20 to the third line of verse 19.

chüeh	*chêng*	*ch'i*	*chih*	*min*	*li*	*pai*	*pei*
1. Abandon	holiness	discard	cleverness	the people	benefit	100	times
chüeh	*jên*	*ch'i*	*yi*	*min*	*fu*	*hsiao*	*t'zu*
2. Abandon	benevolence	discard	righteousness	the people	return	piety	love
chüeh	*hsüeh*	*ch'i*	*li*	*min*	*yu*	*wu*	*yu*
3. Abandon	learnedness	discard	etiquette	the people	have	no	sorrow
chüeh	*ch'iao*	*ch'i*	*li*	*tao (min)*	*tsê*	*wu*	*yu*
4. Abandon	cleverness	discard	profit	(thieves)	robbers	not	appear

The three images in this verse refer to our true nature, the place of return. The "State of the Infant" is that state of primal unity with all things, the state of pure awareness and pure potential; "No Limits" is the boundlessness of our true nature, that which contains all things; the "Uncarved Block" is the pristine quality of our true nature, pure and simple—yet unlimited in potential, as the simplest block, once carved, can become anything.

Verse 28

Chi'ang (force, "forceful means or actions") is contrary to Tao and brings about a premature end. Force, as it is used here, relates to using one's power in a way that is unnatural, that is contrary to natural law (Tao). Harming others, employing deceptive means to gain position, unnatural living, "trying too hard," "going against the flow," etc., are actions that require force, or an egocentric effort, since the universe is not supporting those actions. Action consistent with the laws of nature, and in harmony with Tao (also known as dharma), does not require force, as the universe lends its power to one who acts in harmony with its laws. Natural action brings fulfillment; forced action brings exhaustion.

Verse 30

Lines 64–75 can be translated as follows: "Force is followed by loss of strength. This is not the way of Tao. That which goes against the Tao comes to an early end." (Feng) / "That which uses force (to gain a place or in its development) will flourish for a while but grow old before its time. This goes against the natural way (Tao). Whatever goes against the natural way will come to an early end." (Ming) / "Live fast, die young—this is not the way." (Janwu) / "Things that use force to hasten their rise will, by that same means, hasten their demise." (Star)

Here are some additional translations:

"(For) things age after reaching their prime. That (violence) would be against the Tao. And he who is against the Tao perishes young." (Yutang) / "A thing in its prime soon becomes old; This is not Tao. Not being Tao, it is sure to die early." (Lin) / "When things are full grown, they age. This is called not following Tao. Not following Tao they perish early." (Chen) / "If you peak in strength, you then age; this, it is said, is unguided. The unguided soon come to an end." (Cleary) / "That things with age decline in strength, you may well say, suits not the Way; And not to suit the Way is early death." (Blakney)

"Things age after reaching their prime," "things with age decline in strength," and "a thing in its prime soon becomes old" are all conditions in harmony with Tao. Saying that these natural conditions of life "go against the Tao" does not make sense. The point here is that things that use "force" to gain an unnatural position or speed up development (both of which go against the natural order of things and require individual effort) bring about exhaustion, isolate a person from the support of the universe, and lead to growing old "before one's time." It weakens a person. It is not so much the use of force or one's strength that brings about an early end, but "wrong effort"—using one's force in an unnatural way, for personal gain, which goes against the flow of the universe. It is like using one's efforts to swim against the current: one may make progress for a while; but, in the end, he will fail.

Verse 31 The first three characters, *fu chia ping*, meaning "even an excellent warrior," "master of excellent arms," or "a truly fine warrior," is a very unusual word combination. This appellation resembles names given to Arjuna, warrior-hero of the Bhagavad Gita, who was often described by a three- or four-word combination, such as "Chief of Men," "Oppressor of the Foes," "Winner of Wealth," "Best of the Bharatas," "Mighty-Armed One," and "Wielder of the Bow." In addition, the whole content of this verse reflects sentiments and teachings found in the Gita. Specifically, a warrior is truly void of action; he does not rejoice in victory or mourn in defeat. He fights in accordance with his duty, seeing God as the performer of all action. In this regard, he is not the doer, he does not have attachment to action, he does not slay, nor is he slain—he is merely an instrument that acts in accordance with the Will of God.

Chi ta hsiang: "Apprehend the imitable conception" (Medhurst); "Hold fast to the idea of 'The Great'" (Mears); "Hold fast to the Great Idea, the Formless Form that is Tao" (Ould); "Hold fast to the great primal image"; "Embody your True Nature" (Ming)   **Verse 35**

By holding to the Great Form . . . (a) the Sage will "attract all things to him" (Wu); (b) "you roam where you will" (Blakney); "you can go anywhere" (Au-Young); (c) one "goes about his work in the empire" (Waley); one is not affected by the world, one is not harmed by the world, one is not caught up in its illusion.

Shi wei wei ming   **Verse 36**

   shi: This

  wei: is called

  wei: minute / tiny / small / trifling / insignificant / imperceptible / fading away / obscure due to smallness // secret / dark / hidden / mystery / subtle / conceal / obscure due to darkness / (profound) / (abstruse) // fade or dwindle away / reduce / waning // not / without

  ming: light / enlightenment / to enlighten / one who is enlightened / mystical vision / shine / luminous / illumined / brilliant // insight / discernment / awareness / understanding / wisdom // shine / shines forth / conspicuous

The various translations of *wei ming* reflect the interplay between darkness (hidden) and light (revealed). This is the same root as the Sanskrit word "guru" (*gu* = darkness, *ru* = light), which refers to the divine power of grace that dispels the darkness of ignorance with the light of truth.

"Making small one's enlightenment" / "hiding one's enlightenment" / "making the obscure quite obvious" / "the secret of illumination" / "hiding the light" (Legge) / "perception of the nature of things" (Feng) / "wonderfully minute and obscure, yet brilliant" (Cheng) / "subtle wisdom" (Wing) / "concealment and enlightenment" (Mears) / "revealing what has been concealed" (Ming)

Verse 39   Here is a fanciful account by Chuang-tsu (Chapter 6) that tells about Tao and the power it imparted to various Chinese gods and legendary rulers:

> Tao is both real and evident yet it has neither form nor action. Its power can be transmitted but it cannot be received on its own. It can be realized but not seen; it can be known but not heard. Without support, it has its source and its foundation in itself. Before heaven and earth, before time existed, Tao has stood, unchanged. It gave spirits their light and gods their power. It gave birth to heaven and to earth. Although it reaches beyond the highest point, it is not lofty. Although it penetrates to the lowest point, it is not low. It was here before all creation, yet it has not been here for long; it is more ancient than all of antiquity, yet it is not considered old.

> Emperor Hsi-wei got it and established order in the universe.
> Fu-hsi got it and the elements of creation revealed themselves.
> The Big Dipper got it and never once erred from its course.
> The Sun and Moon got it and have never ceased to revolve.
> K'an-p'i got it and established the K'un-lun mountains.
> P'ing-i got it and was able to flow in all directions like the great river.
> Chien Wu got it and lived forever on Mount T'ai.
> The Yellow Emperor got it and soared with the clouds of heaven.
> Chuan-hsu got it and dwells in the Dark Castle, knowing the mysteries
>   of all worlds.
> Yu-ch'iang got it and stands atop the North Pole.

The goddess Hsi Wang Mu got it and sits securely in the Western
regions—no one knows her beginning, no one knows her end.
P'eng-tsu got it and lived from the period of Emperor Shun to that of
the Five Lords.
Fu Yueh got it and as minister of Wu Tung came to rule the whole
empire. Then, after his death, he mounted upon a constellation
and, drawn by another, established himself among the stars of
heaven.

Ch'ing (purity) and *ching* (still, spotless) are the world's standard (*chêng*) because **Verse 45**
it is through purity of vision and a still mind that the true nature of the world
can be perceived. One could translate this passage as: "With silence and tranquility, make your vision perfect. With your vision perfect, you will see the whole
world as perfect." This relates to the opening line, which states, "great perfection
seems imperfect." Why? Because one's vision is imperfect. In sum, the world is as
you see it, according to your own vision and understanding.

> While your understanding is imperfect, *maya* (this world), *jiva* (the indi-
> vidual soul), and God seem different. When your understanding is
> perfect, you will see the world as a blissful drama of God.
>
> —MUKTANANDA, *Mukteshwari* II, v. 82

> Do not defile your heart by seeing the world that God created as
> impure. The Lord of the universe is in the form of the universe. That
> which you see as impure, is pure.
>
> —MUKTANANDA, *Mukteshwari* II, v. 89

The notion of a "side path," or things that deviate one from one's true course, is **Verse 53**
found in many spiritual traditions. This side path, or that which leads a seeker
astray, can refer to novelty ("Beware of novel affairs, for surely all innovation is
in error"—Muhammad), false prophets (as stated by St. Matthew), or even the
countless thoughts of one's own mind—which can lead one away from the true
vision of the Absolute.

Verse 62   Lines 28–33 can be translated as follows:
"Even if a man is bad, why would (Tao) reject him?" "If a man strays from the true path, it is no reason to cast him away." "If a person is bad, do not get rid of him." The notion here is to honor a person's perfection, even when his actions are contrary to that perfection. This truth is echoed in the words of Swami Muktananda, who said, "If a person is evil, do not get rid of that person, get rid of his evilness; if a person is unkind, do not get rid of that person, get rid of his unkindness."

Verse 69   The scene described here—the meeting of two opposing armies—is the context in which the teachings of the Bhagavad Gita are given. In the Gita, two opposing armies meet for battle. On one side (the side of dharma) is Lord Krishna and the five Pandava Princes (including the famed archer Arjuna); on the other side are the teachers and cousins of Arjuna. Before the battle begins, Krishna and Arjuna ride out between the two armies. Seeing his brothers on one side and his teachers and cousins on the other, Arjuna is taken over by despair and doubt and loses his willingness to fight. Krishna, seeing Arjuna's sorrowful state, proceeds to teach him the lessons of yoga, action, and dharma. "Dharma" is action consistent with the universal will; action free of doership or ego; action that is in harmony with natural law. It is Arjuna's dharma to fight for a righteous cause; it is the Will of God. In the end, Arjuna understands this; he rises for battle, surrenders all his actions to God, and says to Krishna: "I shall do thy bidding."

Verse 70   The wealth of a spiritual seeker is indeed a hidden wealth. Servants cannot know the entire extent of a treasure. They only know the external appearances. Real wealth has been hidden inside, while what appears is merely tinsel. . . . Spiritual experience is indeed like wealth deposited inside a lake which is filled with water. People only look at the water and are unable to get at the treasure.

—RAMDASA (17TH-CENTURY INDIAN SAINT), FROM
Mysticism in India, p. 410 (Ranade)

Verse 71   *Ping* (disease, sickness, suffering) commonly refers to physical illness, but it can also be a metaphor for the disease of worldly existence—which is the disease of wrong understanding, of seeing the world-illusion as being real. This faulty vision is described as a disease because it is something that needs to be "cured" so that the "patient" can recover from his false reality and see the world as it truly is. The Guru, or master, is often described as "the physician who cures the disease of worldly existence."

Although each element of nature can be likened to the Absolute, water has **Verse 78** always been the most endeared by the Taoist and the one closest to the nature of Tao. Water not only represents humility, gentleness, and a mind in perfect repose, but it is the element that gives birth to all life. Witness this brilliant passage on water from the *Kuan-tzu*—a Taoist work of the fourth century B.C.:

> Water is the blood of the Earth; it flows through its muscles and veins. Therefore it is said that water is something that is complete in itself. . . . It is accumulated in Heaven and Earth and stored up in the various things of the world. It comes forth in metal and stone and is concentrated in living creatures. Therefore it is said that water is something with a spirit. Being accumulated in plants and trees, their stems gain orderly progression, their flowers obtain proper number, and their fruits gain proper measure.
>
> Water gathers in jade, and the nine virtues appear. It congeals to form man . . . this is its most refined essence. . . . What is it then that has complete faculties? It is water. Nothing is produced without it. Only he who knows how to rely on its principles can act correctly. . . . Therefore when water is uncontaminated, men's hearts are upright. When water is pure, the people's hearts are at ease. . . . Hence the solution for the Sage who would transform the world lies in water. . . . He comes to rule the world, not by teaching men one by one, or house by house, but by taking water as his key.

This is a metaphor, which is often interpreted as if the Sage is owed but does **Verse 79** not demand from others. When a debtor returns the money, he gives but does not expect anything in return. So, the Sage gives as if paying off a debt—without any expectation of a return. However, the Sage gives out of love, and not out of obligation, so the analogy does not hold in this respect. This could also be interpreted as the Sage "attending to his duties" or "performing his part."

Shan jên. The character *shan*, which is variously translated as good, skillful, or virtuous, is closer in meaning to the Sanskrit word *dharma*. This passage can be interpreted as "Heaven is impartial but it is always with the man who follows dharma." Dharma is righteousness, it is the natural law of the universe—and it naturally arises as goodness, virtue, compassion, love, kindness, etc. All the virtues of Heaven are embodied in dharma. Anyone who follows dharma is *simpatico* with Heaven and therefore draws Heaven's power.

The favor of Heaven is impartial and, like the rays of the sun, it shines on everyone. Yet it only falls on those people who are open to receiving it—those who have aligned themselves with Heaven's law, those who follow dharma. Similarly, "God's grace" is offered to everyone in equal proportion (it is impartial); it always reveals itself in exact proportion to the openness of the one receiving it. In this way, it is always with those who are good, those who are open, those who follow the laws of nature.

COMMENTARY ON VERSE 1

Verse 1 is the seminal verse of the Tao Te Ching and can be considered the foundation of the entire text. It is comprised of four distinct, yet related, sections. In these notes, Section A deals with the transcendent nature of the Eternal Tao and the Eternal Name and puts forth the basic duality of "the Eternal Tao" and "the tao that can be named"; Section B explores being and non-being (or "the Named" and "the Nameless") and shows how they relate to the origin and "the Mother of all things"; Section C addresses the nature of the mind and how it relates to the true perception of the Essence (Reality) and the false perception of the manifestation (the world created by mind); and Section D puts forth the notion of unity and recasts all of these supposed distinctions as different aspects of one Absolute Reality.

<table>
<tr><td>**tao**</td><td>Tao / Way / Path / way / path / "That" / "The Absolute" / "Nature"</td></tr>
<tr><td>**k'o**</td><td>can / able to / can be / "becomes"</td></tr>
<tr><td>**tao**</td><td>Tao / path / way / walked / trodden // be told / talked about / spoken of</td></tr>
<tr><td>**fei**</td><td>not / cannot / surely not / opposes / "other than" / "not identical with" [the]</td></tr>
<tr><td>**ch'ang**</td><td>eternal / everlasting / constant / unchanging / always / fixed // the Absolute / the Eternal</td></tr>
<tr><td>**tao**</td><td>Tao / way / path</td></tr>
</table>

Section A1: Tao

The Nature of Tao. The most common interpretation of these opening lines is that anything the mind can conceive, anything that can be limited to a thought, word, or path, is something other than the Eternal Tao—which cannot be bound or limited in any way. The path that you can walk is not the Eternal Path. The truth that you can comprehend is not the Eternal Truth. Just as you cannot fit the ocean into a cup, you cannot fit the limitless universe into your mind.

A less common, and more abstract, approach to the opening line interprets it as an affirmation of unity: "Tao becomes Tao; it is not just an eternal Tao." This reflects the spiritual approach whereby everything in this universe is seen as Tao. Every path is the Eternal Path; every name is the Eternal Name; every thought is the Eternal Thought.

KEY WORDS

Tao (pronounced "dow") represents the Supreme Reality, particularly that aspect of the Absolute Reality which is formless in nature; which is humble and soft; which is fluid; which is returning and ever-becoming.

Tao is both a noun and a verb. It can represent the substance of the entire universe and the process by which the universe functions. Other words representing aspects of the Absolute Reality include "God"—which, unlike Tao, carries a personal quality. "Shiva"—the substance of all things, which comes into being through its power, Shakti. "The Absolute," "the Eternal," "the One"—all capturing universal aspects of the Supreme Reality. "Consciousness," "the Mind," and *Sat-Chit-Ananda* (Truth, Consciousness, and Bliss)—emphasizing the conscious and supremely intelligent nature of the Absolute. And "That"—a reference to the Supreme Reality without making any attempt to limit it to a particular name or aspect. There are thousands of other names, each referring to some sublime aspect of the Supreme Reality. "Tao" has its own unique meaning but is similar in its intent to the English equivalent "That" in that it makes no effort to capture any aspect of the attributeless Absolute—it simply refers to it.

Tao connotes the totality of everything; it operates in all places and at all times. It is distinctly impersonal. When Tao becomes personal, when it manifests through a human form, it is no longer Tao—it becomes Te. Hence, the Tao Te Ching is the Book (*ching*) of Tao—the Supreme Reality and Te, its pure manifestation, its power (to become), its virtue, its perfect expression.

Tao is a key word for the Absolute Reality but literally means "path," "way," or "road." It also means what a person does on a road, such as walk; or how a person conducts himself, such as "to lead" or "to guide." It can also mean "told," "said," or "spoken of." The character for Tao is comprised of a foot, meaning "to go," and a head, representing a person walking on a path.

K'o represents power, ability, ableness. It is variously translated as "able," "is able to," "can," "can be," "has the power to," and "permit." It can also indicate a potential: "what can be done," "what is possible." As a noun it means "a powerful animal," such as a bear. *K'o* comes from the combination of *k'ou* (mouth) and *ting* (cyclical character, adult), suggesting the ableness or capability of an adult.

Fei is an emphatic negative that means "not," "decidedly not," "opposing," "against," etc. It is a special primitive (root word), with two equal sides opposing each other. It represents the "abstract notion of opposition, contradiction, negation, wrong; no, not so."

Fei, as the negative in the first line of verse 1, emphasizes that there is a decided difference or distinction between "the tao that can be walked" and the "Eternal Tao."

The character *fei* is formed from the two wings of a bird that oppose each other. Although the two wings oppose each other, they are both needed in order for the bird to fly.

A common negative also used in the Tao Te Ching is *wu*, meaning "without, lacking, void of, free of." This is often used in combination with other characters to create special terms, such as *wu-ming* (without name), *wu-yü* (without mental activity), and *wu-wei* (without action). There is also *pu*, which is a simple negation, comparable to the English "un-" or "not." This is also used in combination, forming such terms as *pu-te* ("un-virtue") or *pu-shan* (not good).

Ch'ang means "constant," "unchanging," "enduring," "eternal," "lasting," "everlasting," "permanent," "fixed," etc. It can also mean "a rule or principle," both of which are enduring. One aspect of the Absolute Reality is its eternal existence. Hence, *ch'ang* can also represent the Absolute Reality, with such terms as "the Eternal," "the Unchanging," and "the Absolute."

Ch'ang is composed of the characters *shang* (roof, house) + *chin* (banner, flag, hanging cloth). *Shang* means "house" or "roof" but also connotes the peak of a roof, the highest part. Hence, it can mean "add to," "elevated," or "superior." *Chin* is a banner used to lead troops, a flag representing authority; it is also the cloth that once hung at both sides of an imperial dress, the part that is saved as a souvenir. The character can be associated with authority (such as a dynasty) which is long-lasting. A flag, which is constantly moving in the wind, can also be seen as representing the eternal movement of the universe or the eternal law that says that all things change.

TRANSLATION 1

a) *The Tao that can be told (/walked/perceived) is not the eternal (/unchanging) Tao.*

b) *A way that can be walked is not the eternal way.*

c) *The Tao that can be trodden is not the enduring and unchanging Tao. (Legge)*

d) *The Tao (that your mind) conceives of as Tao, is decidedly not the True Tao. (Ming)*

These interpretations emphasize the separation or difference between the transcendent and immanent reality, between the changing and permanent reality. This reflects the Vedantic dictum *neti neti* ("not this, not this")—whatever can be perceived by the senses, whatever can be comprehended, is "not this, not this"—not the Eternal Tao.

TRANSLATION 2

a) *The way that can be walked is not the way to the Eternal.*

b) *Paths can be walked but not the Eternal Path.*

c) *The Tao that can be expressed is not the Tao of the Absolute. (Wing)*

Here, *ch'ang* is taken to mean "the Eternal, the Supreme Reality." Tao, in this interpretation, is simply a term meaning road, way, or path, and not a special term for the Supreme Reality. The term *ch'ang* also appears in Section C and can mean "the Absolute" in that context as well.

Treating *ch'ang* as a special term for the Absolute, and *tao* as a regular term, translated as "way," "path," or "walk," solves a problem that has disturbed some interpreters. In the traditional interpretation ("The *Tao* that can be *trodden* is not the Eternal *Tao*"), the character *tao* appears three times, yet it is treated in the first and third instances as a special term for the Absolute, while in the second instance it is translated as a regular term meaning "path." Some interpreters have tried to resolve this issue by treating Tao similarly in all three instances. Results of such an approach are: "If Tao can be Taoed, it's not Tao" (Maurer); "TAO called Tao is not TAO" (Addis).

TRANSLATION 3

a) *Tao becomes Tao; it is not just an eternal Tao.* (**Ming**)

b) *Let the Tao become your Tao. It is not just an Eternal Tao.*

c) *Tao is ever-becoming Tao; there is no fixed Tao.*

These translations emphasize Tao as a process, as something "other than the permanent way." Tao is not something "fixed" or "unchanging" but the ever-becoming process of life. That is its nature. In verse 40, it is said that the "action of Tao is returning." Returning to what? To itself. *Tao k'o tao* is the process of ever-becoming, Tao returning to itself at every moment. *K'o*, which is usually translated as "can," "able," "power," or "has the power to become," is translated here as "becomes" or "ever-becoming." This interpretation of the opening line treats Tao as the most humble thing: as a "path"—something that stays below your feet—and not as some lofty goal to be reached at the end of a long journey.

SOME INTERPRETIVE AND IMPROBABLE TRANSLATIONS:

a) *Tao can, Tao cannot—this is always* [**the nature of**] *Tao*

b) *Tao becomes* [**itself**], *Tao opposes* (/ *appears "other than"*) [**itself**]—*this is the absolute* [**nature of**] *Tao.*

In (a), the first line is punctuated as three sets of two characters (*tao k'o—tao fei—ch'ang tao*) as opposed to the more common punctuation of two sets of three characters. This is an improbable translation that means: Tao (in its Absolute nature) can do everything; Tao (in its limited nature as a person) feels as though it connot do certain things; this limitation imposed on the unlimited Tao is the way Tao operates, it is the nature of Tao.

In (b) the same unlikely punctuation is used, and here the nature of Tao is seen as a pulsation, the eternal play of ever-becoming itself in the form of the universe, and ever separating itself, so that it can become itself once again. This reflects the Indian notion of the expansion and contraction of the universe known as *spanda*:

> The absolute oscillates between a "passion" to create, and dispassion from the created. This is the eternal pulsation—*Spanda*—of the absolute. Through it, the absolute transforms itself into all things and then returns back into emptiness of its undifferentiated nature. Both poles of this movement are real; both are equally absolute.
>
> —DYCZKOWSKI, p. 41

Section A2: The Name

ming	Name / names / the Name
k'o	can / can be / able / "becomes"
ming	named / name / given a name / spoken of / ~divided
fei	not / surely not / opposite to
ch'ang	eternal / everlasting / fixed / constant // the Absolute / the Eternal
ming	Name / names / the Name

The first and second lines of the Tao Te Ching are inescapably paired, given their proximity and similar structure—and so, therefore, are the terms *tao* and *ming* (name). Most commonly, *tao* and *ming* are established as supreme principles: the Eternal Tao and the Eternal Name. The Eternal Name, in this context, is the power of Tao that creates the world, the sound vibration by which the entire universe comes into being. Tao and ming are, in this context, inseparable—two aspects of the one Supreme Reality. ("The Name" is also mentioned in Section B, where Tao is the "Nameless" Reality, the origin of all things, while the Name (*ming*) is the Mother, the creator of all things.) The notion of the Name, or the Word, as the supreme power that creates the universe is found in other spiritual texts as well. We see this in the famous opening line of St. John: "In the beginning was the Word, and the Word was with God, and the Word was God." It is also found in the Greek word *logos*, which represents the Creative Power inextricably bound to its source; in Shakti, which creates the world out of its own being; and in God's Spirit.

An oddity of the Tao Te Ching is that the principle of the Eternal Name is established in verse 1—in the first two sections—but never mentioned again. *Ming*, as used throughout the Tao Te Ching, has an opposite connotation: Far from being a supreme principle, it is associated with words, and with limitations; it is something that breaks up the unity, something that opposes, and even disrupts, the true nature of Tao.

KEY WORD

Ming means "name," "to name," "one's name" (such as a title), and can also refer to what a name or word does: divide, separate, or make distinctions. According to the contemporary scholar Wing-Tsit Chan, "In the philosophy of Lao Tzu, names, whether in the sense of analytical concepts or in the sense of fame and titles, break up original unity and simplicity and give rise to intellectual cunning and social discrimination" (p. 157). In this sense, *ming* is interpreted as a product of the mind that artificially divides the essential unity.

TRANSLATION 1

> *(The way that can be walked is not the Eternal Way).*
> *The name that can be named is not the Eternal Name.*

Here, the transcendent and supreme nature of the Eternal Tao and the Eternal Name is established.

TRANSLATION 2

> a) *(Paths can be walked, but not the path to the Eternal)*
> *Names can be named, but not the name of the Eternal.*
>
> b) *The name that can be named is not the Eternal's name.*

wu Without / no / nothing / free of / void / empty // non-being / non-existence

ming name / is named / "manifests as" / the Name

t'ien Heaven

ti earth   }]>Alt: replace *t'ien ti* (Heaven and earth) with *wan wu* (all things)—MWT

Section B: The Origin and the Mother

chih	's / of / its
shih	origin / beginning / starting place // "maiden" (Pine) / "virgin" / ~that which gives birth
yu	with / having / possessing // being / existence
ming	name / names / the Name / the Word
wan	ten thousand / myriad / all
wu	things / creatures / beings
chih	's / its / of
mu	mother / the Mother

THE NATURE OF BEING AND NON-BEING / THE NAMED AND THE NAMELESS

This section tells of *wu ming* (without name / non-being's name) and *yu ming* (with name / being's name) and how these two aspects relate to *shih* (origin) and *mu* (mother). Non-being, or the Nameless (that which cannot be named or divided), is the beginning or original stuff of the universe. Being, or that which can be named and divided, is the mother that gives birth to the universe. This section, as we saw in Section A, puts forth two aspects of the Absolute: (a) *wu ming*, the Nameless, the undivided Supreme Reality, the origin of all things, and (b) *yu ming*, the Named, the creative power that gives birth to the universe, the mother of all things.

KEY WORDS

Wu ming ("without name") is a special term meaning "the Nameless," "the undifferentiated Absolute," "that which cannot be divided by names." It represents Tao in its unmanifested form, as the substratum of all things, existing before Heaven and earth; the unnameable or indivisible nature of Tao. *Wu-ming*, the Nameless, reaffirms the unity of Tao, that Supreme Reality that cannot be named or divided. It is that which cannot be limited by names, that which cannot be comprehended by the words or concepts of the mind (which result from words). It is That which is beyond name and form.

Yu ming ("with name") can be interpreted as a special term meaning "the Name." It is the power of the Absolute that creates this entire world. It also creates the words and thoughts in the mind which create our own experience of the world. Words have the power to superimpose a conceptual reality upon the one, undivided Reality—and this causes a person to think that all things are different and distinct. *Yu ming*, in this context, refers to all that can be named, all that can be limited and conceived by the mind.

T'ien ti (lit.: "Heaven and earth") refers to the universe, all creation, that which is above and below.

Wan wu (lit.: "the ten thousand things") refers to all things, the myriad things, the whole world of creatures. It refers to all life, but can also mean "the whole of creation."

TRANSLATION 1

> *Without name (the Nameless) is the origin of all things;*
> *With name (the Named) is the mother of all things.*

TRANSLATION 2

> *Non-being is the name of all things' origin.*
> *Being is the name of all things' mother.*

In Translation 2, *wu* and *yu* are treated as specialized terms meaning "being" and "non-being"—terms that carry a meaning similar to "Name" and "Nameless." The concept of "being" and "non-being" is also found in verse 40: "Heaven and earth and the ten thousand things are born out of being (*yu*). Being is born out of non-being (*wu*)." Both Translations 1 and 2 can come to mean the same thing, as both depict the two principal aspects of the One, Absolute Reality that are the origin and mother of all things.

An Islamic dictum states: "All creation is a sin." Sin, in this regard, is not a moral concept but is related to the Latin root *sin*, which means "without"; sin is anything that takes place without God. Hence all of creation, and all that we perceive of as the world, takes place only because the true nature of God is hidden by the concepts created in our minds. This is *yu ming*—that which covers the true nature of God and creates our limited experience of the world. With *wu ming*—without name, without the world divided by the concepts in our mind—

the nature of God can be perceived. In this state we see the true nature of God; we see the universe as the interplay of One, undivided Absolute. Even though we see a difference, the origin and the mother remain dual aspects of one reality.

<table>
<tr><td rowspan="11">Section C: The Nature of the Mind</td><td>ku</td><td>Therefore / thus / hence / for / indeed / now / (reason)</td></tr>
</table>

Section C: The Nature of the Mind

ku   Therefore / thus / hence / for / indeed / now / (reason)

ch'ang   always / ever / constant / permanent / unchanging // the Eternal / the Absolute // ~a permanent state / ~established in / ~identified with

wu   without / free of / not having / rid // non-being / non-existence

yü   deep-seated desire / mental patterns / desire / longing / attachment / thought-constructs / "paradigm"

yi   then / what follows / "so we may" / "in order to"

kuan   perceive / see / truly see / recognize / observe / witness / behold // display / reveal / manifest / make evident

ch'i   its / his / 's / ~Tao's / ~the world's / ~the mind's

miao   essence / mystery / subtlety / secret / true nature / wonderfulness / excellence / spirituality / marvels // the Essence / the nature of the Absolute // one's true nature

ch'ang   always / ever / constant / permanent / unchanging // the Eternal / the Absolute

yu   have / possess / ~identify with // being

yü   deep-seated desire / attachment / mental activity / thought-constructs / mental patterns

yi   then

kuan   perceive / see / truly see / recognize / witness // display / reveal / make evident

ch'i   its / his / 's / ~Tao's / ~the world's / ~the mind's

chiao   outer forms / manifestations / outcome / outer shell / end / limit / external / bounds / border / world appearance

PERCEPTION OF THE ESSENCE AND THE MANIFESTATION

This section explores the nature of the mind and how the condition of one's mind dictates the way one perceives the universe. A person whose mind is established within and free from the limited identifications created by thoughts (*wu yü*) realizes his own true nature and is able to see himself as God, as the Absolute, as the Eternal Witness of the unfolding universe. Such a person sees "the Essence," the world as it truly is (*miao*). He sees the whole universe as a play and creation of one Consciousness. A person whose mind is outwardly focused, who identifies with the objects he perceives, who is ego-dictated (*yu yü*)—what we consider our normal state of mind—sees the world as the world, as made up of many different objects. He misses the underlying unity and considers this world, comprised of different things, to be the true reality (*chiao*).

Describing this vision of unity in *A Book for the Mind*, Swami Muktananda writes:

> We perceive the world as world, only as long as our mind looks outward.
> When the mind turns within and dissolves into the Self,
> We see the world, not as the world,
> But as an expansion of God.

> Until the mind loses itself in the inner Self, you cannot attain anything.
> When the mind becomes free from thoughts, when the mind loses
>   itself in itself,
> You become the very form of God.

The same basic concepts appear in both Sections B and C. In Section B, *wu ming* (without name) = all things' **origin**, while *yu ming* (with name) = all things' **mother**. In Section C, *wu yü* (without thoughts) = perceive the **essence**, while *yu yü* (with thoughts) = perceive the **manifestation**.

KEY WORDS

Ch'ang means "always," "constant," "permanent," "unchanging." In one context, *ch'ang* modifies the terms *wu yü* and *yu yü* and becomes a part of a special term for (a) one who is completely identified with, or permanently established in, the thought-free, egoless state of awareness (*ch'ang wu yü*) or (b) someone established in the everyday, thought-filled state of awareness (*ch'ang yu yü*).

Wu means "without," "free of," "no," "none." In this passage, as well as in other passages of the Tao Te Ching (vv. 2, 40), *wu* can be interpreted as a specialized term meaning "non-being" or in combination with other characters to create specialized terms, such as *wu-ming* (Nameless) or *wu-wei* (non-action).

Yü, commonly translated as "desire" or "attachment," may also be understood as a strong and impelling kind of thought. Although *yü* encompasses desire, in this context it suggests a broader and less ephemeral meaning, such as thoughts, mental activity, limited thinking, limited awareness, one's paradigm, thought-constructs, modifications of the mind, *samskaras* (Sanskrit)—mental grooves created by repetitive thoughts.

A further examination of the character *yü* may be of use in understanding the two technical terms it comprises, *wu yü* (without thought-constructs) and *yu yü* (with thought-constructs).

Yü, most often translated as "desire," refers to a deep-seated desire, attachment, longing, mental pattern or tendency, limitations or modifications of the mind, a store of past impressions, or a repetitive history of thoughts, longing, or habit. Many commentators place emphasis on the character *yü*, and translate *wu yü* as "without desire." This is a correct but limited translation, as "desire" in this context means "desires and all other mental tendencies that limit a person's mind."

Yü is derived from (a) *ku*, a deep hollow, gorge, torrent, "the cutting of a deep ravine by the constant flow of water" and (b) *k'ien*, to owe, to breathe, to be exhausted. It is a deep-seated impression cut in the mind by a mental pattern or habit; a mental tendency, disposition, or concept; a *samskara*—a mental scar, "a latent, self-reproducing impression of past actions."

The mind, by nature, is ever-free; *yü* is a limited condition of the mind that is formed by attachment and that perpetuates additional attachments—the result being that the mind is pulled outward toward the senses and away from its inner nature. It is the mind stuck in a rut. In Chinese, the word *hsin* (heart / mind) does not distinguish between the heart and the mind; thus there is no distinction between deep impressions of the heart (emotional attachment) and habitual thought-constructs of the mind.

Yü can be seen as a deep-seated desire, but also as the result of desire or an attachment. Unlike regular desires, which can be satisfied with the object of desires, *yü* can be seen as the state of desiring, the feeling of lack wherein a person wants things (outside himself) in order to feel complete. This condition cannot be satisfied like a regular desire. *Yü* is a mental pattern that binds a person to forms and objects, that pulls a person away from his center, from his true nature, from the awareness of his true self, and binds him to the forms of this world. Desiring something implies that you do not have it; hence, *yü* relates to the false notion of one's self, the notion that one is limited, that one is an individual, that things exist in this world that are other than you. In sum, *yü* refers to any mental state that limits a person—and is based on a false notion of self. In regards to desire, Swami Chinmayananda writes:

> To realize and experience our all-fill Spiritual Nature, is to feel the full-ness of life. So long as this is not experienced one feels a sense of sad imperfection, and man's intellect suggests methods of regaining his sense of fullness, which are called desires. Each desire in the bosom of man is an attempt of his intellect to discover a fuller satisfaction in his own life.

The character *yü* (desire, lust, passion) shares the same root as *yü* but adds *hsin* (heart), thus implying a state that is more emotional, more fleeting, and more circumstantial than *yü*—and one that may be temporarily satisfied.

Wu yü can be interpreted in three ways: (a) as one term (*wu yü*) referring to a thought-free state of mind, (b) as non-being (*wu*) + desires (*yü*), or (c) as without (*wu*) + desires (*yü*).

If *wu yü* is interpreted as a single term, it refers to the thought-free state that is free of desires, where the mind merges back into the Self. *Wu yü* ("no mental activity") is similar in meaning and construction to the Zen term *wu-shin* ("no mind"). It can be compared to the yogic state of *unmana* (beyond the mind), *nir-vakalpa* (free of thought-constructs), or *samadhi* (pure or undivided awareness). This is the state beyond thought; it is the state of pure "I" awareness, the boundless state or unity that is free of ego and limitations. This is the mental state of an En-lightened Being, of one in perfect harmony with Tao. In this state, a person real-izes that he is perfect, that he is whole, that he is the Essence of everything.

> Still water becomes a mirror that gives back a clear reflection of the beard and eyebrows. Reposing at a perfect level, it becomes the stan-dard for a great carpenter. If water gains such clarity from stillness, how much more so one's own mind? The mind of the Sage, reposing in perfect stillness, becomes the mirror of the universe, and the eye that sees all creation.
> —CHUANG-TSU, Chapter 13

Interpreting *wu yü* as without (*wu*) desire (*yü*), it can be seen as a state com-pletely free of desire; a state of dispassion, beyond attachment and aversion. This is a state of perfect equanimity and contentment in which a person is completely fulfilled. Desires can only arise when the mind is divided; when it is outside itself. Desires arise when a person does not realize that he is everything, and therefore he desires things (outside himself) in order to feel complete. The state of *wu yü* (without desires) is one where a person feels complete, where he does not desire anything outside himself; the state of *yu yü* (having desires) is where one feels incomplete and seeks things in the world in order to feel complete.

Yu yü can also be interpreted in three ways: (a) as one term (*yu yü*) referring to our normal state of mind, filled with attachment and aversion, (b) as being (*yu*) + desires (*yü*), or (c) as with or having (*yu*) + desires (*yü*).

Interpreted as a single term, *yu yü* refers to the outwardly focused mind, limited by attachment and aversion, bound by ego and thought-constructs—a mind whereby a person sees himself as a limited individual. This is our normal state of mind, filled with thoughts and desires, having its "ups" and "downs," and swayed by attachment and aversion. In this state, a person sees the world as an interplay of many different objects (*chiao*)—some good and some bad—and not as the manifestation of one Supreme Reality; he is convinced that this false view is the true reality—and he does everything to perpetuate this false view. Herein lies all his pain.

Miao When a person's mind is completely still, he can see his own nature and the nature of the Absolute. In this thought-free state, a person is able to perceive the true nature of the universe, the essence, *miao*. *Miao* variously translates as "the essence," "mysterious," "subtle," "secret," "spiritual," "wonderful," "marvelous," "excellent," "difficult to fathom," and "beautiful." As used in the Tao Te Ching (vv. 1:32, 1:57, 15:08, 27:91), it can be seen as the Essence of all things, the one reality that makes up all things, the pure "I-am" awareness. *Miao* is the true nature of Tao, the Self, That, the Supreme Reality, the Unchanging, Consciousness, God. It is the underlying Truth of all existence, the unifying principle, the oneness, the substratum upon which this whole universe is based. It is the world as it truly is. This one principle manifests as the entire universe. There is nothing other than this.

The true nature of the Absolute is consciousness, truth, freedom, and love. Yet, to become the world, the Absolute assumes countless other natures; it takes on a new nature for each form it assumes. In water, its nature becomes cool and flowing; in fire, its nature becomes hot; in a tree, its nature becomes tall and upright. The Absolute superimposes a particular nature over itself. Though it assumes every nature, its own perfect nature does not change; its own immaculate purity is never lost.

Chiao is the world's appearance, the manifestation of the One Reality, without the perception of the underlying unity. It is the multifarious world, the world that seems to be made up of many different objects and forms; it is the world as it appears to be. But this is a limited and false view of reality.

Chiao, which appears only once in the Tao Te Ching (v. 1:39), can mean "the outer," "outer forms," "forms of this world," "manifestation"; "outcome," "outer shell," "end," "limit," "external," "world appearance"; "that which is outside—or apart from—one's true nature"; "the particular or superimposed nature of a thing," "that which is superimposed upon the Absolute"; "that which limits"; and "the ego." It can also mean "the 'outer shell' or 'cage' of one's own thoughts"; "the limits imposed on one's true nature by thoughts and concepts."

Suppose everything in the world—every shape and form—was made out of gold. There might be an ugly face that you avoid, and there might be a pretty face that you like. As you interact with this world of gold, as your mind begins to form concepts and paradigms about this world of gold, as you become attached to particular forms of gold, you begin to lose the awareness that everything is made out of gold. You create a whole new reality in your mind. The gold is the essence—the one, underlying reality (*miao*); the forms and shapes we get involved with—forgetting that they are made of gold—is the manifestation (*chiao*). In the same way, everything in this world is made out of one Supreme Consciousness but through our continual involvement with, and attachment to, the forms created by that Consciousness (which include our thoughts, feelings, body, etc.), we lose sight of the underlying essence; we cannot see that everything is the interplay of one Consciousness.

The essence (*miao*) can be seen as one's pure awareness, as the perfect "I-am" consciousness; while the outer manifestation can be seen as everything added to the awareness, everything that pure awareness is aware of (*chiao*).

The awareness of being, the "I-am" consciousness, is the same in everyone; it is the same awareness that is with you from the moment you are born until the moment you die. It is the same awareness by which God perceives the universe and hears your prayers. As the medieval Christian mystic Meister Eckehart said: "The eye (awareness) by which you perceive God is the same eye (awareness) by which God sees you." There is only one eye in this universe; there is only one Consciousness, only one awareness. That awareness is in you and in everyone else; it is the Essence of the Universe, and it never changes.

Ch'i ("its," "his," "one's") is used to modify both *miao* and *chiao*. "Its manifestation" (*ch'i chiao*) can refer to (a) Tao's manifestation, which is the world, (b) a person's manifestation, which is one's individual form (body, personality, etc.) or one's ego, or (c) the mind's manifestation, which is "the world created by thoughts and words," the boundaries or limits of the mind, the cage of one's own thoughts.

Kuan translates as "perceive," "examine," "look at carefully," "observe," "behold" and also "display," "reveal," "manifest," "make evident," "prove." *Kuan* implies a perception, a lasting view, as opposed to a glimpse or merely to see something. It comes from the combination of "bird" and "to see" and literally means "to see the world as does a bird." It implies a true vision, to truly see, to see from an objective or divine perspective.

Ku ("thus, therefore, hence"), which appears at the beginning of this section, is often placed within the text of the Tao Te Ching as a device to link unrelated passages. Adding *ku* between unrelated sections can serve to make the verse more cohesive and suggest some link between sections.

TRANSLATION 1

> *Ever without desires (/attachment) then perceive its essence (/your true nature)*
> *Ever with desires (/attachment) then perceive its manifestation (/your individual form)*

TRANSLATION 2

> *Identifying with* [the mind's] *pure awareness reveals its true nature*
> *Identifying with* [the mind's] *limited awareness reveals the world of thoughts*

> *The state of wu yü reveals, "I am the Essence"*
> *The state of yu yü reveals, "I am the body"*

In the context of Translation 1, *miao* is the Essence of the Universe, which is the one underlying principle of all things and/or one's own essence, one's own true nature. In Translation 2, *miao* is the mind's essence, it is the place of the Self where all thoughts arise. In Translation 3, *miao* is the identification with one's unlimited Self; it is the awareness of one's own essence being the Essence of the Universe; it is the realization that "I am That," "I am the Supreme Reality."

Chiao translates as "the body" but can also refer to the false identification that limits a person—mind, personality, individuality, ego, doership, etc.

TRANSLATION 4

a) *The Eternal, [seen] through one's pure awareness, reveals its essence*
   The Eternal, [seen] through one's ego-concepts, reveals its outer forms

b) *The Eternal appears in its true wonder to one whose mind is*
      perfectly still
   The Eternal appears ordinary, as the apparent forms of this world,
      to one whose mind is dictated by its thoughts

Here, *ch'ang* is interpreted as a term for the Eternal, Unchanging Reality—the Absolute.

TRANSLATION 5

a) *By constant Non-being, we desire to perceive its essence*
   By constant Being, we desire to perceive its manifestation

b) *Therefore let there always be non-being, so we may see their*
      subtlety, and let there always be being, so we may see their
      outcomes. (**Chan**)

c) *In eternal non-existence, therefore, man seeks to pierce the*
      primordial mystery; and, in eternal existence, to behold the
      issues of the Universe. (**Chalmers**)

This interpretation is problematic for two reasons: First, translating one term (*wu* and *yu*) with another (non-being and being) does not bring additional clarity to our understanding; and we are never clear what "non-being" or "being" really means. ("Non-being" may refer to non-individual existence or non-attachment to a limited form. "Being" may refer to individual existence, attachment to limited existence, separateness, or a state dictated by ego.) Second, this interpretation suggests that a person in the state of *wu* (non-being) *desires* to perceive the unifying principle of the world (the essence); and a person in the state of *yu* (being) *desires* to perceive the things of this world (the manifestation). A person in the state of non-being does not *desire* to perceive the essence—he just perceives it; similarly, a person in the state of being does not desire to see the world's appearance—he just sees it.

TRANSLATION 6

> a) *By constant identification with the pure "I-am" consciousness,*
> > *a person attains the boundless, egoless state. He realizes,*
> > *"I am That; my essential nature is the Supreme Reality."*
>
> > *By the constant identification with what is added*
> > *to the pure "I-am" consciousness,*
> > *a person remains in the state of ego.*
> > *He thinks, "I am separate, I am limited, I am this body."*
>
> b) *The thought-free awareness, brought about by the mind turned within,*
> > *lets a person behold his true nature—*
> > *eternal, wondrous, the manifestation of one reality.*
>
> > *The awareness that results from the mind turned outward*
> > *lets a person see his life in this world—*
> > *passing, ordinary, filled with differences.*
>
> c) *A mind that is perfectly still and turned inward*
> > *reflects the pure awareness of its boundless nature;*
>
> > *A mind that is restless and turned outward*
> > *lives in the cage of its own thoughts.*

d) *When a person is established in his own nature,*

When his mind merges into itself,

When it no longer identifies with its own thoughts,

When it becomes aware of its own awareness,

Then he sees the one, unchanging Reality
that has become everything in this world.

He sees the world as it truly is—as the perfect expression of Tao,
as the supreme play of one Consciousness.

When a person identifies with what he perceives
and not with the one who perceives,

When his mind is focused outwardly and assumes limitations,

When he remains in the state of separateness and limitation,

Then he sees the varied forms of this world,

He sees the world as the world, as an interplay of objects,

He misses the underlying unity and perfection.

t'zu	These / this	**Section D1: The Unity of Duality**
liang	two / both / pair / pairs / dual / duality / sameness	
chê	those / (they are) / >makes the preceding character or clause into a noun	
t'ung	alike / the same / one / together / unified / unity / merged / "issue from the same" // the One	
ch'u	origin / source / birth // manifest / issue forth / arise / emerge	
erh	but / yet / though	
yi	differ / different / diverge [in]	
ming	name / what they are called / ~how they are / ~how they are called forth / ~how they manifest	

t'ung	unity / oneness / likeness / sameness / together / both / "being the same" / "commonality" // the One / ~the Absolute	**Section D2: The Essential Unity**
wei	call / they are called / called forth / "appear as"	
chih	its / (the) / (____)	
hsüan	mystery / secret / profound / hidden / dark / deep / obscure / mysterious / abyss // incomprehensible >Alt: *yüan* (origin, first cause, original or primal principle)	
hsüan	mystery / secret / profound / hidden / dark / deep / obscure >Alt: *yüan* (origin, first cause, primal)	

chih	it is // (passes) / (becomes)
yu	again / also / ~to a higher degree / ~more
hsüan	mystery / mysterious / profound / secret / obscure / dark / deep
	>Alt: *yüan* (origin, primal)
chung	all / everything / "manifold"
miao	essence / mystery / subtlety / wonder / excellence // ~one's true nature
chih	's / of / its
mên	gate / gateway / door / opening / entrance // house / abode

The Nature of Unity

The universe and I came into being together; and I, and everything therein, are one. —*Chuang tzu*, Giles, p. 41

Infinite consciousness alone appears as one thing in one place and another in another place. There is no division between that consciousness and its power, as there is no division between a wave and water, limbs and body. —*Yoga Vasistha*, Venkatesananda, p. 74

The man of humanity regards Heaven and Earth and all things as one body. To him there is nothing that is not himself. —*Reflection on Things at Hand*, Chan, p. 19

This section espouses the principle of Unity and asserts that there is no difference between the Supreme Reality and the universe it creates—it is just that we call them by different names. This is the fundamental truth that, although there are different aspects and forms in this universe they are all made of the same substance, they all operate according to one underlying principle—which has the nature of Being or Consciousness. There is only one substance, one Consciousness, which forms this entire universe.

In the first three sections of verse 1, fundamental dualities are established. These make distinctions between the real and the unreal, the permanent and the changing, the immanent and the transcendent. In this section, however, all these distinctions are refuted and the notion of unity is established. Here Tao is both the immanent and the transcendent, both the changing and the permanent reality. This affirmation of Unity is also found in the Indian philosophy of Kashmir Shaivism, which states, "Nothing exists that is not Shiva." Chuang-tsu also describes this all-inclusiveness of the Tao in the following story:

> Tung Kuo-tsu asked Chuang-tsu, "This thing you call 'Tao'—where is it?"
>> "It is in the near and the far, the high and the low," replied Chuang-tsu.
> "The high we know about, but is Tao also in the low?" asked Tung Kuo-tsu.
>> "It is in an ant."
> "Only that low?"
>> "It is in a blade of grass."
> "Only that low?"
>> "It is in broken tiles that you walk on."
> "Only that low?"
>> "It is in the stuff that comes out when you squat after eating."
> And Tung Kuo-tsu asked no more—that was low enough for him.
>
> —CHUANG-TSU, Chapter 22

KEY CONCEPTS

Tz'u liang ("these two," "this pair")

For centuries, scholars have held different positions on what "these two" refers to. It could refer to the two central terms in the previous section, *miao* and *chiao*—the essence and its manifestation; the Absolute and the universe it creates; one's true nature and one's ego. Or it could refer to (a) the *tao* that can be walked and the Eternal Tao, (b) the Nameless and the Named, (c) non-being (non-existence) and being (existence), (d) the origin and the Mother—this is Wang Pi's interpretation, or (e) *wu yü* (the thought-free state; the awareness of unity) and *yu yü* (one's normal state of mind; the awareness of the world).

Tz'u liang can also mean "this pair," "these pairs," or "this duality." So instead of referring to two specific characters that appear in the preceding lines, *tz'u liang* could refer to a general principle, a quality or an aspect that is found in *all* the previous character pairings. These pairings (listed below) all relate to the fundamental duality of the Immanent and the Transcendent, the Absolute and the universe it creates, Tao and the world.

The following pairs appear, or are suggested, in the first three sections of verse 1:

Transcendent	Immanent
The Eternal Tao/way	The tao/way that can be walked
The Eternal Name	The name that can be named
The Nameless (*wu ming*)	The Named (*yu ming*)
The origin (*shih*)	The mother (*mu*)
Thought-free state (*wu yü*)	Normal state of awareness (*yu yü*)
The pure awareness	That which is perceived
Non-being (*wu*)	Being (*yu*)
The Essence, inner (*chiao*)	The world manifestation, outer (*miao*)

TRANSLATION 1

t'zu liang chê t'ung ch'u erh yi ming

a) These two are alike in origin but differ in name.

b) These two are the same but we think of them in different ways.

c) These pairs of opposites form a unity though we think of them as being different.

The *Yoga Vasistha*, an Indian scripture, describes this fundamental unity as follows:

> Know that the universe has arisen from Brahman [Absolute Reality] and it is Brahman alone. In the scriptures words have been used in order to facilitate the imparting of instruction. Cause and effect, the self and the Lord, difference and non-difference, knowledge and ignorance, pain and pleasure—all these pairs have been invented for the instruction of the ignorant. They are not real in themselves. As long as words are used to denote a truth, duality is inevitable; however, such duality is not the truth. All divisions are illusory. —*Yoga Vasistha*, p. 87

Key Words

Hsüan refers to the darkness of deep water or the unfathomable heavens. It is a term for "the mysterious," "impenetrable," "ineffable," and "indescribable." In many texts, *yüan* (origin, primal principle) is used instead of *hsüan*.

Mên (gate) refers to a door, a gate, or that into which a door leads. Symbolically it can mean "an opening into a higher reality or state of consciousness."

The Arabic term *fut āh* (opening), as used by Ibn al Arabi in the title of his magnum opus, *Meccan Revelations*, refers to an opening into, or revelation of divine realities, and is similar in meaning to *mên* (gate). It can also mean "unveiling," "tasting," "witnessing," "divine effusion," "divine self-disclosure," and "insight," all of which designate a mode of gaining direct access to God and the unseen worlds. The Persian word *raunagh* (splendor) signifies the opening of the path of Truth. The Sanskrit term *unmesha* (unfolding) refers to the unfolding of divine vision.

Translation 2

a) *Unity is its (the world's) primal origin (first beginning).*
   It is the origin of the origin,
   The opening that leads to (/reveals) the true nature of the Absolute.

b) *That which we call "the One" is hidden.*
   It is hidden within the hidden yet it is the Essence which reveals
      everything (/yet it is the One, Underlying Principle that
      becomes everything).

c) *Oneness (t'ung) is the principle that underlies (yüan) all things.*
   It is the origin of the origin, the root of the root, the cause of all causes,
   It is that which reveals the essence of everything.

Line-per-Line Translations

t'ung wei chih hsüan (yüan)

> Unity, by what we call it, cannot be known (*hsüen*)
> This unity can be spoken of, but remains a mystery
> This unity is incomprehensible, beyond the reaches of the mind

T'*ung wei* (the One and what it calls into being) is a mystery
The One, Absolute (*t'ung*) is its (the world's) origin
There is only one Original Substance (*yüan*)
Oneness is the nature of its origin

hsüan (yüan) chih yu hsüan (yüan)

Mystery is again a mystery
There is a secret within this secret
It is the origin of the origin

This unity is hidden.
It is the hidden within itself, it is . . .

chung miao chih mên

"the gate to the essence of everything"
"the door to all spirituality"
"the opening to the essence of existence"
"the gate to the true nature of everything"
"the opening into all things divine"
"the insight that leads to wonder"

"the door of all subtleties!" (Chan)
"the gateway to all indescribable marvels" (Cheng)
"the gateway of the manifold secrets" (Lau)
"the Gate to the Secret of All Life" (Yutang)
"the door to inwardness" (Maurer)
"the gateway through which all miracles emerge" (Wilhelm)
"the portal leading to the realization of Cosmic Divinity"
    (Au-Young)
"the door to all beginnings" (Pine)

TAO TE CHING: DEFINITIONS, CONCORDANCE, AND WADE-PINYIN CONVERSION

Each selection contains five parts:

a) Wade-Giles spelling (as found in the verbatim text)

b) Character's radical

c) Pinyin spelling (which appears in the first selection of each new English spelling group)

d) Short definition of the Chinese character

e) Concordance, with the verse and line number

A (170), *a*—Yeah, "alright," hesitant reply, exclamation, alas!
20-04

AI (30), *ai*—Lament, grieve, grief, sorrow, distress.
31-107   69-51
AI (61)—Care for, love, cherish, adore, the exhibition of humanity in one's actions.
10-26   13-71   27-81   44-19   72-37

AN (40), *an*—Still, quiet, content, peaceful, tranquil, calm, at ease.
15-74   35-11   64-02   79-08   80-52

AO (37), *ao*—Storehouse, "hidden reservoir," source, refuge // southwest corner of the hall where the wares used to be placed and where one can be quiet // deep, mysterious, obscure.
62-06

CH'A (40), *cha*—Sharp, clear-sighted, discern, examine, scrutinize, survey.
20-93   20-94   58-11   58-12

CHAI (149), *zhai*—Error, attack, blame, scold, find fault.
27-10

CH'AI (142), *chai*—Tail, sting.
55-10

CHAN (62), *zhan*—War, battle, to fight // fear, tremble, alarmed, terrified.
31-111   67-85   68-08
CHAN (85)—Deep, dark, abyss, clear // tranquil as water, calm, serene.
04-28

CH'AN (120), *chan*—Slow, patient, calm.
73-52

CHANG (1), *zhang*—Large, a term of respect, revere // an elder, a senior.

38-109

CHANG (57)—Expand, stretch, open, extend, draw a bow // display, proclaim, to grant.

36-07   77-06

CHANG (59)—Distinguished, prominent, outstanding, well-known, beautiful, elegant // exhibit, show.

22-38   24-18   57-52

CH'ANG (50), *chang*—Eternal, everlasting, long-lasting, constant, always, ever, frequent.

01-05	01-11	01-26	01-33	03-46
16-35	16-37	16-42	16-47	27-39
27-47	28-15	28-38	28-61	32-02
34-31	37-02	46-37	48-27	49-04
51-35	52-72	55-56	55-58	61-15
64-78	65-46	74-14	74-29	79-37

CH'ANG (168)—Long time, increase.

02-31	07-02	07-10	07-21	09-15
10-62	22-49	24-28	28-81	44-38
51-45	51-65	54-41	59-51	59-59
67-66				

CHAO (10), *zhao*—A sign, omen // manifest.

20-49   64-07

CHAO (30)—Call, summon, ask, invitation.

73-48

CHAO (72)—Bright, brilliant, luminous, splendid // display, manifest, show forth.

20-85   20-86

CHAO (74)—Morning, dawn // palace, seat of government, royal court.

23-10   53-23

CHAO (87)—Claw of an animal, talons of a bird // to scratch, hold in the claws.

50-66

CH'AO (156), *chao*—Indifferent, undisturbed, aloof, unattached, avoid, to step over.

26-26

CHÊ (125), *zhe*—It, that, this // "the one" / >a final particle that makes a noun of the preceding character or clause; it is often left untranslated.

01-42	03-56	07-13	13-46	13-66
13-77	14-24	15-06	15-84	19-31
22-69	23-19	23-38	23-40	23-45
23-50	23-57	23-66	23-75	24-02
24-06	24-11	24-16	24-21	24-26
24-45	27-62	29-24	29-28	30-06
30-34	31-04	31-16	31-31	31-58
31-67	33-03	33-07	33-11	33-16
33-20	33-24	33-31	33-37	38-87
38-98	39-05	40-02	40-07	41-34
42-63	49-13	49-19	49-27	49-33
50-42	54-03	54-08	56-02	56-06
61-03	61-72	61-79	62-02	62-64
64-53	64-57	65-06	65-42	66-10
68-04	68-09	68-15	68-21	69-52
70-34	70-38	73-14	74-20	74-33
74-39	74-52	75-48	76-29	76-35
77-10	77-14	77-19	77-24	77-60
78-12	81-10	81-14	81-18	81-22

CH'Ê (60), *che*—Claim, payment.

79-32

CH'Ê (159a)—Carriage, cart, wheel.

11-11

CH'Ê (159b)—Track, rut, wheel ruts // precedent, example, follow a precedent.

27-04

CHÊN (109), *zhen*—Real, genuine, true, essence, purity, virtue, worth.

21-44   41-66   54-25

CHÊN (154)—Pure, virtuous, chaste, undefiled // moral, of high principle.

39-40

CHÊN (157)—Restrain, suppress, press it down, protect, keep // guard, keep in order, protect, oversee.

37-26

CH'ÊN (32), *chen*—Dust, dust of the world, lowly.

04-27   56-26

CH'ÊN (131)—Rule over, subject, minister, master // employ, use, subjugate.

18-26   32-12

CH'ÊN (170)—Wear, don, display, exhibit.

80-36

CHÊNG (66), *zheng*—Government, administration, governing, politics, rule // laws, regulations.

58-02   58-10

CHÊNG (77)—Standard, in order, correct, proper, rectitude, norm // ruler, guide.

08-35   45-40   57-02   57-74   58-35
58-36   78-61

CHÊNG (87)—Contend, compete, quarrel, wrangle, contest.

03-07   08-12   08-47   22-53   22-61
66-68   66-76   68-28   73-38   81-57

CH'ÊNG (4), *cheng*—Chariots // to ride, ascend a chariot, mount // take advantage of, seize the right moment.

26-31   80-28

CH'ÊNG (62)—Complete, finish, perfect, accomplish, succeed, fulfill one's part // entire, whole, filled.

02-30   02-77   07-47   15-97   17-35
25-04   34-19   34-59   41-76   41-95
45-02   47-36   51-11   63-54   64-81
67-64   77-70

CH'ÊNG (115)—Titles, refer, call, designate, talk about, a name.

42-40

CH'ÊNG (149)—True, real, sincere, honest.

22-74

CH'ÊNG (187)—Too much, excess, override, gallop.

12-20   43-07

CHI (9), *ji*—Artful, skill, talent, crafty, clever.

57-43

CHI (29)—To reach, effect, till //>past tense.

13-51   21-51   43-38   48-32

CHI (30)—Fortunate, lucky, happy, auspicious, prosperous, joyful.

31-78

CHI (32)—Foundation, base, a beginning, starting point // property, land.

39-99

CHI (40a)—Tranquil, silent, vast, calm, still.

25-09

CHI (40b)—Be trusted with, confide, deliver // stay, remain, to lodge.

13-68

CHI (49)—Himself, oneself, it, he, I, myself.

81-33   81-40

CHI (52)—Comes close, near, nearly, about, approximate // subtle, hidden, few.

08-20   20-07   64-80   69-42

CHI (61)—Restrictions, fear, shun, avoid, cautious.

57-27

CHI (71)—End, finish, exhaust // since, already, when.

32-46   35-43   52-10   52-18   81-29
81-36

CHI (75a)—Thorns, brambles, thorny bushes, thickets // troublesome, like thorns.

30-22

CHI (75b)—Highest, utmost, ultimate, climax, apex // very, extremely, the end.

16-03   28-46   58-32   59-36   59-40
68-43

CHI (85)—Meddle, be busy, engage // aid, relieve, succor.

52-43

CHI (113)—Sacrifice, an offering.

54-14

CHI (115a)—Soil, grain, millet, earth, land.

78-50

CHI (115b)—Standard, model, pattern, rule, norm, agree with // examine, scrutinize.

65-44   65-48

CHI (115c)—Accumulate, store up, gather, hoard, add, increase.

59-20   59-23   81-28

CHI (120)—Order, system, thread, unbroken strand // a history, annals, chronicle.

14-94

CHI (162)—Trace, footprints, hoofprints // vestiges, results.

27-05

CHI (172)—Rooster, bird.

80-62

CHI (184)—Starve, dearth, scarcity, famine, hunger.

75-03   75-13

CH'I (9), qi—On tiptoes, stand erect.

24-01

CH'I (12)—It, he, she // his, they // that, the one.

01-31   01-38   03-35   03-38   03-41
03-44   04-17   04-20   04-23   04-26
05-25   07-15   07-28   07-34   07-41
07-48   09-07   09-31   11-08   11-20
11-33   14-34   14-38   14-70   14-76
15-39   15-51   15-56   15-61   16-22

17-07   17-13   17-17   17-31   20-27
20-47   20-101   21-21   21-29   21-37
21-41   21-45   21-53   24-29   25-31
25-70   27-78   27-82   28-02   28-05
28-25   28-28   28-48   28-51   29-11
30-13   33-29   34-05   34-51   34-60
35-26   38-112   38-116   38-119   38-123
39-41   42-66   45-05   45-13   47-13
47-17   49-51   50-32   50-59   50-65
50-71   50-77   52-12   52-16   52-20
52-24   52-31   52-34   52-41   52-44
52-59   52-63   54-22   54-30   54-38
54-46   54-55   56-10   56-13   56-16
56-19   56-22   56-25   57-19   58-01
58-05   58-09   58-13   58-31   58-33
58-47   59-35   59-39   60-13   60-18
60-22   60-28   61-75   63-21   63-26
63-55   64-01   64-05   64-10   64-14
65-20   66-12   66-66   67-22   71-22
72-11   72-16   73-25   74-57   75-05
75-19   75-33   76-07   76-21   77-04
77-74   78-17   80-47   80-50   80-53
80-56

CH'I (30)—Vessel, tool, instrument, utensil // useful.

11-18   11-23   28-73   29-18   31-08
31-35   31-40   36-51   41-74   57-36
67-65   80-10

CH'I (37a)—Abnormal, unnatural, strange, new, surprise, unexpected, extraordinary // deceit, trickery, stratagem.

57-06   57-45   58-39   74-19

CH'I (37b)—Contract, agreement, covenant // deed, tally.

79-19   79-28

CH'I (75)—Reject, discard, relinquish, abandon, push aside, break, throw off, forget.

19-03   19-11   (19-18a)   19-23   27-45
27-53   62-33

CH'I (84)—*Ch'i*, breath, vital force, power, spirit.
10-11   42-22   55-67

CH'I (85)—Weep, cry, lament.
31-109

CH'I (150)—Valley, ravine, canyon.
28-10   28-14

CH'I (151)—How? why? what?; how can it be?
22-70

CH'I (156)—Arise, occur, begin, appear, produce, originate, raise up.
57-48   64-40

CHIA (9), *jia*—Excellent, fine, elegant, beautiful, superior.
31-02

CHIA (19)—Add, accomplish, confer upon // meet.
62-26   69-50

CHIA (40)—Families, household, clans, home.
18-21   54-29   54-65   54-67   57-38

CHIA (102)—Arms, weapons // soldier, military.
50-53   80-32

CHIANG (22), *jiang*—Artisan, workman.
74-45   74-50

CHIANG (41)—If, about to, then, will // take in hand, receive, follow, approach.

15-47	29-01	31-87	31-92	32-22
32-50	36-01	36-09	36-17	36-25
37-17	37-25	37-39	37-48	39-48
39-55	39-62	39-69	39-77	39-86
42-69	65-11	67-93		

CHIANG (85)—Great rivers, river.
32-70   66-01

CHIANG (170)—Fall, descend, send down, come into this world, drop // degrade.
32-30

CH'IANG (57), *qiang*—Force, strong, compel, strength, stiff, violent, headstrong, determined, firm.

03-43	15-21	25-37	29-42	30-10
30-42	30-63	33-17	33-22	36-15
36-41	42-61	52-57	55-69	76-11
76-28	76-42	76-47	76-50	78-11
78-25				

CHIAO (8), *jiao*—United, unified, combine, integrate, blend, join.
60-46   61-09

CHIAO (60)—Outer forms, outcome, end, limit, external, frontiers, the end of.
01-39

CHIAO (66)—Teachings, doctrine, lesson.
02-60   42-56   42-59   42-72   43-30

CHIAO (106)—Bright, light, dazzle, brilliant.
14-37

CHIAO (148)—Horn.
50-60

CHIAO (159)—Contrast, compare, examine.
02-34

CHIAO (163)—Outside the city, waste or forest land near the frontier, open common beyond the city, border // place to have a sacrifice, altar.
46-18

CHIAO (187)—Proud, haughty, arrogant // wild horse, ungovernable; disdainful, self-confident.
09-28   30-54

CH'IAO (48), *qiao*—Skill, cunning, clever, shrewd, ingenious, talented, wily, crafty.
19-22   45-22   57-44

CHIEH (9), *jie*—Little, insignificant, small, subtle.
53-03

CHIEH (106)—Everyone, all, altogether, all at once.

02-03	02-12	17-40	20-65	20-111
49-55	67-03			

CHIEH (117)—Finish, utmost, reach its end, exhaust.

39-71

CHIEH (120)—Knot, tie, bindings, tied knots // make a contract, bind by an agreement, united, banded together.

27-27   80-41

CHIEH (148)—Loosen, unravel, undo, untie // open, take apart, extricate, sever // dissipate, scatter, dispel // release from bonds.

04-19   27-34   56-18

CHIEH (149)—Scrutinize, investigate, inquire // demand, ask for with authority.

14-28

CH'IEH (1), qie—And, but, moreover, further, and now, still, also, yet; thus, so, this.

07-11   41-94   67-70   67-74   67-78

CHIEN (9), jian—Frugal, thrift, economy, sparing, moderation.

67-39   67-52   67-73

CHIEN (12)—Unite, together, bring together, join, connect, annex // comprehend, embrace.

61-59

CHIEN (18)—Weapon, sword, a blade.

53-37

CHIEN (32)—Hard, solid, firm, stiff, rigid // stable, immovable, strong // constant, determined, resolute, unwavering // establish, confirm.

43-12   76-10   76-27   78-10

CHIEN (54)—Establish, firm, to set up, erect, confirm.

41-32   41-61   54-02

CHIEN (75)—Bar, keys, bolt.

27-21

CHIEN (147)—Display, show, see, look, recognize // opinion.

03-20	14-04	14-69	14-75	19-42
22-31	24-10	29-10	35-33	47-10
47-30	52-50	72-35	77-77	

CHIEN (154)—Low, humility, humble, put down // common man, commoners // worthless, cheap, poor in quality.

39-92   39-113   56-61

CHIEN (169)—Space, crevice.

05-24   43-17

CH'IEN (18), qian—First, in front, ahead, before, advance, progress // leader, chief.

02-43   38-96   66-51

CH'IEN (24)—Thousand, many.

64-44

CHIH (4), zhi—Its, 's, he, she.

01-17	01-23	01-50	01-53	01-58
02-06	02-15	02-54	02-59	03-12
03-32	04-05	04-14	04-37	04-41
05-23	06-11	06-23	08-16	09-04
09-12	09-22	09-38	10-51	10-53
11-12	11-24	11-37	11-41	11-46
12-30	13-20	13-24	14-02	14-09
14-16	14-56	14-60	14-67	14-73
14-80	14-85	15-02	15-23	15-46
15-69	15-78	17-06	17-12	17-16
17-20	20-02	20-10	20-18	20-53
20-76	21-03	21-10	21-67	22-60
22-63	22-78	23-62	23-71	23-80
24-41	25-34	25-39	26-32	27-66

27-71	27-74	28-77	29-08	29-26
29-30	30-18	30-27	31-07	31-12
31-34	31-39	31-46	31-57	31-101
31-104	31-110	31-117	32-19	32-35
32-61	32-68	34-12	35-21	35-30
35-35	35-40	36-04	36-08	36-12
36-16	36-20	36-24	36-28	36-32
36-49	37-14	37-27	37-31	37-35
38-29	38-37	38-45	38-53	38-56
38-63	38-90	38-94	38-100	38-104
39-02	39-43	40-04	40-09	41-08
41-23	41-35	42-27	42-45	42-50
42-54	42-60	43-03	43-10	43-24
43-29	43-33	43-39	46-35	48-10
49-16	49-23	49-30	49-37	49-57
50-06	50-12	50-18	50-21	50-35
51-03	51-06	51-09	51-12	51-25
51-28	51-32	51-41	51-44	51-46
51-48	51-50	51-52	51-54	51-56
54-19	54-27	54-35	54-43	54-51
55-03	55-34	55-40	55-50	55-75
58-20	58-26	58-45	59-18	59-63
61-08	61-12	62-05	62-09	62-14
62-29	62-34	62-58	63-74	64-19
64-24	64-30	64-38	64-46	64-55
64-59	64-75	64-84	64-104	64-112
64-119	65-02	65-14	65-16	65-29
65-37	66-15	66-31	66-39	66-75
67-33	67-95	67-99	68-23	68-29
68-35	68-42	73-20	73-33	73-35
74-10	74-26	75-02	75-09	75-15
75-21	75-29	75-36	76-02	76-16
76-31	76-37	77-02	77-12	77-16
77-21	77-26	77-37	78-14	78-21
78-23	78-27	78-45	80-09	80-29
80-37	80-45	80-64	81-44	81-52

CHIH (18)—Ruler, governor, govern, regulate // tailor, cut.

28-84

CHIH (32)—Hold, take hold of, grasp, seize // manage, retain, to keep, maintain.

14-78	29-27	35-01	64-56	64-70
69-31	74-23	79-17		

CHIH (61)—Ambition, will, resolution, resolve, determination.

03-42	31-73	33-26

CHIH (72)—Cunning, craftiness, knowing.

03-50	03-55	18-08	19-04	27-85
33-04	65-21	65-25	65-33	

CHIH (77)—Stop, stand, remain, abide, dwell, that in which the mind rests.

20-108	32-52	32-54	35-19	44-33

CHIH (85)—Rule, govern, order, way of ruling.

03-33	03-67	08-37	10-28	32-41
57-03	59-01	60-01	64-23	65-18
65-26	65-34	75-17	75-27	

CHIH (109)—Truth, justice, correct, straight, rectify.

22-06	45-18	58-63

CHIH (111)—Perceive, know, recognize.

02-04	02-13	04-35	10-32	(10-48)
14-88	16-36	16-41	16-46	17-04
21-64	25-30	28-01	28-24	28-47
32-51	32-53	33-01	33-06	33-18
43-21	44-28	44-32	46-24	46-33
47-04	47-18	47-28	52-15	52-19
53-06	54-85	55-31	55-53	55-57
56-01	56-08	57-18	58-30	59-34
59-38	59-47	65-39	65-47	70-05
70-13	70-26	70-31	70-32	71-01
71-03	71-06	71-07	72-32	73-24
78-34	81-17	81-24		

CHIH (122)—Appoint, arrange, install, establish, to place.

62-40

CHIH (133a)—Utmost, at its height, zenith, epitome, perfection // greatest degree of, much, very, highly.

| 43-04 | 43-11 | 48-14 | 55-41 | 55-51 |
| 65-67 | 72-08 | 80-69 |

CHIH (133b)—Cause, reach, bring about, achieve, produce.

| 10-12 | 14-27 | 16-01 | 39-42 | 39-120 |

CHIH (154)—Real, genuine, solid, the substance, matter // simple, plain, honest, sincere, true.

41-65

CH'IH (32), chi—Clay.

11-15

CH'IH (44)—A foot, ~refers to fingers and the unit of measure equal to two hands opened to their widest extent.

69-19

CH'IH (64)—Hold, grasp // manage, maintain, direct with a firm hand.

| 09-01 | 64-04 | 67-30 |

CH'IH (155)—Infant.

55-07

CH'IH (187)—Chasing, racing about, gallop, go quickly.

| 12-19 | 43-06 |

CHIN (9), jin—Now, the present, at this time.

| 14-84 | 21-52 | 67-67 |

CHIN (118)—Muscles, sinews, tendons, strong.

55-25

CHIN (162)—Advance, move forward, enter, progress, go, bring in.

| 41-40 | 62-54 | 69-15 |

CHIN (167)—Gold, metal, bronze.

09-17

CH'IN (19), qin—Effort, exertion, labor, toil // to exhaust.

| 06-25 | 41-05 | 52-39 |

CH'IN (147)—Love, affection, sympathy, kinship // intimate, personal, belonging to myself.

| 17-09 | 18-14 | 44-05 | 56-36 | 79-36 |

CHING (60), jing—By-paths, side roads, deviations, sidetracked.

53-22

CHING (110)—Brag, boast, proud, self-approve, arrogant, proud // complacent.

| 22-47 | 24-25 | 30-46 |

CHING (119)—Spirit, essence, life force.

| 21-40 | 21-42 | 26-05 | 55-39 |

CHING (140)—Briars, brambles, thorns.

30-21

CHING (174)—Still, quiet, tranquil, in repose, peaceful, silent, at rest.

| 15-68 | 16-05 | 16-27 | 37-45 | 45-32 |
| 45-36 | 57-70 | 61-17 | 61-21 |

CHING (187)—Fear, dread, afraid, anxiety, terrify, alarmed, perturbed, astonished.

| 13-04 | 13-15 | 13-22 | 13-26 | 13-32 |

CH'ING (9), qing—Support, lean on, incline toward.

02-38

CH'ING (85)—Clear, pure, unsullied, clarity // peaceful, calm, still, settle, make clear, purify.

| 15-71 | 39-10 | 39-47 | 45-35 |

CH'ING (159)—Lighthearted, lightly, frivolous, easy, levity, make light of // disregard, to slight.

| 26-03 | 26-37 | 26-40 | 63-58 | 69-38 |
| 69-40 | 75-30 | 75-40 |

CHIU (4), jiu—Lasting, ancient, enduring.

| 07-04 | 07-12 | 15-76 | 16-63 | 23-27 |
| 33-32 | 44-39 | 58-50 | 59-52 | 59-61 |
| 67-20 |

CHIU (5)—Nine // to the end; the highest, perfect.

64-36

CHIU (30)—Downfall, calamity, misfortune // a fault, a defect, an error // evil, criminal, unfavorable.

09-32   46-26

CHIU (66)—Rescue, save, take care of, liberate // stop, cease.

27-41   27-49   52-49   67-94

CH'IU (85), *qiu*—Seek, pursue, those who seek, seeker, beg, aim for.

62-69   75-34

CH'IUNG (116), *qiong*—Exhaust, the end, the limit, to the last degree, termination.

05-41   45-16

CHO (64), *zhuo*—Unskilled, clumsy, stupid, crude, inept.

45-24

CHO (69)   Hew, cut, carve, chop, cut to pieces, hack.

74-46   74-51

CHO (75)—Sharpen, point, pointed, acute, temper.

09-11

CHO (85)—Muddy, murky, disturbed water // thick, impure, viscous // dull, stupid.

15-63   15-66

CHO (159)—Cease, end, finish, be suspended // rest, stop.

54-17

CHOU (30), *zhou*—Complete, surround, everywhere, extend // dynasty.

25-17

CHOU (137)—Boat, ship, vessel.

80-24

CHOU (187)—Violent // quick, urgent, rapid, sudden.

23-11

CH'OU (118), *chou*—Count, tally, calculate counter // devise, arrange, to plan, a time.

27-15

CHU (3), *zhu*—Master, ruler, lord, chief, the head // to rule; to make one chief.

26-33   30-05   34-30   34-45   69-09
78-51

CH'U (17), *chu*—Origin, source, birth // produce, give out, go forth.

01-44   05-37   10-52   18-09   35-22
47-02   47-14   50-01   51-43

CH'U (140)—Straw, grass.

05-09   05-19

CH'U (141)—Stop, rest, stay, dwell, occupy // live by, manage, do what is proper.

02-51   02-84   08-13   24-47   26-25
30-20   31-18   31-100   31-116   38-111
38-118   66-44   66-50   76-52   76-56
77-73

CH'U (170)—Purify, clean // splendid, splendor // deduct, take away.

10-19   53-25

CH'UAI (64), *chuai*—Sharpen, temper, knock, handle.

09-09

CHUAN (41), *zhuan*—Concentrate, focus, control, engross // one, singular.

10-10

CH'UAN (47), *chuan*—River, stream, flow.

15-30   32-66

CHUANG (33), *zhuang*—Flourish, reach prime, full-grown, abundant, strong, overdevelop.

30-65   55-71

CHUANG (94)—Form, shape, state.

14-55   14-57

CHUI (154), *zhui*—Extraneous, excess, superfluous, waste, useless // tumor, growth, wen, excrescence, useless appendage, parasite.

24-36

CH'UI (30), *chui*—Breathe in, blow cold, breathe hard, chide // praise, puff up.

29-40

CH'UN (72), *chun*—Spring, springtime // wanton, lustful, joyous, glad.

20-41

CHUNG (2), *zhong*—Within, middle, center, inside.

05-45   21-22   21-30   21-38   21-46
25-63   41-09

CHUNG (61)—Loyal, devoted, faithful, patriotic, devoted, sincere.

18-25   38-88

CHUNG (120)—Outlast, the end, last to the end, utmost, extreme, the end of one's days, deceased.

23-09   23-14   26-13   34-52   52-36
52-46   55-43   63-48   63-76   64-86

CHUNG (143)—All, everything, many, majority, the people, the masses.

01-56   08-14   20-31   20-63   20-109
21-59   21-65   31-105   64-110

CHUNG (166)—Heavy, weighty, solid // gravity, important, severe, grave, give weight to.

26-01   26-19   59-19   59-22   66-49
80-16

CH'UNG (40), *chong*—Favor, honor, esteem, kindness // welcome, accept.

13-01   13-12   13-16   13-29

CH'UNG (85)—Blend, merge, union, combine // shake, agitate, combine, dash against // empty, vacant.

04-02   42-21   45-12

CHÜ (44), *ju*—Occupy, dwell, inhabit, stop, stay, reside // dwell on it.

02-80   08-23   25-69   31-21   31-89
31-94   38-115   38-122   72-13   80-54

CHÜ (61)—Threaten, scare, frighten, fear, regard with reverence or awe, apprehensive.

74-09

CHÜ (64)—Seize, pounce, attack, claw.

55-18

CHÜ (134)—Raise, lift up, go up, promote, lift.

77-15

CH'Ü (28), *qu*—Abandon, avoid, leave, reject, discard, dismiss, remove, withdraw // depart, die.

02-88   12-46   20-06   20-14   21-56
29-53   29-55   29-57   38-126   72-42

CH'Ü (29)—Take hold of, capture // win, conquer, rule, govern.

12-48   29-03   30-41   38-128   48-24
48-38   57-12   61-32   61-42   61-49
61-53   72-44

CH'Ü (44)—Exhaust, fall in, collapse // grievance, wrong, affliction.

05-33

CH'Ü (73)—Bend, yield, give in, bow down // crooked, crippled, scheming, false, tortuous, to wrong.

22-01   22-66   45-20

CH'ÜAN (11), *quan*—Perfect, whole, complete, all, preserved whole, do all that is required.

22-03   22-68   22-75   55-37

CH'ÜAN (94)—Dog.

80-63

CHÜEH (64), *jue*—Carnivorous, prey, predatory.

55-19

CHÜEH (120)—Abandon, eliminate, banish, renounce, break off, interrupt, sever, exterminate, utterly destroy, terminate, end.

19-01   19-09   19-17   [20-01]   19-21

CHÜEH (157)—Fall, topple, stumble.

39-88

CH'ÜEH (26), *que*—Curb, turn back, draw back, reject.

46-05

CH'ÜEH (121)—Imperfect, broken, defective, incomplete, lacking.

45-04   58-15   58-16

CHÜN (30), *jun*—Master, lord, prince, ruler, a sovereign // honorable, exalted, superior.

26-08   26-47   31-19   31-37   70-22

CHÜN (32)—Harmony, peace, "equal vision," impartiality, fair, just, evenly.

32-39

CHÜN (159)—War, battle, campaign // general, soldier, army, troops.

30-26   31-88   31-93   50-50

ERH (7), *er*—Two, duality, to duplicate.

42-06   42-07   67-37

ERH (10)—Child, infant.

10-16   20-52   28-23

ERH (126)—And, yet, but, still, as if.

01-45	02-65	02-69	02-73	02-78
04-03	05-31	05-35	07-30	07-36
08-10	09-02	09-10	09-27	10-55
10-59	10-63	14-31	17-10	20-68
20-114	20-125	22-76	23-28	25-19
25-29	25-67	26-34	27-22	27-31
29-06	30-36	30-44	30-48	30-52
30-56	30-61	31-44	31-52	31-55
32-37	33-34	34-13	34-15	34-27
34-42	35-08	37-05	37-21	38-22
38-30	38-38	38-46	38-54	38-61
38-67	38-72	38-77	38-82	38-92
38-102	41-06	42-18	42-35	42-46
42-51	47-27	47-31	47-35	48-20
51-21	51-34	51-58	51-62	51-66
53-19	55-27	55-36	55-46	56-35
56-40	56-45	56-50	56-55	56-60
57-29	57-64	57-71	57-78	57-85
58-56	58-60	58-64	58-68	61-52
64-82	64-122	66-46	66-52	66-62
67-31	69-10	69-17	73-39	73-44
73-49	73-54	73-62	74-17	74-24
77-32	77-66	77-71	78-08	79-20
80-11	80-18	80-43	81-47	81-55

ERH (128)—Ear // side.

12-11

ERH (184)—Cake, pastries, food, tasty food // eat.

35-16

FA (9), *fa*—Boast, show off, brag // cut down, chastise, destroy.

22-41   24-20   30-50

FA (85)—Follow, imitate, take after, model, emulate // the law, a rule, natural law, follow a rule.

25-74   25-77   25-80   25-83   57-49

FA (105)—Become, turn, manifest as // send forth, to issue, go out.
12-26   39-57

FAN (29), *fan*—Return, revert, reverse, turn back.
25-51   40-01   65-62   78-64

FAN (85)—All-pervading, universal, broad, overflows, floods over // cyclical.
34-03

FANG (38), *fang*—Hinder, impede, impair, entangle.
12-35

FANG (70)—Square // place, region, space, range.
41-70   58-55

FEI (53), *fei*—Abandon, forget, give up, lose, abolish // neglect, ruin, destroy, corrupt, discard, degrade.
18-03   36-19

FEI (154)—Waste, squander, overuse, cost, expense, spend.
44-22

FEI (175)—Not, surely not, not so.
01-04   01-10   07-39   31-36   39-111
39-117   53-49   60-17   60-27   65-07

FÊN (119), *fen*—Haul, haul manure, remove dirt // filth, ordure, muck, dung.
46-09

FÊN (120)—Knots, fetters, tangles // disorder, confusion, perplexed.
04-21   56-20

FÊNG (37), *feng*—Offer, give to, supply, serve // receive with respect.
77-46   77-54

FÊNG (142)—Poisonous insect, bee, wasp, hornet.
55-09

FÊNG (151)—Abundant, abound, copious, prolific, affluent.
54-49

FÊNG (182)—Wind, squall, gust, gale.
23-07

FU (9), *fu*—Conceal, hide, secret // prostrate, put beneath, subdue, suppress, lie in ambush.
58-28

FU (37)—Above all, forasmuch, truly, to the extent // master, scholar, distinguished man.
02-81   03-54   08-44   15-15   15-88
16-15   22-50   31-01   31-63   32-48
37-37   38-85   38-110   41-89   50-28
50-73   51-30   59-08   60-39   61-70
63-57   67-11   67-25   67-82   70-23
71-09   72-19   74-35   74-47   75-42

FU (40)—Wealthy, rich, abundant, enrich, provide.
09-25   33-21   57-81

FU (57)—Not, does not.
02-79   02-83

FU (60)—Return, revert, reverse, restore, again, reiterate, recover.
14-47   16-14   16-20   16-30   16-32
19-14   28-19   28-42   28-65   52-22
52-61   58-37   58-41   64-109   80-40

FU (74)—Clothe, dress in, clad in, wear, clothes.
53-32   59-14   59-16   80-51

FU (88)—Father , beginning, precept, a rule, one who is the ruler of a family.
42-73

FU (101)—Beginning, origin, creation, Creator, father.
21-60   21-66

FU (113)—Happiness, luck, blessings, good fortune, prosperity.

58-19   58-23   65-38

FU (130)—The inner, soul // stomach, belly.

03-39   12-41

FU (146)—Protect, guard, cover, shelter.

51-55

FU (154)—Carry, carry on one's back // rely upon, take refuge.

42-16

FU (159a)—Help, assist, minister, support, restore.

64-116

FU (159b)—Spokes of a wheel.

11-03

HAI (39), *hai*—Child, infant // a child about to smile.

20-55   49-56

HAI (40)—Loss // injure, hurt, harm, damage, offend, fearful of, anxious about.

35-10   56-51   66-55   73-18   81-49

HAI (85)—Ocean, sea // large river.

20-103   32-71   66-02

HAN (30), *han*—Possess, contain, embody, hold, maintain.

55-01

HAN (40)—Cold, shiver, wintry.

45-31

HAO (38), *hao*—Usual, usually, liable to, likely to, prefer, invite // good, right, excellent, highest degree.

30-15   53-21   57-69

HAO (82)—Tiny, small, soft part of plants.

64-34

HAO (141)—Cry, wail.

55-45

HEI (203), *hei*—Black, blackness, dark, obscure // evil, wicked.

28-29

HO (9), *he*—What is, why, how.

13-10   13-33   13-57   20-08   20-16
21-62   26-29   50-29   50-74   54-83
57-16   62-32   62-65   74-06

HO (30a)—Join, combine, unite, match, meet, come together, harmonious, in unison.

32-28   55-35   64-28

HO (30b)—Harmony, blend, soften, agree, union, concord.

02-42   04-22   18-16   42-25   55-49
55-54   56-21   79-01

HO (145)—Coarse clothes, wool, "poor man's garb."

70-45

HO (169)—Close, behind closed doors // whole, complete, family, all.

10-37

HOU (9), *hou*—Prince, baron, duke.

32-14   37-09   39-32   39-80   39-102

HOU (27)—Solid, thick, heavy, much, real, substance // liberal, kind, generous.

38-113   44-26   50-36   55-04   75-37

HOU (60)—After, then, back, behind, to postpone // the second.

02-44   07-27   14-77   30-28   38-68
38-73   38-78   38-83   65-65   66-38
67-77

HSI (12), *xi*—Oh, !, ~very.

04-10   04-29   15-32   15-38   15-43
15-50   15-55   15-60   17-30   20-26
20-46   20-58   20-82   20-100   20-105
21-18   21-20   21-26   21-28   21-34
21-36   25-10   25-12   34-04   58-18
58-24

HSI (50)—Soundless, inaudible, very faint // rare, few, seldom, infrequent // disperse, scatter.

14-14	23-01	41-79	43-37	70-35
74-53				

HSI (60)—Move, move away, migrate, change residence.

80-21

HSI (72)—Old, ancient.

39-01

HSI (76)—Peaceful, shy, with reserve, humble, shy // contract, shrink.

36-03	49-45	49-46

HSI (86)—Joyful, merry // busy, active // light, bright, splendid, intelligent, prospering, ample.

20-33	20-34

HSI (120)—Small, thin, fine, slender.

63-27	63-43	67-23

HSI (124)—Practice, follow, custom.

52-71

HSI (145)—Follow, practice // conceal, cover // penetrate, force, steal, invade, make a foray // inherit.

27-57

HSIA (1), *xia*—Below, under // lowly, inferior // the people, lower classes.

02-02	02-36	13-18	13-65	13-70
13-76	13-81	14-39	17-03	22-27
22-56	25-26	26-39	28-09	28-13
28-32	28-36	28-55	28-59	29-05
29-16	30-12	31-76	32-09	32-64
35-05	37-47	38-09	38-26	39-39
39-97	40-12	41-17	43-02	43-09
43-36	45-39	46-02	46-11	47-06
48-26	48-40	49-44	49-49	52-02
52-08	54-54	54-78	54-81	54-87
56-65	57-14	57-25	60-12	61-04
61-07	61-11	61-23	61-28	61-38
61-47	61-51	61-82	62-79	63-29
63-37	64-51	66-14	66-30	66-59
66-71	67-02	67-46	67-60	68-24
70-10	76-53	77-13	77-56	78-02
78-31	78-59			

HSIA (94)—Squeeze, make narrow, restrict, reduce, cramp, constrict.

72-10

HSIA (95)—Flaw, blemish, slip up.

27-09

HSIANG (8), *xiang*—Enjoy, accept, take part in, celebrate, present in sacrifice, receive gratefully, confer.

20-36

HSIANG (109)—Mutual, both, together, reciprocal, blend with // help // examine, inspect.

02-25	02-29	02-33	02-37	02-41
02-45	20-05	20-13	32-27	60-42
69-49	80-60	80-66	80-73	

HSIANG (113)—Blessing, fortune, good omen, auspicious.

31-06	31-33	55-64	78-55

HSIANG (152)—Image, figure, form, reflection // seems, appears // elephant.

04-39	14-61	21-24	35-03	41-82

HSIANG (163)—Village, district, town, community // region, country.

54-37	54-69	54-71

HSIAO (39), *xiao*—Filial piety, duty, respect and obedience to parents.

18-18	19-15

HSIAO (42)—Small, subtle, insignificant, trifling, petty, narrow.

32-07	34-37	52-51	60-06	61-29
61-33	61-35	61-62	63-11	80-01

HSIAO (118)—Laugh, ridicule, belittle.

41-22   41-25

HSIAO (130)—Resemble, like, similar, seeming // worthy.

67-10   67-17   67-19

HSIEH (76), *xie*—Give out, end, dissolve, stop, wither away // rest, desist, halt, stop.

39-64

HSIEH (163)—?, ~a question.

07-44   39-116   62-75

HSIEN (10), *xian*—Precede, before, begin, in front, first, early, soon // forefather, the ancients.

04-42   07-32   25-05   62-48   66-33
67-47   67-61   67-79

HSIEN (154)—Worthy, good, virtue, talent, moral; one whose virtue, talents, power, and actions exceed others.

03-03   **75-50**   77-78

HSIEN (169)—See CHIEN (169)

HSIEN (195)—Fish.

60-07

HSIN (9), *xin*—Truthful, loyal, faithful, sincere, honest, trust, trustworthy, a man of his word, believe in, confide // be in accord with, follow.

08-34   17-21   17-27   21-48   23-81
23-87   38-89   49-26   49-29   49-32
49-36   49-39   63-62   81-01   81-08

HSIN (61)—Heart, mind, heart-mind // the will, intention, motive, affections // the center, middle.

03-25   03-36   08-26   12-25   20-77
49-05   49-09   49-11   49-52   55-65

HSIN (69)—New, renew, restore // improve, add, increase.

15-96   22-12

HSING (38), *xing*—Families, surname.

05-17   17-39   49-08

HSING (59)—Shape, form, material, body, substance, contour // appear, make manifest, show.

41-84   51-08

HSING (134)—Raise, raise up, uplift, promote, exalt, elevate // establish, fashion // flourish, prosper.

36-23

HSING (144)—Practice, act, effects // go out, actions, progress.

02-56   12-34   24-08   24-37   25-18
26-15   27-02   29-34   33-23   41-07
47-26   50-44   53-07   62-23   64-47
69-22   69-24   70-08   70-16   78-37

HSIU (9), *xiu*—Cultivate, practice // adorn, clean up, renovate, repair.

54-18   54-26   54-34   54-42   54-50

HSIUNG (17), *xiong*—Disaster, calamity, misfortune, unlucky // malignant, cruel.

16-45   30-31   31-82

HSIUNG (172)—Male, manhood, masculine, brave, heroic // cock bird.

28-03

HSÜ (60), *xu*—Gradual, slow // reserved, dignified, serious, grave, slow, tardy.

15-70   15-79

HSÜ (76)—Sigh, breathe out, blow hot.

29-38

HSÜ (102)—Nourish, feed, care for, nurse, rear, nurture.

51-05   61-60

HSÜ (141)—Empty, vacant, hollow.

03-34   05-30   16-02   22-71   53-31

HSÜAN (96), *xuan*—Mystery, secret, profound, hidden, dark, deep, obscure. See YÜAN (10)

01-51	01-52	01-55	06-07	06-09
10-20	10-68	15-09	51-71	56-29
65-52	65-54			

HSÜEH (39), *xue*—Knowledge, learning, study, school.

19-18	[20-02]	48-02	64-106	64-108

HU (4), *hu*—!, indeed, oh, ?.

05-29	10-09	10-17	10-25	10-33
10-41	10-49	23-32	35-25	39-118

HU (61)—Vague, obscure, confused, indistinct, abstruse, inexplicable, minute.

14-64	21-16	21-17	21-27

HU (63)—Door.

11-27	47-03

HU (141)—Tiger.

50-47	50-61

HUA (21), *hua*—Transform, evolve, change, alter, influence.

37-19	37-20	57-67

HUA (140)—Flower, flowery, embellishments, trappings, ornament // splendor, glory, blooming, charming, beautiful.

38-101	38-124

HUAI (61), *huai*—Hide inside, hold, cherish, conceal, bear, carry // bosom.

70-46

HUAN (61), *huan*—Trouble, misfortune, calamity, affliction, tribulation, distress, grief, affliction // fearful.

13-07	13-37	13-45	13-58

HUAN (85)—Yield, supple // dissolve, spread, expand, dissipate.

15-42

HUAN (162)—Return, requite, revert, rebound, come back, retaliation.

30-16

HUANG (61), *huang*—Evasive, illusive, vague, abstruse // disturbed, mad, flustered.

14-65	21-14	21-19	21-25

HUANG (140)—Reckless, confused, indulgent, without restraint // barren, desolate, deserted, neglected.

20-25

HUI (61), *hui*—Intellect, intelligence, wit, wise, clever // strategies.

18-07

HUI (142)—Serpent.

55-11

HUI (149)—Prohibit, conceal, taboo, shun.

57-28

HUI (170)—Fail, give in, succumb, fall, destroy, dismantle, end.

29-48

HUN (72), *hun*—Dark, dusk, dim // confound, disorder, confuse, disrupt, benighted, throw into the dark.

18-22	20-89	20-90	57-40

HUN (85a)—Merge, blend, mingle, mixed, confused, turbid, nebulous, chaos // containing everything.

14-30	15-59	25-03

HUN (85b)—Universal, oceanlike, harmonious, united, whole // undifferentiated, nebulous, chaotic, confused, blended.

49-50

HUO (61), *huo*—Confused, bewildered, perplexed, delusion // doubt, deceive, suspicion.

22-18

HUO (62)—Likely, perhaps, apparently // sometimes, seems to // capacity.

04-06	04-31	24-39	29-33	29-35
29-37	29-39	29-41	29-43	29-45
29-47	31-10	42-43	42-48	61-46
61-50	73-15	73-17		

HUO (85)—Life, live, survive.

73-11

HUO (113)—Calamity, misfortune, curse, disaster, injure, bring calamity // guilt.

46-19	58-17	58-25	69-34

HUO (154)—Wealth, goods, merchandise, treasure.

03-13	12-31	44-08	53-42	64-105

JAN (86), *ran*—So, being so, like, manner, is so, as such, "as it is."

17-44	21-68	23-04	25-85	26-27
51-37	53-04	54-88	57-20	64-121
65-64	73-53	77-41		

JANG (64), *rang*—Seize, stretch, bare // reject.

38-59	69-25

JÊ (86), *re*—Heat, warm, hot, feverish // restless, ardent, energetic.

45-34

JÊN (9a), *ren*—Person, man, men, human.

02-50	03-31	05-12	07-26	08-15
12-04	12-10	12-16	12-24	12-33
12-39	20-17	20-32	20-64	20-75
20-84	20-92	20-110	20-124	22-22
23-31	25-73	26-12	27-38	27-42
27-46	27-61	27-65	27-70	27-73
28-75	29-52	30-04	31-62	31-66
31-103	33-02	33-10	36-56	42-26
42-53	47-24	49-02	49-41	49-54
50-17	57-41	57-59	58-44	58-54
59-02	60-26	60-32	60-34	60-38
61-61	61-69	62-08	62-13	62-27
62-28	63-47	63-71	64-63	64-96
64-111	66-43	68-20	68-34	70-43
71-18	72-30	73-30	76-01	77-36
77-64	78-41	79-16	79-24	79-40
80-39	81-26	81-32	81-39	81-51

JÊN (9b)—Humanity, with human preference, benevolent, humane, kind.

05-04	05-14	08-31	18-05	19-10
38-35	38-74	38-76		

JÊN (18)—Blade, sword, point, weapon, sharp-pointed.

50-72

JÊNG (64), *reng*—Force, enforce, apply force, urge along.

38-62	69-28

JIH (72), *ri*—Every day, daily, day // sun.

23-15	26-14	48-03	48-07	55-44
58-48				

JO (57), *ruo*—Tender, weak, gentle, yielding, soft.

03-40	36-11	36-38	40-06	55-24
76-06	76-34	76-55	78-05	78-22

JO (140)—Is like, seems, resembles, appears // barely visible // with.

06-20	08-03	13-03	13-08	13-14
13-21	13-25	13-31	13-38	15-27
15-33	15-40	15-44	15-52	15-57
15-62	20-15	20-59	20-71	20-102
20-106	32-16	37-11	41-13	41-15
41-38	41-42	41-46	41-50	41-54
41-58	41-63	41-67	45-03	45-11
45-19	45-23	45-27	59-06	60-04
67-18	74-11	78-63		

JOU (75), *rou*—Soft, tender, gentle, yielding, pliant, flexible, mild, kind, soft, meek, limp.

10-13	36-37	43-05	52-55	55-26
76-05	76-19	76-33	76-54	78-04
78-26				

JU (11), *ru*—Enter, penetrate, go in.

43-15	50-03	50-49	61-67

JU (38)—Likely, like, as, as well as, also // resemble.

05-43	09-06	20-35	20-39	20-50
39-129	39-133	62-52	64-87	

JU (160)—Dishonor, disgrace, insult, disappoint, shame, degrade, defile.

13-02	13-13	13-30	28-52	41-55
44-31				

JUI (167), *rui*—Sharp, point, edge, acute // zealous, ardent.

04-18	56-17

JUNG (40), *rong*—Appearance, attitude, demeanor // all-embracing // enter, pierce, insert // receive, contain, endure.

15-24	15-41	16-48	16-49	21-04
50-70				

JUNG (62)—War, army, soldiers, weapon.

46-14

JUNG (75)—Glory, honor, illustrious, beautiful, splendor, prosperous.

26-22	28-49

KAI (66), *gai*—Change, alter, reform, amend, correct, to exchange, make as new // another.

25-16

KAI (140)—Indeed // for, since, for that, now then.

50-37

K'AI (169), *kai*—Open, begin // unfold, explain, reveal, disclose.

10-36	27-25	52-40

KAN (66), *gan*—Dare, venture, presume, risk, intrepid, rash.

03-58	30-39	64-124	67-43	67-57
69-07	69-14	73-03	73-09	74-28

KAN (99)—Enjoy, delight in, relish, sweet.

32-31	80-46

KANG (18), *gang*—Hard, stiff, unyielding, adamant, firm.

36-40	78-29

K'ANG (64), *kang*—Matched, oppose, two sides, resist, equal.

69-47

KAO (75), *gao*—Dry, rotten, decayed, shriveled.

76-25

KAO (189)—High, superior, lofty, noble, high position, exalted, excellent, to a high degree.

02-35	39-85	39-95	77-09

KÊN (75), *gen*—Root, origin, cause, foundation.

06-17	16-23	16-25	26-04	59-56

KO (18), *ge*—Injure, harm // mutilate, cut, cut into pieces, split, sever // affliction, calamity.

28-86	58-58

KO (30)—Each, each one, every, all.

16-19	61-73

K'O (10), *ke*—Overcome, subdue, prevail over, master, sustain.

59-28 59-31

K'O (30)—Can, able, fit.

01-02	01-08	03-21	09-14	13-67
13-78	14-26	14-45	15-13	15-18
20-22	25-22	27-24	27-33	29-20
31-70	32-56	34-06	34-34	34-46
36-44	36-53	44-36	56-33	56-38
56-43	56-48	56-53	56-58	59-41
59-49	62-19	62-24	79-09	

K'O (40)—Stranger, people, guest.

35-18 69-12

KOU (32), *gou*—Dishonor, disgrace, humiliation // immorality, sin.

78-46

KOU (94)—Dog.

05-10 05-20

K'OU (30), *kou*—Mouth, palate, taste buds.

12-17 35-23

KU (30), *gu*—Old, primeval, ancient, first.

14-79	14-89	15-01	21-50	22-62
62-57	65-01	68-41		

KU (31)—Necessary, strong, firm, assuredly // strengthened, fortified, impervious, fixed.

36-06	36-14	36-22	36-30	55-29
58-49	59-57			

KU (39)—Orphans, alone, fatherless, solitary, no protector.

39-106 42-31

KU (66)—For, therefore, thus, hence // cause, reason, purpose, therefore.

01-25	02-22	07-19	07-45	08-19
08-48	11-39	12-45	13-59	14-29

15-20	15-92	19-37	22-32	22-37
22-42	22-48	22-54	23-05	23-33
24-42	25-52	27-43	27-51	27-59
28-82	29-31	31-13	34-57	38-64
38-125	39-89	39-119	41-31	42-41
44-17	46-32	50-30	50-75	51-38
54-59	56-31	56-62	57-57	60-44
61-24	61-45	62-36	62-76	63-52
63-75	64-66	64-71	65-23	66-16
66-69	67-14	67-49	67-53	67-62
67-91	69-46	72-41	73-26	76-26

KU (115)—Worthy, virtuous, goodness // grain, cereals // real, substantial.

39-109 42-34

KU (150)—Valley, ravine, mountain gorge, chasm // empty, hollow.

06-01	15-58	28-56	28-60	32-67
39-21	39-65	41-51	66-08	66-20

KU (159)—Hub of a wheel.

11-06

KU (188)—Bones, frame, body.

03-45 55-23

K'U (75), *ku*—Rigid, decayed, withered, dry, brittle.

76-24

KUA (40), *gua*—Diminish, lessen, curb, small, few, moderate, seldom // a widow, lacking, solitary, friendless, alone.

19-48 39-107 42-32 63-61 80-03

K'UA (37), *kua*—Pride, brag, "show off," boast, vanity, extravagance.

53-48

K'UA (157)—Straddle, stride forward, step across.

24-05

KUAN (40), *guan*—Officer, an official, magistrate, the authorities, ruler.
28-80

KUAN (147)—Perceive, examine, see, recognize, observe, witness // contemplate // display, manifest, evidence, proof.

| 01-30 | 01-37 | 16-13 | 26-23 | 54-62 |
| 54-66 | 54-70 | 54-74 | 54-79 | |

KUAN (169)—Bolt, barrier // bar the door, fasten.
27-20

KUANG (10), *guang*—Bright, brilliant, shine, light, illumined, enlightened // distinguished person.

| 04-24 | 52-60 | 56-23 | 58-67 |

KUANG (53)—Large, broad, liberal, generous, abundant, ample, extensive, wide, spacious.

| 41-56 | 67-55 | 67-75 |

K'UANG (72), *kuang*—Open, empty, broad, wide, vacant, spacious.
15-54

K'UANG (85)—Much less so, moreover.
23-29

K'UANG (94)—Mad, wild, crazed, deranged // rash, excitable, impudent.
12-27

KUEI (77), *gui*—Return, revert, restore, again, revert to the original place or state.

14-48	16-21	16-24	20-62	22-77
28-20	28-43	28-66	34-40	52-62
60-47				

KUEI (154)—Honor, value, esteem, exalt, treasure // to favor, give preference.

| 03-09 | 09-26 | 13-05 | 13-35 | 13-60 |
| 17-32 | 20-126 | 27-77 | 31-23 | 31-28 |

39-84	39-90	51-22	51-29	56-56
56-66	62-61	62-80	64-101	70-39
72-40	75-52			

KUEI (194)—Dark spirits, evil spirits, demons, spirits, ghosts, specter, apparition. // evil.

| 60-14 | 60-19 |

K'UEI (18), *kui*—Hurt, pierce, injure, disfigure, behead.
58-62

K'UEI (61)—Vast, wide, great, cast wide, liberal, enlarge, magnify.

| 73-59 | 73-60 |

K'UEI (169)—Look, watch, peep, glance at, view.
47-08

KUNG (12a), *gong*—Broad // impartial, just // ministers, officers, officials, dukes.

| 16-51 | 16-52 | 42-37 | 62-42 |

KUNG (12b)—Unite, all, altogether, share, have in common, public, same, alike.
11-04

KUNG (19)—Merit, service, work, achievement, reward, credit, actions that deserve praise, honor or reward, a service that will bring reward.

| 02-76 | 09-33 | 17-34 | 22-44 | 24-23 |
| 34-18 | 77-69 | | | |

KUNG (57)—A bow.
77-07

KUNG (64)—Revere, precious, priceless, pay tribute, reverently hold or take with both hands.
62-45

KUNG (66)—Attack, assault.
78-09

K'UNG (39), *kong*—Vast, all-embracing, highest, great, grand // hole, orifice, cave, opening, hollow.

21-01

K'UNG (61)—Fear, apprehensive, anxious, agitated, alarmed // suspicious of, to doubt.

39-49	39-56	39-63	39-70	39-78
39-87				

KUO (31), *guo*—Country, state, kingdom, dynasty, community, empire, nation // rulers or government.

10-29	18-20	36-48	54-45	54-73
54-75	57-04	57-37	59-44	59-46
60-03	61-02	61-26	61-30	61-34
61-36	61-40	61-44	61-55	61-63
65-27	65-28	65-35	65-36	78-44
78-53	80-02	80-59		

KUO (75)—Resolute, resolved, aims, effects, get results, achieve one's purpose, do as one promises, determined, courageous.

30-35	30-43	30-47	30-51	30-55
30-60				

KUO (162)—Pass, pass by, passing, go beyond, exceed.

35-17	61-57	61-65	64-114

LAI (9), *lai*—Come, appear, attracts, come to // gone.

73-51	80-75

LAN (147), *lan*—Vision, behold, perception, insight, understand, perceive.

10-21

LAO (93), *lao*—Feast, sacrificial feast, ox feast.

20-38

LAO (125)—Grow old, become old, aged, decay, exhaustion.

30-67	55-73	80-70

LEI (9), *lei*—Weary, exhausted, worn down, despondent, lazy.

20-56	20-57

LEI (120a)—Accumulating, heap, a pile of.

64-42

LEI (120b)—Rugged, rough, knotty, uneven // difficult.

41-47

LEI (123)—Weak, weakness, feeble, thin, emaciated, decay.

29-44

LI (18), *li*—Benefit, profit, gain, advantage // sharp, acute.

08-07	11-44	19-06	19-24	36-50
53-36	56-46	57-35	73-16	81-46

LI (19)—Strength, force, power, ability, capacity, physical strength, effort.

33-13	62-37	68-36

LI (113)—Propriety, ceremony, rites, rules of behavior, principles of conduct, etiquette.

(19-18b)	31-99	31-115	38-51	38-84
38-86			

LI (117)—Stand, stand firm, steady, poised, set, established, fixed, upright.

24-04	25-14

LI (140)—Govern, rule, oversee, approach.

60-10

LI (166)—Unit of measurement, the Chinese mile, ~a third of a mile.

64-45

LI (172)—Separate, disintegrate, divide, disperse, scatter // leave, depart, dismiss.

10-08	26-17	28-18

LIANG (1), *liang*—Two, both, pair.

01-41	60-40	61-71	65-41	73-13

LIANG (75)—Aggressive, fierce, violent.

42-62

LIAO (40), *liao*—Formless, void, bodiless, vast.
25-11

LIEH (94), *lie*—Hunting.
12-22

LIEH (145)—Split open, crack, disrupt.
39-50

LIEN (53), *lian*—Angular, corner, pointed.
58-59

LIN (163), *lin*—Near, neighboring.
15-36   80-58

LING (9), *ling*—Make, cause, bring about,
command, law, order.
12-03   12-09   12-15   12-23   12-32
19-38   32-36   57-50

LING (173)—Divine, spiritual power, spirit.
39-20   39-61

LIU (12), *liu*—Six.
18-13

LIU (85)—River, delta, stream // flow, spread.
61-05

LIU (182)—Whirlwind, gale, high winds.
20-104

LO (75), *le*—Enjoy, joy, rejoice, happily, glad,
pleased.
23-60   23-69   23-78   31-60   31-64
35-14   66-60   80-55

LO (95)—Let down // necklace.
39-131   39-132

LU (95), *lu*—Shine // respect.
39-127   39-128

LU (170)—Land, on land.
50-43

LU (173)—Dew, rain.
32-32

LUAN (5), *luan*—Trouble, discord, disorder,
anarchy, chaos, confusion.
03-27   18-23   38-93   64-27

LUNG (128), *long*—Deaf.
12-12

MA (187), *ma*—Horse.
46-07   46-15   62-50

MAN (85), *man*—Fill up, full, complete.
09-19

MANG (109), *mang*—Blind.
12-06

MEI (72), *mei*—Dark, dim, obscure, hidden.
14-41   41-39

MEI (123)—Beautiful, good, fair // delight in,
enjoy, pleasing.
02-05   02-08   31-54   31-56   62-17
80-49   81-04   81-05

MÊN (61), *men*—Confused // dull, dejected,
depressed.
20-97   20-98   58-03   58-04

MÊN (169)—Gate, door, opening, entrance.
01-59   06-12   10-35   52-35   56-14

MÊNG (94), *meng*—Wild, fierce, ferocious.
55-15

MI (57), *mi*—Very much, full, complete,
increase, more and more.
47-15   47-19   57-31

MI (162)—Confuse, delude, perplex, misguided.

27-87   58-46

MIAO (38), *miao*—Essence, mystery, subtlety.

01-32   01-57   15-08   27-91

MIEH (85), *mie*—Die, destroy, perish, exterminate.

39-79

MIEN (10), *mian*—Save, free, forgive // spare.

62-74

MIEN (120)—Continual, enduring // soft, silky.

06-18   06-19

MIN (83), *min*—The people, common, multitudes, populace.

03-05	03-15	03-24	03-48	10-27
19-05	19-13	(19-18c)	32-33	53-20
57-30	57-33	57-65	57-72	57-79
57-86	58 06	58-14	64-74	65-10
65-15	66-26	66-34	66-47	66-53
72-01	74-01	74-13	75-01	75-14
75-28	80-04	80-15	80-68	

MING (14), *ming*—Dark, obscure, dim.

21-35

MING (30a)—Name // to name // the Name.

01-07	01-09	01-12	01-14	01-20
01-47	14-05	14-12	14-19	14-46
21-54	25-32	25-40	32-04	32-43
32-44	34-21	34-35	34-47	37-30
37-34	41-88	44-01	47-32	

MING (30b)—Destiny, fate, life, original nature.

16-31   16-33   51-33

MING (72)—Bright, illumine, enlighten, shine, luminous, brilliant.

10-42	16-39	22-33	24-13	27-58
33-08	36-36	41-36	52-53	52-64
55-60	65-09			

MO (75), *mo*—Seed, rootlet, shoot, sprout.

64-35

MO (85)—End, till the end, throughout.

16-64   52-26

MO (140)—No one, none, not, without.

09-21	22-57	32-10	32-34	38-55
46-20	46-27	51-17	51-31	59-05
59-33	59-37	66-72	69-35	70-11
70-14	78-03	78-13	78-32	78-35

MOU (149), *mou*—Plans, lay plans, plot, scheme.

64-09   73-56

MU (75), *mu*—Tree, wood.

64-31   76-15   76-46

MU (80)—Mother.

| 01-24 | 20-128 | 25-27 | 52-09 | 52-13 |
| 52-25 | 59-48 | | | |

MU (93)—Male, the male.

55-33   61-19

MU (109)—Eye.

12-05   12-44

NAI (4), *nai*—This, thus, is.

16-50	16-53	16-56	16-59	16-62
28-63	54-24	54-32	54-40	54-48
54-57	65-66			

NAI (37)—Means, resource, in accordance with // endure.

26-28   74-05

NAN (172), *nan*—Difficult, hard.

02-27	03-10	12-28	63-19	63-30
63-67	63-73	63-78	64-102	65-17
73-32	75-16	75-26		

NÊNG (130), *neng*—Can, able, ability, power.

07-09	07-20	07-46	08-40	09-23
10-06	10-14	10-22	10-30	10-38
10-46	14-87	15-65	15-73	15-93
22-58	23-26	32-11	32-17	34-58
37-12	63-53	66-05	66-17	66-73
67-50	67-54	67-63	70-12	70-15
77-50	78-15	78-36		

NIAO (196), *niao*—Birds.

55-20

NIEN (51), *nian*—Crops, harvest // years.

30-32

NING (40), *ning*—Peace, rest, repose, serene, tranquil // settled, stabilized, firm.

39-15   39-54

NO (149a), *nuo*—Stutter, stammer, inarticulate, "tongue-tied."

45-28

NO (149b)—Promise, agreement.

63-59

NU (61), *nu*—Anger, wrath, furious, rage, mad.

68-11

PA (64), *ba*—Uproot, eradicate, draw out, pull up // topple, fall down.

54-05

PAI (66), *bai*—Ruin, destroy, defect, mar, spoil, fail.

29-25	64-54	64-68	64-83	64-91

PAI (106a)—White, pure, clear.

10-43   28-26   41-53

PAI (106b)—Hundred.

05-16	17-38	19-07	49-07	66-07
66-19				

P'AN (85), *ban*—Melt, dissolve.

64-13

PAO (9), *bao*—Keep, preserve, protect, guarantee // last, maintain.

09-16   15-81   62-16   67-32

PAO (32)—Requite, respond with, compensate, return, repay, reward.

63-14

PAO (40)—Treasure, valuable, honor.

62-10   67-29   69-45

PAO (64)—Embrace, enfold, carry, hold within, cling to.

10-04   19-44   22-23   42-19   54-07
64-29

PAO (140)—Thin, thinness, wearing thin // husk, superficial.

38-91   38-117

PEI (9), *bei*—Double, times, -fold.

19-08

PEI (61)—Sorrow, grief.

31-108

PEI (145)—Flee from, try to escape, avoid, shun // wear, cover, clad.

50-52   70-44

P'EI (164), *pei*—Comply, pair, mate, match, unity, ~live in accord with.

68-39

PÊN (75), *ben*—Root, origin, foundation, support // minister, subject.

26-43   39-94   39-115

P'ÊNG (86), *beng*—Fry, cook, boil.

60-05

PI (55), *bi*—Exhausted, worn-out, impaired, grow old, end.
45-08

PI (60)—The latter, the one, this, that.
12-47   38-127   72-43

PI (61)—Surely, certainly, must, must needs.
30-29   36-05   36-13   36-21   36-29
44-20   44-25   63-32   63-40   63-60
63-65   66-27   66-35   79-04

PI (66)—Worn out, old, grow old // abuse, batter, defraud.
22-10

PI (81)—Compare, examine // join.
55-05

PI (98)—Jade, gem.
62-46

PI (130)—Arms.
38-60   69-27

PI (140)—Grow old, wear out.
15-94

PI (163)—Rustic, unrefined, base.
20-119

PI (169)—Shut, close, shut a door, lock, safe.
27-18   52-33   56-12

P'I (149), *pi*—Compare, illustrate, thus, analogy, in the same way.
32-59

P'IAO (182), *piao*—Whirlwind, gusty // adrift.
23-06

PIEN (160), *bian*—Dispute, debate, oratory, eloquent.
45-26   81-12   81-13

P'IEN (9), *pian*—Assistant, second in charge.
31-86

PIN (154), *bin*—Honor, pay homage, honor like a guest // submit, yield.
32-24

P'IN (93), *pin*—Female, woman.
06-08   06-10   55-32   61-13   61-14

P'IN (154)—Impoverished, poor, become poor.
57-32

PING (1), *bing*—Together, in unison, united, alike.
16-09

PING (12)—Arms, weapons, military, warfare // soldiers.
30-09   31-03   31-26   31-30   50-54
50-67   57-08   69-02   69-33   69-48
76-41   76-49   80-33

PING (15)—Ice.
15-45

PING (104)—Sick, illness, disease, sick of // difficulty, pain.
44-15   71-08   71-11   71-12   71-16
71-20   71-23   71-24   71-28

P'ING (51), *ping*—Peace, peaceful, harmony // even, equal.
35-12

PO (9), *bo*—Hundred.
80-08

PO (24)—Learned, wide learning, universal in knowledge, ample.
81-20   81-21

PO (64)—Grab, grasp, seize // strike, pounce, attack, maul.
14-15   55-22

P'O (85), *po*—Calm, placid, still, inactive.
20-45
P'O (194)—Physical soul, spirit, sexual fluid.
10-03

PU (1), *bu*—Does not, not.

02-19	02-57	02-66	02-70	02-74
02-87	03-01	03-06	03-08	03-16
03-19	03-26	03-57	03-66	04-07
04-34	05-03	05-13	05-32	05-42
06-03	06-24	07-16	08-11	08-46
09-05	09-13	10-56	10-60	10-64
12-42	14-03	14-10	14-17	14-25
14-36	14-40	14-44	14-68	14-74
15-12	15-17	15-85	15-90	15-95
16-40	16-66	17-22	17-26	18-15
19-35	20-21	20-23	21-55	22-29
22-34	22-39	22-45	22-52	23-08
23-13	23-25	23-82	23-86	24-03
24-07	24-12	24-17	24-27	24-46
25-15	25-20	26-16	27-13	27-23
27-32	27-63	27-68	27-76	27-80
28-17	28-40	28-85	29-12	29-19
30-07	30-38	30-57	30-70	30-72
31-05	31-17	31-32	31-41	31-53
31-69	32-57	33-27	33-35	34-16
34-20	34-28	34-43	34-53	35-09
35-31	35-36	35-41	36-43	36-52
37-07	37-42	38-03	38-11	38-114
38-121	39-108	39-125	41-24	41-26
41-59	42-33	42-64	43-27	44-30
44-34	45-07	45-15	46-23	47-01
47-07	47-25	47-29	47-33	48-22
48-35	49-17	49-31	50-45	50-51
51-18	51-59	51-63	51-67	52-28
52-38	52-48	54-04	54-09	54-16
55-13	55-17	55-21	55-47	55-76
55-78	56-03	56-07	56-32	56-37
56-42	56-47	56-52	56-57	58-57
58-61	58-65	58-69	59-27	59-30
60-15	60-20	60-24	60-30	60-36
60-41	61-56	61-64	62-11	62-30
62-51	62-66	63-49	64-98	64-100
64-107	64-123	65-31	66-48	66-54
66-63	66-67	67-09	67-16	67-42
67-56	68-05	68-10	68-16	68-27
69-06	69-13	70-29	71-02	71-05
71-15	71-19	71-27	72-02	72-21
72-25	72-33	72-38	73-08	73-37
73-42	73-47	73-63	74-02	74-55
76-44	77-22	77-34	77-40	77-43
77-67	77-72	77-75	78-33	78-54
79-21	80-12	80-19	80-72	81-03
81-07	81-11	81-15	81-19	81-23
81-27	81-48	81-56		

PU (145)—Complete, mend, patch, add on, supplement, replenish.
77-25   77-33

P'U (72), *pu*—Universal, grand, large, everywhere, pervasive.
54-58
P'U (75)—Pure, simple, natural, plain, "uncarved block of wood," uncut jade, "pristine simplicity."

15-53	19-45	28-68	28-69	32-05
37-32	37-36	57-88		

SAI (32), *sai*—Close, stop, cork, block.
52-30   56-09

SAN (1), *san*—Three, trinity.

11-01	14-23	19-30	42-09	42-10
50-10	50-16	50-27	62-41	67-28
67-40				

SAN (66)—Scatter, disperse, separate, dismiss, shatter, break up, diversify.

28-70   64-17

SANG (30), *sang*—Funeral, mourn, die.

31-98   31-114   69-43

SÊ (30), *se*—Moderation, thrift, sparing, frugal, "restraint," save // the harvest.

59-07   59-10

SÊ (139)—Color, sight.

12-02

SHA (30), *sha*—Hoarse voice.

55-48

SHA (79)—Slay, kill, slaughter.

31-61   31-65   31-102   73-05   74-25
74-32   74-34   74-38   74-40

SHAN (30), *shan*—Good, virtuous, excellent, skill.

02-14   02-17   02-20   08-02   08-06
08-24   08-27   08-30   08-33   08-36
08-39   08-42   15-03   20-09   27-01
27-06   27-11   27-17   27-26   27-40
27-48   27-60   27-64   27-69   27-72
30-33   41-92   49-12   49-15   49-18
49-22   49-25   50-39   54-01   54-06
58-40   62-07   62-12   62-31   65-03
66-13   68-01   68-07   68-12   68-18
73-40   73-45   73-55   79-12   79-39
81-09   81-16

SHANG (1), *shang*—Superior, high, upright, supreme, highest // superior man.

08-01   14-35   17-02   31-50   31-91
38-01   38-18   38-34   38-42   38-50
41-01   41-48   66-25   66-45   71-04
75-06   75-20   76-57

SHANG (9)—Harm, injure, wound, cause distress.

60-25   60-31   60-37   60-43   74-56

SHANG (42)—Honor, exalt, esteem, praise, elevate // even, if // wish, add to.

03-02   23-24   31-80   31-84

SHAO (42), *shao*—Reduce, lessen, few.

19-46   22-13   47-20   63-13

SHÈ (37), *she*—Extravagant, extreme, elaborate.

29-56

SHÊ (64)—Preserve, safeguard, sustain, nourish, maintain.

50-40

SHÊ (85)—Wading, ford, crossing.

15-29

SHÊ (113)—Altar, shrine, sacrifice.

78-49

SHÊ (135)—Discard, renounce, forsake, shun.

67-68   67-72   67-76

SHÊ (142)—Serpent.

55-12

SHÊN (61), *shen*—Careful, cautious.

64-85

SHÊN (85)—Profound, deep, abstruse, intense.

15-11   59-55   65-56

SHÊN (99)—Very, excess, extreme, exceed.

21-43   29-54   44-18   53-17   53-24
53-27   53-30   70-03   70-06

SHÊN (113)—Sacred, soul, spirit, divine, transcendent.

06-02   29-17   39-16   39-58   60-16
60-21   60-23   60-29

SHÊN (158)—Self, person, oneself, body, own life.

07-29	07-31	07-35	07-37	09-35
13-09	13-39	13-50	13-54	13-62
13-73	16-65	26-36	44-03	44-06
52-27	52-37	52-47	52-67	54-21
54-61	54-63	66-37		

SHÊNG (19), *sheng*—Win, conquer, victory, overcome, outdo, sustain.

31-51	31-112	33-09	33-15	36-39
45-30	45-33	61-18	67-87	68-13
69-53	73-41	76-45	78-16	78-24
78-28				

SHÊNG (100)—Life, produce, gives life, bear, birth, come forth, live.

02-26	02-68	07-18	07-22	10-50
10-54	15-80	25-08	30-23	34-14
39-31	39-76	40-15	40-19	42-02
42-05	42-08	42-11	46-16	50-02
50-05	50-19	50-33	50-34	50-41
51-02	51-40	51-57	55-62	59-60
64-32	72-18	75-35	75-46	75-53
76-03	76-17	76-36		

SHÊNG (120)—Continuous, infinite, boundless // cord, tie, string.

14-42	14-43	27-29	80-42

SHÊNG (128a)—Holy, saintly.

02-49	03-30	05-11	07-25	12-38
19-02	22-21	26-11	27-37	28-74
29-51	47-23	49-01	49-40	49-53
57-58	58-53	60-33	63-46	63-70
64-62	64-95	66-42	70-42	71-17
72-29	73-29	77-63	78-40	79-15
81-25	81-50			

SHÊNG (128b)—Voice, melody, sound, music, tone.

02-40	41-80	80-65

SHIH (6), *shi*—Activities, dealings, work, deeds, business, affairs.

02-55	08-38	17-36	23-35	30-14
31-79	31-83	48-30	48-31	48-34
52-45	57-11	57-77	59-03	61-68
63-04	63-06	63-31	63-39	64-77
64-92	70-20			

SHIH (9a)—Ten times, tenfold.

80-07

SHIH (9b)—So that, causes, thus, because // direct, order, control.

03-04	03-14	03-23	03-47	03-53
53-01	55-66	74-12	80-05	80-14
80-38				

SHIH (19)—Circumstances, environment, surroundings.

51-10

SHIH (24)—Ten.

11-02	50-08	50-14	50-25

SHIH (33)—Master, ruler, officer // leader of troops, captain, general // scholar, student, class of person.

15-05	41-02	41-10	41-18	68-03

SHIH (37)—Loss, failure, abandon, renunciation, lose, be separated from.

13-23	23-49	23-53	23-74	23-76
26-42	26-46	29-29	33-28	38-12
38-65	38-70	38-75	38-80	38-120
64-58	64-73	73-64		

SHIH (38)—Origin, beginning, starting place, first cause.

01-18	14-90	32-40	38-105	52-04
64-48	64-88			

SHIH (40a)—A room, house.

11-31	11-36

SHIH (40b)—Fill, make solid.

03-37

SHIH (50a)—Sell, buy, a market.

62-21

SHIH (50b)—Teacher, instructor, tutor, model // master, sage, leader // army, troops.

27-67   27-79   30-17

SHIH (56)—Model, standard, pattern, example, role model // protector, master, shepherd.

22-28   28-33   28-37   65-45   65-49

SHIH (61)—Claim, rely upon, trust, presume, expect, assert, hold to.

02-75   10-61   34-11   51-64   77-68

SHIH (70)—Stray // do, act, give, use.

53-12

SHIH (72a)—As a pronoun: this, these, that, which // As a verb: is, to be, am // right, correct, positive // such, thus.

02-47	02-85	03-28	06-05	06-13
07-23	10-66	12-36	13-27	14-52
14-62	14-91	16-28	21-07	22-19
22-36	24-15	26-09	27-35	27-55
27-88	29-49	30-68	31-59	36-33
38-05	38-14	38-106	39-100	43-19
44-16	47-21	51-13	51-69	52-69
53-13	53-45	56-27	58-51	59-11
59-53	63-44	63-68	64-60	64-93
65-50	66-22	66-40	66-56	68-25
68-31	68-37	69-20	70-27	70-40
71-13	71-25	72-23	72-27	73-27
74-41	75-11	75-24	75-38	75-49
76-39	77-61	78-38	78-47	78-56
79-13				

SHIH (72b)—Timing, time, the moment, opportunity.

08-43

SHIH (112)—Stone, rock.

39-134

SHIH (113)—Show, reveal, display.

36-55

SHIH (142)—Sting.

55-14

SHIH (147)—Insight, perception, vision, perceive, consider.

14-01   35-29   59-62

SHIH (149)—Understand, comprehend, know.

15-14   15-19   38-97

SHIH (162)—Functioning everywhere, far-reaching, moving away // receding, pass away, depart.

25-45   25-46

SHIH (165)—Melt, thaw, loosen.

15-48

SHIH (184)—Food, nourishment, sustenance, consume.

20-127   24-35   53-40   75-07   80-48

SHOU (29), shou—Hold, keep to, stay, guard, receive, protect, preserve // suffer, bear.

78-43   78-52

SHOU (33)—Live long, longevity // immortal.

33-38

SHOU (40)—Keep, by keeping, hold, cling, hold firm // maintain, abide in, observe, preserve, sustain.

05-44   09-24   16-04   28-04   28-27
28-50   32-18   37-13   52-23   52-54
67-89

SHOU (64)—Hands.

74-58

SHOU (94)—Beasts, animals.

55-16

SHOU (185)—Head, face, front, beginning.

14-71   38-95

SHU (39), shu—Which, who, what.

15-64   15-72   23-16   44-04   44-09
44-14   58-29   73-23   74-27   77-49

SHU (44)—Rely upon, depend on, attach, follow.

19-41

SHU (66)—Calculate, plan, numerous, much, count // accountant.

05-40   27-12   39-121

SHU (103)—Hate, shun // far, space, open, "meshed."

56-41   73-61

SHUANG (89), *shuang*—Dull, blunt // spoiled, ruined.

12-18

SHUI (85), *shui*—Water.

08-04   08-05   78-07

SHUI (115)—Tax, tax-grain, duty on merchandise.

75-08

SHUI (149)—Whose, who.

04-36

SHUN (85), *shun*—Simple, pure, genuine, wholesome, honest.

58-07   58-08

SHUN (181)—Harmony, oneness, conform.

65-69

SO (63), *suo*—That, which, the reason why, because // place, position, spot, "mark."

07-07	08-17	13-41	19-40	20-19
20-61	22-64	30-19	32-55	33-30
42-28	42-55	50-57	50-63	50-69
58-21	58-27	61-76	62-15	62-59
64-113	66-03	72-12	72-17	73-21
80-27	80-35			

SSU (9), *si*—Resembles, seems like, similar.

| 04-11 | 04-30 | 20-118 | 67-08 | 67-15 |

SSU (10)—Rhinoceros, wild buffalo.

50-48   50-55

SSU (30)—Master, official, officer // keep, attend, hold to, take charge of, control.

74-31   74-37   79-27   79-31

SSU (31)—Four, the four directions, on all sides, surround.

10-44   15-35   25-65

SSU (69)—Because of, causes, thus, this.

02-09   02-18

SSU (78)—Die, death, dead.

06-04	33-33	42-67	50-04	50-11
50-22	50-79	67-80	74-04	74-08
74-16	75-31	75-41	76-08	76-22
76-30	80-17	80-71		

SSU (113)—Sacrifice // year.

54-15

SSU (115)—Self-interest, personal concern, ego, selfishness.

07-43   07-49   19-47

SSU (129)—Extend, overreach, severe, straining.

58-66

SSU (187)—Four, a team of four.

62-49

SU (9), *su*—Worldly, common, everyday, practices, customs.

20-83   20-91   80-57

SU (120)—Simple, plain, genuine, unadorned // white silk.

19-43

SUI (162), *sui*—Complete, establish, succeed, achieve.

09-34   17-37

SUI (170)—Follow, imitate, comply with.

02-46   14-72   29-36

SUI (172)—Though, although, even if, rather than.

26-20   27-84   32-06   62-43   80-22
80-30

SUN (39), *sun*—Grandchildren, grandsons.

54-12

SUN (64)—Loss, lose, diminish, decrease, reduce // spoil, harm.

42-52	48-08	48-09	48-12	77-20
77-29	42-44	77-42		

TA (37), *da*—Great.

13-06	13-36	13-44	18-01	18-11
20-37	25-42	25-43	25-54	25-56
25-58	25-61	25-66	27-86	28-83
30-25	34-01	34-49	34-56	34-61
35-02	38-108	41-21	41-52	41-69
41-73	41-77	41-81	44-21	45-01
45-09	45-17	45-21	45-25	46-21
46-28	53-09	53-15	60-02	61-01
61-25	61-39	61-43	61-54	61-78
63-10	63-24	63-38	63-51	63-56
65-68	67-07	67-13	69-36	72-06
74-44	74-49	76-51	79-02	

TA (162)—Penetrate, reach, comprehend, open up.

10-45

TAI (9), *dai*—Instead of, for, substitute, take the place of.

74-36	74-43	74-48

TAI (50)—Carry, carry at one's side // ribbons.

53-35

TAI (78)—Danger, peril // hinder, exhaust, tired.

16-67	25-21	32-58	44-35	52-29

TAI (154)—Give, lend, confer, provide, bestow.

41-93

T'AI (37), *tai*—Great, superior, supreme.

17-01

T'AI (85)—Excessive, broad, abundant, liberal.

29-58	35-13

T'AI (133)—A tower, lookout platform, terrace.

20-42	64-39

TAN (85a), *dan*—Tasteless, flat, insipid, dull // quiet, detached.

31-48	35-24

TAN (85b)—Tranquil, placid, calm.

20-99

TANG (102), *dang*—Because of, by way of.

11-07	11-19	11-32

T'ANG (32), *tang*—Hall, court, residence.

09-20

TAO (108), *dao*—Rob, robbery, theft // thieves, highwaymen.

03-18	19-25	53-47	57-53

TAO (162)—Tao.

01-01	01-03	01-06	04-01	08-22
09-39	14-81	14-93	15-83	16-60
16-61	18-02	21-06	21-09	23-37
23-39	23-43	23-56	23-58	24-31
24-44	25-36	25-53	25-81	25-82
30-02	30-71	30-73	31-15	32-01
32-60	34-02	35-20	37-01	38-66
38-99	40-03	40-08	41-04	41-12
41-20	41-30	41-37	41-41	41-45
41-85	41-91	42-01	46-04	46-13
47-12	48-06	51-01	51-20	51-24
51-39	53-10	53-16	53-50	55-77
55-79	59-64	60-09	62-01	62-56
62-63	65-05	67-06	73-36	77-03
77-28	77-38	77-59	79-34	81-45
81-53				

TÊ (60a), *de*—Obtain, gain, possess, benefit, receive, get, attain.

03-11	12-29	13-19	14-18	22-15
23-61	23-70	23-79	29-13	30-58
31-42	31-72	39-03	39-07	39-12
39-17	39-22	39-28	39-34	42-65
44-11	46-31	52-11	56-34	56-39
56-44	56-49	56-54	56-59	61-74
62-70	64-103	74-22		

TÊ (60b)—*Te*, virtue.

10-69	21-02	23-44	23-48	23-65
23-67	28-16	28-39	28-62	38-02
38-04	38-08	38-10	38-13	38-17
38-19	38-27	38-69	38-71	41-49
41-57	41-62	49-24	49-38	51-04
51-23	51-27	51-42	51-72	54-23
54-31	54-39	54-47	54-56	55-02
59-21	59-24	60-45	63-17	65-53
65-55	68-30	79-26	79-30	

T'Ê (61), *te*—Faulty, falter, err, erring, deviate from, go awry, be wanting.

28-41

TÊNG (104), *deng*—Climb, ascend, mount.

20-40

TI (32), *di*—Earth, place, realm, ground, room, spot.

01-16	05-02	05-22	06-16	07-03
07-06	08-25	23-21	23-23	25-07
25-57	25-75	25-76	32-26	39-11
39-51	50-23	50-80		

TI (50)—Lord of Heaven, the Creator, Ancestor.

04-40

TI (66)—Enemy, opponent.

68-14	69-30	69-39	69-41

TI (75)—Stem, stalk, planted // root, basis, foundation, origin.

59-58

TI (85)—Wash, cleanse.

10-18

T'IEN (37), *tian*—Heaven.

01-15	02-01	05-01	05-21	06-15
07-01	07-05	09-37	10-34	13-64
13-69	13-75	13-80	16-57	16-58
22-26	22-55	23-20	23-22	25-06
25-25	25-55	25-78	25-79	26-38
28-08	28-12	28-31	28-35	28-54
28-58	29-04	29-15	30-11	31-75
32-08	32-25	32-63	35-04	37-46
39-06	39-38	39-44	40-11	43-01
43-08	43-35	45-38	46-01	46-10
47-05	47-11	48-25	48-39	49-43
49-48	52-01	52-07	54-53	54-77
54-80	54-86	56-64	57-13	57-24
59-04	60-11	61-06	61-10	62-38
62-78	63-28	63-36	66-58	66-70
67-01	67-45	67-59	67-92	68-40
70-09	73-19	73-34	73-57	77-01
77-27	77-55	78-01	78-30	78-58
79-33	81-43			

T'IEN (61)—Peace, calm, tranquility.

31-47

T'IEN (102a)—Field.

53-26

T'IEN (102b)—Cultivate.

12-21

TING (40), *ding*—Settle, fix, anchor, certain // peace, calm.

37-50

T'ING (8), *ting*—Protect // pavilion.

51-49

T'ING (128)—Hear, listen // a court, tribunal.

14-08	35-34

TO (36), *duo*—More, many, much, abundant, a lot, excess.

05-38	22-16	44-10	44-23	57-26
57-34	57-42	57-55	63-12	63-63
63-66	65-22	75-10	81-42	

TO (37)—Deprive, grasp, take by force, despoil.
36-27

T'O (75), *tuo*—Bellows, sack.
05-27

T'O (130)—Take, leave, separate // escape.
36-45   54-10

T'O (149)—Entrust, care for, guard, guardian.
13-79

T'OU (9), *tou*—Unsteady, frail, "shabby" // fraudulent, remiss, steal.
41-64

T'OU (64)—Butt, thrust, insert, place.
50-58

TSAI (30), *zai*—!, ?, indeed.

20-30	20-79	21-69	22-73	53-52
54-89	57-21			

TSAI (32)—To be, being, exist, presence, alive // govern.
24-30   32-62   49-42

TSAI (40)—Rule, dominate, lord over, control.
10-65   51-68

TSAI (159)—Carry, hold, keep, contain, bear.
10-01

TS'AI (120), *cai*—Clothes, gown // colored clothes.
53-34

TS'AI (154)—Wealth, riches.
53-41

TS'ANG (9), *cang*—Granary.
53-29

TS'ANG (140)—Hoard, store up, pile up, hide.
44-24

TSAO (72), *zao*—Soon, early, morning.
30-74   55-80   59-13   59-15

TSAO (157)—Restless, agitated, rash, hasty, motion.
26-07   26-44   45-29

TS'AO (140), *cao*—Grass.
76-14

TSÊ (18), *ze*—Then, thus // follow, imitate, emulate // on that account, accordingly.

03-64	22-02	22-05	22-08	22-11
22-14	22-17	22-67	26-41	26-45
28-71	28-78	30-66	31-22	31-27
31-68	38-58	55-72	59-25	59-32
61-31	61-41	64-89	67-86	67-90
70-36	72-05	73-04	73-10	76-43
76-48	77-39			

TSÊ (154a)—Make claim, exact one's due, pressure // blame, punish, chastise.
65-30   79-22

TSÊ (154b)—Robber, bandit, thief.
19-26   57-54

TS'Ê (118), *ce*—Bamboo slips, counting rods, calculator.
27-16

TS'ÊNG (44), *ceng*—Stories, levels, layer.
64-37

TSO (9a), *zuo*—Arise, make, work, flourish, come into being, bring about.
02-63   16-10   16-44   37-23   55-38
63-33   63-41

TSO (9b)—Assist, aid, guide.
30-03

TSO (32)—Sit down, kneel, remain still, sitting still, calm.
62-53

TSO (48)—Left, the left side, ~second in command.
31-24   31-81   31-90   34-07   79-18

TSO (167)—Cut out, chisel.
11-26

TS'O (64), *cuo*—Blunt, break, dull, temper // wrong.
04-16   29-46   56-15

TSOU (156), *zou*—Race, galloping, fast, racing.
46-06

TSU (157), *zu*—Adequate, enough, sufficient, content.
17-23   19-36   23-83   28-64   33-19
35-32   35-37   35-42   41-27   41-60
44-29   46-25   46-34   46-36   46-38
48-36   64-50   77-23   77-35   77-44

TS'U (64), *cu*—Put, place, arrange, put in place, fix, attach.
50-64

TSUI (122), *zui*—Sin, crime, wrongdoers, guilty, offend, sinner.
62-72

TS'UI (130), *cui*—Brittle, fragile, crisp, delicate, supple, frail.
64-11   76-20

TSUN (41), *zun*—Esteem, honor, worship, revere, respect, high rank, noble.
51-19   51-26   62-22

TS'UN (39), *cun*—Continue, remain, exist, be.
04-32   06-21   07-38   41-14

TS'UN (41)—An inch.
69-16

TSUNG (40), *zong*—Ancestor, forefather // source, root.
04-15   70-19

TS'UNG (60), *cong*—Follow, comply with, pursue.
21-08   23-34   64-76

TU (80), *du*—Mature, prepare, ripen, cook.
51-51

TU (94)—Alone, single, solitary, isolated.
20-44   20-70   20-88   20-96   20-116
20-121   25-13

TU (118)—Constant, firm, steadfast.
16-06

T'U (31), *tu*—Plan, plan for, prepare, arrange for, deal with, tackle, contemplate.
63-18

T'U (32)—Earth, clay, bricks.
64-43

T'U (60)—Companion, comrade, disciple, ~go on foot with, pursuers.
50-07   50-13   76-32   76-38

TUAN (111), *duan*—Short.
02-32

TUI (10), *dui*—Mouth, opening, passages, apertures, ~senses.
52-32   52-42   56-11

T'UI (64), *tui*—Exalt, praise // support, uphold, push forward.
66-61

T'UI (162)—Retreat, withdraw, draw back, retire.
09-36   41-43   69-18

TUN (66), *dun*—Simple, genuine // thick, solid.
15-49

T'UN (85), *tun*—Confused, chaotic, nebulous, torrent.
20-80   20-81

TUNG (15), *dong*—Winter.
15-28

TUNG (19)—Movement, motion, action, shake, activity, stirring.
05-34   08-41   15-77   40-05   50-20

T'UNG (30), *tong*—Alike, the same, unity, together, identify with, oneness, resemble, be of, becomes one.
01-43   01-48   04-25   23-41   23-46
23-51   23-54   23-63   23-72   56-24
56-30

T'UNG (162)—Penetrate, comprehend, go through.
15-10

TZU (39), *zi*—Philosopher, ruler // child, infant, son, children.
04-38   25-33   31-20   31-38   52-17
52-21   54-11   55-08   62-39

TZU (85)—More and more, multiply, increase, greater amount.
57-39   57-47   57-51

TZU (132)—I, my, self, themselves, himself // naturally, spontaneously, of itself, of its own accord // from, since.
07-17   09-29   17-43   21-49   22-30
22-35   22-40   22-46   23-03   24-09

24-14   24-19   24-24   25-84   32-23
32-38   33-05   33-14   34-54   37-18
37-49   39-104   51-36   57-66   57-73
57-80   57-87   64-120   72-31   72-34
72-36   72-39   73-50

TZU (154)—Material, lesson, resources, raw material, valuables, property.
27-75   27-83

TZU (159)—Baggage, baggage-wagon, ~something heavy.
26-18

TZ'U (61), *ci*—Parental love, affection, compassion.
18-19   19-16   67-36   67-48   67-69
67-83   67-97

TZ'U (76)—The former, the other, next, second.
12-49   17-08   17-14   17-18   38-129
72-45

TZ'U (77)—This, these, then.
01-40   14-22   15-82   19-29   21-71
23-18   39-110   54-91   57-23   62-55
62-62   65-40   73-12

TZ'U (104)—Fault, flaw, stain, malady.
10-24

TZ'U (160)—Refuse, deny, decline, reject, disown, turn away from.
02-67   34-17

TZ'U (172)—Female bird, mother bird, female.
10-40   28-06

WA (116), *wa*—Empty, hollow // field, low ground.
22-07

WAI (36), *wai*—Reject, exclude, put away, outside.
07-33

WAN (72), *wan*—Not yet, late, evening, slow to.

41-75

WAN (140)—Ten thousand, all.

01-21	02-61	04-12	05-06	08-08
16-07	26-30	32-20	34-09	34-25
34-38	37-15	39-26	39-72	40-13
42-12	42-14	51-15	62-03	64-117
76-12				

WAN (181)—Thickheaded, stupid, awkward, stubborn.

20-117

WANG (8), *wang*—Loss, lose // die, cease.

41-16	44-13	44-27

WANG (38)—Error, falsehood.

16-43

WANG (60)—Go, pass, depart // follow // attract.

35-06	35-07

WANG (61)—Die, perish, cease // forget.

33-36

WANG (74)—See, overlook, in sight of // visit.

80-61	80-74

WANG (75)—Crooked, distorted, wronged, bent, bow, curl.

22-04

WANG (95)—King, kingly, royal, noble.

16-54	16-55	25-59	25-68	32-15
37-10	39-33	39-81	39-103	42-36
66-09	66-21	78-60		

WANG (120)—Net, web.

73-58

WEI (9), *wei*—False, hypocrisy, falsehood, pretense.

18-12

WEI (30a)—Taste, tasting, flavor.

12-14	35-28	63-07	63-09

WEI (30b)—Exactly, for this exact reason, only // consent, "yes," definite reply.

02-82	08-45	15-16	15-89	20-01
22-51	41-90	42-30	53-11	59-09
67-12	70-24	71-10	72-20	75-43
77-57				

WEI (38)—In awe, respect, fear, imposing, dreadful, force, power.

17-15	72-04	72-07

WEI (60)—Mystery, secret, subtle, profound // small, minute, trifle, fading away, formless.

14-21	15-07	36-35	64-15

WEI (61)—Only, entirely, exactly, since.

21-05	21-13	21-15

WEI (75)—Not, does not, no.

20-28	20-48	20-54	55-30	64-06
64-21	64-26			

WEI (87)—Act, make, become, being, form, do, practice, work.

02-07	02-16	02-53	02-72	03-17
03-59	03-61	03-63	05-08	05-18
10-39	10-48	10-58	11-17	11-30
11-43	11-48	12-40	12-43	13-17
13-47	13-63	13-74	14-32	15-04
19-33	21-11	22-25	23-17	25-24
25-38	26-02	26-06	28-07	28-11
28-30	28-34	28-53	28-57	28-72
28-79	29-07	29-21	29-23	31-49
34-29	34-44	34-48	34-55	37-04
37-08	38-21	38-25	38-28	38-33
38-36	38-41	38-44	38-49	38-52
39-37	39-93	39-98	39-114	41-29
42-24	42-39	42-71	43-23	43-32
45-37	47-34	48-01	48-05	48-17
48-19	48-23	49-10	49-47	51-61
52-06	56-63	57-63	58-38	58-42
61-22	61-81	62-77	63-01	63-03
63-23	63-50	64-18	64-52	64-65

64-125   65-04   66-06   66-18   67-44
67-58   68-02   68-22   69-08   69-11
74-18   75-23   75-47   77-65   79-11
81-31   81-54

WEI (102)—Fear, dread, afraid of.

15-34   20-20   20-24   53-14   72-03
74-03   74-15

WEI (144)—Guard, protect, save.

67-98

**WEI (149)—Speak, say, call, tell of, describe //
imply.**

01-49   06-06   06-14   10-67   13-11
13-28   13-34   14-53   14-63   14-92
15-22   16-29   17-41   22-65   27-56
27-89   30-69   36-34   39-105 51-70
52-70   53-46   55-74   56-28   59-12
59-17   59-54   65-51   67-04   68-26
68-32   68-38   69-21   74-42   78-48
78-57

**WÊN (67), wen—Decoration, adornment,
ornament, elegant.**

19-34   53-33

WÊN (128)—Hear, listen.

14-11   35-38   41-03   41-11   41-19
50-38   80-67

WO (62), wo—I, we.

17-42   20-43   20-69   20-73   20-87
20-95   20-115 20-120 42-57   53-02
57-61   57-68   57-75   57-82   67-05
67-26

WO (64)—Grasp, hold, shake.

55-28

WU (7), wu—Five.

12-01   12-07   12-13

WU (9)—Insult, despise, revile, contempt, defy.

17-19

WU (20)—Not, without, do not.

30-45   30-49   30-53   30-62

WU (30)—I, me, mine, we, you, they.

04-33   13-40   13-48   13-52   13-55
16-11   21-61   25-28   29-09   37-24
42-68   43-18   49-14   49-20   49-28
49-34   54-82   57-15   69-05   69-44
70-01   70-30   70-33   70-37   74-21

**WU (61)—Detest, loathe, despise, disdain, "ugly-
hearted."**

02-10   08-18   20-12   24-40   31-11
42-29   65-61   73-22

WU (77)—War, warlike, violent, aggressive.

68-06

**WU (86)—Without, nothing, free of, not having,
emptiness // <u>non-being</u>, non-existence.**

01-13   <u>01-27</u> <u>02 24</u> 02-52   03-49
03-51   03-62   03-65   07-42   08-49
10-07   10-23   10-31   (10-39) 10-47
11-09   11-21   11-34   11-45   13-53
14-50   14-54   14-58   19-19   [20-03]
19-27   20-60   20-107 24-22   27-03
27-08   27-19   27-28   27-44   27-52
28-45   32-03   34-32   35-27   37-03
37-06   37-29   37-33   37-40   38-16
38-20   38-23   38-39   39-45   39-52
39-59   39-66   39-74   39-82   39-123
<u>40-21</u> 41-71   41-83   41-87   43-13
43-16   43-22   43-31   46-12   48-16
48-18   48-21   48-29   49-03   50-56
50-62   50-68   50-78   52-65   57-10
57-62   57-76   57-83   58-34   59-26
59-29   63-02   63-05   63-08   63-77
64-64   64-67   64-69   64-72   64-90
69-23   69-26   69-29   69-32   70-25
72-09   72-14   75-44   78-18   79-29
79-35   80-26   80-34

WU (93)—Things, existence, object, substance // creatures, beings.

01-22	02-62	04-13	05-07	08-09
14-51	14-59	16-08	16-16	21-12
21-32	24-38	25-02	27-50	27-54
29-32	30-64	31-09	32-21	34-10
34-26	34-39	37-16	39-27	39-73
40-14	42-13	42-15	42-42	51-07
51-16	55-70	57-46	62-04	64-118
76-13				

WU (140)—Weeds, weedy.

53-28

YANG (37), *yang*—End, limit, utmost, dawn.

20-29

YANG (78)—Misfortune, calamity, danger, distress, peril.

52-68

YANG (170)—Yang, ~positive, male principle, ~complement of yin.

42-20

YANG (184)—Rear, nourish, feed, nurture, care for.

34-24　　51-53

YAO (38), *yao*—Unlucky, bewitch, spooked // evil, ominous, sinister.

58-43

YAO (86)—Shining, luminous, bright, brilliant, blinding, flashy, dazzle.

58-70

YAO (116)—Hidden, deep, profound, secret // dark, obscure, dim, shadowy.

21-33

YAO (146)—Significant, essential, crucial, important, crux.

27-90

YEH (5), *ye*—!, indeed.

03-60	20-78	24-32	29-22	32-13
53-51	55-42	55-52	67-24	76-04
76-09	76-18	76-23		

YEN (9), *yan*—Reserved, grave, reverent // as if.

15-37

YEN (27)—Excessive, extreme, beyond limit, filled with, satisfied // oppressed.

53-38	66-64	72-15	72-22	72-26

YEN (32)—Knead, mold, shape, turn on wheel.

11-14

YEN (86a)—There, in that place // how, why, indeed.

02-64	15-26	17-24	17-28	23-84
23-88	25-72	30-24	34-41	60-48

YEN (86b)—Calm, composed, peaceful, at ease // a swallow, a feast.

26-24

YEN (149)—Words, speech, talking, saying.

02-58	05-39	08-32	17-33	22-72
23-02	27-07	31-96	41-33	43-28
56-04	56-05	62-18	66-29	69-04
70-02	70-17	73-43	78-62	81-02
81-06				

YI (1), *yi*—Unity, one, alike, whole, wholeness, undivided, oneness.

10-05	11-05	14-33	22-24	25-71
39-04	39-08	39-13	39-18	39-23
39-29	39-35	42-03	42-04	67-34

YI (8)—Also, again, moreover, and.

23-59	23-68	23-77	25-60	32-45
32-49	37-38	42-58	49-21	49-35
50-24	60-35	65-43		

YI (9a)—Although, for, that, by means of, by, with, because // thereby, thus, accordingly, a reason, a cause // to use, to aid // >When it precedes a verb, it marks manner, result, or intention; when it follows a verb, it means "reason" or "cause."

01-29	01-36	02-48	02-86	03-29
05-05	05-15	07-08	07-14	07-24
07-40	11-16	11-29	11-42	11-47
12-37	13-42	13-61	13-72	14-82
15-67	15-75	16-12	19-32	20-113
21-57	21-63	21-70	22-20	25-23
26-10	26-35	27-36	29-50	30-01
30-08	30-40	31-71	31-97	31-106
31-113	32-29	34-50	36-54	37-28
37-44	38-06	38-15	38-24	38-32
38-40	38-48	38-107	39-09	39-14
39-19	39-24	39-30	39-36	39-46
39-53	39-60	39-67	39-75	39-83
39-91	39-96	39-101	39-112	41-28
42-23	42-38	42-70	43-20	44-37
46-08	47-22	48-13	48-28	48-37
49-06	50-31	50-76	51-14	52-05
52-14	54-13	54-60	54-64	54-68
54-72	54-76	54-84	54-90	57-01
57-05	57-09	57-17	57-22	58-52
59-42	59-50	60-08	61-16	61-20
61-27	61-37	61-48	62-20	62-25
62-47	62-60	62-68	62-73	63-16
63-45	63-69	64-61	64-94	64-115
65-08	65-12	65-19	65-24	65-32
66-04	66-11	66-23	66-28	66-36
66-41	66-57	66-65	67-84	67-88
67-96	70-28	70-41	71-14	71-21
71-26	72-24	72-28	73-28	74-07
75-04	75-12	75-18	75-25	75-32
75-39	75-45	76-40	77-45	77-53
77-62	78-19	78-39	79-10	79-14
81-30	81-37			

YI (9b)—Support, lean upon, trust, rely on, depend on.

58-22

YI (37)—Invisible, colorless, very dim // straight, level, even, plain // easy, smooth.

14-07	41-44	53-18

YI (40)—Fit, proper, right, should, ought to, fitting, behooves, must.

61-80

YI (49)—Only, alone // end, cease, stop, finish, decline, !, ~a final particle.

02-11	02-21	09-08	29-14	30-37
30-59	30-75	31-43	55-81	

YI (64)—Bring down, press down, keep back, curb, lower // repress, restrain, stop.

77-11

YI (72)—Easy // replace, substitute, change places with.

02-28	63-22	63-35	63-64	64-03
64-08	64-12	64-16	70-04	70-07
78-20				

YI (102)—Differ, different, diverse, foreign // bizarre, unusual // divide, separate.

01-46	20-122

YI (108)—Gain, increase, augment, add to, more and more, to a higher degree // benefit, advance, promote, advantageous.

42-47	42-49	43-26	43-34	48-04
55-61				

YI (111)—!, indeed.

31-77	46-39	63-79	65-57	65-59
65-63	67-21	67-81	69-54	74-59

YI (123)—Virtue, righteousness, justice, morality, rectitude, right, upright // duty, loyalty, "that which enables the heart to rule itself."

18-06	19-12	38-43	38-79	38-81

YI (145)—Clothes, garments // a cover, a husk.

34-23

YI (162)—What follows, bring about //
deficient, at a loss // transmit, bequeath.
09-30   20-72   52-66

YIN (170a), *yin*—Yin, ~female principle,
~complement of yang.
42-17
YIN (170b)—Hidden, concealed, in the
background.
41-86
YIN (180)—Music, sound, musical note, tone.
02-39   12-08   41-78
YIN (184)—Drinks, drinking.
53-39

YING (39), *ying*—Infant, newborn.
10-15   20-51   28-22
YING (61)—Answer, respond // fulfill.
38-57   73-46
YING (86)—Regulate, govern, manage.
10-02
YING (108)—Exhausted, depleted, drained //
full, fullness, replenish, excess.
04-08   09-03   15-87   15-91   22-09
39-25   39-68   45-10
YING (162)—Front // meet, go toward.
14-66

YO (118), *yo*—Pipes, bellows.
05-28
YO (120)—String, bind, tie up.
27-30

YU (29), *you*—Again, and, also, higher degree.
01-54   48-11
YU (30)—Right, right side, ~side of honor.
31-29   31-85   31-95   34-08
YU (43)—Fault, calamity, wrong, error.
08-50

YU (61a)—Reluctant.
17-29
YU (61b)—Sorrow, anxiety, distress.
19-20   [20-04]
YU (74)—Have, own, possess, hold // existence,
being, to be // arise, emerge, appear.

01-19	01-34	02-23	02-71	10-57
11-10	11-22	11-35	11-40	13-43
13-49	13-56	14-86	17-05	17-25
18-04	18-10	18-17	18-24	(19-18d)
19-28	19-39	20-66	20-112	21-23
21-31	21-39	21-47	22-43	23-85
24-43	25-01	25-64	26-21	30-30
31-14	32-42	32-47	33-12	33-25
34-22	38-07	38-31	38-47	40-17
40-18	43-14	43-25	46-03	48-33
50-09	50-15	50-26	51-60	52-03
53-05	53-43	57-56	59-43	59-45
62-35	62-44	62-71	64-22	67-27
69-03	70-18	70-21	74-30	74-54
75-22	77-17	77-30	77-47	77-51
77-58	79-05	79-25	80-06	80-23
80-31	81-35			

YU (91)—Window.
11-28   47-09
YU (94)—Is like, similar, resembles // watchful,
vigilant, alert.
05-26   15-31   32-65   63-72   73-31
77-05

YUNG (19), *yong*—Brave, daring, courageous,
fearless.
67-51   67-71   73-01   73-06
YUNG (101)—Use, utility, function, purpose,
apply, employ, operate, put to use.

04-04	06-22	11-13	11-25	11-38
11-49	27-14	28-76	31-25	31-45
35-39	40-10	45-06	45-14	52-58
57-07	68-19	68-33	69-01	80-13
80-44				

YÜ (32), *yu*—Region, world, universe, realm, country // limit.

25-62

YÜ (60)—Govern, manage, control, direct.

14-83

YÜ (61a)—More, further, exceed, greater // rejoice.

05-36   81-34   81-41

YÜ (61b)—Foolish, folly, ignorant, ignorance, stupid, simple.

20-74   38-103   65-13

YÜ (70)—To, with, compared with, through, in, as, from, become.

08-21	14-49	20-123	23-30	23-36
23-42	23-47	23-52	23-55	23-64
23-73	28-21	28-44	28-67	31-74
32-69	34-36	36-46	40-16	40-20
46-17	46-22	46-29	48-15	53-08
54-20	54-28	54-36	54-44	54-52
55-06	63-20	63-25	63-34	63-42
64-20	64-25	64-33	64-41	64-49
64-79	69-37	73-02	73-07	75-51
78-06	79-23			

YÜ (76)—Deep-seated desires, mental tendencies, habits, desires, thought constructs, mental patterns.

01-28	01-35	03-22	03-52	15-86
19-49	29-02	34-33	36-02	36-10
36-18	36-26	37-22	37-41	37-43
39-126	46-30	57-84	61-58	61-66
61-77	64-97	64-99	66-24	66-32
77-76				

YÜ (85)—Unsteady, changing, fickle, fluid, "melted" // to soil, contaminate.

41-68

YÜ (95)—Jade, jewels, gem.

09-18   39-130   70-47

YÜ (130)—Nurture, bring up, to rear, develop, nourish, educate.

51-47

YÜ (134)—Give, share, supplement, add to, replenish, expand // and, or // unite, join, with.

08-29	20-03	20-11	22-59	35-15
36-31	44-02	44-07	44-12	65-60
66-74	68-17	77-08	79-38	81 38

YÜ (149)—Praise, honor, extol, fame // carriage.

17-11

YÜ (152)—Cautious, hesitant, careful // elephant.

15-25

YÜ (159)—Praise, honor, success, fame // carriage, cart.

39-122   39-124   80-25

YÜ (162)—Meet with, encounter // occur.

50-46

YÜ (170)—Corner, boundary, angle.

41-72

YÜ (173)—Rain.

23-12

YÜ (184)—Surplus, excess, remainder, too much, abundance.

20-67	24-34	53-44	54-33	77-18
77-31	77-48	77-52	79-06	

YÜ (195)—Fish.

36-42

YÜAN (10), *yuan*—Origin, first cause, beginning. (Used instead of HSÜAN [96] in some texts).

(01-51)	(01-52)	(01-55)	(06-07)	(06-09)
(10-20)	(10-68)	(15-09)	(51-71)	(56-29)
(65-52)	(65-54)			

YÜAN (61)—Hatred, grudge, ill treatment, injury, malice, enmity, envy.

63-15   79-03   79-07

YÜAN (85)—Deep, fathomless, profound, abyss.

04-09   08-28   36-47

YÜAN (162)—Far away, distant, removed.

25-48	25-49	47-16	65-58	80-20

YÜEH (73), *yue*—Speak, call, say, said, describe, known as.

14-06	14-13	14-20	16-26	16-34
16-38	24-33	25-35	25-41	25-44
25-47	25-50	52-52	52-56	55-55
55-59	55-63	55-68	62-67	67-35
67-38	67-41			

YÜEH (169)—See, watch, look at, survey, witness, recall.

21-58

YÜN (7), *yun*—Say, speak, declare.

57-60	78-42

YÜN (140)—Flourish, bloom.

16-17	16-18

LIST OF RADICALS

Radicals formed of one stroke

一 (1) YI — One, alike, unite.

丨 (2) KUN — A vertical line, to thread.

丶 (3) CHU — A point, a dot.

丿 (4) P'IEH — A stroke to the left.

乙 (5) YI — A cyclical character.

亅 (6) CHÜEH — To mark.

Two strokes

二 (7) ERH — Two, dual.

亠 (8) WANG — To die, cease, loss.

人 (9) JÊN (a) — Man, person, human.

儿 (10) WU — Stool.

入 (11) JU — To enter, penetrate, go in.

八 (12) PA — Eight.

冂 (13) CHIUNG — Wastelands.

冖 (14) YU — Doubtful, hesitant.

冫 (15) TUNG — Winter, the end.

几 (16) CHI — Small table.

凵 (17) HSIUNG — Unlucky, misfortune.

刀 (18) TAO — Knife.

力 (19) LI — Strength, ability, power.

勹 (20) SHAO — To wrap around, enfold.

匕 (21) PI — Spoon.

匚 (22) FANG — Chest.

匸 (23) HSI — Conceal.

十 (24) SHIH — Ten, perfect.

卜 (25) PU — To divine.

卩 (26) CHIEH — Authority, badge.

厂 (27) HAN — Cliff.

厶 (28) SSU — Private.

又 (29) YU — The right hand, more.

Three strokes

口 (30) K'OU — Mouth.

囗 (31) WEI — Enclosure.

土 (32) T'U — Earth, ground, soil.

士 (33) SHIH — Scholar, officer, warrior.

夂 (34) CHIH — March, progress.

夊 (35) SUI — Walk slowly.

夕 (36) HSI — Evening, end.

大 (37) TA — Great.

女 (38) NÜ — Woman.

子 (39) TZU — Philosopher // child, infant.

宀 (40) MIEN — Roof.

寸 (41) TS'UN — A little, an inch.

小 (42) HSIAO — Small.

尢 (43) WANG — Lame.

尸 (44) SHIH — Corpse.

屮 (45) CH'Ê — Sprout.

山 (46) SHAN — Mountain.

巛 (47) CH'UAN — River, stream, flow.

工 (48) KUNG — Work, labor.

己 (49) CHI — One's self.

巾 (50) CHIN — Handkerchief.

干 (51) KAN — A shield.

幺 (52) YAO — Small, tender.

广 (53) YEN — Covering.

辶 (54) YIN — To move on.

廾 (55) KUNG — Folded hands.

弋 (56) YI — A dart.

弓 (57) KUNG — A bow, a measure.

彐 (58) CHI — Hog's head.

彡 (59) SHAN — Feathers, hair.

彳 (60) CH'IH — To step, walk.

Four strokes

心 (61) HSIN — Heart, mind.

戈 (62) KO — A spear.

戶 (63) HU — Door, window, dwelling.

手 (64) SHOU — Hand, workman.

支 (65) CHIH — Branch, twig.

攴 (66) P'U — To tap.

文 (67) WÊN — Stokes, lines.

斗 (68) TOU — Vessel, peck measure.

斤 (69) CHIN — Hatchet.

方 (70) FANG — Place, region, square.

无 (71) WU — Negative, not.

日 (72) JIH — Sun, days, daily.

曰 (73) YÜEH — Speak, call, describe.

月 (74) YÜEH — The moon.

木 (75) MU — Tree, wood.

欠 (76) CH'IEN — Owe, be wanting.

止 (77) CHIH — Stop.

歹 (78) TAI — Bad, evil, danger.

殳 (79) CH'U — Arm, stick, spear.

毋 (80) WU — Not, do not.

比 (81) PI — Examine, compare // join.

毛 (82) MAO — Hair, feathers, down.

氏 (83) SHIH — Family.

气 (84) CH'I — Vapor, spirit, cloudy.

水 (85) SHUI — Water.

火 (86) HOU — Fire.

爪 (87) CHAO — A claw.

父 (88) FU — Father, beginning.

爻 (89) YAO — Lines of a diagram.

爿 (90) CH'IANG — Wood.

片 (91) P'IEN — Leaf, section.

牙 (92) YA — Teeth.

牛 (93) NIU — Ox.

犬 (94) CH'ÜAN — Dog.

Five strokes

玉 (95) YÜ — Jade, jewels, gem.

立 (96) HSÜAN — Dark, hidden, obscure.

瓜 (97) KUA — Plants.

瓦 (98) WA — Tiles, bricks, pottery.

甘 (99) KAN — Enjoy, agreeable, sweet.

生 (100) SHÊNG — Life, produce, come forth.

用 (101) YUNG — Use, function, purpose.

田 (102) T'IEN (a) — A field, cultivate.

疋 (103) P'I — Roll of cloth.

疒 (104) NI — Disease.

癶 (105) PO — Back.

白 (106) PAI — White, pure, clear.

皮 (107) P'I — Skin, leather, a covering.

皿 (108) MIN — A dish.

目 (109) MU — Eye.

矛 (110) MAO — Halberd.

矢 (111) SHIH — A dart, swift, to shoot.

石 (112) SHIH — Stone, rock.

示 (113) SHIH — To reveal, teach.

禸 (114) JOU — Footprint, step.

禾 (115) HO — Grain.

穴 (116) HSÜEH — Cave, den, cavern.

立 (117) LI — Stand, stand firm.

Six strokes

竹 (118) CHU — Bamboo.

米 (119) MI — Grains of rice.

糸 (120) SSU — Threads.

缶 (121) FAO — Earthenware vessel.

网 (122) WANG — Trap, capture.

羊 (123) YANG — Sheep, goat.

羽 (124) YÜ — Wings, feathers.

老 (125) LAO — Old, decay, exhaustion.

而 (126) ERH — Whiskers.

耒 (127) LEI — A harrow.

耳 (128) ERH — Ear.

聿 (129) YÜ — Pen, pencil.

肉 (130) JOU — Flesh, meat.

臣 (131) CH'EN — Minister, master, rule over.

自 (132) TZU — I, myself // itself.

至 (133) CHIH — To go, to reach.

臼 (134) CHIU — Mortar.

舌 (135) SHÊ — Tongue.

舛 (136) CH'UAN — Error, mistake.

舟 (137) CHOU — Boat.

艮 (138) KÊN — Defy, resist.

色 (139) SHÊ — Color, manner.

艸 (140) TS'AO — Plant, grass.

虍 (141) HU — Tiger.

虫 (142) CH'UNG — Insect.

血 (143) HSÜEH — Blood.

行 (144) HSING — Step, go out // action, do.

衣 (145) YI — Clothes.

襾 (146) HSIA — A cover.

Seven strokes

見 (147) CHIEN — To see, display, show off.

角 (148) CHIAO — Horn.

言 (149) YEN — Words, to speak, say.

谷 (150) KU — Valley, ravine, abyss.

豆 (151) TOU — Vessel.

豕 (152) SHIH — Pig.

豸 (153) CHIH — Reptile.

貝 (154) PEI — Money, valuables, shell.

赤 (155) CH'IH — Infant, naked.

走 (156) TSOU — Walk, march, gallop.

足 (157) TSU — Enough, satisfied // feet.

身 (158) SHÊN — Body, person, oneself.

車 (159) CH'Ê — Cart, track, rut.

辛 (160) HSIN — Bitter, toilsome.

辰 (161) CH'ÊN — Time, planets.

辵 (162) CHO — Going.

邑 (163) YI — Walled city.

酉 (164) YU — Cyclical character.

釆 (165) PIEN — Sort, separate.

里 (166) LI — Third of a mile // village.

Eight strokes

金 (167) CHIN — Metal, gold, bronze.

長 (168) CHANG — Increase, grow.

門 (169) MÊN — Door, gate, entrance.

阜 (170) FU — Mound.

隶 (171) TAI — To reach.

隹 (172) CHUI — Short-tailed birds.

雨 (173) YÜ — Rain.

青 (174) CH'ING — Green, blue, black.

非 (175) FEI — Not, opposing.

Nine strokes

面 (176) MIEN — The face, front.

革 (177) KO — Change, degrade.

韋 (178) WEI — Pliant, flexible, soft.

韭 (179) CHIU — Leeks.

音 (180) YIN — Sound, musical note.

頁 (181) YEH — Head, beginning.

風 (182) FÊNG — Custom, habit, wind.

飛 (183) FEI — To fly, swift.

食 (184) SHIH — Eat, food, nourishment.

首 (185) SHOU — Head, chief.

香 (186) HSIANG — Smell, incense.

Ten strokes

馬 (187) MA — Horse.

骨 (188) KU — Bone, skeleton.

高 (189) KAO — High, lofty.

髟 (190) PIAO — Hair.

鬥 (191) TOU — Quarrel.

鬯 (192) CH'ANG — Sacrificial wine.

鬲 (193) KO — Three-legged pot.

鬼 (194) KUEI — Ghost, spirit.

Eleven strokes

魚 (195) YÜ — Fish.

鳥 (196) NIAO — Bird.

鹵 (197) LU — Salt.

鹿 (198) LU — Deer, stag.

麥 (199) MA — Corn.

麻 (200) MA — Plant fibers.

Twelve or more strokes

黃 (201) HUANG — Yellow.

黍 (202) SHU — Millet.

黑 (203) HEI — Black, dark, evil.

黹 (204) CHIH — Embroidery.

黽 (205) MIN — Toad, make an effort.

鼎 (206) TING — Tripod.

鼓 (207) KU — A drum.

鼠 (208) SHU — Rat.

鼻 (209) PI — The nose.

齊 (210) CH'I — Even, harmony.

齒 (211) CH'IH — Front teeth, mouth.

龍 (212) LUNG — Dragon.

龜 (213) KUEI — Tortoise.

龠 (214) YAO — Pipes.

APPENDIX: SOME OF THE EARLIEST ENGLISH TRANSLATIONS OF VERSE ONE

The *tau* (reason) which can be *tau*-ed (reasoned) is not the Eternal *Tau* (Reason). The name which can be named is not the Eternal Name.

    Non-existence is named the Antecedent of heaven and earth; and Existence is named the Mother of all things. In eternal non-existence, therefore, man seeks to pierce the primordial mystery; and, in eternal existence, to behold the issues of the Universe. But these two are one and the same, and differ only in name.

    This sameness (of existence and non-existence) I call the abyss—the abyss of abysses—the gate of all mystery.

**John Chalmers
(1868)**

1. The Tao that can be trodden is not the enduring and unchanging Tao. The name that can be named is not the enduring and unchanging name.

**James Legge
(1891)**

2. (Conceived of as) having no name, it is the Originator of heaven and earth; (conceived of as) having a name, it is the Mother of all things.

3.   Always without desire we must be found,
               If its deep mystery we would sound;
               But if desire always within us be,
               Its outer fringe is all that we shall see.

4. Under these two aspects, it is really the same; but as development takes place, it receives the different names. Together we call them the Mystery.

Where the Mystery is the deepest is the gate of all that is subtle and wonderful.

G. G. Alexander
(1895)

God (the great everlasting infinite First Cause from whom all things in heaven and earth proceed) can neither be defined nor named.

For the God which can be defined or named is but the Creator, the Great Mother of all those things of which our senses have cognisance.

Now he who would gain a knowledge of the nature and attributes of the nameless and undefinable God, must first set himself free from all earthly desires, for unless he can do this, he will be unable to penetrate the material veil which interposes between him and those spiritual conditions into which he would obtain an insight.

Yet the spiritual and the material, though known to us under different names, are similar in origin, and issue from the same source, and the same obscurity belongs to both, for deep indeed is the darkness which enshrouds the portals through which we have to pass, in order to gain a knowledge of these mysteries.

I. W. Heysinger
(1903)

The way that can be overtrod is not the Eternal Way,
> The name that can be named is not the Everlasting
> Name
Which Nameless brought forth Heaven and Earth, which
> Named, if name we may,
> The Mother of all the myriad things of time and space
> became.
Thereby we sound eternally the mystery divine,
> But only without desire to sound, for if desire abide
The portals of the issuing host our baffled sight confine,
> And deep within the eternal veil the mystery shall hide.
These two, the Nameless and the Named, they differ but in
> name,
For in their vast progression from the deep they are the same,
The deep of deeps, from whose eternal gate all spirit came.

The Providence which could be indicated by words would not be an all-embracing Providence, nor would any name by which we could name it be an ever-applicable name.

E. H. Parker (1903)

"Non-existence" is a name for the beginning of heaven and earth. "Existence" is a name for the genetrix of the innumerable objects of creation.

Hence, "absolute non-existence" suggests to us the miraculous working of what in "absolute existence" has become the resulting essence.

These two emanate from the same, though their namings are dissimilar, and jointly they are termed "state of colourless dissolution." Dissolution, again, within dissolution this connects us with the various miraculous workings.

The Tao which can be expressed in words is not the eternal Tao; the name which can be uttered is not its eternal name. Without a name, it is the Beginning of Heaven and Earth; with a name, it is the Mother of all things. Only one who is ever free from desire can apprehend its spiritual essence; he who is ever a slave to desire can see no more than its outer fringe. These two things, the spiritual and the material, though we call them by different names, in their origin are one and the same. This sameness is a mystery—the mystery of mysteries. It is the gate of all wonders.

Lionel Giles (1904)

The Tao which can be expressed is not the unchanging Tao; the name which can be named is not the unchanging name.

C. Spurgeon Medhurst (1905)

The nameless is the beginning of the Heaven Earth; the mother of all things is the nameable.

Thus, while the eternal non-being leads toward the fathomless, the eternal being conducts to the boundary. Although these two (the Tao and its twofold aspect) have been differently named they come from the same.

As the same they may be described as the abysmal. The abyss of the abysmal is the gate of all mystery.

1. The Reason that can be reasoned is not the eternal Reason. The name that can be named is not the eternal Name. The Unnamable is of heaven and

Paul Carus (1913)

earth the beginning. The Namable becomes of the ten thousand things the mother.

Therefore it is said:

2.   He who desireless is found
       The spiritual of the world will sound.
       But he who by desire is bound
       Sees the mere shell of things around.

3. These two are the same in source but different in name. Their sameness is called a mystery. Indeed, it is the mystery of mysteries. Of all spirituality it is the door.

Isabella Mears
(1916)

              The Tao that can be expressed
                  is not the Everlasting Tao.
              The Name that can be named
                  is not the Everlasting Name.

              He whose Name is "Spirit in Man"
                  is Life-spring of Heaven and Earth.
              He whose name is "outward possessions"
                  is Mother of all created beings.

              Therefore constantly desire Inner Life
                  in order to perceive mysteries.
              Constantly desire possessions
                  in order to perceive limitations.

              These two: One in source but differing in Name
                  are One in being called deep,
                  Deep and yet more deep,
                  Door of many mysteries.

SOURCES

PARTIAL LIST OF ENGLISH EDITIONS OF THE TAO TE CHING

Addis, Stephen, and Stanley Lombardo, trans. *Tao Te ching: Lao-tzu* (Indianapolis, IN: Hackett Publishing, 1993).

Alexander, G. C., trans. *Lao-Tsze: The Great Thinker* (London: Kegan Paul, Trench, Trubner and Co., 1895).

Au-Young, Sum Nung, trans. *Lao Tzu's Tao the King: The Bible of Taoism* (New York: March and Greenwood, 1938).

Bahm, Archie. *Tao the King* (New York: Frederick Ungar Publishing, 1958).

Blakney, Raymond B. *The Way of Life: Lao Tsu* (New York: Mentor, 1955).

Carus, Paul, trans. *Lao-tze's Tao Te King* (Chicago: Open Court Publishing Co., 1898). Contains a Literal Version.**

Chalmers, John, trans. *The Speculations on Metaphysics, Polity, and Morality of "The Old Philosopher," Lau-tsze* (London: Trubner, 1868).*

Chan, Wing-Tsit, trans. *The Way of Lao Tzu* (New York: The Bobbs-Merrill Co., 1963).**

Chen, Ellen M., trans. *The Tao Te Ching* (New York: Paragon House, 1989).*

Cheng, Man-jan. *Lao-Tzu: "My words are very easy to understand."* trans. Tam C. Gibbs (Richmond, CA: North Atlantic Books, 1981).

Chung-Yuan, Chang, trans. *Tao: A New Way of Thinking* (New York: Harper and Row, 1975).

Cleary, Thomas, trans. *The Essential Tao* (San Francisco: HarperSanFrancisco, 1991).

Dalton, Jerry O. *Tao Te Ching: A New Approach—Backward Down the Path* (New York: Avon Books, 1994).

* Primary Sources.

** Essential Sources.

de Bary, William T., ed. *Sources of Chinese Tradition* (New York: Columbia University Press, 1963).

Duyvendak, Jan Julius Lodewijk, trans. *Tao Te Ching: The Book of the Way and Its Virtue* (London: John Murray, 1954).* (Duy)

Erkes, Eduard, trans. *Ho-Shang Kung's Commentary on Lao-Tse* (Ascona, Switzerland: Artibus Asiae Publishers, 1945).

Feng, Giu-Fu, and Jane English, trans. *Tao Te Ching* (New York: Vintage Books, 1972).*

Grigg, Ray. *The New Lao Tzu* (Boston: Charles E. Tuttle, 1995).

Hansen, Chad. *Tao Te Ching* (Internet: http://www.hku.hk/philodep/ch/).

Henricks, Robert G., trans. *Lao-Tzu: Te-Tao Ching: A New Translation Based on the Recently Discovered Ma-wang-tui Texts* (New York: Ballantine Books, 1989). Mau Wang Tui edition.*

Heysinger, I. W., trans. *The Light of China: The Tao Te King* (Philadelphia: Research Publishing, 1903).

Home, A. R. *The Great Art of Laotse* (Exeter, England: Newbard Publication, 1945).

Hua-Ching, Ni, trans. *The Complete Works of Lao Tzu* (Los Angeles: The Shrine of the Eternal Breath of Tao, 1979).

Janwu, Tzu, trans. *Tao Te Ching* (Unpublished manuscript, 1994).

Jiyu, Ren. *The Book of Lao Zi*. He Guanghu, Gao Shining, Song Lidao, and Xu Junyao, trans. (Beijing: Foreign Languages Press, 1993).

Ku-Ying, Ch'en. *Lao Tzu: Text, Notes, and Comments*, trans. Rhett Y. W. Young and Roger T. Ames (Beijing: Chinese Material Center, 1981).**

Kwok, Man-Ho. *Tao Te Ching: The New Translation*, trans. Martin Palmer and Jay Ramsay (London: Element Books, 1994).*

LaFargue, Michael. *The Tao of the Tao Te Ching* (Albany: State University of New York Press, 1992).

Lau, D. C., trans. *Lao Tzo Tao Te Ching* (Baltimore: Penguin Books, 1963).*

——, trans. *Lao-Tzu Tao Te Ching* (New York: Alfred Knopf/Everyman's Library, 1982). Mau Wang Tui edition.

Legge, James, trans. *The Texts of Taoism, Part I* (London: Oxford University Press, 1891).

Le Guin, Ursula K. *Lao Tzu: Tao Te Ching* (Boston: Shambhala Publications, 1997).

Lin, Paul J., trans. *A Translation of Lao Tzu's Tao Te Ching and Wang Pi's Commentary* (Ann Arbor: University of Michigan, 1977).*

Lynn, Richard John, trans. *The Classic of the Way and Virtue: A New Translation of Laozi as Interpreted by Wang Pi* (New York: Columbia University Press, 1999).

Mair, Victor, trans. *Tao Te Ching: The Classic Book of Integrity and the Way* (New York: Bantam Books, 1990). Ma Wang Tui edition.

Maurer, Herrymon, trans. *The Way of Ways* (New York: Schocken Books, 1982).

Mears, Isabella. *Tao Te King by Lao Tzu* (Wheaton, IL: Theosophical Publishing House, 1922).

Medhurst, C. Spurgeon, trans. *Tao Teh King* (Chicago: Theosophical Society, 1905).

Miles, Thomas H. *Tao Te Ching: About the Way of Nature and Its Powers* (Garden City Park, NY: Avery Publishing Group, 1992).

Ming, C. J., trans. *Tao Te Ching* (Unpublished manuscript, 1997).

Mitchell, Stephen. *Tao Te Ching* (New York: Harper and Row, 1988).

Ould, Herman, trans. *The Way of Acceptance: A New Version of Lao Tse's Tao Te Ching* (London: A. Dakers, 1946).

Parker, E. H., trans. *Studies in Chinese Religion* (New York: Dutton, 1905; London: Chapman and Hall, 1910).

Pine, Red (Bill Porter), trans. *Lao-tzu's Taoteching* (San Francisco: Mercury House, 1996).*

Poynton, Orde. *The Great Sinderesis* (Adelaide, Australia: The Hassell Press, 1949).

Ta-Kao, Chu, trans. *Tao Te Ching* (London: The Buddhist Society, 1937).

Tze, Wu-wu, and L. P. Phelps, trans. *The Philosophy of Lau-tzu* (Szechuan, China: Jeh Hsin Press, 1926).

Wai-Tao, Bhikshu, and Dwight Goddard, trans. *Laotzu's Tao and Wu-Wei* (New York: Brentano, 1919; Santa Barbara, CA: Dwight Goddard, 1935).

Waley, Arthur, trans. *The Way and Its Power* (London: George Allen and Unwin, 1934; New York: Grove Press, 1958).*

Wei, Henry, trans. *The Guiding Light of Tao Tzu* (Wheaton, IL: Quest, 1982).

Wilhelm, Richard. *Tao Te Ching,* trans. H. G. Ostwald (London: Arkana/Routledge & Kegan Paul, 1985)

Wing, R. L., trans. *The Tao of Power* (Garden City, NY: Doubleday and Co. / A Dolphin Book, 1986).*

Wu, John C., trans. *Tao Teh Ching* (Honolulu: University of Hawaii, 1939; New York: St. John's University Press, 1961; Boston: Shambhala, 1989).*

Yutang, Lin, trans. *The Wisdom of Laotse* (New York: Random House, 1942; New York: The Modern Library, 1948).*

OTHER SOURCES CONSULTED

Chan, Wing-Tsit. *A Source Book in Chinese Philosophy* (Princeton, NJ: Princeton University Press, 1963).*

Fung, Yu-lan. *A History of Chinese Philosophy* (Princeton, NJ: Princeton University Press, 1953).

Giles, Herbert A., trans. *Chuang Tzu* (London: George Allen and Unwin, 1889; London: Unwin Paperbacks, 1980).*

Wagner, R. G. *Konkordanz zum Lao-Tzu* (München: Publikationen der Fachschaft Sinologie München, 1968).**

Watson, Burton, trans. *The Complete Works of Chuang Tzu* (New York: Columbia University Press, 1989).

Weiger, L. *Chinese Characters* (New York: Dover Publications / Paragon Book Reprint Corp., 1965).**

Williams, S. Wells. *A Syllabic Dictionary of the Chinese Language* (Tung Chou, China: The North China Union College, 1909).**

ACKNOWLEDGMENTS

Grateful acknowledgment is made for permission to reprint from the following:

Ashokananda, Swami, trans. *Avadhuta Gita of Dattatreya* (Madras: Sri Ramakrishna Math, 1981).

Bahirat, B. P. *The Philosophy of Jnanadeva* (Bombay: Popular Book Depot, 1956).

Chan, Wing-Tsit, trans. *Reflections on Things at Hand: The Neo-Confucian Anthology Compiled by Chu Hsi and Lü Tsu-chien* (New York: Columbia University Press, 1967).

Chittick, William C. *The Sufi Path of Knowledge: Ibn al-'Arabi's Metaphysics of Imagination* (Albany: State University of New York Press, 1989).

Dyczkowski, Mark S. G. *The Doctrine of Vibration* (Albany: State University of New York Press, 1987).

Kripananda, Swami. *Jnaneshwar's Gita* (Albany: State University of New York Press, 1989).

Muktananda, Swami. *A Book for the Mind* (South Fallsburg, NY: SYDA Foundation, 1976).

——. *Kundalini: The Secret of Life* (South Fallsburg, NY: SYDA Foundation, 1980).

——. *Mukteshwari II* (South Fallsburg, NY: SYDA Foundation, 1972).

——. *Secret of the Siddhas* (South Fallsburg, NY: SYDA Foundation, 1980).

Ranade, R. D. *Mysticism in India* (Albany, NY: SUNY Press, 1983).

Star, Jonathan. *The Inner Treasure: An Introduction to the World's Sacred and Mystical Writings* (New York: Tarcher/Putnam, 1999).

——. *Tao Te Ching: Definitions Concordance, and Etymologies* (Princeton, NJ: Theone Press, 1999).

Venkatesananda, Swami, trans. *The Concise Yoga Vāsistha* (Albany: State University of New York Press, 1984).